BRITAIN AND LATIN AMERICA
IN THE NINETEENTH AND
TWENTIETH CENTURIES

STUDIES IN MODERN HISTORY

General editors: John Morrill and David Cannadine

This series, intended primarily for students, will tackle significant historical issues in concise volumes which are both stimulating and scholarly. The authors combine a broad approach, explaining the current state of our knowledge in the area, with their own research and judgements: and the topics chosen range widely in subject, period and place.

Titles already published

BRITAIN AND LATIN AMERICA

in the Nineteenth and Twentieth Centuries

Rory Miller

Longman
London and New York

LONGMAN GROUP UK LIMITED,
Longman House, Burnt Mill,
Harlow, Essex CM20 2JE, England
and Associated Companies throughout the world.

Published in the United States of America
by Longman Publishing, New York

©Longman Group UK Limited 1993

First published 1993

ISBN 0 582 218772 CSD
ISBN 0 582 497213 PPR

British Library Cataloguing-in-Publication Data

A catalogue record for this book is available from the British Library

Library of Congress Cataloging in Publication Data

Miller, Rory.
  Britain and Latin America in the nineteenth and twentieth centuries/
Rory Miller.
    p. cm.—(Studies in modern history)
Includes bibliographical references and index.
  ISBN 0–582–21877–2 (hard). — ISBN 0–582–49721–3 (pbk.)
  1. Great Britain—Foreign economic relations—Latin America—History.
  2. Latin America—Foreign economic relations—Great Britain—History.
  3. Great Britain—Commerce—Latin America—History. 4. Latin
America—Commerce—Great Britain—History. 5. Investments,
British—Latin America—History. I. Title. II. Series: Studies in
modern history (Longman (Firm))
  HF1534.5.L3M55   1993
  337.4108—dc20   92–35634
                                           CIP

Set by 5B in 10/12 Bembo Roman
Produced by Longman Singapore Publishers (Pte) Ltd
Printed in Singapore

Contents

List of Tables

List of Figures and Maps

FIGURES

MAPS

Abbreviations

ASAB	Anglo-South American Bank
BAGSR	Buenos Ayres Great Southern Railway
BAPR	Buenos Ayres and Pacific Railway
BAWR	Buenos Ayres Western Railway
BBC	British Broadcasting Corporation
BOLSA	Bank of London and South America
BT	Board of Trade
BW	Balfour Williamson archive
BWC	Brazilian Warrant Company
CAP	Common Agricultural Policy
CAR	Central Argentine Railway
DOT	Department of Overseas Trade
EC	European Community
ECLA	Economic Commission for Latin America (United Nations)
FO	Foreign Office
GWBR	Great Western of Brazil Railway
LBB	London and Brazilian Bank
LBMSA	London Bank of Mexico and South America
LRPB	London and River Plate Bank
MFN	'most favoured nation'
NRC	Nitrate Railways Company
PP	Parliamentary Papers
PRO	Public Record Office
RIIA	Royal Institute of International Affairs
RSF	Recife and San Francisco Railway
SPR	San Paulo Railway
T	Treasury
UCL	University College, London

[A list of journal abbreviations is to be found at the beginning of the Select Bibliography on pp. 282–3]

Glossary

agiotista	speculator in government debt (Mexico)
asiento	slave-trade monopoly
caudillo	political (normally military) leader
caudillismo	political domination by *caudillos*
comissário	coffee-broker (Brazil)
consulado	guild of merchants
estancia	cattle ranch (River Plate)
estanciero	owner of an *estancia*
fazenda	(coffee) plantation (Brazil)
fazendeiro	owner of a *fazenda*
ficha	token
frigorífico	meat refrigerating plant
habilitación	short-term loan
hacienda	landed estate
mestizo	person of mixed race
obraje	textile workshop
oficina	nitrate processing plant
pulpería	grocery/general store

Preface

There were two principal reasons for writing this book. First, several years of teaching undergraduate courses in Latin American history had suggested that while students found the subject of Britain's relations with Latin America interesting it was often difficult for them to come to terms with the literature on the subject. There was an enormous gap between the theoretical writing on imperialism and dependency and the hundreds of historical case studies which frequently concentrated on one country or one topic over a short period of time, and which were difficult to fit into a broader picture. Second, no-one had really attempted to construct a synthesis of the existing literature on Anglo-Latin American relations for scholars whose research interests lie elsewhere. I hope that this book might at least partially fulfil both these needs, and that, by providing some generalisations and arguments from which others can depart, it will stimulate more investigation and debate and thus help to improve understanding of the historical relationship between Latin America and Britain.

To complete such a project properly would demand much more archival research and time than I have been able to devote to it. In several respects this book does not fully achieve what I originally set out to do. It has been difficult for me, without writing a much longer text, to include sufficient background material on Latin American history for non-specialists in the region, to balance British and Latin American perspectives, and to devote the attention I should have liked to the smaller Latin American countries (I regret in particular not being able to include more on Uruguay, Peru and Mexico). Working in a provincial university in the north-west of England, a country whose library facilities, like much else, are concentrated in the south-east, I have also not had the opportunity to consult as much literature published in Latin America as I should have wished. Some Latin American specialists may therefore feel that the viewpoint is a little too 'Anglo'. However, it is difficult, in such a synthesis, to avoid this, for it is economic and business trends and government policies in Britain which provide the cement to hold together the diverse experiences of individual Latin American countries. Constraints of space have also unfortunately meant that footnotes have had to be cut to a minimum. I have normally cited references only where the work of a specific author is mentioned in the text, or to provide sources for statistics and quotations. This does an enormous disservice, for which I apologise, to the many historians and social scientists on whose research I have somewhat parasitically relied, but an indication of the principal sources for each section of the book can be found in the bibliographical essay at the end.

I owe thanks to a large number of people. The Nuffield Foundation and the Research Development Fund of Liverpool University provided the funds to support some archival and library research in London. Many individual colleagues provided an enormous amount of help along the way. My greatest intellectual debt, although I depart from his interpretation of Anglo-Latin American relations in many respects, is to the late Christopher Platt, who encouraged my initial interest in Latin America, supervised my doctoral research in the early 1970s, and answered many queries about sources and archives in the preliminary stages of the research for this book. I deeply regret that he did not live to see it completed. Henry Finch and Robert Greenhill both read the whole of the draft text, in the case of some sections two or three times, a task for which I am extremely grateful. Other friends read individual chapters and made perceptive comments upon them: I should particularly like to thank David Cahill, Cristóbal Kay, John Knape, Walter Little, Carlos Marichal and Guy Thomson for this. Colin Lewis and Raúl García Heras both answered queries about Argentine problems. John Fisher did some of my teaching when I was on leave undertaking some of the research in 1986, and Robert Lee gave me consistent encouragement to complete the project. None of these is of course responsible for the final result.

The arguments developed here were also stimulated and modified by discussions at seminars and conferences which I attended while I was writing the book. For this I am grateful to audiences at the Centre of Latin American Studies in Cambridge, the Liverpool–Manchester Economic History Conference, the University of Bielefeld, and the Ibero-Amerikanisches Institut in Berlin, and in particular to colleagues who shared their ideas at two major conferences, the 1988 International Congress of the Americanists in Amsterdam, where Colin Lewis and I coordinated a symposium on British Business in Latin America, and the conference on Public Debt in Latin America which Reinhard Liehr organised during a memorable week in Berlin in November 1989.

My greatest thanks are due to Gill, who put up with having this book in the house for seven years, and to Sarah and Aidan who were both born while it was being written. Now, perhaps, their father might have more time to play with them.

Chester   Rory Miller
February 1992

CHAPTER ONE
Introduction

THE GROWTH AND DECLINE OF BRITISH INTERESTS

'Spanish America is free,' George Canning, the British Foreign Secretary, asserted in December 1824, 'and if we do not mismanage our affairs sadly, she is English.'[1] Almost at the very moment that Canning wrote, the Latin American wars of independence were drawing to a close with the defeat of the Spanish forces in Peru at the decisive battle of Ayacucho. Britain's future in the region seemed assured. The leaders of the new nations regarded diplomatic recognition by the United Kingdom as essential for both their economic development and their political security. Canning's sense of triumph was motivated by the fact that he had finally persuaded his colleagues to consent to negotiations with Mexico, Gran Colombia and Buenos Aires for commercial treaties which might provide a more solid basis for Britain's trade with the new nations.

Canning's success in advancing Britain's economic interests during the period of Latin American independence marked the culmination of more than two hundred years of attempts by privateers, merchants and ministers to break into the monopoly of the Spanish and Portuguese empires and to promote Britain's influence there against its commercial rivals, particularly the French. Statesmen and businessmen had long believed that the maladministration and inefficiency of the Iberian colonies in the New World concealed tremendous potential wealth, especially in the form of unexploited gold and silver deposits. For mercantilist theorists, who visualised a nation's power in terms of its ability to accumulate bullion, the prospect of breaking into the Iberian monopoly was irresistible. While mercantilism lost its dominance as a mode of economic thought at the end of the eighteenth century, the avaricious capitalists of the early Industrial Revolution were equally tempted by opportunities to sell cheap cottons to people in Latin America who had been starved of access to foreign trade or to gain control of the renowned silver mines of Peru and Mexico.

The first real concessions came in 1810, when the British government negotiated preferential trading privileges in Brazil in return for its support for the Portuguese royal family during the Napoleonic Wars. In the Spanish empire, where the struggle for emancipation lasted from about 1810 until 1825, restrictions on direct trade between the colonies and other countries were gradually dismantled during the conflict. When it finally became clear, in the early 1820s, that Spain could do little to reverse the independence process, Canning took the first steps towards safeguarding Britain's economic interests and recognising the new republics by sending out consular officials. The British mania for Latin America rose in a crescendo early in 1825, just after the government's decision to grant formal recognition to some of the new nations. Merchants with cargoes of manufactured goods, particularly cotton textiles, established themselves in large numbers in ports along the Atlantic and Pacific coasts, while in London eager speculators invested their savings in loans to the young governments and in mining enterprises which promised a new El Dorado.

In practice, the reality proved somewhat disappointing. The speculation in loans and mining stocks turned suddenly into a commercial and financial crisis. Almost all the new governments, unable to raise the revenue they required to pay interest on their bonds, defaulted on the loans they had contracted in London. The mining companies largely failed, and the saturation of markets in Latin America brought ruin to merchants. Many republics lapsed into dictatorship or political anarchy, further hindering the development of economic relations with the outside world and prompting calls in Britain for government intervention to provide some security for business interests. For twenty years commercial relations with Latin America appeared to stagnate. Contemporary estimates of exports to the region in 1845 valued them at only £6.0 million, compared with £6.4 million twenty years before. At least a third of this trade was with one country, Brazil.[2]

The timing of the recovery varied from one country to another. Brazil never defaulted on its debt, and its trade always remained relatively healthy even when that of other countries collapsed. Elsewhere signs of revival began to appear in the 1840s, just at the time when the British government, through the abolition of import duties, colonial preferences and shipping restrictions, was instituting the system of 'free trade' which would endure until the 1930s. Latin America's exports began to grow in value. Products like hides and wool from the River Plate, copper from Chile and guano from Peru found markets in Britain and elsewhere in Europe. The expansion of trade, and hence revenues, permitted governments to start to renegotiate the loans of the independence era.

During the subsequent decades the economic links between Latin America and Britain intensified. British and continental European markets grew rapidly and the costs of shipping began to fall, facilitating the export of bulkier products like wheat. Increasing numbers of British firms offered commercial services to Latin American producers and consumers, expanding the supply of credit, insurance, transport and marketing facilities. Britain's own exports to Latin America rose in value to £13.6 million in 1860.[3] National and provincial governments began to issue new bonds on the London capital market, while, for the first time since the collapse of the mining enterprises in the 1820s, numerous companies were floated on the Stock Exchange to invest in activities like railways, public utilities and commercial banking.

Figure 1.1, which outlines the timing of British economic activities in Latin America, illustrates the significance of the 1860s and 1870s for the growth and diversification of British interests. At the same time a marked change in their geographical focus occurred. While Brazil remained attractive, the old colonial mining centres, Mexico and Peru, lost much of their importance. The Anglo–French intervention of 1861–62, which resulted in the imposition of the Austrian Archduke Maximilian as emperor of Mexico, led to a rupture in diplomatic relations with Britain which lasted for almost twenty years. In Peru the 'guano age' drew to a close in the 1870s with default on the massive foreign debt which the country had incurred, followed swiftly by defeat in war with Chile and the loss of its valuable guano and nitrate reserves. British interest thus came to focus more on Brazil and the three southern republics, Argentina, Uruguay and Chile.

Between 1870 and 1914, despite setbacks caused by commercial and financial crises in the mid 1870s and the early 1890s, Britain's economic interests in Latin America reached their peak. In the major countries their influence appeared pervasive and almost unassailable. Already, in the 1890s, even before the astounding growth of Britain's interests in the River Plate which occurred between 1900 and 1914, the United States consul in Buenos Aires had claimed: 'It almost seems that the English have the preference in everything pertaining

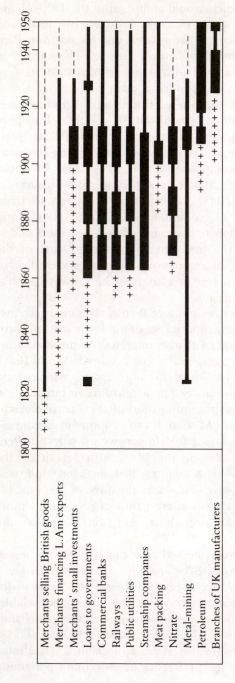

Key: ++++ Sporadic interest

—— Maintenance of existing investments

▬▬ Peak periods of new investment

- - - Declining interest

NB: Any diagram like this is bound to be impressionistic. The chronology of British interests differed in each country. Note too that the thickness of the bars is *not* a guide to the relative size of the investments.

Figure 1.1 Chronology of British economic interests in Latin America

to the business and business interests of the country. . . . They are "in" everything, except politics, as intimately as though it were a British colony.'[4] Apart from their role as Argentina's leading trading partner British businessmen accumulated substantial investments in government loans, railways, public utilities, commercial banks, meatpacking plants, and land in Argentina. These assets represented almost 10 per cent of Britain's total overseas investment in 1913.[5] In Brazil, where the level of Britain's trade grew more slowly, they still appeared to possess a dominant role in public finance, shipping, the import trade, export credit, railways, cables and telegraphs. They had even obtained concessions to install a radio network. British investments in Mexico also expanded noticeably early in the twentieth century, despite the twenty-year hiatus in relations after 1867 and the United States' domination of Mexico's trade. In addition Britain possessed important interests in Peru, Chile and Uruguay, and many smaller investments elsewhere. Commentators in both Latin America and the United States began to believe in the existence of a close alliance of merchant bankers, companies and government officials defending and promoting British interests.

Yet by the middle of the twentieth century Britain's influence had disintegrated. The First World War permitted the United States to gain ground in Latin America at the expense of the European powers. It also transformed Britain from a substantial international creditor into a debtor, making it impossible for the City of London to regain its prewar eminence in the supply of overseas finance. In the 1920s the majority of new foreign investment in Latin America came through New York. The Depression, and the advent of Imperial Preference in Britain in the early 1930s, added further blows. Trade declined, and Britain's investments in the region, with the exception of the petroleum and manufacturing interests which had been growing since the turn of the century, became largely unprofitable. Moreover, the oil companies, railways and public utilities all came under increasing attack from nationalist critics.

The Second World War reduced trade further and put Britain into debt to the major Latin American countries as well as to the United States. By 1945 Britain's exports to the region amounted to less than a quarter of their 1938 level.[6] Over the next few years many of the pre-1914 investments, which had become almost worthless, were surrendered to Latin American governments in exchange for a cancellation of Britain's debts. While a handful of the old railway and utility companies and merchant houses remained in business after 1950, the only truly significant investments left were Royal

Dutch-Shell's interests in Venezuela, the Bank of London and South America's branch network, and a few manufacturing companies. Both for the British government and for many businessmen, Latin America, in contrast to the United States, Europe and the Commonwealth, no longer possessed any real significance.

THE EVOLUTION OF LATIN AMERICA[7]

At the time of independence Latin America was still, in many respects, a frontier of European colonisation. Apart from the principal centres of pre-Columbian civilisation in highland Mexico and the Andes, Spanish and Portuguese settlements were largely concentrated near the coast. Much of the interior – the Amazon and Orinoco basins, the lowlands to the east of the Andes, Patagonia, the deserts of northern Mexico (which then included California, New Mexico, Arizona and Texas) – remained beyond their control. Population was sparse and the principal cities and ports small. The Peruvian census of 1827, for example, suggests a population of about 1.5 million, almost two-thirds of whom were 'Indian'. Lima, the capital, had only 60,000 people.[8] Brazil in 1819 had a population of about 3.6 million, almost one-third of them slaves.[9]

Enormous disparities in wealth, income and social status were evident everywhere in Latin America. Small 'white' elites comprising merchants, bureaucrats and landowners dominated countries in which most people were of *mestizo* (mixed race), African or indigenous descent. In Brazil, the surviving Spanish colonies in the Caribbean (Cuba, Puerto Rico and eastern Hispaniola), and parts of the Peruvian, Colombian and Venezuelan coasts, slavery remained essential to commercial agriculture. Elsewhere both mineral production and primitive manufacturing, as well as the large *haciendas* which often dominated the countryside, depended heavily on the labour of the indigenous population. Yet despite the poverty of many of the region's inhabitants, complex networks of internal trade and migration had developed, especially, but not only, close to the mining centres. Agricultural commodities such as grain, sugar and wine, imported manufactures, artisan products like textiles, and other goods like mules, cattle, salt and, in the Andes, coca were widely traded.

Independence obviously stimulated a wholesale reorientation of Latin America's external economic connexions. The struggles also caused serious disruption to the domestic economies of the new states. The Spaniards fleeing to the remaining colonies in the Caribbean or to Europe and the Portuguese who left Brazil took with them considerable amounts of capital. The warring armies seized cattle, food and mules, and recruited new soldiers in every area through which they passed. The loss of transport animals and money both disrupted existing commercial networks. Arable production normally recovered fairly quickly from the damage caused by war, but mining was more seriously harmed, for the stoppages often caused flooding and hence the need for new capital expenditure to restore output. Moreover, the newly independent governments were faced with a mass of claims upon them, especially from those who had supplied goods to the military or seen their property confiscated.

Despite their success in achieving independence the 'patriots' left the political future of Spanish America undefined. Liberal hopes of political stability and constitutional progress were almost everywhere quickly disappointed. Instead, the new republics, with the exception of Chile, lapsed into what liberals, and many foreign commentators, viewed as the anarchy of the *caudillos*. While some constitutional norms such as periodic elections and sessions of Congress might still be observed, most governments seemed to rise and fall on the whim of the military veterans of the independence wars.

The precise reasons for the political instability and its nature varied from one country to another, but there were some common problems. One was that most governments remained desperately short of money. In the Andes the liberal ideal of eliminating legal distinctions based on ethnicity was quickly reversed; by the end of the 1820s colonial taxes on the indigenous populations had been reimposed under new names simply to raise revenue. These 'contributions', besides confronting liberal sensibilities, were difficult to increase. Apart from minor property and production taxes, therefore, the most obvious source of income for the new states was foreign trade. However, success in collecting import duties in adequate amounts was often limited, for it depended on the probity of officials, their ability to reduce contraband, and the level of economic activity. In addition, many governments incurred much greater expenditure than they had anticipated; the new loans which they obtained to cover the deficits, usually from local merchants, simply added to the claims arising from the independence struggles, thus increasing the internal debt.

Closely associated with these fiscal problems were the problems of external security and the intense civil conflicts which developed after independence. Mexico faced an invasion from Spanish forces in 1829, the secession of Texas in 1835–36, a French intervention in 1838, and war with the United States in 1846–47. Buenos Aires and Brazil fought over ownership of the Banda Oriental (modern Uruguay) from 1825 until 1828. Attempts at federation in Gran Colombia, Central America and Peru–Bolivia all disintegrated in the decade after 1829. Struggles within the republics also increased in bitterness, due to ideological disputes over the role of the church, constitutional questions like the relationships between the executive and legislature or national and provincial governments, and the economic conflicts which developed among different provinces or sectors of the elite. Military *caudillos*, who often possessed considerable popular appeal, allied themselves with particular groups within the civilian elites. As instability increased, power often trickled away from the national capitals towards the regions.

The outcomes of the political struggles varied. Mexico, Peru and Bolivia all provided extreme examples of instability. Between May 1833 and August 1855 the Mexican presidency changed hands thirty-six times; at the peak of the conflict, between 1835 and 1840, twenty ministers of finance held office.[10] In such countries the central government's inability to obtain revenues, and the bitterness of ideological and economic conflicts within the elite, made it impossible for any one leader to create a coalition powerful enough to preserve order for any length of time. Elsewhere, however, certain *caudillos* did succeed in establishing more stable governments by constructing firmer alliances with landowners and regional leaders, developing their popular support and, at times, eliminating their opponents by force. In Paraguay José Gaspar Rodríguez de Francia remained in power from 1814 until his death in 1840, creating a *mestizo* nation largely isolated from the outside world and under his personal authority. In the River Plate, Juan Manuel de Rosas, a leading *estanciero* (cattle-rancher) who became governor of Buenos Aires in 1829, dominated Argentina by means of alliances with other provincial governors, the support he cultivated among poorer urban groups, and the occasional use of terror, until rival *caudillos* from the littoral provinces, supported by Brazil, overthrew him in 1852.

In British eyes there were two singular exceptions to the instability and *caudillismo* which marked their image of Latin America in the first half-century after independence. One was Brazil, which retained a member of the Portuguese royal house of Bragança as emperor. Despite serious civil conflicts during the nine-year regency which lasted from the abdication of Pedro I in 1831 until Pedro II's assumption of full powers in 1840, Brazil gradually developed a political structure dependent on the ability of bureaucrats and politicians to mediate between the landowners of the provinces and the imperial government in Rio de Janeiro. The other exception was Chile, where a leading conservative merchant, Diego Portales, established an authoritarian constitution at the beginning of the 1830s. With the exception of two short civil wars in the 1850s, Chile then remained internally peaceful until 1891, aided by its small size, a steadily growing economy, the low level of conflict among landowners, and the elite's ability to absorb other families, often immigrants, who had acquired wealth in commerce and mining.

The formation of strong national political structures thus proved more difficult than either the Latin American or British proponents of independence had expected. Yet slowly political institutions became more stable, and power began to pass from military *caudillos* to civilian presidents. Liberalism, which essentially consisted of opening markets, freeing land and labour from colonial restrictions, ending slavery, and reducing the power of the church, came to predominate. Respect for constitutions, which took a more permanent form in several countries in the 1850s and 1860s, increased. Gradually more powerful national states were constructed, though not without some major conflicts in the middle of the century. In Mexico the Liberal Constitution of 1857 precipitated a civil war in which the proclerical Conservatives were supported after 1861 by the French. Only in 1867 did the Liberals, under Benito Juárez, succeed in ending the foreign occupation. By coopting, dividing or eliminating regional *caudillos*, Juárez and his successor, Sebastián Lerdo de Tejada, then began to augment the power of the national president. This process culminated in the rule of Porfirio Díaz, a Liberal general who took power in a coup in 1876 and who, except for four years after 1880, remained in control until 1911. In Argentina the fall of Rosas in 1852 resulted in the division of the country between the province of Buenos Aires and the Argentine Confederation. They were not reunited until 1862, after a brief war. Disputes between the province and the nation nevertheless remained potentially serious until they were solved by the federalisation of the city of Buenos Aires in 1880 and the establishment of a new provincial capital at La Plata after 1882.

The increasing power of national governments depended on economic growth. The expansion of trade led to a rise in customs revenues. Their growing credit in London and other European financial centres provided access to foreign loans. Governments thus acquired resources to pay their debts, expand the bureaucracy, satisfy the armed forces and commence public works. Both the telegraph and the railway made it easier for them to control outlying provinces.

National states could now incorporate provincial landowners through cooptation rather than violence, often by aiding them with construction projects and allowing them considerable autonomy over their own affairs. In several countries key groups of export producers – the *estancieros* of Argentina, coastal planters of Peru, silver miners in Bolivia – obtained a greater degree of control over national affairs, either directly by themselves supplying their countries with political leaders or through interest-group associations. The major families in the capitals and ports strengthened their connexions with foreign investors and local politicians and lawyers, and developed more sophisticated business networks, often combining financial, commercial and agricultural activities. Once-significant provincial elites, in contrast, lost their influence as economies became more oriented towards Europe and the United States and railways permitted the cheaper transport of imported supplies.

Despite their outward constitutionalism the political systems of Latin America in the late nineteenth century tended to be relatively closed and undemocratic. Literacy and property requirements normally excluded the mass of the population from participation in elections. Particularly in the provinces voters were few and easily controlled, and new methods of electoral fraud were grafted on to the regional *caudillismo* of the past. Congressmen frequently became brokers between the national government and local landowners. Moreover, civil war and dictatorship did not totally disappear, even in the larger countries. The Brazilian empire collapsed in November 1889, eighteen months after the abolition of slavery. Five years of rule by military presidents then followed, until naval and regional revolts in 1893–94 provided the opportunity for the coffee planters of São Paulo to lead a transition to civilian rule and impose a decentralised federal structure of government. In Chile the term of office of President Balmaceda (1886–91) culminated in a bloody civil war, at the end of which Balmaceda committed suicide. In Mexico Porfirio Díaz overrode the provisions of the 1857 constitution prohibiting the re-election of the president, and constructed an authoritarian regime based on his personal control of elections, appointments and government expenditure.

While enriching and strengthening sectors of the commercial and landowning elites, economic growth brought in its train other significant social changes. There is strong evidence that in many rural areas standards of living for the majority deteriorated. The growth of the economies gave landowners greater incentives to control land and labour; at the same time population began to increase, further squeezing the rural poor. *Gauchos* in Argentina and former slaves in Brazil were marginalised by immigrants, most of them Europeans whom landowners preferred as employees or tenants because of their apparent eagerness to work, as well as for racial reasons. Many of the older artisan groups, who had formed the core of the urban population in the middle of the century, also declined or disappeared under the pressure of changing patterns of consumption and the increase in imports.

Most cities grew very rapidly during the export boom. Buenos Aires, which had a population of almost 80,000 in 1869, had increased to nearly 1.6 million by 1914; by then ten cities in Latin America had over 200,000 inhabitants.[11] These urban centres contained a growing middle class, consisting primarily of clerks, bureaucrats and small businessmen, artisans concentrated in the clothing, footwear and construction industries, an increasingly organised and vocal proletariat employed in large enterprises like the docks, railway or tramway companies, and a mass of residents who were largely unskilled and worked in domestic service or on a casual basis as day-labourers. As they grew in size and changed in social composition, middle-class and working-class groups in the cities threatened the structures of oligarchic politics. Politicians like José Batlle y Ordóñez (president of Uruguay, 1903–07 and 1911–15), or Hipólito Yrigoyen (president of Argentina, 1916–22 and 1928–30) took the opportunity to tailor their rhetoric and policies to appeal to popular discontent and aspirations.

In Mexico, almost uniquely among the major countries, rebellion in the countryside provided the more powerful stimulus for political change. The personalist political structures Díaz had established proved unable to contain pressure from dissident landowners and the urban middle class to open up the political system. A small revolt in the north late in 1910 rapidly developed into a more broadly based movement comprising small property-owners, artisans and large sectors of the rural poor. Díaz resigned a few months later and, as the central government's power to control events disintegrated, the country entered the decade of civil war known as the Mexican Revolution.

During the First World War some of the problems arising from the liberal model of development based on foreign trade and capital began to become more intense. Although exports boomed immediately after 1918 and remained superficially healthy until the crash of 1929, there were severe difficulties beneath the surface. Some export sectors such as rubber in northern Brazil or nitrate in Chile declined due to competition from new producing areas and synthetic substitutes.

Other producers, in sugar, wheat, coffee and minerals, found prices weakening. Although they often tried to maintain their incomes by increasing output, this tended to exacerbate the medium-term problems. Moreover, in 1918–19 working-class protest reached a climax in a wave of strikes which spread throughout Latin America. Although such actions generally met with violent repression from the state, the social changes which the economic boom had stimulated continued to undermine the legitimacy of the political structures established by the elites in the late nineteenth century. The Depression which followed the Wall Street Crash thus marked a watershed in the history of Latin America. Almost everywhere governments collapsed.

There was no clear pattern to the subsequent political developments. In Argentina a coalition known as the Concordancia, essentially consisting of leading landowners and military officers, maintained conservative politicians in power through fraudulent elections until the overthrow of President Castillo in a military coup in 1943. From this group of officers Juan Domingo Perón emerged. Making use of a powerful nationalist and populist rhetoric to strengthen his connexions with the urban working class he succeeded in winning the presidency in the elections of 1946. In Brazil Getúlio Vargas, the former provincial governor of Rio Grande do Sul, led a successful revolt in 1930. After overcoming a serious rebellion from São Paulo in 1932, Vargas instituted a constitutional and increasingly centralised regime, but in 1937, with the support of the military, he closed Congress and commenced a period of authoritarian rule known as the Estado Nôvo. This lasted until the calling of elections in 1945. In Mexico the attempts of Presidents Obregón (1920–24) and Calles (1924–28) to rebuild the state after the Revolution encountered serious problems. After the assassination of Obregón in 1928, the domestic political and economic pressures on the regime mounted. Only in the following decade, after the 'election' of Lázaro Cárdenas to the presidency, did stability return, but in a form which hardly suited either the landowners or foreign investors in Mexico. During his six-year term (1934–40) Cárdenas instituted far-reaching changes, including a radical agrarian reform, the empowerment of worker and peasant confederations under the umbrella of the state, and the nationalisation of the railways and foreign oil companies.

Yet while there was no clear pattern to the political changes which occurred in Latin America during the 1930s and 1940s, the economic policies followed by the leading countries did share certain common features. The traditional concentration on exports and welcome for foreign investment began to come seriously into question. Many governments responded to the crisis of the early 1930s by partially or wholly defaulting on their loans, and limited foreign firms' ability to repatriate profits. Gradually, through a combination of exchange and credit controls, protectionist tariffs and import quotas, they then started to focus on the need to transform their domestic economies and to introduce deliberate policies of import substitution industrialisation. At the same time the economic role of the state grew, as governments themselves took control of more of the infrastructure, in particular the transport systems in which the British had invested so heavily.

QUESTIONS AND CONTROVERSIES

For historians of the British connexion with Latin America two sets of questions arise from this survey. The first concerns the dynamics of the British role: the reasons for the rise and decline of different business activities, the part played by government, and the growing concentration of British interest in particular sectors and countries. These are of relevance to both the imperial and the economic history of Britain in the nineteenth and twentieth centuries. There is an obvious contrast between the extension of British rule in other areas of the world and the lack of a formal empire in Latin America (apart from the relatively insignificant colonies founded in the Falkland Islands and British Honduras).[12] The evolution of British trade and investment in Latin America also offers important evidence to economic historians debating the reasons for Britain's long-term decline as an industrial and commercial power. For specialists in Latin American history a second set of questions is more important. These concern the interaction between the British economy, officials and businessmen on the one hand, and the development of Latin America on the other. How much influence did individual British firms exercise within Latin America, for example over national and local governments? What were the economic, social and political consequences of their activities? How did Latin America respond to the growth of the British economy, and did the region suffer long-term harm from the specialisation which this encouraged? Such issues lie at the heart of both the criticisms directed at the British by contemporary observers and the intense debate which has subsequently developed about Britain's role in the region.

Early Latin American critiques

In the immediate aftermath of independence significant groups within Latin America soon began to criticise the rapid growth of British influence. Local merchants who had hoped to gain from the removal of the Spaniards were frequently swept aside by the influx of cheap British goods and foreign traders. Domestic producers, particularly artisans, found themselves unable to compete with European products (in some cases landowners were also harmed by food imports from the United States). Artisan riots directed at foreign goods and firms became commonplace in the mid nineteenth century, but they gained considerable support from other social groups. There was certainly no automatic acceptance of the doctrines of free trade and comparative advantage (the idea that certain countries were best suited to the production of raw materials and foodstuffs, others to manufacturing, and that each would benefit from the abolition of commercial restrictions and from minimal tariffs) which British consuls and merchants propounded, especially after Britain's own adoption of liberal commercial policies in the 1840s. Latin American officials also expressed considerable scepticism about the benefits of the British connexion. 'The commerce between the two countries is carried on with English capital, on English ships, by English companies,' the Brazilian minister in London wrote in 1854. 'The profits . . . the interest on the capital . . . the payments for insurance, the commissions and the dividends from the business, everything goes into the pockets of Englishmen.'[13]

While liberal ideas did gradually gain ground at the expense of the conservative nationalism of the early nineteenth century, even at the peak of the relationship between Latin America and Britain several writers still questioned the influence of the British and the direction in which their countries were heading. A leading Chilean historian, Francisco Encina, published a short book in 1911 entitled *Nuestra inferioridad económica* (Our economic inferiority), in which he complained about the poor progress of industry in Chile and the consumption habits and values of an elite which preferred European goods and travel.[14] In Argentina towards the end of the First World War, Alejandro Bunge criticised the outward-directed development, based on free trade, the British market and foreign capital, to which his country seemed excessively committed. Just over a decade later, as the Depression highlighted many of the disadvantages of Argentina's commitment to comparative advantage and foreign investment which had concerned Bunge, nationalist writers in Buenos Aires began to publish a series of scathing attacks on British 'imperialism'. Led by Raúl Scalabrini Ortiz and the Irazusta brothers, they denounced the dominance which they believed the English had established, with the compliance of the Argentine landowning elite, through their control of the market for Argentina's exports, the loans they supplied to governments, and their ownership of crucial sectors of the economy like the railways.

Alongside these dissenting views from elite intellectuals and right-wing nationalists, criticisms of the relationship with Britain also began to appear from the left. The development of Marxist theories of imperialism in Europe in the early twentieth century linked the industrial countries' needs for cheap raw materials and food and for outlets for manufactures and capital to the growth of finance capitalism in Europe and the scramble for colonies in Africa and Asia which had occurred since the 1880s. Most European Marxists, though, ignored Latin America, despite its significance for British and German trade and investment, because they tended to identify imperialism with the colonial rivalries associated with a particular stage of capitalism and no scramble for exclusive concessions had occurred in the region. Latin America receives scarcely a mention in the works of Lenin, Hilferding or Luxemburg.

Despite this neglect Latin American writers influenced by Marxist ideas began themselves to develop a radical critique of British influence. The Peruvian José Carlos Mariátegui argued in *Seven Essays on Peruvian Reality* (1928) that the independence of Spanish America was essential for the growth of English capitalism and that Peru had subsequently mortgaged its guano, nitrate and railways to English financiers. The elite of his own country had, he claimed, remained subservient, semi-feudal and exploitative as a result of a century of compromise with foreign interests. In Argentina Rodolfo Ghioldi, a leader of the Communist Party, denounced British investment during the nineteenth century for 'deforming the development of the Argentine economy, and impeding the evolution of a national process of growth'. The British-owned railways, he alleged, were allied to the landowners and cattle-breeders, and 'an instrument for the oppression of the rural masses'. The recently signed trade agreement (the notorious Roca-Runciman Pact of 1933) was viewed by Ghioldi simply as 'a pact signed by Argentines to benefit British capital'.[15] Over the following generation historians such as Hernán

Ramírez Necochea in Chile developed interpretations which centred on the growth of an anti-nationalist alliance between British capitalists and Latin American elites, and the adverse consequences which this had produced for the economic and social development of their own countries.

These two streams of criticism, the nationalism of the right and the Marxist analyses of the left, together created a series of popular heroes, key events and central themes concerning the relationship between Latin America and Britain. Studies of nineteenth-century leaders like Francia and Rosas concentrated on their attempts to restrict the growth of British interests and to lead their countries on an autonomous road to development. Later nationalist presidents like Balmaceda or Batlle could be interpreted in a similar light. Historical episodes in which the British government or commercial interests were supposed to have encouraged and intervened in domestic struggles also became symbols of imperialism. These included events like the Anglo–French intervention in Mexico (1861–62); the Paraguayan War of 1865–70, in which Paraguay fought the Triple Alliance of Argentina, Brazil and Uruguay; the Pacific War of 1879–83 between Peru, Bolivia and Chile; the Chilean Civil War of 1891; the Anglo–German blockade of Venezuela in 1902–03; the Mexican Revolution; and the Argentine coup of 1930. In other instances, such as the mid nineteenth-century renegotiations of the post-independence loans, or later settlements of debt crises in Peru, Argentina and Brazil in the 1890s, British investors were assumed to have used their financial leverage to extract unfair concessions or to determine policy.

A number of ideas about Britain's historical role therefore became popular in Latin America. Many believed that the British had destroyed the opportunities for autonomous and balanced development by intervening in internal political conflicts and exercising influence over tariff and monetary policies. It was often assumed that British merchants and investors had extracted the majority of the profits from Latin America's export boom, and that local elites, captivated by liberal economic ideas of comparative advantage and the benefits of foreign investment and free trade, had willingly participated in the subjugation of their countries to British hegemony.

The debate on informal imperialism

Many historians in the United Kingdom were unaware of the literature being published in Latin America. Instead, interest in Britain's relationship with the region arose largely out of discontent with the way in which imperial historians had concentrated on the colonial empire and ignored other areas of British influence. For John Gallagher and Ronald Robinson, writing in 1953, this was 'rather like judging the size and character of icebergs solely from the parts above the water-line'.[16] Gallagher and Robinson quarrelled with the conventional assumption, shared by imperial historians and Marxists alike, that imperialism had entered a new phase in the late nineteenth century. They claimed instead that there had been a fundamental continuity in British policy throughout the century. In their view British governments always aimed to secure hegemony through 'informal' means of obtaining influence, and they resorted to force and annexation only where this proved impossible. The case of Latin America, where no colonial scramble had occurred, was central to this interpretation. While Britain did use force in the early nineteenth century to safeguard its interests there, Gallagher and Robinson claimed that it stopped short of annexation and that by 1913 there was 'no need for brusque and peremptory interventions on behalf of British interests . . . [because] once [the Latin American] economies had become sufficiently dependent on foreign trade the classes whose prosperity was drawn from that trade normally worked themselves in local politics to preserve the local political conditions needed for it'.[17] H.S. Ferns also concluded in the early 1950s that coercion and intervention had become unnecessary in Argentina because the elite had developed the 'institutional means and the will to engage in an economic and financial relationship with Great Britain'. Such an arrangement he termed 'informal empire'.[18] However, these reinterpretations of Britain's relationship with Latin America gathered dust for a decade. Robinson and Gallagher turned to work on Africa and India. While Robinson developed the concept of a 'collaborating elite' which mediated between local society and the British, he did not apply it to nineteenth-century Latin America.

When the attack on Gallagher and Robinson eventually came, it focused on three issues: their assumption that British officials successfully supported businessmen; their claim of continuity in official thinking and policy (which is less relevant to this discussion); and the significance of Latin America to Britain. Ferns himself seemed to retreat from his earlier discourse of 'informal empire'. In *Britain and Argentina in the Nineteenth Century* (1960) he argued that while British commercial and financial interests had exercised 'great influence', it was an interdependent rather than an exploitative relationship in which the dominant interests in Argentina had taken the lead. Moreover, he asserted, 'the British government has never had the power to oblige Argentina to pay a debt, pay a dividend, or to export or import any commodity whatever'.[19] A few years later D.C.M. Platt and W.M. Mathew both argued that there were significant differences of interest between government and business. Platt, in particular, claimed that the British government had played little part in the relationship with Latin America. He also began to question the assumption that Latin America was ever important to British businessmen in the mid nineteenth century. 'There are, indeed,' Platt asserted in 1973, 'absurdities in attributing a modern, neo-colonial relationship between subordinate primary producers and developed industrial powers, to a period and to trades where primary products were not, as yet, in demand, and where exports of British produce and manufactures to the entire continent of Spanish America and Brazil, 1841–50, averaged £5.7 million per annum.'[20]

This reinterpretation of the British government's role gained acceptance from many historians outside Latin America, but it left open other questions concerning the relationship between British businessmen and Latin American governments and elites. Much research in the United Kingdom began to concentrate on 'business imperialism', defined by Platt, rather narrowly, as the extent to which business interests had exercised control or derived excessive profits from Latin America. Initially Platt identified some possible areas of control or exploitation: the denial of credit; the influence of merchant bankers like the Rothschilds or Barings; the profits of monopolies in railways or public utilities. However, he believed that the emphasis of such research would 'likely . . . be on the limitations to the discretion and authority of the foreign entrepreneur [rather] than on the breadth of his "control"'.[21] Summing up the contributions to *Business Imperialism* (1977), which he edited, he concluded that the level of returns was not excessive and that there was no strong element of control in the business relationship. Instead, he argued, 'the case against British enterprise and capital in Latin America seems rather that it consistently outstayed its welcome, and came ultimately to serve as a barrier to, rather than promoter of, Latin America's economic development. It reinforced tendencies which turned out to be not in Latin America's best interests.'[22]

While case studies on business activities proliferated after 1970, there were many problems with this research. The British debate was hardly known in Latin America, for none of the key contributions was translated except for Ferns' book and a few of Platt's later articles. For the most part Latin American and British historians continued to talk past one another rather than to one another. There were also difficulties with the bias introduced by reliance on official and business archives in Britain; the perspective of historians in the United Kingdom (what looked marginal to the British could be central to a small Latin American country); the definitions (what exactly did terms like informal, economic or business imperialism mean?); the selection and evaluation of case studies; the fact that much of the research, including Platt's, stopped in 1914; and the generally narrow focus of the debate on the direct links between the home government, British businessmen and host governments. More radical writers, critical of the approach of the business historians, were concerned about the dominant position occupied by British interests collectively rather than the behaviour of individual firms. Others considered broader issues like the exclusion of Latin American investors from potentially profitable activities, the reinforcement of 'particular patterns of investment, production, distribution and consumption', and the internalisation of British values by Latin Americans (a particularly problematic area to research) just as important as individual examples of 'exploitation'.[23]

Latin American development theories: structuralism and dependency

The theories of Latin American development economists and sociologists provided a further input into the debate, first through the influence of the 'structuralists' working in the United Nations' Economic Commission for Latin America in Santiago (ECLA) in the 1950s and 1960s, and subsequently through that of 'dependency' writers.

Structuralists rejected the doctrine of comparative advantage to which Latin American elites and governments before 1930 had largely adhered, and thus began to rationalise the policies of import substitution and state intervention which had become dominant since the Depression. In the development of their arguments Raúl Prebisch, the Argentine economist who was the key figure in the early days of ECLA, made two points of significance for the debates about Britain's role in Latin America. First, he believed that since the 1870s the terms of trade had been moving against the primary-producing countries (the periphery) in favour of the industrial nations (the centre). This would mean that Latin American nations had to export more, simply to maintain their capacity to import. Second, under the Gold Standard, to which several Latin American countries adhered both before the First World War and during the 1920s, gold tended to drain out of the peripheral countries when the centre (London and then New York) encountered a crisis. This threw the costs of adjustment disproportionately on to peripheral states as they lost access to new capital and suffered an outflow of reserves. Over the long term, therefore, and contrary to the assumptions of liberal theorists, the distribution of benefits from increased trade and investment was asymmetrical.

The most developed summary of 'structuralist' views about the historical relationship between Latin America and Britain can be found in Celso Furtado's well-known *Economic Development of Latin America* (1970). In Furtado's view, the developmental effects of foreign trade and investment before 1914 were limited because Britain and other industrial countries retained control of finance and technology, especially the supply of capital goods. This meant that, despite the increase in trade, production techniques in Latin America were hardly transformed. In addition, the instability of raw material prices and of capital flows made the administration of Latin American monetary systems and public finances extremely difficult and created enormous fluctuations in the domestic economy.[24] Arguments such as these put Britain's role in Latin America into a rather different light from the much narrower discussion of government and business behaviour which dominated the British literature. However, for the most part British historians ignored questions like the terms of trade, the volatility of financial markets, the difficulties of policy-making caused by dependence on London, and the transfer of technology, all of which were of importance for the structuralists.

What brought the Latin American approaches and some of the more conservative British historians into real conflict therefore was the controversy over the 'dependency' theories which developed in Latin America after 1965. It is difficult to summarise these briefly. 'Surveying the dependency literature,' Cristóbal Kay writes, 'is like being confronted with a Tower of Babel,' due to the quantity of literature, the variety of approaches, and the fact that many authors changed their position and arguments.[25] However, for most historians there were two central works. English-speaking writers tended to focus initially on André Gunder Frank's *Capitalism and Underdevelopment in Latin America* (1967). Only slowly did they begin to acknowledge the importance of Fernando Henrique Cardoso's and Enzo Faletto's *Dependency and Development in Latin America*, which first appeared in Spanish in 1969 but which was not published in English for another ten years.

Frank drew particularly heavily on the ideas of an earlier Marxist

Introduction

economist, Paul Baran, in order to show that the advance of capitalism and the growth of underdevelopment in Latin America were two sides of the same coin. Through a chain of exploitative relations running from the periphery to the metropolis, he argued, the surplus generated in Latin American economies was captured by national elites, who either indulged in conspicuous consumption or reinvested it unwisely in the external sector, and even more by metropolitan interests, which in the nineteenth century meant the British. The only respites occurred when wars and depressions weakened the industrial countries. In his essays on Chile and Brazil, the core of *Capitalism and Underdevelopment*, Frank reiterated, often simply by means of lengthy direct quotations, many of the criticisms which earlier nationalist and Marxist writers had made of the British. Essentially, however, he made four specific points about the British in nineteenth-century Latin America. First, although there had been a struggle between nationalists and liberals after independence, the British had eventually established in power elites who adhered to the ideals of free trade and comparative advantage. Second, the British had captured most of the surplus from the export sectors, either through direct ownership or by appropriating it through their intermediary functions. Third, they had restricted the opportunities for Latin American development by displacing local entrepreneurs who had begun to develop exports and by buying out their interests in activities like internal trade and transport. Fourth, Frank assumed that the British state would, if necessary, use force to support businessmen in dispute with Latin American governments in order to achieve these ends. The advance of liberal capitalism, he stated explicitly, was underpinned by 'arms, naval blockades, and where necessary direct military intervention and instigation of new wars, such as that of the Triple Alliance versus Paraguay'.[26]

Cardoso and Faletto were much more sophisticated in their treatment of nineteenth-century Latin America. Whereas Frank had tended to assume that the outcome was predetermined by the overwhelming power of the British, they stressed that the relationship between external forces and local elites fluctuated. In some circumstances, and here they differentiated among export sectors controlled by foreigners from the beginning, those where foreigners acquired control, and those where local producers retained ownership, there were real possibilities for Latin American economies to develop. Each country evolved its own unique relationship with foreign capitalists in the nineteenth century, and this determined both the outlook of its elite (and thus later responses to foreign enterprise) and its economic and

21

social development. In this relationship the position of the state, on which, at the time they were writing, there was relatively little research, was crucial, for on the one hand it 'was formally sovereign and ready to be an answer to the interests of the "nation", and [yet it was] simultaneously and contradictorily the instrument of international economic domination'.[27]

This analysis raised very different issues from those discussed by Frank. There was an acknowledgement that Britain's links with each country would differ. The dynamics and extent of foreign trade and investment in individual Latin American economies, and the developing relationships among businessmen, local elites and the state, were crucial variables. Although they were working in isolation from the main currents of British historiography, therefore, Cardoso and Faletto were raising very similar issues to those with which historians in the United Kingdom were concerned. In particular their emphasis on the potentially contradictory roles of the state and exporting elites in mediating between local and foreign interests was very reminiscent of Robinson's concept of the 'collaborating elite'.

These two examples indicate the diversity of 'dependency' theories, and the considerable problems which historians faced in trying to test them. Although many attempted to place research on Britain's activities in Latin America within this context, it is hardly surprising that the results were unsatisfactory, for there was as little consensus about the definition of 'dependency' as there was about the varieties of imperialism. On both sides of the Atlantic eminent historians expressed disillusion. Tulio Halperín Donghi complained of 'ever more frequent use of categories of analysis taken from Marxism with total indifference towards the historical framework for which they were developed', Héctor Pérez Brignoli of the methodology of 'dependency' writers, which, in his view, revealed 'olympian disdain for historical analysis'.[28] In Britain Platt published vehement attacks on the 'dependency school', bringing into his fire not only the work of Frank, Cardoso and Faletto but also the North American historians Stanley and Barbara Stein, who had claimed in *The Colonial Heritage of Latin America* (1970) that the 'informal empire of free trade and investment' which Britain had erected on the ruins of Spanish and Portuguese imperialism had been devastating for 'primitive' Latin American economies.[29]

Certainly there were many problems in using 'dependency' theories to dissect Britain's relationship with Latin America. As Pérez Brignoli hinted, the historical analysis which lay behind them, whether of Frank or Cardoso and Faletto, contained numerous errors, partly because of their often uncritical reliance on earlier nationalist writers and the lack of fresh empirical research. Nevertheless, the 'dependency' literature, like the structuralist interpretations which preceded it, raised questions which were crucial to the discussion of Britain's links with Latin America. The most obvious were those concerned with 'dependency' itself: the extent to which Britain stimulated the Latin American economies, and whether their incorporation into world markets dominated by Britain made them more vulnerable and dependent; the degree to which Latin American countries retained some autonomy or fell under the control of British interests; the financial flows and accumulation of profits which occurred as a result of export growth. In retrospect, however, the most important contribution of this literature was only slowly recognised by historians. Writers like Cardoso and Faletto had emphasised the relationship between the international economy, specific foreign business activities, and domestic class formation in Latin America. This highlighted the need to examine the inter-relationships in each country among three groups of actors: foreign economic interests (which were predominantly British in Brazil and the Southern Cone before 1914 but elsewhere increasingly North American), local elites, and the state. Gradually it became clear that the state was not simply the tool of local elites, and that they in turn were not simply collaborators of British and other foreign interests. The reality was much more complicated.

THE THEMES OF THIS BOOK

Both the historical survey in the first half of this chapter and the discussion of the theoretical and historiographical debates in the second show how difficult the subject of Britain's relationship with Latin America has become. Historians have to confront the problems of generalising about twenty countries over 150 years, the extraordinary complexity of the theoretical and historical controversies, and a mass of empirical case studies, many of them extremely narrow in focus. There is no consensus about what the key questions are, and a clear disjuncture between theoretical debates and the empirical research. How can one make sense of it all?

Debate has taken place at three levels, ranging from the very general to the more specific. The broadest discussion has occurred over the incorporation of Latin America into a world capitalist system dominated, until the First World War, by Britain. However, works such as Bill Albert's *South America and the World Economy* or the various chapters in the *Cambridge History of Latin America*, as well as much of the general literature inspired by 'dependency' theories, have surveyed the relationship between Latin America and the world economy in the nineteenth and twentieth centuries carefully, and for this reason it is not proposed to cover similar ground here.

As far as the relationship specifically between Britain and Latin America is concerned, there have really been two levels of debate, that over structures and that over institutional behaviour. The former is the broader one, picking up many of the questions raised by structuralist and dependency writers, and concentrating on the overall consequences for the Latin American countries of their relationship with the British economy. This considers issues like the distribution of the benefits from trade and investment; the problems of dependence on Britain for the supply of services, markets and capital; and the extent to which the connexions with Britain reinforced structural constraints on Latin American development rather than alleviating them, for example by encouraging particular patterns of consumption and investment. The debate about institutions involves the behaviour of specific British actors, especially government officials or business-men, separately or in combination. Frequently participants in this area of controversy focus on particular incidents or episodes such as international or civil wars or financial crises. In a sense the debate about structures is concerned with long-term issues, that about institutions with short-term questions, but the two overlap, and many historians have been involved at both levels, even if they have not differentiated them.

This book is an attempt to synthesise the mass of literature on Britain and Latin America in the nineteenth and twentieth centuries. The first task is to explain the long-term dynamics of British interests in Latin America – the reasons for their rise and decline and for the geographical concentration of interest which appeared. Beyond that it attempts to summarise and evaluate the behaviour of British officials and businessmen and their relationships with their counterparts in Latin America, and to outline the long-term consequences of the British connexion for the economic, political and social development of the region. The organisation is partly chronological, partly the-matic. Chapter Two surveys the eighteenth-century links between Latin America and Britain and the process of independence. The next five chapters, covering the core period of British influence in Latin America between independence and 1914, concentrate on a number of themes: the role of British government officials; the controversies about the first half-century after independence; the expansion of trade and the role of merchants; the growth of investment and the behaviour of businessmen; and the specific cases of Argentina, Brazil and Chile. Chapters Eight and Nine analyse the rapid decline of British interests after 1914 and the difficulties this created for Latin Americans. Chapter Ten adds some concluding comments about the debates over the rise and decline of British interests and their impact in Latin America, and concludes with an epilogue outlining the changes which have occurred since 1950.

REFERENCES

1. Quoted in Humphreys, *Tradition and Revolt*, p. 143.
2. Mitchell, *British Historical Statistics*, pp. 498–9. The valuation of trade, especially for the early nineteenth century, is very problematic. For further discussion see pp. 72–3.
3. 'Annual Statement of Trade and Navigation, 1860', *PP* 1861, LX.
4. Quoted in Smith, *Illusions of Conflict*, p. 191.
5. RIIA, *Problem of International Investment*, p. 121.
6. Humphreys, *Latin America and the Second World War*, II, p. 223.
7. This section is intended for readers with little knowledge of Latin American history. The Appendix (pp. 254–60) contains a chronology of key events, and suggestions for further reading on Latin American history generally can be found in the Bibliographical Essay (pp. 261–81).
8. Gootenberg, 'Population and Ethnicity', 126.
9. Marcílio, 'Population of Colonial Brazil', 63.
10. Meyer and Sherman, *Course of Mexican History*, p. 324; Platt, 'British Finance', 46.
11. Walter, 'Socioeconomic Growth of Buenos Aires', 67; Mitchell, *International Historical Statistics*, pp. 101–8.
12. For a recent and powerful reappraisal of British imperialism see Cain and Hopkins, *British Imperialism: innovation and expansion 1688–1914* and *British Imperialism: crisis and deconstruction 1914–1990*.
13. Quoted in Graham, *Britain and the Onset*, p. 73.
14. Note that further discussion and full references to the authors and works mentioned in this section are in the Bibliographical Essay and Bibliography. References here are limited to the sources of direct quotations.
15. Ghioldi, *¿Qué significa el pacto Roca?*, pp. 9 and 30–1.
16. Gallagher and Robinson, 'Imperialism of Free Trade', 1.
17. Gallagher and Robinson, 'Imperialism of Free Trade', 10.
18. Ferns, 'Britain's Informal Empire', 63.
19. Ferns, *Britain and Argentina*, p. 488.
20. Platt, 'Further Objections', 84.
21. Platt, 'Economic Imperialism and the Businessman', 308.

22. Platt, *Business Imperialism*, p. 13.
23. Winn, 'Britain's Informal Empire in Uruguay', 121.
24. See Furtado, *Economic Development*, pp. 30–9 and 151–2.
25. Kay, *Latin American Development Theories*, p. 126.
26. Frank, *Capitalism and Underdevelopment*, p. 315.
27. Cardoso, 'Consumption of Dependency Theory', 13–14.
28. Halperín Donghi, '"Dependency Theory"', 121; Pérez Brignoli, 'Economic Cycle', 8.
29. Stein and Stein, *Colonial Heritage*, pp. 134–5 and 155.

CHAPTER TWO

The Origins of British Interest in Latin America: the Colonial and Independence Eras

British commercial interest in the American colonies of Spain and Portugal has a long history, but the relationship was completely transformed in the first quarter of the nineteenth century. Three sets of events provide the context for this change: the growth of industrial production and exports in Britain; prolonged war in Europe, in which Spain was initially allied with Britain but then, from 1796 until 1808, with France; and the process of emancipation in Latin America, which began with the *de facto* independence of Buenos Aires in 1810 and lasted until 1825. The speed with which the situation developed was unexpected, especially after the British victory at Trafalgar in 1805 which destroyed French and Spanish naval power. This was quickly followed by Napoleon's institution of the 'Continental System', which effectively barred British exports from European markets and forced merchants and manufacturers to search for other outlets. Also in 1806 a Royal Navy officer, Commodore Home Popham, launched an unauthorised attack on Buenos Aires. While this episode ended in defeat for the British, it provided a catalyst for the growth of discontent with Spanish rule in the River Plate. Then, in 1807–08, Napoleon invaded the Iberian peninsula, bringing into question the whole issue of Spain's relations with its colonies, and further stimulating the incipient movements for independence.

These events created enormous opportunities for businessmen in Britain and elsewhere, and their response had a profound effect on the Latin American economies. For the government in London the volatility and unpredictability of both European and Latin American politics, together with the pressure of commercial and industrial interests, gave rise to serious strategic and diplomatic problems. Not until the late 1820s did the future outline of Britain's diplomatic and commercial links with Latin America become clear.

BRITISH TRADE AND THE SPANISH EMPIRE BEFORE INDEPENDENCE

The commercial system which brought so much wealth to Spain in the century after the discovery of Mexico and Peru had decayed by 1700. Production of silver had fallen, while Spain could no longer supply the colonists with the goods they desired. Although Spanish merchants maintained their official monopoly of trade with the colonies, most of the goods they exported to America came from other European countries, and they aimed generally to keep supplies short and prices high. Annual fleets continued to operate to Mexico and, via Panama, to Peru, but other regions of the empire remained on the margins of trade. This, together with the poor salaries received by officials who had purchased their posts from the Crown, and the inability of Spain to police the coastline of its colonies, stimulated corruption and contraband. While the Dutch were probably the greatest smugglers of the seventeenth century, English possessions in the Caribbean provided a base for both the plunder of Spanish shipping and the development of trade with Spanish settlements, in which slaves and foodstuffs were exchanged for dyes and bullion. Jamaica, which an English expedition had captured in 1655, possessed a trade with the Spanish colonies worth between £100,000 and £200,000 annually by the end of the century.[1] However, the English were still weaker than their rivals. The French benefited more from the disintegration of the Spanish commercial system during the war of 1702–13, as they seized the opportunity to supply Spanish colonies with slaves and to sail directly to Chile and Peru.

Nevertheless, in 1713, under the Treaty of Utrecht, Spain conceded the *asiento*, the exclusive right to supply slaves to its empire, to England. The South Sea Company would transport to the colonies 4800 adult male slaves (or their equivalent) a year, a quarter of them to Buenos Aires. To facilitate this trade the company was permitted to establish depots at seven ports (Cartagena, Buenos Aires, Vera Cruz, Havana, Santiago de Cuba, Porto Bello and Panama) and import the supplies necessary to maintain the unsold slaves.[2] In addition the company could send one ship to each of the annual trade fairs which Spain hoped to re-establish along with the old fleet system.

The potential for using the *asiento*, which lasted until 1739, to infiltrate American markets was immense. The South Sea Company even allocated funds specifically to bribe Spanish officials. Contraband goods like woollen textiles arrived on both slave ships and supply vessels. Moreover, in the 1720s Spanish administrators permitted company agents to travel overland from Buenos Aires to Chile and Peru to sell slaves there. Both these markets very quickly became saturated with European imports. Although the company sent only nine Annual Ships to fairs in Vera Cruz and Porto Bello during the *asiento*, almost invariably they flooded the markets with cheap goods, provided a cover for contraband trade for themselves and other Europeans, and totally disrupted the legal commerce of the Cadiz merchants.

Through the remainder of the century the British traded with the Spanish empire through both legitimate and illegitimate channels. Despite the high duties imposed by Spain many merchants still preferred to ship regularly through Cadiz. This required less credit, avoided the costs and risks of lawbreaking, and gave them access to Royal Navy ships to consign silver home. The contraband trade followed several different paths. The dominance of English merchants in Lisbon's trade permitted goods to reach Buenos Aires through Brazil and the Portuguese outpost at Colônia do Sacramento on the Plate estuary. A Spanish raid in 1762 found twenty-seven ships loaded with British merchandise there; at the time this commerce was valued at over £200,000 annually.[3] The Caribbean was also a centre of illicit trade, in part encouraged by the British government's Free Ports Act of 1766, which permitted Spanish colonists to sell dyestuffs (logwood, cochineal, indigo), livestock and bullion in West Indian ports in exchange for rum, slaves and manufactures. However, merchants in Kingston traded actively with Spanish colonists on the Caribbean mainland both in peace and in war throughout the century; the coastguard fleet based in Cartagena and responsible for halting smuggling actually relied on Jamaican re-exports of North American flour. Another route for contraband passed through the growing British logwood settlements in Central America. From the Caribbean and Atlantic ports of the Spanish empire foreign goods then reached the Mesoamerican and Andean highlands and the Pacific seaboard.

By the early 1760s the British, through their role in trade and their naval power, had become the principal threat to Spain's control of its empire. Their capture and occupation of Havana in 1762–63 sent shockwaves throughout the imperial structure and provoked a series of Spanish reforms intended to safeguard the empire from further British penetration and ultimate collapse. The strengthening of defence required revenue, and this meant regaining control over colonial trade and increasing its volume. Ports in Spain and the colonies were gradually given greater freedom to trade with each other, breaking the inefficient monopoly of the Cadiz merchants. The creation of the Viceroyalty of the River Plate in 1776 and the capture of Colônia do Sacramento the following year were intended to counter the British threat in the South Atlantic. In the short term the reforms appeared to bear fruit. Revenue and trade increased dramatically, especially after the War of American Independence ended in 1783. Spain's exports quadrupled between 1778 and 1796, while imports from America rose tenfold.[4] To some extent, at least, the Crown had succeeded in diverting exports like hides from the River Plate or Central American indigo from contraband into legitimate channels, even though Britain remained the ultimate market.

This success was partial and short-lived. Investigations by the Spanish government in 1789 showed that contraband was still rampant, foreigners were trading directly with the colonies, and most of the legal trade through Spain consisted of re-exports of goods from Britain and elsewhere. One persistent problem was the demand for labour in certain colonies. Permission for the free entry of slaves was granted to the Caribbean islands in 1789, Cartagena and Buenos Aires in 1791, and Peru in 1795, but it allowed foreigners to introduce other goods into these markets under the cover of slave-trading; in 1794 Spain also permitted its own subjects to trade with foreign ports to buy slaves. The growth of whaling expeditions also brought foreign vessels into the South Atlantic and South Pacific. Six English ships alone visited Chilean ports under this guise between 1792 and 1795.[5]

When war broke out with Britain in 1796, Spain's direct trade with the empire collapsed due to the Royal Navy's control of the Atlantic. Exports began to accumulate in colonial ports, and the demand for imports grew. Britain's own trade with America was diverted rather than halted. In 1797 Spain authorised neutral ships to trade with the empire. This permitted Portuguese, North American, Danish and German ships, sometimes used as flags of convenience by English merchants, to continue to sell British textiles and hardware to Spanish American markets, as well as sugar, grain, wine and manufactured goods from other sources. Contraband trade in the Caribbean continued, and perhaps expanded. In 1804 Jamaica's trade with the Spanish colonies was valued at 1 million pesos (about

£200,000), while Port of Spain in Trinidad, which the British had captured in 1797, exported British manufactures worth 850,000 pesos (about £170,000), 70 per cent of them cotton and linen textiles, to Spanish America.[6]

During the eighteenth century, therefore, the British made increasing commercial inroads into the Spanish empire, but with occasional reverses during wartime and some redirection of trade in the 1780s as a result of Spain's reforms. Spain's weaknesses lay in its maintenance of an outdated and inefficient monopoly system, the corruption which pervaded the imperial administration, and its inability to supply the colonies with shipping facilities, manufactures and slaves. These were gaps which the British, with their colonies in the Caribbean and their close relationship with the Portuguese in Brazil, could fill. As their own industry grew, they also offered a growing market for goods like dyestuffs and hides, and they had a voracious appetite for silver on which they depended to balance their own trade with the Far East. The combination of efficient shipping, a stronger manufacturing base and easier credit enabled them to surpass their two principal rivals, the French and the Dutch.

Some points of significance for the later history of Britain's relations with Latin America are evident. Contacts with different parts of the Spanish empire varied greatly. They were most intense in the Caribbean and the River Plate, less with Mexico (perhaps because of the greater Spanish presence and the low demand for slaves there), and infrequent and generally indirect with the Pacific ports. There were also hints of two problems which would become more obvious in the independence era and its aftermath. Latin American markets could easily become saturated by a sudden influx of imports. By 1810, after contraband valued at 20 million pesos (£4 million) had entered Peru in the previous decade, Lima had sufficient stocks of imported merchandise to satisfy four years' demand.[7] There is also some evidence that imports were beginning to undermine local textile workshops in Mexico and the Andes, as highland producers lost markets on the coast to European goods.

ENGLAND AND THE PORTUGUESE EMPIRE IN THE EIGHTEENTH CENTURY

In most eighteenth-century conflicts Britain fought against Spain. Portugal, on the other hand, had been a consistent ally since the middle of the seventeenth century, although increasingly subject to British dominance. A series of treaties, beginning in 1642, established English privileges in Portugal's, and hence Brazil's, trade. In 1654 English merchants received the right to trade with all its colonies including Brazil, as long as their ships accompanied the Portuguese fleets, and in 1661 they were granted permission to reside in Bahia, Pernambuco and Rio de Janeiro, although this privilege was also granted to the French and the Dutch.

By the end of the seventeenth century, however, the commercial links between England and Portugal were entering a crisis. English restrictions discriminated against imports of Brazilian sugar and tobacco, while the Portuguese were developing some textile production. The famous Methuen Treaty of 1703, in which Portugal granted tariff reductions on the import of woollen textiles from England in exchange for concessions on wine, helped to reverse the trend, though the Dutch also obtained similar concessions. More significantly, gold had been discovered in Brazil shortly before, stimulating an enormous expansion of the colonial market. Portugal consequently bought large quantities of English woollens for export to Brazil (and through Colônia do Sacramento to the Spanish settlements in the Plate). In return Royal Navy ships and the monthly Falmouth packet, both of which were immune from search by the Portuguese, carried gold from Lisbon to England. Even in the late 1760s, when gold mining was in decline, over £1 million a year was estimated to pass through Falmouth alone in exchange for exports to Portugal and Brazil.[8] In many respects this bore out the warning made by the Governor of Bahia in 1701 that the discovery of gold would give England, France and the Netherlands 'all the profit, while we have all the work'.[9] What was not clear in 1701 was that the English would benefit most. The reasons why they did so were much the same as in Spanish America: the unique combination of maritime power and efficient commercial shipping, financial resources, and the growing manufacturing base which they possessed.

This penetration of the Portuguese colonial economy was not an unremitting process. There are signs that Portugal's commercial dependence diminished after the Seven Years' War (1756–63). Although the statistics are very imprecise, it seems that by the 1790s Britain had a negative trade balance with Portugal. This was due in part to the fall in Brazilian gold production and the Spanish capture of Colônia, but also to the vigorous measures taken to reconstruct the Portuguese imperial economy. Like his contemporaries in Spain, Pombal, the chief minister of Portugal, determined to reverse the growing foreign penetration of the empire. Besides attempting to halt the unauthorised export of bullion, restrict contraband, and curtail the privileges of English merchants, he established monopoly companies open only to Portuguese nationals to trade with Pará and Maranhão in the north of Brazil (1755), and with Paraíba and Pernambuco (1759). The government also stimulated industry in Portugal and agriculture in Brazil with some success: domestic manufactures accounted for an increasing share of Portugal's trade, while raw cotton exports from Brazil grew from less than £100,000 in 1785 to over £600,000 in 1791.[10] By 1792 Brazil was supplying 30 per cent of England's growing demand for cotton fibre, and it was partly due to this that the balance of trade had turned round. However, the growth of the Brazilian economy also helped to encourage direct trade in English ships. Eight arrived at Rio in 1791, thirty in 1800.[11] For Portugal, as for Spain, the outbreak of war in Europe halted its attempts to regain control of colonial trade.

THE INDEPENDENCE PERIOD, 1806–1825

The background

In the first part of the war which engulfed Europe between 1792 and 1815 relations between Latin America and Britain were affected chiefly by the reorientation of trade and the growth of contraband. In many respects the tactics of the Anglo–Spanish war after 1796 (British attacks on Spain's shipping and colonial outposts) resembled conflicts earlier in the century. However, the second phase of the war, especially between 1806 and 1815, and the years which followed the restoration of the absolutist monarchy in Spain in 1814 saw much more profound changes.

By 1806 Napoleon, with whom Spain was allied, dominated the continent of Europe while Britain, following the battle of Trafalgar, possessed control of the seas. Napoleon's introduction of the 'Continental System' that year was a deliberate attempt to blockade Britain's trade and curtail its economic power, but the Iberian peninsula, and particularly Britain's ally, Portugal, was potentially a weak link in these efforts. Napoleon therefore launched an attack on Portugal late in 1807 which precipitated the flight of the Portuguese royal family to Brazil on British warships. The following year he intervened in a dispute between Charles IV of Spain and his son,

Ferdinand, and placed his own brother, Joseph, on the Spanish throne. The results were unexpected: revolts broke out in several regions of Spain in support of Ferdinand VII, as well as in Portugal, and British forces were quickly sent to their aid. In 1812 the rebels in Spain adopted a liberal monarchical constitution, which, although rejected by Ferdinand when he returned in 1814, remained a rallying point for dissidents.

In Spanish America the disruption of Spain created conflicts of loyalty for the colonists and provided a catalyst for the first real independence movements. Between 1809 and 1814 revolts occurred in Buenos Aires, Venezuela, New Granada, Peru and Upper Peru, Chile and Mexico, but only the first was successful. Although the United Provinces of the River Plate, led by Buenos Aires, declared their independence in 1816, the firm action of viceroys in Mexico and Peru together with a Spanish military expedition to Venezuela and New Granada quelled the other movements, if not the sentiment, for independence.

After 1815 the major powers of Europe attempted to preserve a balance of power among themselves, and, in Britain's case particularly, to limit the influence of France, but the continuing instability of Spain and its empire provided a serious threat to this. The movements for emancipation regained strength. Victories at Maipo in 1818 and Boyacá in 1819 secured the independence of Chile and New Granada respectively. Then a Spanish expeditionary force assembled in Cadiz to sail for the Plate mutinied at the beginning of 1820 and reimposed the liberal constitution in Spain. Both Mexico and Peru declared their independence in 1821. In Europe concerted action among the powers broke down with the Congress of Verona in 1822. The following year France, much to Britain's disquiet, intervened in Spain to restore absolutist rule.

British policies towards Spanish America

Until Popham's unofficial expedition to Buenos Aires in 1806 British governments had given little thought to the future of the Spanish possessions in America. In eighteenth-century wars attacks against key points, like Havana in 1762, had been intended primarily to secure bargaining counters for the subsequent peace negotiations. Disputes with Spain over the Falklands/Malvinas in 1770–71, and Nootka Sound on the west coast of North America in 1790, had briefly threatened conflict but were soon defused. As long as legitimate trade and contraband were largely unhindered, there was little incentive to force an entry to markets which were less important than those in Europe, the United States and the West Indies. British policy between 1783 and 1806 was, in John Lynch's words, 'diffident' and 'vague', dominated by the negative aim of forestalling the French.[12] Plots to attack different parts of the empire were occasionally hatched by creole exiles such as the Venezuelan patriot Francisco de Miranda, British adventurers and even individual ministers, but they received no support from the government.

The news of Popham's initial success, while causing enormous euphoria in commercial circles, created considerable confusion within the government. By the time news of his surrender arrived, reinforcements had already been despatched, but they too were forced to withdraw from the Plate in July 1807. The commanders had been given no clear instructions about Britain's aims in South America, for there was no agreement among ministers. Some desired conquest, either in the hope of obtaining permanent possessions or for the traditional purpose of acquiring cards to play during peace negotiations. A minority favoured giving encouragement, even physical aid, to creole movements for independence in the hope of obtaining concessions for British trade. Most conservatives, however, fearful of unleashing social revolution in the wake of France and St Domingue, were cautious about encouraging colonial dissidents to revolt against Spanish power.

The first clear statement of policy came in a memorandum written by Lord Castlereagh, the Secretary for War and the Colonies, in 1807, shortly before news of the failure in the River Plate arrived. Asking, in the light of Napoleon's blockade of British goods, how the country might secure 'the opening to our manufactures of the markets of that great Continent [South America]', he rejected the first option, 'the hopeless task of conquering this extensive country against the temper of its population'. He was doubtful too about attempting to foment revolt against Spain, although should it occur British forces might act as 'auxiliaries and protectors'. 'In endeavouring to promote and combine the happiness of the people with the extension of our commerce,' he argued, 'we might, in destroying a bad government, leave them without any government at all.'[13] The subsequent news from Buenos Aires that the creoles had failed to ally with the British forces against their Spanish rulers confirmed doubts about the extent of sentiment for independence in South America.

Over the next few years the strategic principles established by Castlereagh remained the basis of British policy, although tactics altered in accordance with events in Europe and Spanish America.

Arthur Wellesley (later the Duke of Wellington) began to assemble an expedition to attack Mexico, primarily with the aim of obtaining silver to finance the war, although possibly also with the intention of further testing the desire for independence. However, the Spanish uprising in 1808 turned these plans on their head. Britain became allied to the rebels in Spain and the need for military action in Europe became paramount. Wellesley's forces embarked for the Iberian peninsula rather than Mexico.

Policy-making in the subsequent decade was extraordinarily difficult. The wartime alliance with Spain, and then, after 1815, the need to prevent Spain's weaknesses from undermining the European diplomatic system, made it impossible to give overt support to revolutionaries in the colonies, despite pressure from commercial interests and public opinion in Britain. Successive foreign secretaries attempted to persuade Spain to accept British mediation to resolve its conflict with the rebels in Spanish America, in return for commercial concessions in the empire, but without success. Spanish ministers had so much distrust of British commercial ambitions that they would not tolerate British demands for trading concessions and imperial reform. Mediation, they believed, should depend on the threat of coercion, but the British government refused to provide military support for efforts to subdue the revolts. The one positive move which affected the outcome of the revolutions was Britain's decision to station warships in the South Atlantic in 1808, largely to defend the continent from the French. The Navy already had bases in the Caribbean, and it also extended operations into the Pacific in 1812. Britain's naval power thus isolated the revolutions in Spanish America from the struggles in Europe until after the defeat of Napoleon.

After 1815 policy-making remained complicated. Domestically Castlereagh, the Foreign Secretary, faced increasing pressure from commercial interests in favour of Latin American independence, but also the conservatism of many of his cabinet colleagues and the Prince Regent. Spain remained intransigent over concessions to the colonies and began to seek aid from other powers, initially Russia, to subdue the revolts. For all these reasons policy remained extremely cautious. Castlereagh tended to respond to events rather than creating them. His great diplomatic success, at a time when neither Venezuelan nor Argentine independence was secure, came in 1817 when he secured a guarantee from the European powers that no forces other than Spain's would be sent to the New World. However, further problems arose when Spain complained about the recruiting of British mercenaries for Bolívar's armies in Venezuela and New Granada. On this Castlereagh, fearing opposition both in Parliament and from the press to any attempts to halt recruitment, prevaricated, and by the time the British government passed the Foreign Enlistment Act in 1819, over 5000 British soldiers had embarked for Latin America.

The success of the revolutions and the advent of republics demanding international recognition of their independence in the early 1820s made it more difficult to delay decisions. Bolívar's envoy threatened commercial sanctions against nations which did not recognise Gran Colombia (the former viceroyalty of New Granada). The United States, once its treaty with Spain transferring Florida had been ratified in 1821, also declared its intention to recognise the new republics. Yet in London it still seemed important not to alienate Spain. Moreover, while public opinion favoured recognition, the King and some of Castlereagh's cabinet colleagues were still strongly opposed to the idea of giving approval to countries born in rebellion against a monarchy. Castlereagh's solution to this impasse was twofold. First, he decided to allow Spanish American vessels to enter British ports. This provided them with *de facto* recognition and separated the commercial and diplomatic issues. Second, he warned Spain before the Congress of Verona in 1822 that Britain could not wait indefinitely. Recognition of the republics was 'rather . . . a matter of time than of principle'.[14] Shortly after making this statement Castlereagh died.

Canning, his successor, faced the same domestic problems and a deteriorating international situation. Although he favoured recognition of the new republics himself, he did not have the political influence within the cabinet Castlereagh had possessed. His hopes of cooperation with the United States failed, leading to President Monroe's unilateral declaration in December 1823 that the United States would not countenance the establishment of further European colonies or the transfer of European political systems to the New World. Moreover, it was not until October 1823, six months after their invasion of Spain, that the French agreed, in the Polignac Memorandum, not to send forces to aid Spain in the New World.

Gradually Canning gained his case. At the end of 1823 he obtained the cabinet's agreement to send consuls and special commissioners to Spanish America to investigate the reality of independence. Yet formal recognition still required another battle in cabinet, won only when he and the Prime Minister threatened resignation in December 1824. The argument hinged on international factors, the fear that France would extend its influence and that the United States, which had already granted recognition, might gain a preponderant position in the former Spanish colonies, especially Mexico. Recognition took the form of commercial treaties, signed with Gran Colombia and the United Provinces of the River Plate in 1825 and with Mexico in 1827. Both the United Provinces and Gran Colombia, perceiving British recognition as essential for their security, quickly accepted Canning's demands for free access for British shipping and 'most favoured nation' status for their exports.[15] Mexico attempted, unsuccessfully, to obtain guarantes for a loan and support against an anticipated Spanish attack. These treaties did not affect Britain's policy of preference for its own colonies; 'most favoured nation' treatment in the British market did not mean that Latin American countries could compete on equal terms with colonial products, only with other 'foreign' goods. It should also be noted that even the first treaties came well after the expansion of trade and borrowing. The Latin American republics had already gained access to the London capital market three years before the British government recognised independence. Indeed, agreement on the treaties came just as trade was declining and the republics were defaulting on their loans.

Evaluating British diplomacy

British diplomacy was certainly skilful, in the sense that it avoided a break with Spain, kept the other European powers out of Spanish America, and maintained Britain's commercial position in the region while avoiding social revolution there. But how significant was it for the independence process itself? Is there any evidence that the government and the business community were attempting jointly to secure Spanish American independence in order to gain access to its markets, as some have supposed?

Canning's views were certainly closer to those of the merchants than Castlereagh's, but by the time he gained control of foreign policy recognition was simply a matter of time. It was not necessary for Britain's commercial expansion, except in the marginal sense of providing written protection for merchants and guarantees of fair treatment on tariffs. For merchants the most important decisions had been taken earlier, when Britain stationed warships in the Atlantic and Pacific, for these provided them with some protection against physical attack or discriminatory treatment in Latin America itself. Overall, the impact of the government in London on the independence process was a neutral one; it prevented other European powers from interfering and ensured that the conflict was one between 'patriots' and Spaniards.

If British officials did have an impact on the independence process and the expansion of trade, it came from those in the region rather than the foreign secretaries in London. In the early nineteenth century delays in communications, which might amount to several months, meant that what governments in Europe said and what their agents on the other side of the Atlantic did might be very different. Popham had invaded the River Plate without permission, and throughout this episode the government was responding to reports written three or four months earlier. The reinforcements sent in October 1806 did not know of the loss of Buenos Aires until they arrived in the Plate three months later. Moreover, the instructions given to British representatives were often imprecise, and on occasion non-existent. Lord Strangford, the minister in Lisbon, arranged the successful escape of the Portuguese court in 1807 largely on his own initiative. Having followed them to Brazil, where he remained from July 1808 until 1814, he played a central role in restricting Portuguese ambitions in the Banda Oriental (present-day Uruguay), where they came into conflict with the Argentine *junta*, and in preserving free access for British merchants to Buenos Aires and Montevideo. The degree of personal initiative he had to possess is illustrated by the fact that at one stage the Foreign Office left him without instructions for two years.

In fact, for most of the independence period the key officials in Spanish America, though not in Brazil, were responsible not to the Foreign Office, since diplomatic ties did not exist, but to the Admiralty or the Colonial Office. This is one reason why D.A.G. Waddell could write that it was 'one thing to formulate a policy of neutrality in London, but it was quite another matter to implement it in the Caribbean'.[16] The implementation of policy and the protection of merchants were the responsibility of Britain's colonial governors in the Caribbean and naval officers elsewhere. In the early stages of the Venezuelan struggle governors in Curaçao intervened on behalf of the patriots, while those in Trinidad tended to be more pro-royalist. Although neither had much long-term impact, both could upset events in the short run. Naval officers, perhaps because of their connexions with merchants, tended to be sympathetic towards independence, but their overriding task was to protect English commerce rather than support one side or the other.

Finally, the British government could do little to control the activities of either merchants or mercenaries. Hyslops of Jamaica acted as agents for the patriot governments in New Granada throughout the 1810s, while in the struggle to eject the Spaniards from Chile and Peru merchants sold military equipment to both sides, being, in Consul-General Ricketts' words, 'alone influenced by their own temporary advantage'.[17] Although the British government banned the export of weapons directly to Spanish America, rebels could always obtain them by trans-shipment from a third country. Moreover, the government could find no *effective* measures to prevent the recruitment of soldiers and sailors. Lord Cochrane organised the navies of Chile and Brazil, General Miller was a leader of Bolívar's armies in Peru, and later, in the renewed clash between Argentina and Brazil over the Banda Oriental in the 1820s, the two rival navy commanders were both British. Thus the actions of individual British naval captains, merchants and soldiers had much more influence on local independence struggles than the government in London. What is surprising, perhaps, is that they did not undermine the cautious and neutral approach of the latter more frequently.

British trade in the independence period

In Spanish America the renewal of war in 1803 after a short truce made direct trade with Spain almost impossible, while British merchants began to search for alternative markets, especially after the closure of continental Europe to them in 1806. With some encouragement from the government greater numbers of ships began to trade directly with South America. In twelve months in 1808–09 over thirty British vessels arrived in Buenos Aires, while in 1807–08 twelve left British ports for the west coast of South America.[18] For Spanish officials in America, starved of access to the outside world and desperate for revenue, there was little alternative but to permit trade in order to tax it, and as the independence wars proceeded both sides opened the ports. In 1809 the viceroy permitted allied and neutral shipping to enter Buenos Aires; royal officials granted access to Havana the same year, while the patriots opened Caracas in 1810 and Cartagena and Valparaiso in 1811. Under pressure from local interests, officials often attempted to restrict the activities of foreigners, by barring them from the retail or coastal trade and insisting that goods were consigned to native merchants, but it is doubtful whether these limitations were particularly effective.

How important was British trade with Latin America at this time, and what was its impact? For Britain the Latin American market, especially after 1806 when other outlets were closed, was crucial to its growing textile exports. François Crouzet comments that 'the greatest gain to British trade from 1808 onward came from the opening of Brazil and of the Spanish colonies'.[19] Modern recalculations of Britain's commercial statistics suggest that Latin America took exports worth £1.1 million, 2 per cent of the total, in 1804–06, but £5.0 million, 13 per cent of the total, in 1824–26.[20] The optimism about the commercial possibilities of the region was well expressed by Lord Brougham who told the House of Commons in 1817 that 'no field of enterprise [was] so magnificent in promise . . . as the vast continent of South America.'[21] Yet problems persisted. Whenever ports were opened British goods and merchants, along with those from other countries, arrived in floods, quickly satiating demand and creating stockpiles of unsaleable products. As early as 1811 a Parliamentary Select Committee attributed much of the commercial distress in Britain to the 'great and extensive speculations, which commenced upon the opening of the South American markets in the Brazils and elsewhere'.[22] Within six months of the reopening of the ports in Chile in 1817 after a three-year closure the warehouses were filled with foreign merchandise.

One of the major problems for Latin Americans was that the opening of trade coincided with falling prices for key imports, especially cotton textiles. If several foreign ships arrived together, the need to make profits or cut losses as quickly as possible led to the dumping of vast quantities of cheap goods, with adverse consequences for native merchants and local producers. The effects went deeper, however. Spanish American exports were limited. Import bills often had to be settled with bullion, which had long-term implications for the capital and credit resources of the former colonies. The local merchants also suffered from the instability caused by the cyclical shortages and surpluses, and disruption due to blockades and privateers at sea and the civil wars on land.

The British were the most visible and wealthiest of the foreigners. They appeared to be both the cause of the difficulties being suffered by local economies, yet also the principal beneficiaries. Merchants in Buenos Aires complained in 1815 that if the British achieved their supposed ambitions of displacing them in Upper Peru, Paraguay and the Banda Oriental, 'the country will be completely destroyed: we will have nothing to eat, and our children will be even more wretched. The state will have no taxpayers . . .' The foreigners, they added, had established themselves in the retail trade, persisted in contraband activities, and promoted the indiscriminate slaughter of the pampas' livestock.[23] The British appeared to possess overwhelming advantages. In particular a sympathetic naval commander might provide them with protection from a legitimate blockade or prevent a patriotic government in need of funds from levying forced loans on them, as in Buenos Aires in 1818 and Chile in 1820.

It is unclear, however, just how dominant the British were among the foreigners; it seems to have varied over time and from one port to another. 'The power of England,' one French agent wrote in Colombia in 1823, 'is without a rival in America. . . . Her merchandises are bought almost exclusively; her commercial agents, her clerks and brokers, are everywhere to be met with.'[24] Such evidence should not be accepted unreservedly. Merchants from the United States, with their cargoes of foodstuffs, and Europeans like the French and Germans also appeared in large numbers after 1820, while some local merchants took advantage of the changing commercial situation as well. The hundreds of traders who arrived after the opening of the ports were quickly diminished by business failures. By the end of the independence era, although the British were frequently among the wealthiest and most influential merchants, they were far from monopolising trade. Statistics from the period are not very trustworthy, but in 1824, when Britain's exports to the Plate exceeded £1 million, British vessels accounted for only 23 per cent of the shipping tonnage entering Argentine ports. Of forty leading merchants identified in Chile between 1818 and 1828 only fifteen originated in Britain, and some of those had become naturalised Chileans; over half came from peninsular or Spanish American backgrounds.[25]

Britain and Brazil in the independence period

The case of Brazil differed from that of Spanish America in several respects. The greater commercial opportunities which Brazil offered and the experience British merchants possessed of this trade, together with political factors, the long association between Britain and Portugal and the exile of the Portuguese royal family, combined to create a situation in which the British government had more influence and more impact than in Spanish America. In Sir Charles Webster's view, British actions almost certainly meant not only that Brazil achieved independence relatively peacefully but also that it retained a monarch from the Bragança dynasty.[26]

A week after he arrived in Bahia under British protection in January 1808 Dom João, the Prince Regent of Portugal, opened Brazil's trade to all friendly nations, largely to reduce the stocks of sugar and tobacco awaiting export there. The British poured in. By August they had between 150 and 200 merchants and commercial agents in Brazil.

Trade increased fourfold in 1808, although imports quickly saturated the markets.[27] Brazil, however, possessed exportable products other than bullion (cotton, sugar, tobacco, coffee). This, as well as the absence of civil war until the 1820s, permitted commerce to expand more quickly than in Spanish America. The market's importance and Portugal's dependence on Britain also gave the British the opportunity and incentive to negotiate a commercial treaty from a powerful bargaining position.

British diplomats therefore secured privileges in Brazil which they could not obtain elsewhere. In February 1810 the Portuguese agreed to the appointment of special magistrates for British commercial affairs and a maximum import duty of 15 per cent on British goods, compared with the 24 per cent paid by others. Portugal received no special favours in the British market in return; indeed, discrimination against Brazilian coffee and sugar in favour of colonial produce continued. The treaty was intended to be permanent, although subject to revision after fifteen years. 'Odious and impolitic', Canning, who had been Foreign Secretary when Strangford received his negotiating instructions, later called it, claiming that the Board of Trade had forced it on him.[28]

It certainly antagonised the Brazilians, whom Dom João had not consulted. They also complained about British pressure on them to end the slave trade, and the conflict with Buenos Aires over the Banda Oriental further complicated relations. Britain's political influence declined rapidly, especially when Strangford attempted to persuade Dom João to return to Lisbon in 1814. Castlereagh was forced to recall him, leaving Britain's affairs in Brazil in the hands of a consul-general for four years. Yet despite these difficulties trade flourished. In the middle of the decade Brazil was Britain's most important market in South America, taking perhaps three-quarters of all exports to the region (and three-quarters of those were cotton textiles). In some respects it had become the 'Emporium for British Manufactures destined for the consumption of the whole of South America' which Canning had envisaged in his original instructions to Strangford, and an especially useful base for contraband in the Plate.[29]

Dom João was eventually forced by the Portuguese liberals to return to Lisbon in 1821. Dom Pedro, his son, declared Brazil's independence the following year, in an attempt to maintain Bragança control of both countries. This again thrust Brazil into dependence on Britain, now to defend its security against Lisbon, but it created additional difficulties for Canning because of the long-standing alliance between Britain and Portugal. There were other threats to Britain's interests. Brazil was Britain's third-largest foreign market, and the 1810 treaty would become liable to revision in 1825. Moreover, Brazilian independence also threatened British action against the slave trade, since the status of Portugal's colonies in Africa was uncertain. Yet Canning wished not to antagonise the one monarchy still existing in a continent of republics. The situation demanded careful handling in order to isolate Portugal from its potential European allies, and thus compel it to recognise Brazil's independence. As in Spanish America Britain needed to remain on good terms with both sides, but here the stakes were much higher.

The skilful diplomacy of Canning and his envoys took full advantage of Dom Pedro's desperate need for recognition to preserve Brazil's unity and independence against attack from both Portugal and Spanish America. Britain emerged from the process with Bragança monarchs in Lisbon and Rio de Janeiro, the African colonies separated from Brazil, and a treaty which committed the government in Rio to terminate the slave trade three years after ratification. Despite his condemnation of the inequalities of the 1810 treaty Canning insisted that British merchants should maintain their privileged legal status in Brazil. The maximum duty of 15 per cent on imports also remained, although other nations soon gained similar tariff concessions under 'most favoured nation' clauses. Nevertheless, the treaty, which in these respects was quite unlike those negotiated with the Spanish American republics, circumscribed the powers of the Brazilian government to raise revenue or to impose protectionist measures until 1844, when it finally expired. In the Brazilian context, much more than in Spanish America, British policy, in Webster's words, 'sometimes appeared to amount to dictation', and the concessions to Britain were one of the many grievances which led to the alienation of Dom Pedro from the Brazilian elite and his eventual abdication in 1831.[30]

CONCLUSION

What is most noticeable about Britain's relationship with Latin America during the independence era is that government policy and commercial expansion were largely independent of one another. There was certainly no joint 'project', shared by government and merchants, to bring Latin America to independence in order to open it as a market. Commercial interests would have liked the recognition of independence and the negotiation of commercial treaties to have occurred much earlier, but they managed quite well without them, and what really mattered was the presence of warships which could provide some protection. The government in London was much more concerned about the war against Napoleon, and then about the international balance of power. These considerations, coupled with the conservative attitudes of George IV and many ministers, forced it to proceed slowly and cautiously. Commercially, the opening of Latin American markets after 1806 provided the United Kingdom, at least in the short term, with a solution to the closure of outlets elsewhere. What was quite unclear, as the independence era drew to a close, was the long-term potential of South America, which had absorbed substantial quantities of British goods and created enormous wealth for some merchants, but also bankrupted many.

In Spanish America the sharp rise in Britain's, and other foreign nations', commercial presence had a significant impact. Local production was damaged by the influx of consumer imports, especially textiles (although the *extent* of the harm is quite unclear), the old commercial structures were undermined, native merchants found it difficult to adjust, and there was a considerable outflow of bullion, both in payment for imports and accompanying the retreating Spaniards. Some of these outcomes were less apparent in Brazil, where textile manufacturing had not developed on the same scale, and there were other exportable products besides precious metals. There, however, the British could exert diplomatic as well as commercial pressure, and this resulted in the operation, until 1844, of treaties which were more inequitable than those signed with the Spanish American republics.

REFERENCES

1. Fortune, *Merchants and Jews*, pp. 114 and 148; Nettels, 'England and the Spanish American Trade', 8.
2. Caracas was added in 1735.
3. Villalobos, *Comercio y contrabando*, p. 21.
4. Fisher, *Commercial Relations*, pp. 48–61.
5. Villalobos, *El comercio y la crisis colonial*, pp. 141–49.
6. Goebel, 'British Trade', 293.
7. Haitin, 'Urban Market and Agrarian Hinterland', 284.
8. Boxer, 'Brazilian Gold', 471.
9. Quoted in Boxer, 'Brazilian Gold', 458.

10. Manchester, *British Pre-Eminence*, p. 52.
11. Alden, 'Late Colonial Brazil, 1750–1808', 639.
12. Lynch, 'British Policy', 1.
13. Quoted in Webster (ed.), *Britain and the Independence*, I, p. 9.
14. Quoted in Waddell, 'International Politics', 211.
15. Under the 'most favoured nation' clause of a commercial treaty an exporter could claim equal treatment if any concession, for example over tariffs on a particular product, were granted to a third country.
16. Waddell, 'British Relations with Venezuela', 29.
17. Quoted in Humphreys, *Tradition and Revolt*, p. 129.
18. Goebel, 'British Trade', 309 and 316.
19. Crouzet, 'Toward an Export Economy', 72.
20. Davis, *The Industrial Revolution*, pp. 96–101.
21. Quoted in Lynch, 'Great Britain', 15.
22. Quoted in Humphreys, *Tradition and Revolt*, pp. 112–13.
23. Quoted in Segreti, 'La política económica porteña', 66–7.
24. Quoted in Humphreys, *Tradition and Revolt*, p. 144.
25. Ferns, *Britain and Argentina*, pp. 132–3; Rector, 'Transformaciones comerciales', 125–6.
26. Webster (ed.), *Britain and the Independence*, I, pp. 73–5.
27. Bethell, 'The Independence of Brazil', 173.
28. Quoted in Webster (ed.), *Britain and the Independence*, I, p. 54.
29. Quoted in Manchester, *British Pre-Eminence*, p. 78.
30. Webster (ed.), *Britain and the Independence*, I, p. 53.

CHAPTER THREE

The British Government and Latin America from Independence to 1914

Views of the role played by the British government in nineteenth-century Latin America differ substantially. Popular Latin American interpretations, echoed by Frank, take the view that the British government intervened consistently throughout the period to protect and to gain concessions for its businessmen, even initiating wars when faced with a particularly recalcitrant government. Historians in Britain, with greater access to Foreign Office archives, have tended to argue that its activities were more limited. H.S. Ferns, for example, differentiated between the undoubted influence of British commercial and financial interests in Argentina and the British government's inability to mould economic policy there.[1] W.M. Mathew, in a study of mid nineteenth-century Peru, sought examples of 'the employment of [British] economic and military superiority as a means to force concessions, secure privileges, or remove impediments on economic activity', but found 'little in the historical record to justify viewing Peru as the victim of British imperialism'.[2]

Since 1968 the reference point for most research on this topic has been D.C.M. Platt's *Finance, Trade and Politics in British Foreign Policy*, the one attempt of any length to generalise about the British government's role in Latin America between 1815 and 1914. Platt argued that the policy of non-intervention established by Castlereagh during the independence era persisted until the First World War. In his view, the government made little attempt to promote specific business interests. Responsibility for trade was limited to ensuring 'a fair field and no favour', in other words protesting at discrimination against British interests rather than seeking exclusive advantages. For Platt the commercial treaties provided strong evidence for this, since the British demanded nothing more than 'most favoured nation' status, equality of treatment in matters like tariffs and access for their shipping. The exception, the treaties with Brazil, he noted, lasted only until 1844. Investors could not expect active support from Whitehall. Foreign secretaries normally refused official help to holders of Latin American government bonds on the grounds that the higher nominal return they obtained from lending overseas already compensated them for the risks. In order to remain free from entanglement in internal disputes, Britain refused to provide guarantees for loans or for treaties between Latin American states. While recognising that force, in the shape of naval demonstrations, was used on occasion, Platt argued that it was confined to the protection of British subjects or their property against unjust treatment, and that it became infrequent after 1860.

There were several grounds for questioning this interpretation. Platt relied heavily on the correspondence and memoirs of diplomats, and the viewpoint was very much that of policy formulation in London rather than its implementation in Latin America. In an early review Zara Steiner suggested that political instability in countries where British firms were established might draw diplomats into disputes, despite the non-interventionist intentions of London. Moreover, she added, 'there was a large intermediate area which fell between what local agents could do and what the Foreign Office would veto'.[3] Other criticisms have included the points that threats rather than actual coercion could explain Latin Americans' agreement to British demands; that one could not expect others to understand the Foreign Office's fine distinction between applying pressure through 'good offices' (informal conversations with Latin American ministers) and 'official support' (a written note requiring an answer); and that British representatives thousands of miles from London may have misinterpreted their instructions or followed their private interests. Although there has been no overall reappraisal since 1968, the cumulative effect of detailed case studies is to raise doubts about Platt's interpretation.

THE FIFTY YEARS AFTER INDEPENDENCE

The view from London

The institutional background of British policy requires some explanation. Until 1920 the Foreign Office (the staff in London) and Diplomatic Service (those overseas) were separate, with little inter-

change between them. The Consular Service, which contained officials ranging in grade from Consul-General to unpaid Consular
Agent, was distinct from both, though controlled by the Foreign
Office. In the early nineteenth century foreign secretaries tended to
formulate policy themselves, leaving their subordinates with routine
ciphering and copying tasks, but as the volume of work increased
the permanent officials became more important. After Canning's
initial enthusiasm for Latin America many missions there were
downgraded to save on salaries and expenses. Between 1842 and
1872 only Argentina, Brazil and Mexico (until the suspension of
diplomatic relations in 1867) had legations (second-rank missions
headed by a minister). Elsewhere full-time consuls-general acted as
chargés d'affaires. More junior consular officials normally worked
part time, receiving a small salary but earning the bulk of their income
from other activities, generally as merchants.

British policy had two positive objectives. One was to terminate
the transatlantic slave trade to Brazil and to the remaining Spanish
colonies in the Caribbean, most importantly Cuba. The other, in the
words of Palmerston's famous dictum, was 'to open and *secure* the
roads for the merchants'.[4] In Latin America, as in other areas of
the world, this had several facets. First, the Foreign Office sought
treaties of trade and navigation which would provide protection
for British merchants and include a 'most-favoured nation' clause
to ensure fair treatment for British exports. Rather surprisingly, it
took until the 1840s and early 1850s for Britain to obtain treaties with
Bolivia, Uruguay, Guatemala, Costa Rica, Peru, Ecuador and Chile.
Second, the government wished to open the major inland waterways,
the Amazon and the Plate/Paraná system, to international trade. The
latter proved particularly complicated because the viceroyalty had
disintegrated at independence, and Buenos Aires made persistent
efforts to control access to the interior provinces of Argentina and
Brazil and to Paraguay. Third, there were some attempts to acquire
islands or small enclaves for strategic reasons or as commercial
entrepots. This explains the establishment of colonies in the Falkland
Islands in 1833, the Bay Islands in 1852, and British Honduras in
1862. Britain already held Trinidad and British Guiana, both of
which complicated relations with Venezuela. In addition to these
broad objectives, however, other problems arose which the British
government could not ignore.

The optimism of independence quickly degenerated into a trail
of defaulted loans and internecine warfare. An early indication of
these difficulties was the continuing conflict over the Banda Oriental

(the eastern bank of the River Plate), which, after a brief period of autonomy, had been incorporated into Brazil in 1821. Four years later a rebellion, financed by private interests in Buenos Aires, confined the Brazilians to the towns and provoked war between Brazil and the United Provinces. For Britain this was, in Ferns' words, 'an absurd situation. . . . The Brazilian navy, manned largely by British subjects, would be fighting an Argentine navy manned largely by British subjects in the process of which a commerce conducted largely by British subjects would be destroyed.'[5]

Attempts at mediation proved impossible until a military and naval stalemate had developed. Then, however, in 1828 British diplomats succeeded in obtaining agreement to the transformation of the Banda Oriental into the independent state of Uruguay. The episode exemplified the importance of the men on the spot, in this case Woodbine Parish, the consul in Buenos Aires, and Lord Ponsonby, the minister appointed there in 1826, for initially neither side was prepared to compromise. After skilful diplomacy Ponsonby obtained Brazil's agreement to the creation of Uruguay by insinuating that he would withdraw recognition of their blockade of Buenos Aires (which would have rendered it unworkable), meanwhile warning the Governor of Buenos Aires that Britain 'did not want the means, nor the will to interfere with the policy of America' if he reneged.[6]

Civil wars, together with the occasional international conflict, continued to erupt. They were often interconnected, since rebels received support from neighbouring countries, and both caused increasing concern among British officials. Political instability, a consul argued, harmed British interests in several ways: through blockades and military interdicts; constant changes in commercial regulations; the destruction of business confidence; the confiscation of property and demands on local businessmen for forced loans, depriving those with debts to British merchants of the means to pay; and the waste of life and labour.[7]

Impatience with the apparent inability of Latin American states to govern themselves therefore began to accumulate. British representatives resident in the area, many of whom were innately arrogant about southern Europeans, Catholics, blacks and American Indians anyway, added to this their frustration with the living conditions and threats to personal security which they experienced. 'We are mistaken,' one diplomat in Brazil stated in 1835, 'if we regard the South American republics as much better in organisation, national faith, and civilisation than the Barbary States.'[8] Such views were shared in London. In 1850 Lord Palmerston lumped China, Portugal and South America together in asserting that 'these half civilised governments . . . all require a dressing down every eight or ten years to keep them in order. Their minds are too shallow to receive any impression that will last longer than some such period and warning is of little use. They care little for words and they must not only see the stick but actually feel it on their shoulders.'[9]

For several reasons, therefore, a more aggressive and interventionist mood began to develop in the Foreign Office. Some pressure came from ministers and consuls in Latin America, who believed that British interests were harmed by their instructions to preserve neutrality in internal conflicts. For Lord Palmerston, the Foreign Secretary in the 1830s, European considerations also played a part, especially the fear that the French might obtain exclusive privileges in Mexico and Uruguay. In the late 1830s the threat of unemployment and social unrest in England arising from the loss of markets in Europe provided an additional reason for introducing policies aimed at securing sympathetic and stable regimes in Latin America. In 1839 Palmerston, having refused to intervene two years earlier, rather belatedly instructed the chargé d'affaires in Santiago to warn Chile over its attack on the Peru-Bolivian Confederation, which had adopted liberal tariffs and commercial regulations. In 1841 he offered to sign treaties with New Granada, Venezuela and Ecuador providing for British mediation in any war among them.

The reappraisal of policy came to a head in 1841 with a 'Memorandum on South American States', prepared by James Murray, a member of the Foreign Office staff.[10] Murray emphasised the value of Latin American trade to British manufacturers and its potential as a market, and argued for intervention to advance British interests. In Central America, he believed, the way forward might lie in 'judicious support and encouragement to the Mosquito Nation – a Nation virtually English without being a Colony'. In South America Britain might promote order by negotiating alliances to stop politicians from interfering in neighbouring states. An obvious candidate was Uruguay, where the Consul-General could offer protection against rebels led by Manuel Oribe and supported by Rosas, the Governor of Buenos Aires, in return for the commercial treaty Uruguay had so far refused to sign. The government sought comments from three consuls-general on leave in London. All expressed their support for a more active policy, although Hood, from Montevideo, feared that commitments to alliances would entangle Britain in endless disputes. The disastrous decade which followed for Britain in the River Plate confirmed his reservations.

Intervention in the River Plate

In 1841 a Tory government entered office and Aberdeen replaced Palmerston as Foreign Secretary. European considerations, now the desire for a rapprochement with France, provided further reasons for a more active policy in the River Plate. The British also hoped to break Buenos Aires' attempt to monopolise commerce in the river. In cooperation with the French, therefore, the minister, Henry Mandeville, invited Rosas to agree to peace and open the rivers. He also finally signed a commercial treaty with the Montevideo government, which hoped for British protection. Yet policy was somewhat confused; Mandeville did not receive the forces he had been led to expect, and, contrary to his wishes, Royal Navy ships intervened early in 1843 to prevent Oribe, the rebel leader, from blockading Montevideo, thus helping to relieve the city.

In 1845 the situation deteriorated further. With Oribe about to take Montevideo, the new British minister, Gore Ouseley, who had been instructed to threaten Rosas and force a withdrawal of Argentine forces, ordered a blockade of Buenos Aires and organised a naval expedition to force a passage upriver to Paraguay. This stimulated an outcry from merchants and from Barings, who were seeking payments on Buenos Aires' defaulted 1824 loan, and new orders from Aberdeen to preserve British neutrality. When Palmerston returned to the Foreign Office in 1846 Britain's attempts to cooperate with France ceased. Palmerston took the view that blockading Buenos Aires and forcing ships to pay duties in Montevideo was 'piracy . . . equivalent to stopping neutral vessels on the high seas and making them pay blackmail', and in 1847 he approved the actions which Lord Howden, Ouseley's successor, had taken to end this British blockade of their own commerce.[11] Two years later the British agreed to return the island of Martín García, which they had occupied in 1845, and the Argentine warships they had seized, and to salute the Buenos Aires flag in recompense.

The deficiencies of British policy in the Plate are clear: the lack of well-defined objectives and unambiguous instructions from Aberdeen; problems in cooperating with the French; partisan officials (and in the case of Ouseley inexperience and incompetence); and differences of opinion between diplomats and naval commanders. John Lynch concludes that 'gunboat diplomacy as practised in the Río de la Plata in 1843–6 was curiously timed, casually planned, and almost completely ineffective'.[12]

Although armed intervention was over, the interference of British diplomats in Argentina's internal affairs continued. The overthrow of Rosas in 1852 resulted in the country splitting into the province of Buenos Aires and the Argentine Confederation. The Foreign Office, in cooperation with France and the United States, appointed a vice-consul to Buenos Aires and a minister to Paraná, the Confederation's capital, in the hope that withholding full recognition from the province might influence its leaders to rejoin the nation. One immediate result was that the Confederation, in an attempt to gain support against an anticipated blockade by Buenos Aires, agreed in 1853 to the free navigation of the Plate which the British had wanted for so long. William Christie, appointed as minister in 1856, then attempted unsuccessfully to intervene in elections for the governorship of Buenos Aires on the Confederation's behalf, and also publicly stated his support for Urquiza, the *caudillo* who had overthrown Rosas. His successor, Edward Thornton, acted, more neutrally, as a go-between in the final conflict between Buenos Aires and the Confederation in 1860–61. Only the unification of Argentina in 1862, James Scobie concludes, permitted British diplomats to become 'observers of rather than mediators in the political scene'.[13]

Brazil

In Brazil Britain faced rather different problems from the political instability and desire for free navigation which dominated affairs with Argentina and Uruguay. Relations centred on two legacies of the independence period: the privileged commercial position of the British, and Brazil's commitment to terminate the slave trade (see pp. 43–4). Both the commercial treaty and vital clauses of the 1826 slave-trade treaty expired in the mid 1840s. It proved impossible to negotiate a new commercial agreement after 1844, initially because Britain refused to end discrimination in favour of colonial sugar without progress on ending the Brazilian slave trade. Even though the British government did begin to equalise the sugar duties within two years, its aggressive actions over the slave trade had by then alienated Brazilian opinion against concessions to Britain.

The treaty of 1826, which began by defining the slave trade as 'piracy', had continued many of the measures Britain had previously agreed with the Portuguese, including the right to search ships and take them before 'courts of mixed commission' in Rio or Sierra Leone if slaves were found. In 1831 the Brazilian Parliament had also declared the trade illegal. Nevertheless, imports of slaves increased during the 1830s and 1840s, and London became increasingly annoyed at the Brazilians' ability to find new loopholes to continue the trade whenever the Royal Navy and Foreign Office closed old ones. Even the entry of British warships into Brazil's territorial waters after the late 1830s had little effect.

In 1845 the expiry of part of the 1826 treaty ended both the right to search and the Anglo–Brazilian mixed commissions, the principal means of punishing slave-traders. The British responded with the 'Aberdeen' Act of 1845, which unilaterally gave Admiralty courts the power to treat Brazilian slavers as pirates, a measure described later by Sir Richard Burton as 'one of the greatest insults which a strong ever offered to a weak people'.[14] However, Royal Navy ships in the South Atlantic were preoccupied with the blockade of Buenos Aires, and so enforcement was limited until Palmerston increased the pressure in 1848–49, threatening Brazil with occupation of part of its coast and searches of ships in its ports. There was also a growing feeling in Brazil against the slave-traders, many of whom were Portuguese, and fears both of internal risings and of Rosas' ambitions. Thus internal factors and international pressure coincided. In July 1850 the Brazilian government took the decision to suppress the trade immediately, the alternative, according to the Foreign Minister, being war with Britain.

The cases of Argentina and Brazil illustrate a number of points about British diplomacy in the 1840s. First, diplomats, consuls and naval officers became deeply involved in internal politics, in the Plate due to the chronic political instability of Uruguay and Buenos Aires' claims to control shipping on the river, and in Brazil because of the slave trade. There, according to Palmerston's private papers, the British chargé used Secret Service funds to finance informants, bribe officials and subsidise newspapers. Second, the Foreign Office took decisions against the interests of merchants, both in the Plate and in its crusade against Brazilian slavery. Third, British diplomats were frequently ineffective, at least in the short term. Consul-General Wilson had commented in 1842 that 'consuls without cannons' had little impact, yet the use of warships had often inflamed local feelings and been counter-productive.[15] Moreover, the events of the 1840s showed that even Britain had finite naval resources and could not intervene everywhere simultaneously. Finally, the British succeeded most easily when a weak government faced with internal enemies (Uruguay in 1842 or the Argentine Confederation in 1853) made concessions in the hope of obtaining British support, or when domestic developments were also moving towards the same end as the British sought. The dynamics of relations among the different provinces and states of the River Plate were determined internally, although the result, the stabilisation and unification of Argentina, fulfilled Britain's objectives. In Brazil the eventual abolition of the slave trade depended on a favourable conjuncture of political and economic forces within the country as well as Palmerston's threats, although these were crucial to the timing of abolition.

Central America

The case of Central America, which Murray also picked out in his 1841 memorandum, confirms many of these points, in particular the difficulties of making policy in London and implementing it thousands of miles away, and the failure of diplomats to remain neutral in domestic politics. Frederick Chatfield, first sent as consul to negotiate a commercial treaty with the Central American Federation in 1834, dominated British policy in the area until his recall in 1852. Until 1838 he offered advice on financial reform to the Federation's government, which had defaulted on its debt; once it disintegrated into separate nations he worked actively with conservative forces in Guatemala to prevent its revival. He used claims for damage to British property to justify naval action against Guatemala's enemies, and, as Mario Rodríguez shows by comparing the consulate's internal correspondence with his despatches, concealed from London much of his meddling in local politics.[16] Although the government did not always respond to Chatfield's suggestions for British guarantees or mediation, and censured his attempt to seize the island of Tigre in the Gulf of Fonseca in 1849 as a British base, it permitted him to use warships to enforce claims *he* considered legitimate and declared a protectorate over the Mosquito Shore of Nicaragua in 1843. This was largely the work of Macdonald, the superintendent of Belize, who had encouraged expansion in Mosquitia, but it was Chatfield who persuaded Foreign Office officials of the desirability of a protectorate. They in turn persuaded the Colonial Office.

Unlike much of South America, policy in Central America was also influenced by geopolitical considerations. After the defeat of Mexico and the acquisition of California in the 1840s the threat that the United States might construct an interoceanic canal forced London into negotiating the Clayton–Bulwer Treaty of 1850, which aimed to ensure that neither power could claim an exclusive sphere of influence in the Central American isthmus. However, this did not solve the problem, partly because neither government could control its agents in the region. In the 1850s there were two serious clashes with the

United States over the Mosquito protectorate. Moreover, Britain's objectives were confused. In 1852 the Colonial Office actually created the colony of the Bay Islands without informing the Foreign Office, which gave it up seven years later without consulting the Colonial Office. Britain rationalised its position in Central America only between 1859 and 1862, when it surrendered its protectorate over the Mosquito Shore to Nicaragua, made a treaty with Honduras to withdraw from the Bay Islands, and formally transformed the settlement at Belize into the colony of British Honduras.

A reappraisal of British policy before 1870

Britain's long-term objectives, as noted earlier, concentrated on the ending of the slave trade, guarantees of equal access for shipping and exports, and protection for its merchants. By 1870 these had been achieved. There were also two points on which the Foreign Office was normally cautious: providing territorial guarantees which might commit Britain to intervening in internal disputes, and interfering in problems arising from loans to Latin American governments. The Foreign Office's support for bondholders' claims, which might have involved it in constant arguments, was limited. In 1829 Aberdeen authorised British diplomats and consuls to make verbal representations on bondholder issues, but refused to support them with official notes of protest.

However, in both cases policy wobbled: over the question of alliances and territorial guarantees in the early 1840s, after Murray's memorandum, and over the bondholders in 1848, when Palmerston addressed a circular to Britain's representatives overseas. This made it clear that tactical considerations, rather than principle, had hitherto restricted support for the bondholders, since the government believed that capital was better employed at home. While it therefore discouraged loans to foreign states and would *normally* abstain from offering creditors official support, Palmerston argued that on occasion 'it might become the duty of the British Government to make these matters the subject of diplomatic negotiation', and he requested that diplomats and consuls communicate this to foreign governments.[17]

In its implementation British policy often departed from these overall principles for several reasons. First, Foreign Office instructions were not always unambiguous or consistent. The broad outlines of policy could be affected by the preconceptions, misunderstandings, or arrogance of a particular foreign secretary. Second, both the Colonial Office and the Admiralty had an interest in Latin America and possessed their own representatives in the region. Third, the general lines of policy could not cover all eventualities, especially if crises like a war or blockade broke rapidly. Finally, London was dependent on agents thousands of miles away, with whom an exchange of despatches might take six months, for both accurate reporting and the implementation of instructions.

Inconsistencies in British policy, especially over the use of force, can therefore be found through the 1850s and early 1860s. In 1857, during a dispute with Peru over the repudiation of bonds, the Foreign Office produced a memorandum entitled 'Our Case for Going to War with Peru', and contemplated blockading Callao or seizing the Chincha Islands. In 1863 the British chargé in Santiago authorised a naval demonstration without consulting the merchants in Valparaiso. However, more important examples of ill-considered behaviour and subsequent withdrawals, both during Lord John Russell's term as Foreign Secretary, were the participation in the early stages of the French intervention in Mexico in 1861–62, largely out of frustration with the persistent neglect of British claims, and the 'Christie Affair' in Brazil in 1862–63, where the impulsive actions of the British minister and naval commander after an incident involving Royal Navy officers, coupled with an ill-considered response from Russell to their complaints, led to a short blockade of Rio. Both these episodes culminated in the rupture of diplomatic relations, the break with Brazil lasting only two years, but that with Mexico seventeen. Both reflect an unwillingness by the Foreign Office and its diplomats to recognise the sensitivities and difficulties of independent Latin American states, and in neither case did the crisis bring any benefit whatsoever to Britain's commercial interests.

The question of claims for damage to property or mistreatment of British subjects raised enormous problems. Such incidents were obviously more frequent in civil and international wars, but even in peacetime the behaviour of a customs official or a xenophobic colonel or crowd could precipitate a dispute. The Foreign Office depended on its representatives to ascertain the justice of these claims, many of which came from firms and individuals which possessed British nationality but had only tenuous connexions with Britain itself. For reasons of ignorance, incompetence, over-zealousness or self-interest, officials made errors. London could compound them by impolite protests or the impetuous use of force.

There were other explanations for inconsistencies. Within Latin America the implementation of policy might be distorted by rivalries among chargés, consuls and naval officers, or by a consul and naval commander together exceeding Whitehall's instructions. Britain's representatives abroad had no experience in the Foreign Office itself, and did not always interpret the 'official mind' correctly, especially if their instructions were vague. Often they did not have time to ask London for advice on a particular case, and were persuaded to enter immediate protests against apparently arbitrary government actions. The longer they stayed in a country the more they became liable to establish business or social relations with local entrepreneurs or politicians, which could compromise their neutrality, and few were far-sighted or independent enough always to resist manipulation by their domestic allies. The rivalry David Walker depicts between Ewen MacKintosh and the Martínez del Río family in Mexico City for the ear of successive British ministers illustrates the importance of their support in a situation of extreme economic and political instability.[18] Few could avoid becoming partisan; some, indeed, arrived at their posts with their prejudices about local politicians already formed. Every minister in the River Plate in the 1840s and 1850s, for example, had strong views for or against Rosas, the rival *caudillos* in Argentina and Uruguay, and the regime in Paraguay. Finally, the individual competence of diplomats and consuls, whatever their views, varied from the outstanding to the catastrophic.

What of the impact of British policy? Both for British merchants and for Latin American governments it was the realities, rather than the theory, that were significant. The commercial treaties seem to have operated without real problems, with the exception of a rumbling dispute with Venezuela over the duration of the agreement. In practice, however, they were not, as the examples of Brazil after 1844 or Chile before the 1850s suggest, essential for trade. Businessmen continued to operate independently of government, and even the suspension of diplomatic relations did not necessarily deter trade or investment. It is doubtful also whether the 1848 circular on bondholders' claims had much impact in Latin America. Generally bondholders sorted out their own affairs, often using merchants as their agents. They too depended on a lack of obstacles to trade, the source of most government revenue, and a favourable political climate in Latin America to obtain payments or a renegotiation of the debt. Blockades and interventions, by depressing trade and inflaming nationalism, probably did bondholders, as well as merchants, more harm than good.

It is more difficult to evaluate the influence of British officials at the local level, in the absence of much research in Latin American diplomatic archives or on the correspondence of British legations and consulates overseas. The examples of Pakenham in Mexico, Chatfield in Guatemala, or successive ministers in the Plate, however, suggest that officials participated in domestic decision-making to a much greater extent than their despatches to London imply. Thus the Latin American perspective on British power was (and is) very different from London's. Moreover, some of the distinctions drawn by the British government must have appeared incomprehensible to Latin Americans. In theory the Foreign Office separated the business activities of a vice-consul from his official functions, treating him almost as two distinct individuals. Yet how could a Latin American government negotiate properly with a consul in his private capacity as a bondholders' agent one day and in his official capacity the next without confusing the two, and how could it be expected to distinguish between 'good offices' forcefully expressed and full government support for a claim?

The final, though under-researched, factor in the equation is the naval presence. British warships stationed in the Atlantic and Pacific called frequently at Latin American ports. In 1848 the Pacific squadron alone had twelve ships, and there were also sizable forces in the South Atlantic and Caribbean.[19] Commanders had instructions not to interfere in local politics, but they were also expected to follow diplomats' instructions and to defend British lives and property. During a civil conflict the line between non-intervention and protection was difficult to draw. While the Royal Navy often did not have the resources to mount a full blockade, retaliation or a demonstration of power using one or two ships was always feasible. Thus all Latin American governments lived under the shadow of its presence. Consul-General Wilson noted that the blockade of Cartagena (in New Granada) in 1836–37 had a salutary effect on the *Peruvian* government. Twenty years later Anglo-French naval movements coincided with internal political struggles to push the Peruvian government into recognising a debt. In time the frequent use of naval demonstrations might become counter-productive by inflaming nationalism, but often a chargé d'affaires could judiciously use the information that he had requested naval support to obtain concessions. To a Latin American minister, with a knowledge of his own country's history and events elsewhere, the consuls' power to summon cannons appeared a reality.

THE GOVERNMENT AND LATIN AMERICA, 1870–1914

The growth of non-intervention

Although it did not explicitly reassess its policies, after 1870 the British government enjoyed a much smoother relationship with Latin America. There were several reasons for the change. Increasing commitments elsewhere, in Asia and Africa, distracted attention from the New World. After the French imbroglio in Mexico the threat that another European power might establish an exclusive sphere of influence disappeared. Indeed, the Foreign Office usually tried to cooperate with other European countries over issues like claims. There seemed little to fear from the United States either. Washington's sporadic attempts at an expansionist policy were hindered by the inconsistency which stemmed from political changes every four years. When the United States did begin to assert its interests in the Caribbean basin at the turn of the century, Britain gave way there for both ideological and pragmatic reasons. As Paul Kennedy explains, the primary aim of British foreign policy was then to avoid conflict with any Great Power. War with the United States, in particular, was considered not only likely to be expensive and difficult, but peculiarly immoral.[20] Thus when, in 1895–96, a crisis over the demarcation of the Venezuelan – British Guiana frontier coincided with the Jameson raid in South Africa, a much more serious threat to British imperial interests, the cabinet agreed to US demands that it should mediate the dispute. Shortly afterwards, under the Hay-Pauncefote Treaty of 1901, Britain in effect relinquished its rights under Clayton-Bulwer, leaving the way open for the United States to complete and fortify the Panama Canal. Yet this withdrawal reflected strategic and economic realities within Latin America itself. US commercial and geopolitical objectives were still confined to the Caribbean basin, while Britain's interests had become concentrated south of the Equator.

Technological and economic developments also contributed to a smoother relationship. From the mid 1870s the submarine cable helped London to control the actions of diplomats overseas. Steamships also made communication by mail quicker. The growth of trade gave governments more resources, and the desire for capital, especially for large projects like railways or port improvements, compelled them to renegotiate and repay previous loans. Economic growth also aided political stability and permitted the state to consolidate its control over national territory, reducing the dangers of domestic conflicts and the claims they stimulated. When such problems did occur, it became customary to establish joint commissions to adjudicate compensation.

In London other government departments lost interest in Latin America, leaving the Foreign Office with a monopoly over policy. It was supervised by a succession of highly competent under-secretaries, beginning with Sir Julian Pauncefote in 1876. The quality of diplomats may have improved too, especially in Rio and Buenos Aires, where several who later became ambassadors to major European countries served in mid-career. The Foreign Office did use less important countries as places where it could post the more incompetent until they retired, but the lack of rivalry with other powers meant that the chances of them causing serious damage were minimal. The telegraph allowed London to issue them rapidly with detailed instructions if a crisis did erupt. In determining policy the Foreign Office generally became more cautious and legalistic, referring all doubtful cases to the Law Officers of the Crown, and its attitudes towards the more common problems it confronted became more closely defined.

For trade Britain continued to rely on the 'most favoured nation' clause of the commercial treaties which it had signed. Yet even in Brazil, where the treaty had lapsed in 1844, no real problems occurred, except for a short period between 1891 and 1894 when the United States attempted to obtain reciprocal concessions. The gap between government and commercial interests remained wide. Merchants never induced a fundamental shift in official attitudes, although they occasionally influenced policy on specific issues, one example being the pressure from Chambers of Commerce which led to the re-establishment of diplomatic relations with Mexico in 1884. The government's efforts at trade promotion were generally limited to publishing information in consular reports and the *Board of Trade Journal*, although it did sponsor a commercial mission (the Worthington Mission) to the major countries of South America in 1898, and another (the Milne Mission) to Colombia, Venezuela and Central America in 1911.

Investors with grievances could expect little help. In 1871 the Foreign Office tightened its policy and denied official support to bondholders except where a government gave preferential treatment to other creditors, alienated property hypothecated to the bondholders, or ignored their claims in a transfer of territory or treaty negotiations. Despite several loan scandals and defaults in the mid 1870s a Parliamentary Select Committee rejected the suggestion that officials should supervise investment. The government made no effort to tie loans to the purchase of British products or to encourage merchant banks to issue loans simply to increase British influence. 'Generally speaking, and especially in South America,' Sir Edward Grey stated in 1914 when asked about a Brazilian loan, 'these are things in which the Foreign Office does not interfere.'[21] Particularly after the formation of the Corporation of Foreign Bondholders in 1869 investors developed their own methods of dealing with defaults.

In the case of companies operating in Latin America the Foreign Office would permit its ministers to make informal representations on their behalf but would not provide official support unless the local courts had been unjust. The distinction between 'good offices' and 'official support' sometimes remained blurred, but generally, it seems, governments which did try to restrict the activities of foreign firms, through legislation or the revision of concessions, gradually realised how limited the weapons at the British diplomats' disposal actually were.

The Foreign Office could not stand completely aloof. It still had to investigate incidents in which companies alleged unfair treatment by local officials or judicial authorities, and it did not always possess the knowledge to act in an even-handed manner. Due to ignorance about the ownership of bonds and shares issued in London, or reliance on partial information supplied by the companies themselves, diplomats sometimes supported a company whose British links were at best tenuous. A further problem was that as direct investment increased it became more likely that the Foreign Office would find it difficult to aid one British company without discriminating against others.

The use of force or threats of it became rare after the mid 1860s. Three occasions in Haiti, naval actions in Nicaragua in 1895 and Guatemala in 1913, and the Anglo-German coercion of Venezuela in 1902–03 provide almost the only examples. Noticeably, too, force was used only against weak states in the Caribbean. The government always cleared the action with the United States beforehand, and operated in conjunction with other European powers where possible.

In South America the Foreign Office's responses to emergencies illustrate the limitations of the role to which it now aspired. The near-coincidence of the Baring crisis in Argentina in 1890 and the civil war in Chile in 1891 (see below, pp. 65, 153–5 and 171–2) provoked demands for action. However, in a major speech in the City of London Lord Salisbury categorically refused to become involved. 'We have been pressed, earnestly pressed,' he stated, 'to undertake the part of arbitrator, of compulsory arbitrator in quarrels in the west of South America. . . . We have been earnestly pressed, also . . . to undertake the regeneration of Argentine finance. On neither of these subjects are Her Majesty's Government in the least degree disposed to encroach on the function of Providence.'[22] Few in Britain could have doubted the message, given the seriousness of the Argentine problem. Whether Latin American interests fully comprehended it is not so clear, for the Brazilian President claimed later in the decade that Rothschilds had threatened him with British intervention over the Brazilian debt (see p. 165).

This overall interpretation of the *late* nineteenth century is closer to Platt's than to much of the Latin American historiography. To justify it more fully requires some consideration of the major incidents in the period in which Britain is often assumed to have intervened: the Paraguayan War of 1865–70, when Paraguay fought against the Triple Alliance of Brazil, Argentina and Uruguay; the Pacific War of 1879–83, in which Chile defeated Peru and Bolivia; the civil wars in Chile in 1891 and Brazil in 1893–94; and the Anglo-German intervention in Venezuela in 1902–03.

The Paraguayan War

Controversy has surrounded Britain's involvement in the Paraguayan War. J.A. Fornos Peñalba, for example, talks of 'the role of British diplomacy and money as the major assets which the Allied powers utilised in their destruction and dismemberment of Paraguay'. 'All three,' he asserts, 'were profoundly influenced by British policy and her financial dictates.'[23] The reasons put forward to explain why Britain should wish to wipe out Paraguay range from the theory that Britain was trying to open the country to investment and manufactured exports to one emphasising the need for new cotton supplies during the US Civil War.

Nobody has produced evidence from the Foreign Office archives to support these charges. The suggestion, made by some, that Britain worked through Brazil overlooks the fact that when the war began diplomatic relations with Brazil were suspended due to the Christie Affair. The British minister in Buenos Aires, Edward Thornton, was undoubtedly partisan towards President Mitre of Argentina and antagonistic towards Paraguay, and he accompanied Argentine and Brazilian representatives to a crucial meeting in Uruguay in 1864. However, he was on leave in London for a critical sixteen months in 1862–63, and in his absence the chargé d'affaires protested against Mitre's actions in Uruguay (the country whose civil conflicts eventually sparked off the war), and attempted to use gunboats to stop arms reaching Mitre's clients. British policy appears confused rather than Machiavellian. There is some evidence of private diplomacy, which perhaps had a marginal impact, but not of a deliberate Foreign Office policy against Paraguay. In fact the Foreign Office was so incensed when it received information about the secret treaty agreed between the Triple Alliance powers which arranged for the dismemberment of Paraguay that it published it.

The question of private financial aid is a separate matter. Both Brazil and Argentina did issue bonds in London during the war, although the British government, as normal, played no part in them. However, the papers of Barings, Argentina's financial agents, indicate the reverse of what nationalist historians might expect, namely that it was extremely difficult to raise money precisely because of the war. This does not deny the significance of foreign loans for the eventual victory of Brazil and Argentina; rather that British businessmen, especially during the financial crisis of 1866, did not fall over themselves to bankroll the defeat of Paraguay.

The War of the Pacific

The background to Chile's war with Peru and Bolivia was a severe economic crisis in Peru, due largely to the decline of its guano resources and economic mismanagement. This led to default on its external debt in 1876, which primarily affected English and French bondholders. Just before this, over-supply and falling prices in the nitrate industry had led to its partial nationalisation. Peru paid the owners, many of whom were British, with certificates on which it also defaulted in 1877. During the war there was strong public support for Chile among British merchants, and the ease with which British firms came to dominate the booming nitrate industry in the 1880s after the Chileans had captured and privatised it added to the *prima facie* case for British involvement.

In fact the first allegations against Britain came from the US Secretary of State, James Blaine, in 1882 when he stated that 'it [was] a perfect mistake to speak of this as a Chilian war on Peru. It [was] an English war on Peru, with Chili as its instrument.'[24] There is little in the British government archives to support this. V.G. Kiernan, after a meticulous study of the documents, concluded that the Foreign Office was 'always calm and correct, usually alert, and sometimes notably good at masterly inactivity'.[25] He found no case against either the Foreign Office or its representatives in South America.

If the evidence absolves the British government, it again leaves open the role of private interests. The key firm was Antony Gibbs & Sons, the leading merchants on the west coast, who, after making their fortune in the guano trade, had become successful nitrate entrepreneurs. Besides administering Peru's state nitrate company between 1875 and 1878, Gibbs were also minority partners in the Antofagasta Nitrates and Railway Company (then in Bolivia), the taxation of which provided the *casus belli*. Fortunately the house left a massive archive in London, research in which has shown that Gibbs themselves had little control over the Santiago government and indeed much reason to quarrel with it. Instead, it seems, the close connexion between the Antofagasta Company's Chilean shareholders and their government, coupled with the adroit use of propaganda, propelled Chile into a war in which the results, for British interests, seemed far from clear until 1882.

The civil wars

Similar conclusions about the role of the British government apply to the civil wars. In the 1891 revolution against the Balmaceda government in Chile there is no evidence that the British minister in Santiago had detailed foreknowledge of the conspiracy, and his early despatches suggest that he saw the rebels' action as unconstitutional, unjustified, and unlikely to succeed. Although one should differentiate between the origins of the war and what happened during it, since the British representatives refused to recognise Balmaceda's declaration of a blockade against rebel-held ports in the nitrate zone, the evidence against the British minister is still weak. Under prevailing principles of international law a blockade could be recognised only if it was effective, and Balmaceda, after the secession of his navy, had no means of enforcing it. The real problem was that while the British minister desperately tried to remain neutral himself, he had no control over naval officers, who traditionally had close links with their Chilean counterparts, or the merchants, a few of whom also held consular appointments. 'There is no doubt,' he admitted after the war to the Foreign Office, 'that our naval officers and the British community of Valparaiso and all along the coast rendered material assistance to the opposition and committed many breaches of neutrality'.[26] He himself, however, had never advised the Foreign Office to recognise the rebels as belligerents, and it did not do so.

This example shows up two key problems: whether to recognise rebels as belligerents (which would make it easier for them to obtain arms and mount blockades affecting foreign interests), and whether to recognise blockades declared by either side as effective. These decisions would always create allegations of partiality, for in such circumstances one side would inevitably take umbrage. The Foreign Office generally adopted a cautious approach, especially for fear that the outcome of the conflict might be disadvantageous for British firms if their government appeared to take sides. Rather late in the Brazilian naval revolt of 1893–94 the British minister did advise that the insurgents, who were attempting to blockade Rio and with whom he personally sympathised, should be recognised as belligerents. In contrast, significant sections of British commercial opinion were requesting intervention to end the blockade. In the absence of agreement with the United States and the European powers, which were divided on the issue, London in the end refrained from aiding either side.

The Venezuelan intervention

In the light of these earlier episodes the Anglo-German coercion of Venezuela in 1902–03 appears somewhat anomalous, especially as the Foreign Office had already effectively recognised US hegemony in the Caribbean. However, relations with Caracas were quite abnormal, due to Venezuela's indignation over Britain's repeated refusals to renegotiate the commercial treaty, the use of Trinidad by smugglers and anti-government rebels, the frontier with British Guiana, and the claims arising from civil wars. Venezuela had suspended diplomatic relations from 1887 until 1897.

The normal view of the 1902 intervention is that it was undertaken on behalf of bondholders, whose claims were included in the British demands. Platt's analysis of Foreign Office archives shows, however, that the bondholders did not appeal to Whitehall until it had already decided to use force, and that the Foreign Office privately gave priority to claims regarding shipping and injury to British persons and property. It could not, for tactical reasons, acknowledge publicly that some claims were more important than others.[27] In many respects the allied coercion of Venezuela, like the intervention in Mexico in 1861–62, resulted from a decade's exasperation at unfulfilled promises and arbitrary action over claims resulting from civil conflict. The outcome was that most of the claims were submitted to arbitration, while the bondholders simply obtained a commitment that the

Venezuelan government would negotiate with them. The affair was much more important for its long-term effects on international relations: the unpopularity in Britain of cooperation with Germany, and the fact that it stimulated the United States into attempting to control the finances of Caribbean and Central American states and thus prevent the Europeans from justifying the use of force in the future.

CONCLUSION

Whereas both Frank and Platt tend to emphasise continuity, the argument here is for discontinuity in the British government's relations with Latin American states, with a watershed around 1870. Before then, British policy is best understood in the context of its worldwide attempts to open up countries and rivers to commerce and to halt the slave trade; an increasing irritation with the way in which the political instability and nationalism of Latin American countries impeded the achievement of these aims and hindered trade; and as a consequence a willingness to take a more active role, especially marked among diplomats and consular officials in the region. Implementing policy before the development of modern communications was difficult. The broad aims of the Foreign Office were distorted by Britain's diplomatic and naval representatives in Latin America, with the result that what looked to London like a policy based, with occasional exceptions, on non-intervention appeared very differently in Latin America, where partisan British ministers could frequently make their views felt and have them supported by warships.

After the failure of the joint intervention in Mexico in 1861–62 the outlook began to change. Having achieved the opening of the rivers and the ratification of commercial treaties with most countries, the government became much more unassertive, especially in promoting trade. In this its attitude contrasted with its main rivals, the United States and Germany, which made more conscious efforts to encourage trading and financial links with Latin America. The introduction of better communications, more sustained economic growth, the establishment of clearer rules regarding intervention, and the ability of business to look after itself all helped to make Latin America less problematic for the British government. By 1914 most diplomatic correspondence possessed 'a humdrum character'.[28] While there was some anxiety, but little action, about the growing competition faced by Britain's trade, the main territorial disputes (Guatemala/British Honduras, Venezuela/British Guiana, the Falklands/Malvinas) were dormant, and imperial rivalries in Asia and Africa had not spread to the western hemisphere.

Between 1870 and 1914, therefore, the key actors in the relationship between Latin America and Britain were businessmen, not the government. It was only with the outbreak of the First World War that the Foreign Office had to give the region more attention, a process which continued afterwards due to concern about British trade and the need to support investment interests in an era of growing economic nationalism. This, however, brought into the policy-making process other departments like the Board of Trade and Treasury, together with the Bank of England. Thus there is a paradox. The Foreign Office dominated policy most completely in the half-century before 1914, when Latin America's political, though not its economic, significance to Britain was least.

REFERENCES

1. Ferns, *Britain and Argentina*, p. 488.
2. Mathew, 'Imperialism of Free Trade', 563 and 579.
3. Steiner, 'Finance, Trade, and Politics', 547.
4. Quoted in Cain and Hopkins, 'Gentlemanly Capitalism, I', 523. Emphasis added.
5. Ferns, *Britain and Argentina*, p. 158.
6. Quoted in Ferns, *Britain and Argentina*, p. 194.
7. Wilson to Canning, 27 August 1842, FO 97/284 (PRO).
8. Quoted in Bethell, *Abolition of the Brazilian Slave Trade*, p. 116.
9. Quoted in Bethell, *Abolition of the Brazilian Slave Trade*, p. 345.
10. 'Memorandum on South American States by Mr Murray', 31 December 1841, FO 97/284 (PRO).
11. Quoted in Cady, *Foreign Intervention*, p. 231.
12. Lynch, *Argentine Dictator*, p. 292.
13. Scobie, 'Los representantes británicos y norteamericanos', 166.
14. Quoted in Bethell, *Abolition of the Brazilian Slave Trade*, p. 266.
15. Wilson to Canning, 27 August 1842, FO 97/284 (PRO).
16. Rodríguez, *A Palmerstonian Diplomat*, pp. 214–24 and 365–6.
17. The circular is printed in Platt, *Finance, Trade, and Politics*, pp. 398–9.
18. Walker, *Kinship, Business, and Politics*, pp. 76–8.
19. Wu, *Great Britain and Peru*, pp. 9–10.
20. Kennedy, *Strategy and Diplomacy*, pp. 23–4.
21. Quoted in Platt, *Finance, Trade, and Politics*, p. 20.
22. Quoted in Ferns, *Britain and Argentina*, p. 465.

23. Fornos Peñalba, 'Draft Dodgers', 468–9.
24. Quoted in Kiernan, 'Foreign Interests', 23.
25. Kiernan, 'Foreign Interests', 17–18.
26. Quoted in Smith, *Illusions of Conflict*, p. 196.
27. Platt, 'Allied Coercion of Venezuela', 3–28.
28. Ferns, *Britain and Argentina*, p. 372.

CHAPTER FOUR

Latin America and British Business in the First Half-Century after Independence

There is little consensus about Britain's economic links with Latin America in the first half-century after independence. At the centre of the debate lie the linked problems of continuity (did British trade increase steadily after the end of the independence era, or was there a hiatus?) and dependency (was dependence on Britain growing or did Latin American countries have real opportunities for autonomous development?). Cardoso and Faletto, and the Steins, suggest that there was little scope for escaping incorporation, on a subordinate basis, into the international capitalist system dominated by Britain, although they accept a period of transition between independence and the establishment of fully fledged export economies.[1] 'To Latin America, Britain was the most important of all trading partners,' the Steins write. 'The impact of British goods upon each of the economies of Latin America was critical to their growth.'[2] Yet Frank argues that real opportunities existed immediately after independence for national-industrial interests within the region to initiate a pattern of autonomous rather than dependent growth; only their defeat condemned their countries to imperialist exploitation and under-development.[3] Platt also presents a case for autonomy, but with very different implications. After independence, he writes, 'Latin America could sell nothing to Europe, so that it could buy nothing in return. . . . Spanish America retired over the edge of the periphery. It remained outside world markets . . . for the first half century of political independence.'[4] The result, in his view, was that Spanish America, but not Brazil, stagnated until production began to outgrow domestic demand. Export growth then stimulated foreign investment and immigration, leading to a more rapid expansion.

To some extent all these writers are attempting to make sense of *this* period within the context of interpretations derived from their views of the colonial era or the later nineteenth century. However, the disagreements reflect deeper problems. This is probably the most under-researched period in Latin American history, due largely to the paucity and difficulties of the archival material. Quantitative data are particularly sparse and unreliable. A further difficulty, as Platt recognises in excluding Brazil from his model, is that of generalising about British interests in twenty countries. Yet in some ways generalisations are easier for this than for subsequent periods, for the disparities of wealth within Latin America were nothing like as great as they later became, and British interests, which were centred primarily on merchants and trade, were much less diversified.

THE TRADE

Problems of analysis

One persistent cause of misunderstanding has been the tendency to make inaccurate assumptions about the British economy and economic policy. The acceleration in Britain's industrial growth which began in the late eighteenth century was initially concentrated in a few manufacturing sectors, most importantly in *cotton* textiles, which accounted for almost half Britain's global exports between 1800 and 1850.[5] A succession of innovations reduced production costs after the 1780s, when power-driven machinery was applied to spinning. However, the really sharp decline began in the 1820s due to the mechanisation of weaving and a steep fall in raw material costs. By 1856 the price of cotton piece-goods had dropped to less than a quarter of its 1815 level.[6] Technological change in other textile industries took longer, especially in woollens, the traditional export staple, where mechanisation proved more difficult. Here the major cost reductions began in the 1830s, due to the greater use of mixtures of cotton and woollen fibres, and falling prices for wool, but the power loom did not become widespread until the 1850s. In other sectors of industry – metals, hardware and ceramics, for example – modernisation also occurred slowly. Moreover, Britain supplied only part of Latin America's demand for imports. Luxuries like furniture, silks and glass continued to come mainly from France. It is essential, therefore, not to transpose the mid nineteenth-century image of Britain as 'workshop of the world' to the 1820s and 1830s.

It is also important not to exaggerate Britain's commitment to 'free trade'. The term had different meanings, and it was some time before it acquired the sense of 'low or non-existent tariffs' as opposed to the 'freedom to trade' with which Britain's early commercial treaties with Latin American nations were concerned. At the end of the Napoleonic Wars Britain still retained the Navigation Acts, which restricted foreign shipping, and high tariffs, which discriminated in favour of the colonies. The real liberalisation of trade commenced during Sir Robert Peel's administration (1841–46), with a general reduction of import duties in 1842. Three years later tariffs on raw cotton and wool were abolished and those on coffee and sugar reduced. These measures also eroded colonial preferences, partly to respond to criticisms that discrimination against foreign produce made it difficult to obtain return cargoes from Latin America. The view that Britain was committed to free trade principles at the time of independence is misleading.

A further difficulty lies in the quantitative material available, particularly the trade statistics. The sharp fall in prices, especially of textiles, makes it essential to differentiate clearly between trends in value and in volume. The *value* of British exports to the Americas (excluding the United States) increased at only 0.2 per cent a year between 1814 and 1846, but the growth in *volume* was 3.4 per cent; between 1846 and 1873 the *value* of exports rose by 4.4 per cent annually but the increase in *volume* stayed at 3.4 per cent.[7] This confusion explains some of the disagreement about the significance of British trade to Latin America following independence; what may look like a stagnating or disappointing level of trade from the British perspective seemed like a flood of ever cheaper imports to Latin Americans.

Latin American statistics for these years are sparse and of dubious accuracy. Almost everywhere customs officials engaged in contraband. This often created an enormous gap between official figures for imports and exports (especially where the principal export was bullion) and the actual shipments. Recent 'guesstimates' put contraband at up to 40 per cent of the official figures for imports in Mexico, and between 25 and 50 per cent in Venezuela; in some years it may have been much greater.[8] As a result historians generally turn to the British figures, despite their drawbacks. One source of error in them was identifying the destination of exports and origin of imports, since trade was often routed through third countries; much British commerce with Argentina passed through Montevideo, with Bolivia via Chile or Peru. A second problem was valuation; government officials in Britain recorded the declared value of exports from 1798 but did not attempt to list imports at current values until 1854. A third was classification; while goods like raw cotton, sugar or wool could be measured by volume and classified with some accuracy, customs officials could not define complex manufactured products with any consistency. In addition, the British import figures before 1859 omit precious metals, whether unminted bullion or coin. For Mexico, Peru and Chile, silver was an important export, and its exclusion can lead to a serious underestimation of British commerce with those countries.

British exports

Despite these reservations British statistics can provide some information about the volume and value of trade with Latin America. The most useful source is the recalculation of the figures which Ralph Davis made for the middle years of each decade between the 1780s and 1850s, although this choice of years raises some problems for Latin American specialists, because British exports to the region in 1824–26 were almost certainly much higher than earlier or later in the decade as a result of the ending of wartime blockades and a temporary flurry of investment. It must be remembered, too, that these are estimates for the *current value* of exports. They mask the steep decline in prices, especially for the cotton textiles which comprised over half Britain's exports to Latin America.

Table 4.1 British exports to Latin America, 1804–1856
(annual averages, £000)

	Cottons	Linens	Woollens	Metal products	Others	Total	Proportion of total British exports
1804/06	595	35	115	94	286	1125	2.3%
1814/16	1353	89	426	177	431	2476	5.2%
1824/26	2825	366	751	409	658	5009	12.6%
1834/36	3206	270	720	333	518	5047	10.9%
1844/46	3037	524	1023	440	610	5634	9.7%
1854/56	4522	593	1266	1016	1577	8974	8.8%

Note: These figures do not include those exports which passed through colonial entrepots in the Caribbean or through continental Europe or the United States.

Source: Davis, *Industrial Revolution*, pp. 96–101

Do these figures bear out Platt's contention of limited trade in the fifty years following independence, except for the furious activity of the mid 1820s?[9] It certainly seems true that Latin America lost some significance as a market. However, an analysis which concentrates on the value of trade provides only part of the story. François Crouzet, in contrast to Platt, emphasises that Latin America, 'though an uncertain, expensive, and disappointing market . . . still made a notable contribution to the growth of British exports' after 1825.[10] The backwardness of textile industries in the region, except in Mexico after the late 1830s, made it an especially important outlet for Lancashire's cotton mills. Unlike Europe, where trade concentrated on semi-finished goods, especially yarn, Latin America offered a growing demand for cheap finished piece-goods which were losing markets elsewhere. In 1840 it took 32 per cent of Britain's exports of cotton cloth, buying 'per head of population more than sevenfold as much cloth as the average inhabitant of the world'.[11] Although the value of cotton exports shown in Table 4.1 hardly increased between the 1820s and 1840s the volume actually grew two and a half times. By the mid 1850s the value was only 60 per cent greater than thirty years before but the volume had risen by 325 per cent. In 1860 British exports of cotton cloth directly to Argentina and Chile exceeded 30 yards per inhabitant, while Brazil and Peru bought around 20 yards a head.[12] Bearing in mind the growth of linen and woollen exports, as well as the indirect trade through Europe, the Caribbean and North America, it seems unlikely that Woodbine Parish exaggerated much when he commented in 1852 that British textiles had 'now become articles of the first necessity to the lower orders in South America'.[13]

What of the geographical distribution and composition of British exports? Davis does not disaggregate the figures for Latin America, but the official statistics for 1860, when they had become more reliable and there were no major wars to disrupt trading patterns, provide some indications (Table 4.2). These show that Brazil took one-third of Britain's exports to the region, the two principal countries on the west coast (Chile and Peru) 23 per cent, and the River Plate nations 20 per cent, with 11 per cent going to the Spanish Caribbean. The apparently low level for Colombia (New Granada) and Venezuela may be misleading. In both countries there were few British merchants, and textiles probably reached them through Germany or British colonies in the Caribbean. Mexico probably received some exports through the United States, but the low figure is also due to the reduction of textile exports caused by the construction of modern cotton mills, an early example of import substitution.

Table 4.2 British exports to individual Latin American countries, 1860 (£000)

	Cottons	Linens	Woollens	Hardware	Iron	Machinery	Others	Total
Brazil	2360	215	258	124	301	94	1095	4447
Argentina	874	50	372	79	69	12	326	1782
Chile	1023	53	173	52	123	16	263	1703
Cuba & Puerto Rico	463	354	46	74	172	98	323	1530
Peru	801	70	221	38	31	15	205	1381
Uruguay	453	26	195	44	28	—	177	923
New Granada	531	54	45	23	6	4	148	811
Mexico	253	63	51	16	9	9	62	463
Venezuela	224	44	31	4	2	1	18	324
Central America	100	5	6	8	7	5	51	182
Ecuador	48	3	2	5	3	—	13	74
Total	**7132**	**938**	**1401**	**468**	**750**	**256**	**2681**	**13620**
Percentage of total	52.4	6.9	10.3	3.4	5.5	1.9	19.7	

Notes: Some totals may not add due to rounding.

Some countries, especially those at the bottom of the list, may have received considerable quantities of British exports through entrepots. Bolivia and Paraguay do not appear in the British statistics at all.

Source: 'Annual Statement of Trade and Navigation', *PP*, 1861, LX

Table 4.2 also shows how import requirements in the larger markets were beginning to diversify, as demand grew for metal manufactures (a category which included iron plates, rails, tubes and pipes), and in the cases of Brazil and Cuba machinery (probably for the sugar mills). This trend away from textiles and towards capital goods would become more significant as the nineteenth century progressed.

Latin American exports

Analysing trends in British imports is more difficult due to the variety of products involved and Britain's use of other entrepots in Europe to obtain raw materials. It should also be remembered that Britain re-exported some of its imports, including coffee, sugar and even raw cotton. However, Table 4.3, using Davis' estimates, does provide some guidance.

Comparing this with Table 4.1, Latin America seems, on the surface, much less important as a supplier of foodstuffs and raw materials than as a market. After a brief flurry of activity based on cotton and hides at the end of the Napoleonic Wars the trade subsided as Britain rebuilt normal patterns of peacetime supply. Until the mid 1840s, when the guano trade grew, Latin America was essential to Britain only as a source of hides; Brazil's importance for cotton diminished as prices fell after 1815. Argentina's growing exports of sheep's wool went primarily to France and Belgium. British colonies in the Caribbean and the East, rather than Latin America, continued to supply tropical products like sugar and coffee.

However, there is a crucial omission from these statistics: gold and silver bullion and coin. The Mexican and Peruvian mining industries both recovered surprisingly quickly from the disasters of the independence wars, while Chile became a major silver producer for the first time. Although there is no complete study of the trade, Admiralty records show that British warships carried considerable quantities of silver, much of it contraband, from Peru and the west coast of Mexico up to the 1850s (little is known about such shipments from the River Plate, Brazil, and the Caribbean and Gulf coasts). It is difficult to escape the conclusion that a considerable portion of Britain's exports was paid for with precious metals omitted from the British import statistics.

Table 4.3 British imports from Latin America, 1804–1856 (annual averages £000)

	Sugar	Coffee	Tobacco	Cotton	Wool	Copper	Dyes	Hides & Skins	Guano	Others	Total	Proportion of total British imports
1804/06	20	10	5	584	2	8	43	130	—	468	1270	2.3%
1814/16	188	92	41	3018	1	—	110	2012	—	765	6227	8.7%
1824/26	120	92	—	1315	15	39	312	648	—	568	3109	4.7%
1834/36	172	106	2	1449	182	42	274	724	—	429	3380	4.8%
1844/46	441	279	18	493	254	128	425	1596	404	867	4905	6.0%
1854/56	609	333	200	626	232	978	445	1100	2503	2672	9698	6.4%

Note: These figures do not include Latin American exports which came to Britain by way of ports in Europe or North America. They also exclude silver and gold.

Source: Davis, *Industrial Revolution*, pp. 114–25

The question of trade stagnation

The view that British trade with Latin America stagnated or diminished for much of the half-century after independence thus overlooks two crucial points: the difference between the volume and value of trade (the volume of imports was critical to Latin Americans, especially if prices were falling rapidly), and the importance of bullion exports to Britain. The stagnation of imports from Latin America in the British market lasted little more than a decade after 1825, although the speed of recovery varied greatly from one country to another. From the 1840s the reduction and then the removal of colonial preferences stimulated a rise in imports of sugar, coffee and tobacco. At the same time economic growth created a demand for new imports like Peruvian guano and Chilean and Cuban copper. In addition there were increasing shipments, for example of Argentine hides and wool, to continental Europe, which helped to increase demand for British exports.

The British figures provide only part of the picture. One should not assume that trade was normally bilateral and balanced. A much more complex pattern was already emerging. Some of Britain's exports passed through continental Europe, the United States, or its own colonies in the Caribbean, and were imported into Latin America by merchants of other nationalities. Britain re-exported much of its imports of Brazilian sugar and coffee, yet obtained hides from the River Plate via Antwerp. British merchants frequently traded in products not destined for the British market. This was especially so in Brazil, where, in 1843, it was estimated that they handled almost 40 per cent of the sugar exports, half the coffee, and over 60 per cent of the cotton.[14] What tied the system together was the growing use of the bill of exchange drawn on a London or Liverpool merchant house for international payments. This made it unnecessary for a Latin American country to export directly to Britain to acquire sterling to purchase Lancashire textiles, thus permitting English manufacturers and merchants to benefit from the growth of Latin American exports to Europe and the United States.

THE MERCHANTS

For many historians the power of British merchants in Latin America after independence goes without question. The Steins believed that the

British *entrenched* themselves in trade *throughout* the region.[15] Charles Pregger Román writes of the destruction of the small Latin American petty bourgeoisie and of the dominance of British merchants in 'foreign commerce, the shipping industry, and local trade'.[16] The place which the British held in Brazil's export trade would seem partially to justify such views. Further supporting evidence comes from the River Plate where, according to Tulio Halperín Donghi, the British continued to control credit and marketing, even though continental Europe became the most important destination for Buenos Aires' exports of hides.[17] It is, however, misleading to assume that what applied in one country was true elsewhere. In fact the influence and interests of British merchants changed considerably in the fifty years after independence and their strength varied across the region.

The influx of British merchants during the independence era resulted in immense profits for a few but disappointment and bankruptcy for most. Thereafter the British were rarely more than a minority within the merchant community of the major ports and capital cities. Rather than displacing domestic merchants, they relied heavily upon them for access to local markets (providing them with imports on credit) and for the supply of produce from the interior for export. One study of the 1827 census in Buenos Aires concludes that 80 per cent of wholesalers came from either Spanish or creole backgrounds, although the British did comprise the largest and richest group within the foreign community.[18] In most ports other foreign nationals were also significant. Of the sixty-four merchant houses in Valparaiso in 1849, forty-nine were foreign but only seventeen were British (nine were German, eight French, with fifteen of other nationalities).[19] These figures, moreover, come from markets – Mexico, Brazil, Buenos Aires and Montevideo, Valparaiso and Lima – which exercised greater attractions for the British. Elsewhere they were much fewer in number. In Venezuela only one house of British origin, founded by John Boulton in 1826, survived the century, and that principally on the basis of trade with the United States. Reports from Caracas in the late 1840s suggest that German firms dominated commerce, even in British goods, although it may be that some British merchants preferred to trade from the security of Trinidad (Belize played a similar role for Central America). In Colombia local entrepreneurs rather than foreigners dominated mercantile activities.

Initially merchants concentrated on the import trade where the barriers to entry were low (so were the barriers to exit, though it might take some time to wind up accounts). At first most merchant houses in Latin America were simply agencies and warehouses operated by an individual or partnerships with a limited life. They sold goods on commission for exporters and manufacturers in England, returning to them produce, specie or bills of exchange in payment. Most worked on credit supplied from England and invested little themselves in either stocks of imports or purchases of exports. Rather than capital they required good connexions with textile exporters, Liverpool merchants, and if possible an acceptance house in London like Barings which would provide them with credit and whose name would attract business. However, the low barriers to entry meant that other foreign and local entrepreneurs could easily participate in trade, and merchants in London, many of whom were themselves recent immigrants to England, had few reservations about dealing with agents of other nationalities.

Each commercial crisis caused a shake-out of those who had overextended themselves or who could not collect debts owing to them. The more speculative houses disappeared, leaving behind a few more permanent residents, both British and foreign, who survived because of their increasing reputation for stability, their resources, and their minimal exposure to commercial risks. Gradually the British merchants divided into different types. By the 1850s some had been absorbed into Latin American societies as permanent immigrants, often landowners, rather than expatriate traders. Sometimes, as the founders gave way to their sons, houses became more local than foreign. By the end of the nineteenth century Boultons, which had never possessed more than tenuous links with Britain, could be considered fully Venezuelan. The Edwards family in Chile followed a similar path. In becoming absorbed into local society, merchants like this resembled many of their French, German, Spanish, and Italian counterparts. Some British merchants formed partnerships with immigrants from elsewhere in order to improve their business with the United States or Germany. A few independent commission houses remained, working on manufacturers' credit. Other partnerships depended on an agency or correspondent relationship with a firm in London or Liverpool – perhaps, for example, a line of credit which permitted them to draw bills on a house like Barings – and began to concentrate on shipping Latin American exports. Some were quite clearly junior partners of London and Liverpool firms, the best examples being the west-coast subsidiaries of houses like Antony Gibbs & Sons and MacLean Rowe (later Graham Rowe), both of which appeared at independence.

Merchants who survived faced the problem of employing the

capital they accumulated. This explains why some, especially in Argentina and Chile, became landowners. Most, however, looked for other activities where they could use their contacts and expertise. The drawback was that moving away from the commission trade exposed them to greater risks. Survival and growth therefore became a question of balancing the rewards and hazards of a particular activity with the need to preserve liquidity and not tie up too much capital.

Two obvious uses for surplus funds were providing short-term credit to export producers, a logical progression from buying produce on behalf of merchants in England, and to governments. Loans to producers could be secured on crops, minerals or land. Gibbs, who became a leading exporter of Chilean copper, provide a good example. By the 1860s they were financing over twenty miners, recouping their advances from minerals sold on consignment in Britain. Between 1860 and 1864 their commissions in this trade alone exceeded £120,000.[20] Nevertheless, activities like these often led partners in Latin America into conflict with more cautious principals in London or Liverpool. Had it not been for the slowness of communications, which made it impossible to reverse decisions taken several months before, much of this export financing might not have been undertaken. In the early 1840s the Lima house of Gibbs began to participate in the Peruvian guano trade, which they dominated for the next twenty years, despite the reluctance of the London partners who preferred to concentrate on the safe commission business. Gibbs' activities in guano in fact combined export finance with loans to governments, for guano was a state monopoly, and Lima demanded increasing sums in advances from its guano consignees in order to cover fiscal deficits.

The Peruvians were not alone in looking to merchants for credit. Except for Chile, a country of stable government, balanced budgets (at least until the 1860s) and a wealthy domestic elite, most states desperately needed money. The domestic and foreign commercial community was an obvious source. The high interest rates offered (sometimes 12–15 per cent) were one attraction for the merchants, but in addition their advances were normally guaranteed by customs duties and sometimes by state monopolies like tobacco manufacture and marketing. They themselves were responsible for paying the customs revenues which would service and amortise the loans, and the state often permitted them to do so with treasury notes acquired at a discount. They also knew that they were, in effect, the lenders of last resort for the state and that in theory it could not alienate them.

The extent of British involvement in internal debt transactions is unclear. Parish estimated that British merchants held half the public debt of Buenos Aires in 1824, but it seems unlikely that the proportion remained that high in the following decade.[21] In Brazil in the 1840s they held just over 20 per cent of the internal debt.[22] The example of Mexico, which had the greatest debt problem of all, is instructive, for it shows both the relative importance of local and foreign businessmen and also the consequences of unwise speculation. By the 1840s, although British houses certainly participated in the business, the most notorious *agiotistas* (speculators in government debt) were local businessmen like Escandón, Iturbe or Rubio who used their power to obtain government concessions. Moreover, in this extreme case of political and financial instability, lending to the government did carry risks. Three of Barings' agents in Mexico, two of them British houses, collapsed due to their participation in government loans between 1828 and 1860.[23] Even diplomatic support and the threat of armed intervention in the 1850s could not force impecunious Mexican governments into recognising and paying their predecessors' debts.

There were other paths for diversification. The merchants' participation in the local credit market, coupled with an increasing demand for facilities to discount bills of exchange, led them towards supporting more formal banking institutions. The British apparently controlled the short-lived Banco de Buenos Aires in the 1820s. Thirty years later they contributed much to the management of Chilean banking in its early stages, although they never held more than a minority of shares. Merchants also invested in land, sometimes following foreclosure on loans, or, in the River Plate in the 1830s and 1840s, as a means of employing capital during blockades. In Mexico there are even two examples of British merchants (and vice-consuls) in Tampico and San Blas investing in textile factories.

British businessmen possessed certain advantages. Their closer links with the London money market gave them access to cheap credit, as well as risk-free business such as arranging shipping or insurance or collecting debts on which they could earn commissions. Thus some firms acquired the stability and wealth to withstand commercial depressions. Gibbs' eventual success in the guano trade arose in part from the difficulties their rivals faced in the 1847 crisis in Peru, but which with the support of their London parent they could overcome with ease. Moreover, houses like the west coast or River Plate ones which spread their interests across different countries and activities obtained some insurance against problems in a particular state or economic sector.

As foreigners the British possessed some immunity from civil conflicts. Wilfrid Latham, who abhorred Rosas, conceded that during his government British landowners were 'absolutely exempt from forced contributions, horses excepted . . . and any injury to their properties, or the taking of their cattle in intestinal warfare, constituted claims for compensation under the existing treaties'.[24] Merchants obtained similar dispensations, including a freedom to move not granted to others. In the final campaign against Rosas the only people permitted to cross the siege lines around Buenos Aires were the English, whose cricket ground lay outside the city! Their immunity provided the British with opportunities to trade in times of civil war and to avoid the forced loans which weighed on their local competitors. In the last resort they could also appeal for diplomatic help, for example when government measures made it more difficult to collect business debts in Venezuela in the late 1840s, or when the British minister's protests allowed them to resist forced loans in Mexico in 1843 and 1847.

British merchants also proved adept at circumventing restrictions. There are reports of them running blockades, bribing ministers, presidents and officials, making fraudulent declarations on documents to reduce duties, smuggling, and evading the limits which many countries placed on their participation in retailing. One angry Chilean summed up their behaviour in 1828 with the comment: 'These merchants' only rule of conduct is to consider legitimate anything which will not peremptorily and inevitably take them to the gallows.'[25] Weak Latin American governments, themselves riddled with corruption, found it almost impossible to control the British merchants' activities, especially on isolated parts of the coast.

Yet in the end British merchants were not omnipotent. Even where they remained influential – in Buenos Aires, Rio, Valparaiso or Lima – the composition of the community changed considerably as new firms replaced the failures. Few houses survived twenty, let alone fifty, years in the uncertain business climate of post-independence Latin America. The advantages they possessed reduced, but did not eliminate, the immense risks of trade in an era of difficult communications, political instability and periodic commercial crises. Every recession brought a stream of failures. Even a merchant working mainly on commissions might find it difficult to endure a war or blockade, or a series of forced loans from which he himself was exempt, due to his inability to collect debts from local traders. Moreover, commissions depended on obtaining business in a competitive environment, and this encouraged consignees to extend credit to untrustworthy wholesalers or producers. Both in 1835–37 in Lima and in 1844 in Buenos Aires the bankruptcy of local firms caused British merchants and manufacturers substantial losses. In such situations commercial houses might simply be left with unsaleable stocks of imports and exports, uncollectable private debts and depreciated government paper. The more they had speculated with their surplus funds or on credit the greater the risk that poorly secured loans would bring them down. The result was a rapid turnover of firms, the most durable being those which possessed the best links with London and Liverpool, and which often fortuitously achieved the difficult balance between diversification and liquidity.

LATIN AMERICA AND THE BRITISH COMMERCIAL PRESENCE

British merchants and trade

One important consequence of the influx of British merchants and manufactures at independence was a shortage of capital and money in Latin America. British warships carried large quantities of bullion to Europe in payment for imports or on behalf of Spaniards wishing to repatriate their wealth. Consul-General Ricketts in Lima estimated that the Royal Navy transported 27 million *pesos* from Peru alone between 1819 and 1825.[26] In many regions the shortage of coin grew, limiting trade and, coupled with the removal of colonial restrictions on usurious lending, increasing the cost of credit. Interest rates in Buenos Aires, for example, rose from 6 per cent at the time of the revolution to 18 per cent in the 1820s.[27] It became difficult to obtain anything but short-term loans. The desire of the British merchants who survived the traumas of the 1820s to maintain liquidity did nothing to alleviate the shortage of funds, particularly for activities which needed long-term support. Their exports of silver, frequently untaxed, in fact continued to drain currency from countries like Peru and Mexico. However, the controversies about the British commercial presence in these years have not really considered these problems but concentrated on other issues: the degree to which British merchants displaced creoles; the extent to which imports undermined local producers, preventing a transition towards a modern industrial sector; and the influence of British merchants on governments.

The evidence of censuses and commercial reports shows that the

British did not totally displace local entrepreneurs, even in the short term. Almost everywhere creole and Spanish merchants continued to make up the majority of the international and wholesale merchants. On occasion local firms attempted to persuade governments to reserve particular areas of business for them. In Lima, for example, a revived *consulado*, composed entirely of Peruvians, succeeded in keeping foreign houses out of retailing and government finance for almost the whole of a twenty-year period. The British houses which remained in Latin America certainly included the richest and most durable firms. Yet wealth was not equivalent to political influence, and the British do not seem to have acted as a separate group but rather as part of a wider commercial community. There is no evidence of them, for example, attempting to block a local or foreign merchant of another nationality from developing his own business contacts in England, and several did so, as Barings' papers show. On the whole the British tended to enter a symbiotic relationship with local traders, on whom they relied for the marketing of their imports and often for the collection of export produce; in this, as in any transaction among merchants, there was also the potential for conflict over prices and debts. The long-term problem for local merchants, apart from the greater vulnerability to civil war and forced loans, was that the British, by becoming key intermediaries in international trade, at least in some countries, were concentrating their activities in potentially the most dynamic sectors of the economy.

Industry and Tariffs

The debate over the consequences of British trade for Latin American industry has normally focused on textiles. It involves two distinct questions: the extent and speed with which local industries collapsed, and the suggestion that British merchants deliberately and successfully fostered a policy of free trade, preventing the modernisation of existing industries in order to defend the import market they had established. 'Foreign merchants,' Eugene Ridings states, 'were in a position to thwart or delay government programs favouring industrialisation or other forms of autonomous economic development.'[28]

Many of the complaints that cheap British cottons caused the demise of domestic textile industries have come from Argentina, with echoes from highland Peru and Mexico, but the process was more complex than a sudden influx of British goods at independence. Miron Burgin argues that in the River Plate British competition was only one problem faced by textile producers in the interior; they also lost markets, as a result of independence and endogenous economic changes, in Bolivia and Chile.[29] Jonathan Brown provides evidence that until the middle of the century the trade in woollen cloth from Córdoba to the Argentine littoral and Buenos Aires remained strong.[30] In Peru the problems had begun under Spanish rule. The principal result of the independence wars was to confirm the loss of coastal markets to highland producers, but artisans there survived. Elsewhere domestic industry also remained important until mid-century. Even in Chile there were still 80,000 people employed in spinning and weaving in 1855.[31]

Thus the effects of cheap textile imports were felt, in Tulio Halperín Donghi's words, 'more gradually and partially than the apocalyptic versions of today's critics would have us believe'.[32] Without doubt the influx of cottons and woollens from Britain did, eventually, undermine the greater part of Latin America's traditional textile industries, but the process was much slower than many would suggest. Rather than collapsing suddenly after independence they suffered a lingering death, until the combination of ever cheaper foreign goods and lower transport costs finally killed them in the third quarter of the century. A further reason why the decline of national textile production was slowed is that some governments tried to use tariffs to protect producers. To state this, however, is to contradict the frequent assertion that free trade came at the behest of British merchants and the Foreign Office along with independence.

Analysing tariffs is not easy. Changes were frequent, and each country had particular priorities. However, it was normal to establish a standard level of import duties, 15 per cent in the case of the 1822 Buenos Aires tariff, 30 per cent in the 1826 Peruvian one, and then to specify exceptions: reduced duties for some essential inputs and high levels on imports which competed with local production. Thus Peru in 1826 set a 90 per cent duty on coarse woollens, hats, footwear and furniture.[33] Some governments even took the step of completely banning the importation of certain products, although prohibitions lost the state revenue from import duties and, like high tariffs, encouraged contraband.

Governments had to balance their fiscal requirements (which might include the need to approach merchants for short-term loans and hence to appease them) against domestic pressure for protection from imports. British merchants undoubtedly did, at times, use their financial or political influence to secure concessions on duties or commercial laws. The liberal regulations of the Peru–Bolivia Confederation were drafted by a committee of advisers which included several British merchants nominated by Consul-General Wilson. What is not so clear is whether these representations had much effect, except in the short term, for they could easily provoke a nationalist response. Although Peru retained a reasonably low tariff after the end of the Confederation this was, according to Paul Gootenberg, due to the need for income, not a lack of protectionist sentiment.[34] It is also worth noting that, contrary to the expectations of the British official sent to Brazil to negotiate a new commercial treaty there in the early 1840s, the merchants had no strong wish to maintain the maximum level of tariffs established in 1810.

There is considerable evidence that the crucial struggle between protection and free trade was fought by domestic interest groups. Every country had artisans, landowners and prospective industrial entrepreneurs who favoured protection and utilised nationalist arguments against the commercial interests (including local merchants who acted as wholesalers) and consumers who desired cheap access to foreign goods. It seems to have been the failure of protectionists to deliver on their promises which turned the trend towards liberalism in country after country. For example, in Buenos Aires the inability of local industry to respond to the combination of high duties (imposed in 1835) and a French blockade caused general disillusionment about such measures, which had simply caused shortages and high prices. Gootenberg explains the failure of a protectionist crusade in Peru between 1848 and 1852 in terms of conflicts of interest between industrialists and consumers, and the inability of new factories to respond quickly to the opportunities offered to them.[35] In Chile, Robert Will argues, government policy before 1856 represented 'an attempt to stimulate the development of national industry with all the means at the government's disposal', but the minimal results achieved discouraged further experiment.[36] In 1861 the president actually declared that protection harmed the majority of the population, and Chile began to adopt more liberal policies.

The Mexican textile industry provides a key example of the limits to manufacturing. It had been strong in the colonial period and both *obrajes* (large workshops using semi-free labour) and artisans successfully increased production during the Napoleonic Wars. After 1830 the industry received official support through the Banco de Avío, which was financed by the duty on cotton textile imports, and from the Dirección General de la Industria Mexicana. Successive governments proved willing to offer not only financial aid but high levels of protection and, on several occasions, complete prohibitions of competitive imports. By 1844 there were forty-seven cotton spinning and weaving mills.[37] Yet the industry's performance was disappointing, except at the end of the 1830s when import prohibitions, a French blockade, and the protection offered by a depreciating copper coinage coincided. The obstacles to sustained growth were overwhelming. Cotton supplies were expensive and inadequate (because landowners also demanded protection against US cotton exports, and when imported cotton was available it fell under the control of merchant oligopolies); individual provinces protected their own factories, discouraging internal trade; there were rivalries between spinners and weavers; and the national government's financial dependence on the merchant *agiotistas* meant that policy was subject to sudden reversals. Demand was also limited. Mexican factories could not supply efficiently the range of higher-quality cloth that the wealthier consumers required. The mills established between 1838 and 1842 remained sufficient to supply the demand for cheap textiles until the 1870s.

As a rule high tariffs and import prohibitions resulted in more extensive contraband, falling government revenues and higher prices for consumers, while only rarely achieving positive responses from industry. In many countries governments moved towards more liberal foreign trade policies in the 1850s. In some cases – Argentina in 1853 and Mexico in 1857 – new constitutions actually included clauses which outlawed prohibitions of imports.

It is therefore difficult to interpret the failure of industry in Latin America in this period in terms of concerted pressure from British merchants or indeed their government. The assumption that the existing textile industry was proto-industrial, with the potential for transformation into a modern manufacturing sector, even with government assistance, is questionable. Policies to foster completely new factories also ran into problems. The reasons did lie partly in the flood of cheap imports from Britain, but also in other aspects of the colonial heritage outlined by the Steins: a long history of government failure to control contraband or official corruption; the inadequacies of internal taxation and financial institutions; the elite's preference for commercial, mining and agricultural investments; enormous disparities in income; and the weakness of most Spanish American states as a result of the regional, class and ideological antagonisms unleashed by independence.[38] Even in Chile, which possessed the most stable regime in Spanish America and a growing export sector to stimulate capital accumulation and the development of a domestic market, attempts at diversification had limited success. 'If growth did not result in self-sustained economic development',

Luis Ortega concludes, 'this was the consequence of the decisions taken by Chileans themselves concerning the allocation of profits accumulated over several decades.'[39] Probably the most significant contribution which British merchants made to this disappointing process was not deliberately to hinder developmental policies but rather their desire for liquidity. By constraining their lending and providing a model of risk avoidance, this helped to reinforce the elite's predilection for investment in land, mineral exports, banking and commerce rather than long-term industrial projects.

BRITISH INVESTMENT

Loans to governments

Loans to governments and investments in mining companies are the other significant features of British interests in the post–independence period. The City of London had just become accustomed to foreign investment through loans to France, and an institutional structure to channel finance overseas had begun to develop. As interest rates fell in Britain, investors responded eagerly to the opportunities offered by Latin America, encouraged by optimistic publications about its economic prospects. Between 1822 and 1825 Latin American governments indebted themselves to the tune of £21 million in London, although, due to the practice of issuing bonds below par value and the deduction of commissions and fees, the amount they received was rather less (see Table 4.4).

The method of floating loans followed a fairly standard pattern. A firm of London merchants would contract with the agents of the government to issue a loan at a fixed price in return for a commission. It would then use the press to 'puff' the prospects of the country in order to improve the market. A successful campaign could secure significant additional profits for the merchants by allowing them to sell bonds at a higher price than that stipulated in their contract. They also normally retained enough of the proceeds to cover interest and amortisation for a couple of years. So great was British investors' ignorance of Latin America that as the boom built up the task became easier. Indeed, in one case promoters managed to issue bonds for a fictitious country, Poyais, with a face value of £200,000.

The governments which raised these loans were heavily criticised at the time. One problem was that they could not control their

Table 4.4 Loans to Latin American Governments, 1822–1829

	Date	Nominal amount (£)	Price	Interest rate	Date of default	Date of settlement
Brazil	1824	1,000,000	75	5	—	—
Brazil	1825	2,000,000	85	5	—	—
Brazil	1829	769,000	54	5	—	—
Buenos Aires	1824	1,000,000	70	6	1828	1857
Chile	1822	1,000,000	70	6	1826	1842
Central America	1825	163,000	73	6	1828	*
Mexico	1824	3,200,000	58	5	1827	1888
Mexico	1824	3,200,000	86.75	6	1827	1888
New Granada	1822	2,000,000	84	6	1826	*
New Granada	1824	4,750,000	88.5	6	1826	*
Peru	1822	450,000	88	6	1826	1849
Peru	1824	750,000	82	6	1826	1849
Peru	1825	616,000	78	6	1826	1849
Total		**20,898,000**				

*Responsibility for the New Granada loans was later divided between Venezuela, Colombia and Ecuador and for the Central American loan between Guatemala, El Salvador, Honduras, Nicaragua and Costa Rica.

Sources: Marichal, *Century of Debt Crises*, pp. 29 and 59; Dawson, *First Latin American Debt Crisis*, p.249

agents in London. The Bogotá government had withdrawn the powers of Vice-President Zea some months before he negotiated the first Colombian loan. Irisarri deliberately defied the orders of the Chilean government to sign the contract for its loan, leaving ministers with money they could not spend. Yet because of their need for recognition, neither Colombia nor Chile could disavow these actions. A second criticism was the issue price and the profits made in London. In this, however, there were two phases. The early loans were issued at very low prices, the worst sufferer being Mexico in its contract with Goldschmidt (see Table 4.4). As a result true interest rates were much higher then nominal ones. During much of 1824, however, the demand for Latin American loans was so great that governments could negotiate much better terms, and the commissions they paid fell (Mexico had paid Goldschmidt 8 per cent). Surprisingly, the real sufferer in this phase was Buenos Aires, which contracted for its loan with a consortium of Anglo–Argentine merchants at 70, who then negotiated with Barings for it to be placed in the market at 85. A third problem was the use made of the loans. Almost invariably governments spent the proceeds to repay earlier advances or to cover general administrative or extraordinary wartime expenditure. The Chilean Congressional Commission spoke for many when it reported in 1825 that it had found it impossible 'to conceive one single useful purpose to which any part of the money . . . has been appropriated'.[40]

Revenues might have been sufficient for most states to meet interest payments, but unexpected military outlays and the failure to control contraband made it impossible to balance budgets. Moreover, a depression began in England late in 1825, causing the collapse of several banks and ruining business confidence. Trade fell off and within three years every government, except Brazil's, had defaulted on interest payments. Apart from Barings and Rothschilds, who had restricted themselves to the Buenos Aires and Brazilian loans respectively, almost all the issuing houses – Goldschmidt, Barclay Herring & Richardson, Herring Powles & Graham, and Thomas Kinder – also foundered.

Although unable to meet further interest payments, Latin American governments did not repudiate liability. After the partition of Gran Colombia, for example, Venezuela, New Granada and Ecuador divided the responsibility for the defaulted debt, and a similar process later occurred in Central America. Occasionally, in the hope of regaining access to the London market, a government might even temporarily resume payments, as Mexico did in the early 1830s and

Rosas a decade later. This in turn encouraged continued trading of the bonds in London, in the hope that renewed payments, or, even better, arrangement of the arrears, would result in speculative capital gains.

By 1870 it was evident that the borrowers of the 1820s could be divided into three groups. Brazil, first, had never defaulted, although it had survived 1829 only with the aid of another £769,000 loan arranged by Rothschilds, partly to cover interest payments. It had then been able to raise new money in 1839, and by 1875 had floated bonds to a nominal value of £25 million. The second group consisted of Chile, Peru and Buenos Aires, which had all renegotiated their debts, normally by recommencing payments on the principal and capitalising the interest arrears into 3 per cent bonds. The Chilean settlement of 1842 provided the model for Peru in 1849 and Buenos Aires in 1857. These governments then maintained payments on the renegotiated debt, restored their credit, and eventually raised new loans. Chile resumed borrowing in 1858 and floated almost £10 million in the next seventeen years, while Argentina followed in 1866. Peru, with the benefit of its new wealth from guano, had succeeded in raising new money on the London market in 1853. Many countries in the third group – Colombia, Venezuela, Ecuador, Guatemala and most importantly Mexico – also renegotiated their debts but failed to maintain payments for more than a short period. Without a restoration of credit they could not raise fresh loans, for the Stock Exchange had agreed in 1827 not to sanction the sale of new bonds by countries in default. Revenue shortfalls, extraordinary expenditure (often military), and the preference given to domestic creditors (who were lenders of last resort) did not permit such governments to satisfy speculators thousands of miles away. And without aid from the Foreign Office the bondholders could do little, with the result that the defaulting governments, for a time at least, 'enjoyed a considerable degree of economic autonomy from the great powers of the day'.[41]

Mining and other investments

The welcome given to government loans also encouraged entrepreneurs to market shares in companies to work in Latin America. These included schemes to send Scottish milkmaids to churn butter in Buenos Aires and the opening of pearl fisheries in Colombia. The only substantial investment, however, was in mining. Promoters claimed that modern English mining and refining techniques would revolutionise primitive industries in Latin America. The investment occurred relatively late in the boom; although authorised capital totalled £24.2 million, only about £3.5 million was actually paid up, partly because after December 1825 shareholders could not obtain bank loans to meet calls on their shares.[42] The results generally proved as disappointing as the government bonds. Bolívar commented that the mining associations, which frequently had no specific concessions to work, demonstrated only that 'the English capitalists . . . did not know what to do with their riches'.[43] Few companies survived, the most important being Real del Monte in Mexico (founded 1824) and St John d'El Rey in Brazil (founded 1830).

There is no simple explanation for the failure of most mining investments and the success of a few, beyond the risks inherent in the sector. Two Brazilian gold-mining companies managed to find good deposits which allowed them to use Cornish deep-mining expertise. The companies in Mexico suffered from labour and fuel shortages and high prices for explosives and mercury as well as poor ores. In the case of Chile, Claudio Véliz believes, the problem lay in the late timing of the companies' foundation which left them financially unstable.[44] In Peru, at the 15,000-feet altitude of Cerro de Pasco, inappropriate and expensive technology – the use of steam engines which were vulnerable to mechanical breakdown and fuel shortages – appears to have been at the root of the failure.

CONCLUSION

Does the evidence suggest a continued process of growth and integration into the international economy during the fifty years which followed Latin American independence, or a thesis of stagnation and autonomy? Did the British merchants who arrived during the independence era withdraw before returning in force late in the century, or did they remain and adapt to the Latin American environment? How much influence did they exercise?

The recession which followed the mid 1820s, exacerbated by renewed warfare in Latin America, did mark a break with the growth many regions had experienced in the late colonial period. Moreover, the influx of British and other foreign merchants, and of cheap imports, totally disrupted the old commercial structures. But did the depression last half a century? In the minor countries, perhaps. Bolivia's silver-mining industry recovered much more slowly than those in Mexico and Peru. However, where the political turmoil lasted only a few years, in Chile and Brazil, the economy revived on the basis of a growing export sector surprisingly quickly. To a large extent, therefore, the question of continuity depends on the countries chosen to illustrate the argument, and the disjunctures appear especially marked in Mexico, Venezuela and Colombia, all of which had experienced rapid growth in the late colonial period.

The prospects for Latin American economies depended largely on the path of British and European industrialisation. This created an uneven demand for raw materials and foodstuffs, and not all could respond while Britain retained colonial preference. As a result the principal groups to benefit from *British* demand in the first half of the century were Argentine landowners exporting hides (often via Antwerp), the Peruvian government with its monopoly over guano, and silver and copper miners. However, after the liberalisation of British commercial policy in the 1840s the range of imports from Latin America broadened, and other producers began to rely more heavily on the British market.

As for trade in the reverse direction, the falling prices for British textiles certainly undermined local production and harmed many artisan producers. The process, though, was much slower than many have suggested. Moreover, as a result of the immense drop in import prices many people achieved small material gains, if only because clothing, one of their major items of expenditure, cost less. Some artisans like tailors also benefited. It is not clear what protection for traditional industries might have achieved beyond the short term, and the assumption that they could have been transformed is questionable. Shane Hunt concludes his complex economic analysis of the guano period in Peru with the comment that an indiscriminate policy of protection might have saved some industries but would have implied extensive losses for others, and overall a real cost in welfare.[45] There may have been some prospects for some modern industries, but just as they were coming into existence, in the late 1840s and early 1850s, the protectionist coalitions, which had not really differentiated among primitive workshops, artisan production and factories, began to disintegrate. In addition the size of many national markets encouraged monopoly and oligopoly, making the long-term gains to the economy more dubious.

Important changes occurred in the organisation of international trade which should not be overlooked. In two significant respects the British merchants laid foundations for the later and fuller integration of Latin America into the world economy. The first was their move away from importing on a commission basis towards the provision of credit, albeit short term, to producers, and their search for other outlets for investment. The second was the increasing use of bills of exchange to settle transactions. Initially remittances for imports took the form of specie or produce as well as bills, but gradually merchants separated the finances of the import trade from their export business. Textile wholesalers in Manchester did not want to have to dispose of consignments of hides, tallow, coffee or sugar. It made more sense for merchants in Latin America to ship exports on consignment or on their own account directly to partners or associates in London or Liverpool (or in Europe or the United States), while paying for imports with bills of exchange purchased in Latin American commercial centres. These changes provided the basis for multilateral trade, for further specialisation of merchant functions, and for the growth of commercial banks later in the century.

The presence of British merchants was uneven. In many countries they occupied an important, but not usually a dominant, position. Their interests obviously lay in looser restrictions on their activity and lower duties. But governments had to balance these demands with domestic political pressures and their own need for revenue. Thus there seems little evidence that British merchants had sufficient influence deliberately and consciously to push Latin American governments and elites into a pattern of development contrary to their long-term interests. More important for Latin American economies may have been the investment preferences of the merchants. While commercial instability and political turmoil pushed British merchants towards a desire for liquidity and short-term lending, they also impelled Latin American entrepreneurs towards 'safe' activities like landholding. These preferences came together in the provision of loans secured on export crops or shipments. When it began to appear that protectionist policies were leading nowhere, therefore, the structures were in place for an expansion of international trade and investment.

REFERENCES

1. Cardoso and Faletto, *Dependency and Development*, pp. 38–39; Stein and Stein, *Colonial Heritage*, pp. 134–6.
2. Stein and Stein, 'D.C.M. Platt', 137.
3. Frank, *Capitalism and Underdevelopment*, pp. 313–14.
4. Platt, 'Dependency in Nineteenth-Century Latin America', 115–16.
5. Davis, *Industrial Revolution*, pp. 14–16.

6. Davis, *Industrial Revolution*, p. 16.
7. Crouzet, 'Toward an Export Economy', 73.
8. Walker, *Kinship, Business, and Politics*, p. 13; González Deluca, 'Los intereses británicos', 103.
9. Platt, 'Dependency in Nineteenth-Century Latin America', 115.
10. Crouzet, 'Toward an Export Economy', 75.
11. Farnie, *The English Cotton Industry*, pp. 93–4.
12. Exports from 'Annual Statement of Trade and Navigation', *PP* 1861, LX; population from Mitchell, *International Historical Statistics*, pp. 51–2.
13. Quoted in Lynch, *Argentine Dictator*, p. 254, and Ferns, *Britain and Argentina*, p. 79.
14. Manchester, *British Pre-Eminence*, p. 315.
15. Stein and Stein, *Colonial Heritage*, p. 135 (my emphasis).
16. Pregger Román, 'Dependence, Underdevelopment, and Imperialism', 417.
17. Halperín Donghi, 'La expansión ganadera', 60.
18. Robinson, 'Merchants of Post-Independence Buenos Aires', pp. 116–17 and 121–3.
19. Oppenheimer, 'Chilean Transportation Development', 358.
20. Mayo, 'Commerce, Credit and Control', 35–7.
21. Pratt, 'Anglo-American Commercial and Political Rivalry', 306.
22. Manchester, *British Pre-Eminence*, p. 315.
23. Liehr, 'La deuda exterior de México', 429.
24. Quoted in Lynch, *Argentine Dictator*, p. 68.
25. Quoted in Véliz, 'Egaña, Lambert, and the Chilean Mining Associations', 661.
26. Humphreys, *Tradition and Revolt*, p. 128. 27 million *pesos* were equivalent to about £5.4 million.
27. Halperín Donghi, 'La expansión ganadera', 71.
28. Ridings, 'Foreign Predominance', 18.
29. Burgin, *Economic Aspects*, p. 119.
30. Brown, *Socioeconomic History of Argentina*, p. 217.
31. Bauer, 'Consumption and Development', 232.
32. Halperín Donghi, *Aftermath of Revolution*, p. 52.
33. Burgin, *Economic Aspects*, p. 70; Mathew, 'Imperialism of Free Trade', 565; Hunt, 'Guano y crecimiento', 58.
34. Gootenberg, *Between Silver and Guano*, pp. 109–10.
35. Gootenberg, 'Social Origins of Protectionism', 347–54.
36. Will, 'La política económica', 251–2 and 255.
37. Thomson, 'Continuity and Change', 278.
38. Stein and Stein, *Colonial Heritage*, pp. 134–8 and 159–60.
39. Ortega, 'Economic Policy and Growth', 168.
40. Quoted in Véliz, 'Irisarri Loan', 15.
41. Marichal, *Century of Debt Crises*, pp. 66–7.
42. Rippy, *British Investments*, p. 24.
43. Quoted in Halperín Donghi, *Aftermath of Revolution*, p. 73.
44. Véliz, 'Egaña, Lambert, and the Chilean Mining Associations', 663.
45. Hunt, 'Guano y crecimiento', 60.

CHAPTER FIVE

The Merchants and Trade, 1870–1914

A British merchant of the 1820s returning to Latin America forty years later would not have felt out of place. Although overseas trade had grown considerably, the goods imported had not altered much: textiles, especially cottons, still dominated. The export trade contained new products but earlier staples like hides, sugar and cotton remained significant. Foreign investment had begun to increase during the 1860s but it was still concentrated largely in government loans. Although some short railways had been constructed, the means of transport and communication, both overland and across the Atlantic, had changed little since independence.

The next forty years saw enormous changes. Railways, steamships and telegraphs revolutionised communications. Investments became the main focus of British interests in Latin America, and the emphasis shifted from government loans to a host of companies organised to operate railway concessions, urban services, banks, *haciendas*, mines, oilfields and factories. British interests became much more concentrated in certain countries, Argentina and Brazil particularly, and to a lesser extent Chile, Uruguay, Mexico and Peru. Yet while attention has generally focused on the problems of investment, both at the time and in subsequent historical research, merchant activities and trading patterns were also transformed after the 1860s.

THE MERCHANTS

The transformation of the merchants' business

In Chapter Four it was argued that after independence British merchant houses became a wealthy minority in many trading centres in

Latin America but that their presence was uneven across the region. While their business initially concentrated on imports, those firms which survived had begun to diversify by the middle of the century, although they still attempted to maintain a high level of liquidity. These trends – the uneven presence of British merchants and their diversification – both became more marked after 1870.

In some countries, Mexico and Venezuela among them, British houses had totally disappeared by 1900. In Peru, however, they accounted for perhaps a third of the leading merchants after 1880, and Graham Rowe and Duncan Fox were two of the most active firms.[1] In Chile both these houses, along with Antony Gibbs & Sons, Balfour Williamson, and Wm & Jno Lockett, played a substantial role in the economy. One reason for the continued presence of British houses on the west coast may be that both Chile and Peru sent a substantial proportion of their exports to Britain. Yet British merchants also remained significant in Brazil, whose direct trade with Britain stagnated during the final quarter of the century. In Buenos Aires, in contrast, by 1914 there were few diversified British merchant houses of the type found on the west coast, even though exports were becoming more orientated towards the British market. It became clear at the beginning of the First World War that British houses played little role in the grain trade and had fallen behind US firms in meat exports, the two major branches of Argentina's commerce with Britain.

The differences arose in part from the merchants' responses to the communications revolution of the late nineteenth century. The greater speed and reliability of steamships, which began to replace sailing ships from the 1850s, enabled commercial houses to carry smaller stocks of imports. The development of railways and modern port facilities further reduced the need to invest in inventories. The transatlantic cable, which connected South America with Europe in the 1870s, permitted orders and market information to be transmitted overnight. As a result merchants in Buenos Aires needed only forty-five days to replenish stocks rather than the 160 which had been customary.[2] This reduced their capital and credit requirements, lowering the barriers to entry into general importing. Many small entrepreneurs, often immigrants from other European nations, therefore began to move into this business, especially in the wealthier and more accessible markets. Portuguese traders, for example, became numerous in Brazilian ports. Commissions on imports were consequently reduced, forcing the well-established British houses to look elsewhere for more profitable alternatives. Expertise, resources and

Table 5.1 Merchant activities in the nineteenth century

Activity	Barriers to entry		Risks and Rewards			
	Capital/credit requirements	Specialised knowledge/ contacts	Level of risk	Short-term profits	Speculative profits potential	Long-term income potential
General importing	Low	Low	Low	Moderate	Low	Declining
Specialised importing	Low	High	Low	Moderate	Low	Moderate
Landowning	Moderate	Moderate/high	Moderate	Moderate	Moderate/high	Moderate
Industrial investment	Moderate	High	Moderate	Low	Moderate	Moderate/high
Mining investment	High	High	High	Low	High	High
Advances to governments	High	High	Moderate	High	High	Moderate
Merchant banking	Very high	High	Declining	High	High	High
Exporting on own account	Moderate	Moderate/high	High	Moderate	High	Moderate
Exporting on consignment	Moderate	Moderate/high	Low	Moderate	Low	Moderate
Advances to exporters	High	Moderate/high	Moderate	Moderate	Moderate	Moderate

Note: This analysis is clearly quite subjective. It is intended simply to provide an idea of the barriers to entry to different types of business behind which British merchant houses might shelter, and of the risks and potential rewards of different kinds of activity. Any activity which involved advancing money to governments or investing in mining brought with it the risk of conflicts with government. Other merchant activities were not normally the concern of governments.

the opportunities available in the countries where they were located provided the parameters within which they reorganised. Table 5.1 summarises the possible paths they could follow, the barriers to entry, and the potential risks and rewards of each type of activity.

British merchants did not, first, relinquish the import business entirely, but rather than handling goods like textiles which offered diminishing returns they began to specialise, to acquire exclusive rights to market branded goods, or to act as purchasing agents for large enterprises in Latin America. In Brazil, for example, Wilson Sons & Co concentrated on coal imports, while Henry Rogers Sons & Co handled textile machinery. Both these activities made use of specialised contacts and required some investment, in the case of coal in storage and lighterage facilities, and in machinery in spares and a staff of skilled fitters. In Chile Graham Rowe acquired sole rights to sell Nobel explosives and Chubb locks and safes, while Gibbs became the purchasing agents for the state railways. Second, merchants used their connexions with Liverpool and London to secure shipping and insurance agencies, which, in conditions of expanding trade, offered a dependable source of income. The senior partners of merchant houses often later became directors of such firms. Members of the Williamson, Gibbs and Huth families, all of whom belonged to leading firms on the west coast, occupied positions on the boards of life insurance companies. Third, their specialised knowledge led merchants into acting as company promoters and investors. Often they initiated or acquired ventures which then needed an injection of capital from London for further expansion. In Argentina, for example, British merchants took a leading part in the promotion of the Buenos Ayres Great Southern Railway, one of the best known of all British transport enterprises in Latin America. Balfour Williamson floated nitrate, oil and flour-milling companies operating in Chile and Peru on the London Stock Exchange early in the twentieth century. The advantage of such ventures was that the merchants were well paid for the original investment, and, while obtaining funds from the public for expansion, they normally retained the management of the company and its profitable sales and purchasing agencies. As their contacts with the City of London increased, some houses of humble origin made the transition into becoming merchant banks, concentrating their activities on the acceptance of bills of exchange, loan issues and company flotations. Both Gibbs and Kleinworts, who were recognised as merchant banks rather than merchants by 1914, had begun by trading extensively in Latin America.

Probably the most significant move for those who remained

primarily merchants was into the export trade, which grew rapidly as a result of the astounding growth of population and industry in Europe in the late nineteenth century. As well as increasing in scale, commodity markets also became much more sophisticated; specialised brokerage firms, more intricate categorisation and grading of produce, and systems like futures quotations developed for most trades of importance. British merchants were often at an advantage because their location in London and Liverpool allowed them to acquire knowledge and contacts in European markets fairly easily, while they also possessed reliable information about the credit-worthiness of producers and merchants within Latin America. Export merchants also required greater resources of capital and credit than importers because they generally needed to supply advances to local traders who collected produce, or else *habilitaciones* (short-term loans against crops) and long-term mortgages to landowners. Access to the City of London gave British merchants the benefit of cheap credit. All these factors raised the barriers to entry to the commodity trades, thus permitting the British houses to take advantage.

Specialisation was enhanced by the differences which developed in the credit and marketing systems of each trade. In Peru, for example, cotton-growers needed finance for each annual crop and they repaid their loans by selling the cotton to the merchants, who thus took the profits (and occasionally the losses) on the difference between Peruvian and Liverpool prices as well as earning interest on the loans. Sugar, however, which was produced throughout the year, was much more capital intensive and increasingly dominated by a few large landowners. Merchants needed the resources to offer planters facilities to borrow by drawing bills of exchange up to an agreed credit limit and normally sold the sugar on consignment. Wool exports from the south (particularly alpaca) demanded investments in processing, a network of agents in the *sierra*, and close contacts with specialised brokers in Liverpool.

As merchants concentrated on exports, their reputation often came to depend on particular businesses: Johnstons on coffee, Gibbs on nitrate, Duncan Fox on cotton and wool, Balfour Williamson successively on wheat, nitrate and oil. This involvement in export finance and shipment could also lead to more sophisticated and integrated operations. Some merchants began to produce raw materials themselves (often after foreclosing on loans) or to process them for either local or export markets. Duncan Fox owned cotton gins and textile mills in Peru and sheep farms in Chile; Graham Rowe one of the two major sugar refineries in Chile; Balfour Williamson (in Chile and

Peru) and Knowles & Foster (in Brazil) both developed extensive interests in flour-milling. It was this type of diversification which led eventually to the flotation of small companies in London to raise further capital. By 1914 some merchants had become, in effect, incipient multinational enterprises, with the merchant partnership at the core of the business controlling inter-related companies in different countries and activities.

Evaluating the merchants

Because merchants diversified in so many directions, depending on their individual perceptions of the risks and opportunities, it is extremely difficult to evaluate the effect of these changes. Even in exports, the focus of much criticism of their role, the organisation of each trade differed. In some cases they dealt directly with producers, in others with a chain of local middlemen to whom they provided credit. Clearly there was potential for conflict in any such arrangement over the prices they paid and the interest or commissions they charged. Critics also suggested that over time they accumulated greater control over trade and in some cases created local oligopsonies, reducing the prices paid to local producers.

In the most extensive study of these questions Robert Greenhill concluded that 'the equation of power persistently favoured overseas shippers at the expense of local intermediaries'.[3] As transport links improved British merchants extended their influence inland from the ports, gradually forcing formerly independent middlemen into becoming their agents or replacing them altogether. In the Brazilian coffee trade, for example, Johnstons increasingly dealt directly with *fazendeiros*, bypassing the once important *comissários*. In southern Peru the merchants who dominated the Arequipa wool trade made many formerly independent traders into their agents, as well as purchasing directly from large *haciendas*; the traditional commercial fairs of the region collapsed. If these changes helped to reduce transaction costs or interest rates they may have benefited the producer, but they did eliminate potentially significant sources of local capital accumulation and entrepreneurship. Investments in warehousing facilities and processing machinery (to clean coffee or wool or gin cotton, for example) and their control of grading also extended the merchants' influence.

The producers' power to negotiate with merchants varied according to their credit requirements. If they needed to borrow money annually against individual harvests they might be able to play traders off against one another, but long-term mortgages would tie them to

particular merchants more permanently. Producers also risked foreclosure and total loss where they borrowed against land rather than
the crop. Much also depended on the degree of competition among
merchants in a particular locality. In many export trades the barriers
to entry, although higher than for imports, were still relatively low,
and good margins might attract rivals. Nevertheless, within Latin
America commodity trades only rarely resembled the perfect and
equitable markets of classical theory. Differing access to knowledge
and credit meant that market imperfections increased along the chain
of intermediaries from exporter to peasant or small grower, while
large landowners had greater opportunities to negotiate better interest
rates or prices than their smaller neighbours, especially if they could
delay releasing their crops. Moreover, there are signs that in the big
Latin American export trades – coffee, grain, rubber, sugar, meat –
concentration among the export houses in each country was increasing
after 1900, although the British were not always the dominant foreign
element.

Collusion among exporters did occur on occasion. The Arequipa
wool dealers, faced with a limited and difficult market for alpaca,
their principal product, attempted from time to time to establish
export quotas and set prices, but these arrangements rarely lasted
long. In the Argentine frozen meat trade there is evidence that at
the end of the nineteenth century the three leading exporters (two
of whom were British) met weekly to discuss market conditions,
but the growth of the trade and the entry of Chicago meat-packing
firms after 1907 brought about a vicious price war which severely
weakened the British while temporarily benefiting producers.[4] In
nitrate the merchants who dominated the production companies
made persistent attempts to regulate output and raise prices. While
the Chilean government initially opposed these combinations because
they reduced tax revenues and employment, eventually it began to
support them in order to stabilise the industry. The Brazilian coffee
trade, in which German merchants predominated but British houses
shared, saw an official attempt to protect planters by restricting output
and funding buffer stocks after 1906 in order to raise prices.[5] Thus the
effect of collusive arrangements was not always adverse to producers;
at times it was consumers who suffered. Moreover, very few cartels
survived for more than a short time without attracting competitors
or disintegrating. In relative terms the inequality between British
merchants and Latin American producers or middlemen was probably
greater in the minor export trades and more remote localities, which
historians have tended to ignore, rather than the major trades where

national governments and powerful producers could exert influence.

Other criticisms of the merchants centre on their priorities and outlook. In his *Seven Essays on Peruvian Reality* José Carlos Mariátegui echoed a common complaint that British merchants lent only on export crops, and had done nothing to develop other forms of agricultural credit.[6] In this way Latin American economies became oriented towards the North Atlantic world rather than integrated national markets. In Mariátegui's eyes, however, Peruvian governments and elites were also guilty for collaborating with the British merchants in building up the export sectors at the cost of more widespread development. Part of the problem lay in business perceptions. Most export prices held up until the 1920s, apparently justifying the concentration on international trade, before turning against primary producers. However, by then the commercial infrastructure of which the British merchants formed part had attracted elites towards export production, contributing towards an allocation of resources which hindered more balanced development.

Did the merchants restrict the growth of progressive entrepreneurship by setting an example of conservatism? John Mayo argues that the merchants in Chile before 1880 emphasised caution, kept their funds liquid, and offered little incentive to producers to modernise techniques. Their influence over the early banks there further restricted innovation.[7] British merchants in Chile have also been criticised for the lack of technical innovation in nitrate after 1880, the result of which was that the industry proved unable to withstand competition from synthetic substitutes in the 1920s.[8] Yet the case for merchant conservatism is not so clear cut. After the communications revolution the merchants could not continue earlier policies of maintaining liquidity. In order to survive they were forced to tie up capital in fixed assets or loans, and apart from nitrate, where they had in fact encouraged extensive innovation before 1880, and perhaps also copper mining, they do not seem to have been reluctant to finance change. Bill Albert demonstrates the extent to which houses also involved in Chile welcomed and funded the mechanisation of Peruvian coastal agriculture, especially of sugar.[9] And merchants themselves innovated, by investing in activities such as oil or manufacturing, or introducing new agricultural techniques. Rather than criticising merchants before 1914 for their lack of innovation, a stronger case against them might be constructed on the grounds that ventures like flour-milling or textile production might permit them to establish a monopolistic or oligopolistic position sheltered by tariff barriers, against the interests of consumers, or that the degree of vertical integration they created might reduce the options available to local producers or late-coming domestic entrepreneurs.

THE LATIN AMERICAN EXPORT TRADE

The British market

Except for Cuba and a few coffee producers, the leading export of every Latin American country changed during the second half of the nineteenth century as new production possibilities, technologies and demands appeared. For some the British market was significant, for others not. Its importance continued to vary from one product to another, depending on British demand and the availability of other supplies (though in this period Britain did not impose tariffs on imports and Latin American producers could compete on equal terms with suppliers from within the British empire). Some goods, like coffee, found better markets in continental Europe and North America, while other producers, of short-staple cotton for example, found it difficult to compete with supplies from elsewhere on grounds of price, quality and transport costs.

The trends in tropical and temperate crops, livestock products and minerals were all different. Until 1900 very few tropical or semi-tropical crops from Latin America, apart from sugar, found good markets in Britain, and cane-sugar producers suffered from severe price falls after 1880, caused largely by competition from European sugar beet. After the turn of the century, however, British imports of coffee and bananas from Central America, cocoa from Ecuador, and rubber from Brazil and Peru all increased, due partly to the diversification of demand but also Britain's role as an entrepot, especially for rubber. Some cotton producers also found niches in the British market. The minerals trade shifted in emphasis from bullion to non-ferrous metals like copper and tin, demand for which increased as the electricity and food-processing industries grew. Until the discovery of copper resources within the empire, and the construction of tin smelters elsewhere, Britain remained a good market for both. Nitrate imports from Chile were also significant throughout the period after 1880, although more went to continental Europe.

Table 5.2, which shows British trade in 1913 with four of the major countries, illustrates many of these points. Now that the

British statistics differentiated retained from total imports, its role
as an entrepot for commodities like coffee and rubber is clear.
The wide range of products imported is apparent as well. Most
marked, however, is the size of the trade with Argentina in temperate
agricultural goods and livestock products, which was also reflected in
Chile's exports of grain, frozen meat and wool. This was probably the
most significant change during the period.

Table 5.2 Principal British imports from Argentina, Brazil, Chile and
Peru in 1913 (£)

	Retained	*Total*
Argentina		
Fresh and frozen beef	12,379,656	12,815,002
Maize	10,665,360	10,851,874
Wheat	6,135,810	6,137,518
Flax and linseed	2,398,315	2,398,635
Wool	1,986,811	2,140,647
Fresh and frozen mutton	1,895,124	1,908,255
Oats	1,886,831	1,892,186
Hides	860,649	881,552
Others	2,518,140	3,459,722
Total	40,726,496	42,485,391
Brazil		
Raw cotton	1,839,806	1,992,268
Rubber	1,337,292	5,940,700
Coffee	339,359	793,582
Cotton seed	326,360	326,369
Cocoa	321,384	387,939
Others	422,265	567,509
Total	4,586,466	10,008,367
Chile		
Nitrate	1,317,551	1,439,981
Copper	928,471	1,002,406
Corn and grain	631,953	651,172
Frozen mutton	293,133	293,133
Tin ore★	282,833	347,982
Sheep's wool	66,842	788,962
Others	746,468	835,699
Total	4,267,251	5,359,335

Peru

Raw cotton	1,268,018	1,280,210
Alpaca wool	273,141	288,951
Rubber	272,494	445,681
Sugar	255,455	266,137
Sheep's wool	162,136	212,300
Others	629,438	684,982
Total	2,860,682	3,178,261

*Tin ore arriving in Britain from Chile almost certainly originated in Bolivia.

Source: 'Annual Statement of Trade and Navigation, 1913', PP, 1914, LXXXIII

As its population increased in the late nineteenth century Britain had begun to rely more heavily on imports of foodstuffs. This created a market first for Chilean and then for Argentine grain; its arrival during the northern hemisphere spring significantly filled a seasonal shortfall in supplies. Demand for livestock products, while remaining reasonably strong for industrial inputs like hides and wool, also tended to move towards meat. Here Latin American producers gained from technical improvements in canning and refrigeration and from their proximity to the market. Initially the trade was restricted to meat extracts, canned meat and live cattle, but in the thirty years before the First World War it became possible to ship first frozen mutton, and then frozen and finally chilled beef. After 1900 meat from the River Plate possessed significant advantages in the British market. The United States' export surplus declined due to the growth of domestic demand, while Australian producers did not overcome the technological problems involved in carrying frozen beef over such a distance until the 1930s. In 1908 Argentina supplied over 60 per cent of Britain's imports of frozen and chilled beef, and 35 per cent of its frozen mutton.[10]

This massive growth in trade in temperate products meant that Latin America became more important overall as a supplier to Britain. In 1880 Central and South America had provided only 4.5 per cent of Britain's imports, in 1900 only 5.2 per cent, but the proportion rose in the early twentieth century to 9.9 per cent in 1913 and 10.6 per cent in 1929, before falling to 7.7 per cent in 1938.[11] This was largely a consequence of the enormous growth in Britain's imports from Argentina, which by 1913 dwarfed those from other countries, in contrast to the middle of the century when they had been of little significance except for hides. Nevertheless, in the pre-1914 boom, as Table 5.3 shows, all Latin American countries increased their exports to Britain.

Table 5.3 British imports from Latin America, 1860–1913[a] (£000)

	1860	1880	1900	1913[b]	
				T	R
Argentina	1110	887	13080	42485	40726
Brazil	2269	5261	5947	10008	4586
Chile	2582	4146[de]	4828	5359	4267
Peru	2581	2160[de]	1307	3178	2861
Uruguay	867	695	490[c]	2749	2519
Bolivia & Paraguay	199	131	—	2259	1883
Colombia, Venezuela					
& Ecuador	587	1683	559	2118	1326
Central America	225	1339	673[c]	2060	1213
Spanish Caribbean	3288	1752	96[ce]	3802	3706
Mexico	490	628	472[c]	1880	1700
Total	**14298**	**18353**	**27452[c]**	**75898**	**64787**

a   These figures exclude gold and silver bullion

b   Total and retained imports were not differentiated until the early twentieth century: for the 1913 columns T = total, R = retained.

c   It is known from Platt, 'Problems in the Interpretation', that in 1900 large quantities of Liebigs' exports from Uruguay were arriving in Britain via Belgium (and are therefore not included in these figures), and that goods from Mexico, Central America and Cuba were included as imports from the United States.

d   The figures for Peru and Chile for 1880 have been adjusted to take account of the fact that Chile, apparently unknown to British customs officials, had captured the Peruvian nitrate deposits.

e   In 1880 Peru and Chile were at war, and in 1900 Cuba was still devastated after the independence war against Spain.

Source: 'Annual Statements of Trade and Navigation'

Questions of dependence

To what extent, then, was Latin America dependent on Britain for its export trade? Obviously the importance of the British market varied according to the products a country could export, but it could be vital for particular countries and regions. Some republics, especially Chile and Peru, relied greatly on it throughout this period, as Table 5.4 shows. Sugar, cotton and wool, Peru's principal exports apart from copper, all depended on markets in Liverpool or Bradford. While Peru supplied only 1.7 per cent of Britain's imports of cotton in 1910–14, these shipments made up 70 per cent of Peru's cotton exports.[12] The growth of the British entrepot trade in rubber, gathered in the Amazon rain-forest, deeply affected the north of Brazil. When prices collapsed after 1910 as a result of the British success in domesticating wild rubber and producing it on colonial plantations in Asia, the economy of the region disintegrated. Most importantly for the future, as grain and meat exports grew, Argentina (and also Uruguay) became *more* dependent on the United Kingdom, and specialised in accordance with the demands of the British market.

Table 5.4   British share of Latin American countries' exports, 1880–1913 (%)

	Argentina	Brazil	Chile	Peru	Uruguay
1880	9.1	n/a	45.5	n/a	21.7
1885	15.5	n/a	37.0	n/a	19.4
1890	18.8	n/a	31.9	68.3[a]	13.4
1895	12.5	n/a	35.1	55.8[b]	15.1
1900	15.5	12.9[c]	73.2	46.7	6.8
1905	13.9	18.4	37.0	51.7	5.8
1910	21.7	24.8	35.3	35.2	8.3
1913	24.9	13.1	34.6	37.4	17.1

[a] 1891   [b] 1894   [c] 1901

Note: Latin American export statistics are notoriously unreliable, partly because of the practice of shipping goods like wheat without stating a specific destination. These figures are intended only as a guide to trends and relative proportions. The 1891 figure for Peru and the 1900 one for Chile look particularly dubious.

Source: Mitchell, *International Historical Statistics*, pp. 593–609

To restrict the analysis, however, to the direct export trade is to take too narrow an approach. Britain was such an important market for so many commodities in the late nineteenth century that the value of Latin American exports might depend on prices determined there even if they were not sold directly to Britain. The telegraph made such market information readily available. Thus, for example, purchasers in Latin America based quotations for sugar and cotton on

Liverpool prices, for wool on Bradford, for minerals on the London Metal Exchange.

The question of export prices has been fundamental to structuralist critiques of Latin American development. Prebisch believed that commodity prices had been declining faster than those for manufactured goods from the 1870s, with the result that Latin America's terms of trade (the ratio of export to import prices) had steadily deteriorated. Certainly British consumers and industrialists enjoyed lower food and raw-material prices in the final quarter of the nineteenth century, while the decline in the cost of manufactured goods generally slowed. However, part of the explanation lies in the substantial falls in intermediate costs (commissions and shipping) that occurred, which would not affect the prices paid to Latin American producers.

Empirical evidence on terms of trade is sparse. Very few historians have attempted the difficult task of quantifying trends for individual Latin American countries. Of those who have, Carlos Manuel Peláez and Nathaniel Leff both conclude that Brazil's overall terms of trade improved slightly in the half-century before the First World War, although Leff notes an important regional distinction. Unstable prices for sugar and cotton almost certainly meant a deterioration for the north of the country, in contrast to an improvement for the coffee-producing regions.[13] Shane Hunt estimates that between 1855 and 1900 the buying power of Peru's exports fell by one-third.[14] Much therefore depended on the products a region or country exported; those concentrating on silver and sugar probably suffered most. But conclusions also vary according to the period over which terms of trade are measured. Export prices for many products, including coffee and meat, seem to have improved in the twenty years preceding the First World War before turning down again in the 1920s.

It was not only British demand and British prices which affected exporters in Latin America. Some were dependent in other ways on changes in the British economy or on British firms, even if they did not export there. The dominant role of sterling in international payments meant that a financial crisis in London quickly affected the availability of credit, the level of interest rates, and the ability to discount bills of exchange. Since a substantial proportion of Latin America's exports to Germany were financed by accepting houses in the City, these were also affected by changes in the London money market. Moreover, Latin American producers still used the services of other British intermediaries. Brazilian coffee went primarily to New York, but London-based railway companies, banks, trading houses and shipping lines played a considerable role in the trade. Chilean nitrate found its major market in Germany, but for much of the 1880s and 1890s British-registered companies produced over half of it.[15] It is hardly surprising, therefore, that in considering the export trades Latin Americans frequently complained about 'the grip which the British held upon the railroad, the exporting firm . . . the shipping company, the insurance agency, the financial bank', for all were significant intermediaries, especially in the major countries of South America.[16] For Britain the growth of Latin American exports meant that the credit offered by British merchant houses and commercial banks financed much trade which never touched British ports but provided a valuable source of invisible earnings.

THE DEBATE ABOUT BRITISH EXPORTS

On both sides of the Atlantic historians have tended to concentrate on problems associated with their own countries' exports. Thus

Table 5.5 British exports to Latin America, 1860–1913 (£000)

	1860	*1880*	*1900*	*1913*
Argentina	1782.4	2450.6	7142.7	22640.9
	(13.1%)	(13.6%)	(28.9%)	(40.9%)
Brazil	4446.8	6681.7	5820.4	12465.1
	(32.6%)	(37.1%)	(23.6%)	(22.5%)
Chile	1702.8	1919.5	3254.7	6010.5
	(12.5%)	(10.7%)	(13.2%)	(10.9%)
Peru	1381.4	312.8	948.6	1487.8
	(10.1%)	(1.7%)	(3.8%)	(2.7%)
Uruguay	922.7	1381.3	1690.9	3012.1
	(6.8%)	(7.7%)	(6.8%)	(5.4%)
Bolivia and Paraguay	—	78.3	15.9	555.8
		(0.4%)	(0.1%)	(1.0%)
Colombia, Venezuela, Ecuador	1208.8	1820.2	1245.9	2932.8
	(8.9%)	(10.1%)	(5.0%)	(5.3%)
Central America	182.3	658.5	962.9	1734.5
	(1.3%)	(3.7%)	(3.9%)	(3.1%)
Spanish Caribbean	1530.0	1469.5	1345.4	2280.8
	(11.2%)	(8.2%)	(5.4%)	(4.1%)
Mexico	462.6	1225.6	1998.3	2233.1
	(3.4%)	(6.8%)	(8.1%)	(4.0%)
Total	**13619.8**	**17998.0**	**24695.6**	**55353.4**

Source: 'Annual Statements of Trade and Navigation'

while Latin American commentators have been much more concerned about British intermediaries and British markets, they have paid little attention to imports from Britain (in contrast to their worries about the flood of British manufactures in the early nineteenth century). For many British economic historians, however, trends in exports to Latin America in this period provide important evidence for debates about industrial competitiveness and marketing methods, and hence the roots of Britain's relative decline as a trading nation.

Although statistical problems remain in this period, especially in the accurate identification of destinations (as the figures for Bolivia and Paraguay illustrate), the basic trends are clear from Table 5.5. Much of Central America, northern South America and the former Spanish colonies in the Caribbean were of declining significance. In contrast, Brazil and Chile remained important markets, and Argentina grew spectacularly after 1880. By 1913 four countries – Argentina, Brazil, Chile and Uruguay – were taking 80 per cent of Britain's exports to Latin America.

Table 5.6   Composition of British exports to Latin America (%)

	1860	1880	1900	1913
Cotton textiles	52.4	49.7	30.0	23.1
Linens	6.9	4.2	2.1	1.8
Woollen textiles	10.3	6.6	7.3	6.3
Coal	1.7	2.9	9.6	11.8
Hardware	3.4	3.8	2.2	0.8
Iron and steel	5.5	10.8	12.2	12.9
Machinery	1.9	3.2	8.0	9.5
Others	17.9	18.9	28.6	32.8

Source: 'Annual Statements of Trade and Navigation'

The composition of exports (see Table 5.6) altered substantially. Cotton textiles still formed the largest single group but their relative importance was declining, and after 1895 the volume exported to Latin America also began to fall. One problem was competition from other industrialising countries. British manufacturers lost good markets in Cuba and Puerto Rico to the United States. Import substitution, especially in Mexico and Brazil, also became a serious threat. By 1910 both these countries produced over 400 million yards of cloth annually. This largely explains the rapid fall in exports of piece-goods to Brazil after the early 1890s shown in Figure 5.1,

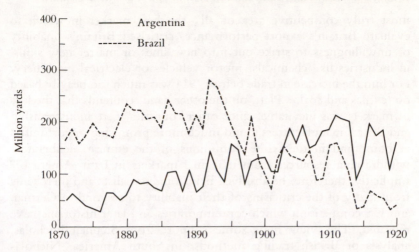

Figure 5.1 British cotton textile exports to Argentina and Brazil, 1870–1920.

Source: 'Annual Statements of Trade and Navigation'

although it was partly offset by rising exports of yarn and machinery. Moreover, domestic production tended to replace the cheaper textiles first, leaving British trade in more expensive dyed and printed cloths intact. The Argentine market for textiles, in contrast, which was only slightly affected by import substitution, rose steadily to a peak in 1912. The sectors of significant export growth were coal (intended principally for steamships and railways) and a wide range of iron and steel products and machinery, as well as chemicals, paint, branded foodstuffs and pharmaceuticals, all of which fall into the category of 'others' in Table 5.6.

Nevertheless, Britain was losing its leading position in the import trade. The Germans began to make substantial inroads in the 1880s, but the long-term threat came from the United States. Even in Argentina, its strongest market, Britain's share of imports fell from 37 per cent in 1885–86 to 31 per cent in 1910–12, while Germany's rose from 8 to 17 per cent and the United States' from 8 to 15 per cent.[17] By the beginning of the First World War Britain retained the lead in only four countries – Chile, Brazil, Uruguay and Argentina – and in both Uruguay and Brazil its share of imports had fallen to less than a quarter.

This experience has been a major issue in the debate over Britain's decline. S.B. Saul, for example, who considered South America 'the

113

most truly competitive area of all', the best market in which to evaluate Britain's export performance, criticised Britain's 'inability or unwillingness to strike out into new lines or master new skills' in industries like chemicals, motor vehicles or electrical machinery. For him the increase in trade before 1914 was much too heavily based on textiles and coal.[18] Platt, on the other hand, contends that the loss of markets was inevitable, since other countries were industrialising and British manufacturers found much more promising opportunities at home and in the white dominions of the empire, deliberately withdrawing resources from marginal markets in Latin America.[19] Implicitly, therefore, he absolves British industrialists and merchants from many of the criticisms of their inability to respond to German and US competition which contemporaries and later historians have repeated. This view finds some support from Stephen Nicholas' analysis of British trading methods. In South America, Nicholas argues, the Worthington Mission of 1898 acquitted British merchants and commercial travellers of the frequent allegations that they lost sales through linguistic ineptitude and insufficient credit arrangements, adding that one sign of British success was the envy with which North American commentators regarded the merchant-house system.[20]

The disagreement is due, in part, to the difficulties of evaluating complex qualitative evidence, but it arises also from the high level of generalisation at which debate has been conducted, and the tendency of those who take an 'optimistic' view not to look beyond 1914. There is no doubt, as Platt suggests, that manufacturers and merchants had little incentive to invest much in the smaller and more marginal markets where demands for imports were unsophisticated. In Venezuela British cottons continued to sell well, even though they were marketed by German houses who purchased either through agents in Britain or through commercial travellers in Latin America. However, countries like Argentina and Brazil were not marginal to British businessmen, and their import demands were becoming increasingly complex. The analysis of Britain's export performance should concentrate on these markets and middle-rank economies like Chile's and Peru's, where British merchant houses were still strong. It is also necessary to distinguish four separate issues: the competitiveness of particular products; the overall composition of exports; the adequacy of marketing methods; and the other props on which British trade rested before 1914.

The question of competitiveness has normally been approached by analysing individual export sectors, and here the picture was mixed. While some sectors of British industry were highly efficient exporters, others frustrated merchants and companies abroad by their commercial myopia and inability to adapt. The cotton textile industry was still able to compete on price and to cater to changing demands, but this was not so in hardware or areas of the engineering trades. While Britain dominated Latin American markets for textile or flour-milling machinery, for example, it supplied little agricultural equipment, except for sugar processing, and had only a small share of the market for electrical goods. British manufacturers still dominated the market for caustic soda and soda ash, but they had fallen behind the Germans in supplying organic chemicals. In goods like branded food and drugs, sewing machines and office machinery, the United States was securing a much greater share of the market. It could therefore be argued that the composition of Britain's trade presented serious long-term problems, despite its overall growth during the decade before 1914. The sectors in which Britain was most competitive were often not the most dynamic areas of trade. Cotton textiles were vulnerable to import substitution, as the relatively poor showing of British trade in Brazil illustrated, and coal to replacement by petroleum. In retrospect, despite the pre-1914 boom, British trade looks too heavily dependent on old technologies in transport, fuel, chemicals and consumer goods.

Would better marketing have improved the situation? Nicholas regards the envy that US officials showed for the British merchant houses as a positive sign of their marketing skills. In small countries, he argues, merchant houses must have reduced transaction costs.[21] Yet the discussion of merchant activities earlier in this chapter would suggest that for many British firms importing by itself was not particularly significant. Moreover, merchant houses could not effectively represent twenty or thirty manufacturers in a single market. Their contribution to British manufacturing sales may have arisen more from their functions in the Latin American export trades and their close contacts with producers, to whom they supplied credit for the purchase of goods like machinery. On their behalf the London or Liverpool offices of the merchants could arrange for tenders, confirm orders, and pay suppliers directly. Other manufacturing firms keen to trade in Latin America began to bypass the British houses, either by sending their own travellers abroad to sell directly to the import merchants or by establishing sales offices. Even so, the number who did this, in comparison with US firms like Singer, Remington or Ford, was small, particularly given the importance to them of markets like Argentina. There is clear evidence of only eight British manufacturing companies with their own sales offices or factories in Latin America before 1914.[22]

To some extent, also, the apparent health of Britain's export trade just before 1914 depended on other areas of British strength. The availability of sterling bills in Latin America made it easy to pay for imports from Britain. British dominance of shipping helped to maintain markets for bulk cargoes like coal, cement and alkalies, for which shipping companies offered low outward freights because of their usefulness as ballast. Investment also helped to maintain markets, either indirectly by boosting the level of demand in Latin America, or more directly because many British firms tended, where possible, to purchase equipment in the United Kingdom. Thus there was a boom in trade with Argentina in the late 1880s, when it briefly surpassed Brazil as Britain's most important market in the region, as a consequence of railway investment. As railway companies grew, they came to offer a fairly secure market for coal, locomotives and rolling stock, if not for rails, which were subject to international cartel arrangements. This may have been reinforced, as the US Federal Trade Commission alleged in 1916, by close personal ties between consulting engineers in London and the directors of the railway companies, equipment suppliers and coal exporters.[23] However, in other areas of British investment, such as petroleum, British capital goods were largely unavailable, and the close relationship between the nationality of the investment, technicians and exports much less marked than with the railways.

CONCLUSION

Merchants' business and the pattern of trade were transformed in the late nineteenth century, as the communications revolution reinforced changes which had begun earlier. Importing became much less significant than the British merchants' other activities: the Latin American export trade, the agency services they provided for other British firms, and their own investments. In many parts of Latin America British merchants almost disappeared. Moreover, for several countries, especially in Central America and the Caribbean, Britain was no longer particularly significant as a trading partner by 1914, except perhaps as a supplier of cheap textiles.

British interests were concentrating in Brazil, Argentina and Uruguay, Chile and Peru. Here their commercial influence was substantial, but it showed itself in different ways in individual countries, and it changed over time. In Chile and Peru British merchant houses retained a significant role in the economy. In Argentina and Uruguay merchants were relatively unimportant, although dependence on the British market was growing. In Brazil it was the role of British intermediaries, shipping lines, insurance companies and banks as well as the merchants, which caught the attention, for British trade with Brazil was stagnant for much of this period.

Overall, the merchants and the direct trade with Britain had become much less important in defining the nature of Anglo-Latin American relations by the early twentieth century. In 1914 the most obvious signs of the British presence were the London-based companies which operated in Latin America. Merchants had become just one sector of a group of British intermediaries which also included commercial banks, insurance firms, railways and shipping lines, and the telegraph companies, and which together gave Latin American producers easy access to world markets. In some countries, Brazil especially, Britain's role in these activities had become much more important than its direct trade. Moreover, the infrastructure available for international trade was frequently much more efficient than that available for domestic commerce, enhancing Latin America's orientation towards Britain and the North Atlantic.

Dependence on Britain – on British firms and on the part that Britain played in international trade and its infrastructure – was therefore widespread, especially in the southern part of Latin America, but it took different forms in different countries, and it did not arise from a conspiracy of British interests of the type assumed by writers like Frank. There is little evidence that British merchants deliberately forced Latin American countries into a subordinate relationship, impeding development and extracting most of the profits from exports. Their own investments in manufacturing, their inability to prevent the loss of major markets for textiles, and the substantial income earned by Latin American exporting interests are all evidence against such simplistic explanations. The evidence on trade and the merchants would suggest that writers like Cardoso and Faletto, who recognise both that Latin American elites would have opportunities to profit and that their relationship with British interests would vary from one country to another, provide a more fruitful approach to the problem of Latin American dependence and the role of the British.

REFERENCES

1. Bollinger, 'Rise of US Influence', 73.
2. Reber, *British Mercantile Houses*, p. 80
3. Greenhill, 'Merchants', 170.
4. 'Report of Departmental Committee on the Meat Trade', *PP* 1909, xv, 9–10
5. These cases are discussed in more detail in Chapter Seven.
6. Mariátegui, *Seven Essays*, pp. 68–70.
7. Mayo, 'Before the Nitrate Era', 289 and 298–302.
8. O'Brien, '"Rich beyond the Dreams"', 132–15 and 141.
9. Albert, 'External Forces', 242–5.
10. 'Report of Departmental Committee', 8–9.
11. Mitchell and Deane, *Abstract of British Historical Statistics*, pp. 283–4 and 322–3.
12. Platt, *Latin America and British Trade*, p. 257; Miller, 'British Business in Peru', 83.
13. Peláez, 'Theory and Reality', 280–1; Leff, *Underdevelopment and Development*, I, 81–6.
14. Hunt, 'Guano y crecimiento', 39.
15. O'Brien, *Nitrate Industry*, p. 111.
16. Graham, *Britain and the Onset*, p. 73.
17. Saul, *Studies in British Overseas Trade*, p. 39.
18. Saul, *Studies in British Overseas Trade*, pp. 38–40.
19. Platt, *Latin America and British Trade*, pp. 99–128.
20. Nicholas, 'Overseas Marketing Performance', 493–4.
21. Nicholas, 'Overseas Marketing Performance', 497–503.
22. Greenhill and Miller, 'Merchants, Industrialists, and the Origins'.
23. US Federal Trade Commission, *Report on Cooperation*, I, 174–6.

CHAPTER SIX

The Investment Boom and its Consequences, 1870–1914

In the late nineteenth century, Peter Cain and Tony Hopkins argue, the centre of dynamism within the British economy moved from the manufacturing areas of the Midlands and North towards the commercial and financial interests of the City of London.[1] Nowhere was this shift of emphasis more marked than in the case of Britain's relations with Latin America. Despite the growth in direct trade outlined in Chapter Five the region accounted for only about 10 per cent of Britain's foreign commerce in 1913, whereas it absorbed at least 20 per cent of Britain's overseas investment.

Initially this flow of capital concentrated on government bonds, but from the 1870s numerous companies were founded in Britain to develop concessions and purchase existing businesses in Latin America. By 1913 the British possessed interests, on one estimate, in seventy-seven railways (thirty-five of which were capitalised at over £2 million each), fifty-three utility companies, nine banks, thirty-six nitrate firms, eighty-five other mining companies, fifteen oil firms, and 112 other enterprises in industry, land and commerce.[2]

In those countries where Britain's interests became concentrated, these investments affected almost every group in society. The rhythm of economic life in Argentina, Brazil and Uruguay, Cain and Hopkins claim, was 'dependent on the ebb and flow of London funds'.[3] The need to service government loans and the companies' foreign exchange requirements placed considerable constraints on policy-making. Key sectors of the economy came under the control of firms based in London and potentially outside the influence of governments. For Latin American business elites Britain's investments offered opportunities for profit, yet also the danger that companies might either renege on their commitments or obtain a position from which

119

they could exploit domestic producers and intermediaries. Thousands of people in all sectors of society came into direct contact with British firms, whether as consumers of their services or as their employees. British businessmen's attitudes and actions thus had profound effects on the development of popular nationalism and labour organisations.

THE PATTERN OF INVESTMENT

An intense controversy has developed over the level British overseas investments had reached by 1913, due largely to differences in sources and methodology. Table 6.1 shows the principal estimates for Latin America. Feis drew his figures from Sir George Paish who had based them on the Inland Revenue statistics of the income received from overseas investments before 1907, and then on new issues of bonds and shares in London for 1907–13. Subsequent historians have tended to rely instead on Stock Exchange statistics. Rippy's figure, derived from the *South American Journal*, represents the nominal value of all government loans and companies involved in Latin America quoted on the Stock Exchange, while Stone used the published details of new issues of stocks and bonds in London between 1865 and 1913 to calculate his estimates. D.C.M. Platt, who in 1986 argued that the global estimates for British investment in 1913 were much too high, criticised all these procedures for not taking account of the purchase of securities in London by other foreigners or the amortisation of loans.[4] With this in mind Davis and Huttenback omitted those bonds known to have been sold elsewhere in Europe from their attempt to reach a lower-bound estimate for capital calls, but their figures relate only to *South* America, excluding Mexico. There is thus no precise answer to questions about the stock of Britain's investments in Latin America in 1913 or the capital flows which had occurred. All that can be said with certainty about the level of Britain's assets there is that they had a nominal value in 1913 of between £700 million and £950 million.

There is less dispute about timing. The experiences of the 1820s made British investors wary of Latin America until those debts had been renegotiated. Capital exports before 1860 went principally to continental Europe, the United States and the empire. Thereafter, however, Latin American countries participated in three cycles of overseas lending. The first, which reached a peak in 1872, was terminated again by several defaults on government loans. The

Table 6.1 Estimates of British investment in Latin America, 1913 (£ million)

	Total investment in Latin America	Investment in Latin American government bonds	Comments
Herbert Feis (1930)	756.6		Based on earlier (1914) estimates of Sir George Paish for British holdings of assets overseas (these were themselves based on Inland Revenue returns to 1907, then new issues).
J. Fred Rippy (1959)	999.2	316.4	Based principally on *South American Journal's* estimates, totalling nominal value of all securities traded in London.
Irving Stone (1977)	1179.9	445.5	Total value of new issues in London, based on *Stock Exchange Yearbook*.
Lance E. Davis & Robert A. Huttenback (1986)	623.4	223.4	Minimum value for capital calls for *South America* (excluding Mexico) between 1865 and 1913.

Sources: Feis, *Europe, the World's Banker*, pp. 23–4; Rippy, *British Investments*, p. 67; Stone, 'British Direct and Portfolio Investment', 698; Davis and Huttenback, *Mammon and the Pursuit of Empire*, p.49

second wave commenced at the end of that decade and closed with the Baring crisis of 1890. The third began around the turn of the century and reached a climax in 1913. The supply of capital for overseas lending depended on saving in Britain and the returns on domestic investments; whether it went to Latin America, and if so where, depended on British perceptions of the past record and the potential opportunities in each republic.

Table 6.2 Stone's figures for British investment in Latin America, 1865–1913 (paid-up capital)

(£ million)	1865	1875	1885	1895	1905	1913
Argentina	2.7	22.6	46.0	190.9	253.6	479.8
Brazil	20.3	30.9	47.6	93.0	124.4	254.8
Chile	3.2	10.0	10.1	32.4	42.1	76.1
Peru	3.9	36.2	36.6	22.3	22.5	29.7
Uruguay	1.1	6.2	16.0	33.6	39.2	47.3
Mexico	25.6	28.4	40.8	93.6	119.5	132.1
Others	24.1	40.3	53.4	86.7	87.2	142.1
Total	**80.9**	**174.6**	**250.5**	**552.5**	**688.5**	**1179.9**

Source: Stone, 'British Direct and Portfolio Investment', 695

Even though Stone's figures overestimate total British holdings, they still provide the best guide on their geographical distribution. As Table 6.2 illustrates, Argentina became the most important recipient. However, investment there did not take off before the 1880s. In the first wave of lending Peru borrowed large amounts but defaulted in 1876. In the following cycle Mexico began to attract new capital, even before the final renegotiation of its post–independence debt in 1888, and became a major attraction. Brazil and Chile remained significant throughout. Overall, Britain's investment, like its trade, became concentrated in a few countries. Argentina, Brazil and Chile together accounted for 69 per cent of new issues, Mexico for a further 11 per cent.

Stone's estimates for the distribution of this investment by economic activity appear in Table 6.3. This shows a continuing predominance of government loans until the 1870s; while they always remained significant thereafter, accretions to capital depended more on the growth in railway investment, especially in the 1880s, and, after 1900, on growth in both railways and public utilities. British interests thus shifted quite substantially over the period from portfolio investments (in which they did not exercise managerial powers over the expenditure of the

capital and any enterprises established with it) to direct investments
controlled from the City of London.[5] Both Stone and Svedberg
conclude that about half the total British investment in 1914 was
direct, even though several companies controlled from elsewhere, for
example the Canadian-owned public utilities in Brazil and Mexico,
raised large amounts of loan finance in London, an investment which
was clearly portfolio in nature.[6]

Table 6.3 The distribution of British investments in Latin America

(a) Percentages by sector (accumulated new issues)

	1865	1875	1885	1895	1905	1913
Government	76	74	66	47	45	38
Railways	12	14	22	36	34	34
Public utilities	1	5	4	3	6	12
Shipping	3	3	1	1	1	2
Financial	3	2	2	7	7	8
Raw materials	3	1	3	3	4	3
Industrial & miscellan.	1	1	2	2	3	3

(b) Proportion of new issues accounted for by each sector

	1865–75	1875–85	1885–95	1895–1905	1905–13
Government loans	72	44	33	33	28
Railways	16	43	47	27	35
Public utilities	8	3	2	16	20
Financial	1	1	12	8	9
Raw materials	—	7	3	7	2
Other	3	2	3	9	6

Source: Stone, 'British Long-Term Investment', 323

How important was the London capital market to Latin America?
One attraction was that Britain had the most liberal regulations in
Europe on foreign investment. Unlike France and Germany, the
government did not supervise the Stock Exchange and made no
attempt to tie loans to the purchase of goods from the lending
country. France did take a significant share of Latin American
business when it was still concentrated in government loans before
1875, but it then faded in significance until the decade preceding 1914.
Although Germany also participated quite extensively in public loans

in the 1880s, the list of banks leading each issue suggests that London dominated Latin American government finance between 1870 and the turn of the century but that after 1900 Berlin, Paris and New York began to offer greater competition for this business.[7]

For promoters wishing to finance companies the London market, with its record of investment in railways and other undertakings overseas, was dominant throughout. 'London was near paradise for speculators and company promoters,' Charles Harvey and Jon Press write of mining firms. '[There was] no difficulty in organising new firms and presenting them to the public as worthy investments.'[8] Although many British capitalists still preferred bonds and debentures, they seemed more attuned to risky investments in equities than the French, who disliked anything but fixed-interest *obligations*, or the Germans. US investors in Mexico, Central America and the Caribbean were also prepared to speculate with their capital, but by the time they appeared, in the 1890s, the British interest in these areas, except for Mexico, was relatively small.

LATIN AMERICAN PUBLIC DEBT

Trends in lending

The first cycle of investment, in the 1860s and early 1870s, determined the future pattern of lending to Latin American governments. As noted in Chapter Four, Brazil, Peru, Chile and Argentina had all restored their credit by 1860, and then raised new loans in London, often taking advantage of falling interest rates to convert earlier debts. Other countries like Colombia, Uruguay and the Central American republics also made settlements with their creditors. As a result, between 1860 and 1875 thirty-four loans for fifteen different Latin American countries were issued wholly or partially in London, together with another four in the early 1870s for Argentine provinces. The nominal value exceeded £100 million.[9] The purpose of these loans was threefold: the refinancing of earlier debts; extraordinary fiscal expenditure (particularly military demands); and public works. One would normally expect countries which borrowed for military needs to have incurred the more acute problems of repayment. In fact, though, it was those which raised excessive loans at high interest rates for impracticable public works which soon found continued payments impossible. The consequence was a string of defaults: Honduras and

Santo Domingo in 1873, Costa Rica and Paraguay in 1874, Bolivia and Guatemala in 1875, and Uruguay and Peru in 1876.

In effect this divided Latin American countries into two groups, the defaulters and those which continued to borrow. In the next cycle, during the 1880s, only five states (Argentina, Brazil, Chile, Mexico and Uruguay) were able to raise new loans. Some of the defaults, for example that of Honduras, remained unsettled for years, but the renewed availability of capital during the 1880s encouraged other governments to make settlements with their creditors on the basis of an issue of new bonds. Paraguay, Costa Rica and most, significantly, Peru, conceded national assets, normally land but in the Peruvian case the state railways and guano export rights, in return for a cancellation of their debts. Nevertheless, of the earlier defaulters only Uruguay, which suspended interest payments for just three years, fully regained its credit rating.

The countries which survived the 1870s crash became favourites in the London market. In the 1880s some provinces or states, and a few municipalities, also raised loans besides the national governments. In addition British investors purchased internal debt obligations of Argentina, Brazil and Mexico. Despite problems during the 1890s, when Argentina and Brazil both threatened default, their reputation on the London market remained strong, and they were therefore able to take advantage of the renewed cycle of foreign investment which commenced around 1900.

By then developments in the mechanisms of lending had made it less costly. In 1875 many of the institutions which organised the sale of Latin American bonds had still been commodity merchants and acceptance houses first, and loan issuers second. Although major houses like Rothschilds, Morgans or Schroders seem to have faced few financial problems, others remained vulnerable to a recession, especially if they were over-exposed in a particular region. Thus the crisis of 1890 bankrupted Murrieta and emasculated Morton Rose, both of which had been heavily engaged in Argentine finance, brought Gibbs almost to its knees, and would have bankrupted Barings totally had it not been so large that its collapse would have threatened the entire fabric of the City. During the 1890s merchant banks rebuilt their capital; by 1900 they possessed considerable funds and were concentrating their efforts on finance. Thereafter there were no failures of significance for Latin America.

The increasing specialisation and resources of the merchant banks had advantages for Latin American governments. The big houses became skilled in organising large bond issues, but they could also make short-term advances if necessary. Three other developments reduced the cost and risk of borrowing for the leading countries. First, greater competition among merchant banks meant that governments could seek high prices for loans while interest rates and commissions declined. Second, most loans were syndicated among bankers in several European financial centres, a custom that had been growing since the 1870s, and a proportion of the bonds was issued simultaneously in each. Third, many loan issues were underwritten by commercial banks, insurance companies and investment trusts, further spreading the risk. The appearance of numerous loans for provincial and municipal governments was an indication of increasing confidence and the availability of funds. Often intended for public works projects, these loans allowed the smaller and newer merchant banks to participate in the business at a time when Rothschilds, Barings and Morgans dominated the requirements of the major South American countries. Their growth in turn expanded the opportunities available to Latin American politicians. Thus when Rothschilds, Brazil's traditional bankers, refused to become involved in financing coffee valorisation in 1908, the São Paulo state government obtained funds, at a price, from Schroders in London, who led a syndicate which also included banks in Paris and New York (see pp. 160–1).

Problems and issues

The distinction between the poorer countries which defaulted in the 1870s and the wealthier ones which, despite problems, maintained their credit is crucial in evaluating the balance among the three principal groups of actors: private investors, merchant bankers and Latin American governments. Clearly those individuals who purchased bonds which went into default in the 1870s lost large amounts, whereas those who concentrated on the better-known countries earned a steady income. Merchant banks could also make considerable losses, as the events of 1890 showed, if they were left with unsaleable bonds, but the risks diminished as syndication and underwriting became more common, and in many instances the profits were substantial. Morgans, for example, made £484,500 on two Chilean issues as early as 1867.[10] The management of interest and amortisation payments also provided merchant banks with a substantial commission income. But what of Latin American governments?

In the first lending cycle weaker governments suffered much exploitation. A Parliamentary Select Committee in 1875 discovered, for example, that Honduras had become liable for bonds worth £6 million, in exchange for which it possessed an abandoned fifty-three mile stretch of railway for which the contractors had received about £700,000. The means used to persuade the public to purchase such loans had been, the committee concluded, 'flagrantly deceptive'.[11] Secret dealings before the loan was allocated raised the price of the bonds to a premium, inducing the innocent to buy. In some cases governments authorised the issuing houses to use the initial proceeds of the loan to speculate in the bonds and thus maintain the price in order to sell the remainder. The bankers gained at the expense of both the government responsible and the investing public.

Such governments lay at the mercy of both their own agents in Europe and the financial intermediaries issuing the loan. The price at which their bonds were sold, the commissions they paid, and the interest for which they became liable meant that they gained few long-term benefits from their access to foreign finance. By the mid 1870s Peru, the largest borrower, was devoting its entire guano revenue to servicing the foreign debt, in exchange for which it had acquired some unfinished and unprofitable railways. For such countries default, which relieved the economy of interest payments they could not afford, was much the best policy. The problems came when, in a subsequent lending cycle, governments decided to attempt to regain access to the London market by entering negotiations with speculators who had accumulated semi-worthless bonds. They then often recognised an outstanding debt which far exceeded the bonds' market value, or conceded national assets to bondholders in order to cancel it. This turned portfolio into direct investment and created different problems, because the government relinquished control over the outflow of remittances and had to find means of maximising the benefits from powerful foreign interests which still influenced its credit rating. The clearest example is Peru in 1890. It not only renegotiated its debt too late in the cycle to obtain new loans, but found itself in continuing disputes with the Peruvian Corporation (the company the bondholders established) and other creditors. The national government did not borrow in London again until 1922.

For the countries which maintained their credit the balance of power varied according to the stage of the cycle. In an upswing governments could negotiate better terms as competition for their business increased. All except Brazil, which remained with Roths-childs, deliberately moved issues from one house to another in both the 1880s and 1900s. Argentina, for example, played off Barings and Morgans against one another and against bankers in Europe and the United States. The problems came in a downswing when government income and the supply of foreign exchange diminished, with the result that as a proportion of both government revenues and export earnings interest and amortisation payments rose rapidly. Even without the additional burden of company remittances, increased foreign indebtedness thus exacerbated problems of economic management for the major countries. In particular it made the exchange rate a central issue in policy-making, and one on which the interests of exporters, who preferred a steady depreciation, diverged from the government's.

In such crises the stronger countries, which wished to maintain their access to foreign credit, and their financial agents in London, who needed the business, normally cooperated to maintain payments and prevent default. In 1876 and 1913–14, for example, Argentina obtained short-term advances to pay interest on its loans. More serious crises occurred in Argentina after 1890 and Brazil in 1898 when, in order to avoid default, governments issued new bonds to meet interest payments and other obligations. The terms on which these operations were undertaken and the policy conditions which were imposed created major controversies (see pp. 153–5 and 164–5).

One other point needs to be made. With a few exceptions around 1870, the initiative in seeking foreign loans lay with Latin American politicians. They obtained approval from Congress, negotiated the loan contracts, and disbursed the proceeds. While Richard Graham, in his study of the British in Brazil, concludes that 'most of the foreign loans did little to advance modernization', he adds that 'with rare exceptions, one must blame the Brazilian government rather than the British bankers'.[12] The problem for governments was that they often did not adequately foresee the long-term consequences of access to cheap credit in London. As in the 1970s, the development of the London capital market, by making loans cheaper and easier, encouraged many to borrow more heavily than they could afford.

COMPANY FORMATION

The growth of investment

Unlike the period after 1914, British direct investment in Latin America before the First World War was not normally channelled through multinational companies with interests in several countries. Most enterprises before then were what Mira Wilkins has called 'free-standing companies', firms with small headquarters in the City of London and operations in just one country overseas.[13] Some never used the Stock Exchange to raise finance (the leading petroleum firm in Peru between 1889 and 1913, for example). However, the largest, like the railway companies, banks and public utilities, required much more capital than an individual or a partnership could supply. The stock market also offered entrepreneurs the opportunity to offload on to the public the risks and cost of expanding an existing undertaking while taking profits on their original investment. Generally companies raised finance in one of three ways: ordinary shares, on which returns could range from nil to outstanding; preference stock, which paid a fixed maximum dividend (often 4 or 5 per cent) as long as the company's income permitted; and fixed-interest debentures (bonds), which were a first charge on the company's profits.

Rather less is known about mechanisms of corporate finance than about government loans. It seems clear, however, that both the timing of equity and debenture issues and the ease with which capital could be raised for companies in individual countries were closely related to trends in government borrowing. Thus, for example, Morgans, Barings, Huths, Schroders and Gibbs are all known to have been managing share and debenture issues for companies operating in Argentina, Chile and Mexico in 1889–90. Firms seeking finance for enterprises in countries like Peru, on the other hand, where the experience of lending to government was poor, found it difficult to raise money even in an upswing. 'Peruvian Stocks were not favourably looked upon by the London Financial Houses and Under-writers,' one businessman complained in 1910.[14] The only chance of raising money was through high-interest debentures backed by a government guarantee and hypothecated on a specific tax.

These considerations enhanced the concentration of British invest-ment. Two other features of upswings led in the same direction. First, as a lending cycle progressed, more speculative enterprises in the major countries could be floated in London, often with a high degree of over-capitalisation. Thus, for example, in the first Chilean nitrate boom, only four firms were floated between 1882 and 1887, but a further fourteen, nine of them founded by the infamous Colonel North and his associates, in 1888–89.[15] In the pre-1914 cycle a similar role was played by numerous small mining ventures and some public utilities. Research on one of these, Fred Stark Pearson's Canadian group, which operated in Mexico and Brazil and raised substantial amounts of debenture finance in London, shows how such entrepreneurs deliberately 'watered' capital to provide themselves with profits and to ensure that dividends remained 'reasonable' in the eyes of host governments, thus forestalling pressures to reduce tariffs or invest more in improving services. As a result the actual flow of funds to Latin America in Pearson's enterprises was between only a third and a half of nominal capital.[16] Second, the availability of capital in an upswing encouraged the 'denationalisation' of Latin American enterprises, whether through governments disposing of investments or Latin American businessmen seeking further finance in Britain. In 1889, for example, the Buenos Aires provincial government sold its Western Railway, and Chilean private investors the Antofagasta (Chili) and Bolivia Railway, to British interests. A parallel process occurred in the subsequent cycle.

By 1914 an enormous variety and number of British firms were operating in Latin America, making it difficult to generalise about issues of control, exploitation and dependence. For Latin American governments, however, the most problematic investments, in terms of their scale and economic role, were probably the commercial banks, railways and public utility companies.

Commercial banks

The Companies Acts of 1858 and 1862 offered limited liability to joint-stock banks registered in England. Almost immediately several were founded to operate abroad. The London and Brazilian Bank was incorporated in 1862, and the London and River Plate Bank opened its first branch in Latin America the following January. Subsequent investment booms encouraged the foundation of further banks and the spread of the older ones' branch networks, often into neighbouring countries. Some lasted only a few years before going out of business, while the survivors gradually amalgamated their interests. By 1914 four large and increasingly multinational institutions dominated British commercial banking in Latin America: the London and River Plate Bank with assets of £32.4 million, the London and Brazilian Bank (£22.3 million), the Anglo-South American Bank (£19.8 million) and the British Bank of South America (£14.3 million). They had achieved, in David Joslin's words, 'a formidable position in domestic banking' in the main countries of British interest, controlling one-third of deposits in Brazil and one-quarter in Argentina and Chile.[17]

The banks which survived tended to be those which maintained liquidity and lent cautiously. Initially they saw their role not as providing funds for long-term investment but as offering short-

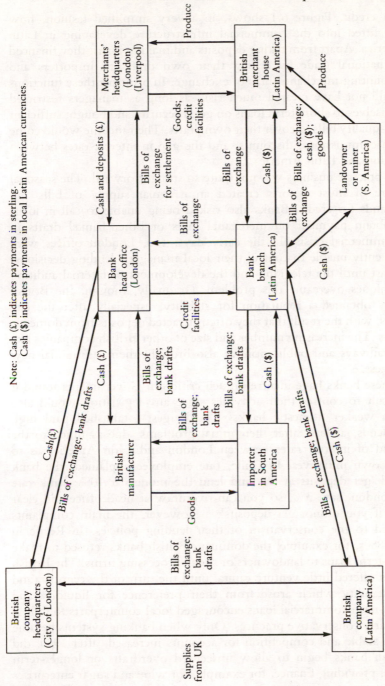

Note: Cash (£) indicates payments in sterling.
Cash ($) indicates payments in local Latin American currencies.

Figure 6.1 A simplified model of the operations of British commercial banks, merchants and companies in Latin America

term credit. Figure 6.1 shows, in a very simplified fashion, how they fitted into the commercial infrastructure developing in Latin America. Apart from taking deposits and making loans, they financed international trade by selling their own drafts to importers and discounting merchants' bills of exchange. In principle these functions should not have created much risk, as long as managers restricted themselves to short-term loans on good security and bought sufficient high-quality bills to cover their own drafts. Their income would come from commissions, discounts, and the gap in interest rates between London and Latin America.

In practice business was not quite so straightforward. The seasonal nature of most exports created an irregular supply of bills and demands for credit. Banks also risked being unable to call in loans or obtain payment on merchants' bills or other banks' drafts in a commercial crisis. In the early days, too, London offices were frequently unable to control their local managers' lending decisions, at least until the telegraph and the development of internal auditing techniques overcame this problem. Gradually, though, the British banks obtained a reputation for stability, especially after the late 1880s, with the result that they often attracted deposits from domestic banks. The increasing number and size of other British companies like the railways and public utilities also brought them substantial new business.

These banks have incurred much criticism. Governments found it difficult to control their activities since any legislation would also harm weaker domestic banks. The longest established paid high dividends, at least after their initial problems, due as much to the spread of interest rates between London and Latin America as to their own initiatives. In Chile, one employee explained, the bank could 'get deposits at 2% and lend the money at 10%; bank rate in London, say, 3%, so you can overdraw at head office and clear 7%, if you cannot get deposits'.[18] However, the main complaints related to the conservatism of their lending policies. In Recife in the 1880s, for example, the dominant British banks refused to make long-term loans to landowners or sugar-processing firms. The British banks offered little venture capital until the turn of the century, and the stability which arose from their preference for liquidity and short-term commercial loans encouraged local counterparts to follow similarly conservative practices. Only when banking systems became more stable and competition for accounts increased, after 1900, did British banks begin to allow unsecured overdrafts or longer-term loans, providing finance, for example, for wine and sugar enterprises in Argentina and textile mills in Brazil. Nevertheless, domestic banking, even in Argentina where interest rates fell to European levels, remained much more cautious than in Europe, in large part due to the conservative model provided by the British. The high liquidity provisions of the Banco de la Nación Argentina compared with those in England and Germany, Charles Jones argues, seriously restricted the extent to which the substantial surpluses of the Argentine export trade might have financed internal growth.[19]

Railways

The railways were the epitome of the 'free-standing' company, accounting for almost half the total quoted British capital in Latin America by 1913. However, despite their experience in financing and constructing railways elsewhere, British investors had not rushed to establish similar enterprises in Latin America. The initiative for many lines came from local businessmen, and in several countries the state then acquired responsibility for further construction when these early enterprises encountered financial problems. Governments themselves used foreign loans to build lines, especially in Chile and Argentina. Even where private investors were willing to build, governments normally had to guarantee returns (usually 7 per cent on capital invested) and provide other concessions like duty-free imports of materials.

Foreigners, the British especially, began to dominate railway financing and operation in Latin America in the 1880s. Local capitalists and governments both sold lines to London-based companies, while British entrepreneurs also scrambled to obtain new concessions backed by government guarantees in countries like Argentina. The move towards private capital was partly for ideological reasons (a belief that the state would be less efficient than private firms) but also because even in a boom governments could not borrow all the capital required for extensive networks. However, the outcome was disastrous, for guarantee payments represented an enormous burden on fiscal revenue, especially in a commercial crisis.

During the 1890s many governments abrogated the existing guarantees and refused new ones. Subsequently several distinct patterns of railway ownership and operation developed in Latin America, with the state, local businessmen and foreign firms playing different roles in each country. By 1914, after a series of amalgamations, the 'Big Four' British companies dominated Argentina, but in Mexico British

133

investors came to own a minority holding in a system dominated first by US firms and then by the Mexican government. In Brazil and Peru foreign companies leased track from the state. In Chile British firms coexisted with an extensive state-operated network.

Whatever their role in the national system, foreign railway companies stimulated similar complaints: the burden of guarantees; the abuse of their monopoly position; the organisation of rate-fixing pools; excessive tariffs and poor services; the cost to the government and economy of duty-free imports; and the railways' employment policies. Many of these criticisms reflect the central dilemma of a government seeking foreign capital: how to motivate capitalists to invest and then reinvest while at the same time maximising the benefits to the country. Once the companies had become established, governments' bargaining powers should have improved; whether Latin American states made the optimum use of this is debatable.

Many problems originated from the first concessions. Most of these included provisions for a guaranteed return, duty-free imports, considerable freedom to set tariffs, and exclusive privileges to construct railways in a specified zone. What made matters worse was that the original economic projections for a railway were frequently unrealistic, either deliberately or through ignorance of Latin American conditions. Engineers, spurred on by politicians or company promoters, constructed railways which could never have made reasonable profits because the traffic available simply would not suffice to cover the fixed costs. Such lines became problems both for their shareholders and for governments which desired adequate railway services.

There were several disadvantages in the guarantee system. It promoted careless and wasteful construction and management, especially as few governments had the expertise to control the companies firmly. Moreover, the combination of political pressure and investor mania in a boom meant that governments frequently approved guarantees without considering the financial consequences. Neither Argentina nor Brazil, for example, controlled their liabilities when new projects proliferated in the 1880s. Railways needed time not only to be built, but also to generate traffic and income. Recession inevitably hit both the companies' profits and government revenues, increasing the demand for guarantee payments just when fiscal crises became acute. Borrowing to meet them was not a solution. These difficulties lay behind governments' attempts to end the system after 1890, although their solutions differed. In Argentina the state issued bonds to the foreign companies to commute the payments. In

Brazil, in contrast, it invoked its right to repurchase the lines, using foreign loans for the purpose, and then leased many back to British companies.

Concessions which gave companies exclusive privileges within a large zone were also ill judged. Platt regards the Santos–São Paulo Railway, one of the most profitable British enterprises in South America, as the most conspicuous example of a foreign monopoly 'holding a nation to ransom' through its domination of the main route for coffee exports.[20] He could have said much the same of the Mexican Railway Company before the construction of competing lines to Mexico City from the Pacific and the United States. However, rate-fixing and pooling arrangements among foreign railways were rare, except where several served an inland market like Mexico City. Most lines radiated outwards from ports rather than converging on an inland centre, thus giving companies local or regional monopolies.

Tariffs, taxes and the standard of services were therefore serious problems, for monopolistic enterprises might charge high prices for very little. In order to attract capital, governments had often abdicated full control over freight rates and allowed them to be tied to gold (a further source of strain in a recession), as well as providing tax concessions. In Uruguay, for example, the state could not intervene until profits reached 8 or 12 per cent of capital invested, depending on the date of the concession, and the Central Uruguay Railway had been exempted from taxes for forty years. The Argentine government did not regularise the position of the railway companies until the Mitre Law of 1907. Even then, in order to attract further investment, it limited taxes to 3 per cent of net profits for forty years, and restricted its power to intervene in setting freight charges unless net profits exceeded 6.8 per cent of authorised capital for three consecutive years. Moreover, railways often did not keep up with the demand for their services. Poor and marginal companies, often dependent on debentures rather than equity finance, had to pay interest on loans before considering reinvestment. Yet even the more efficient companies were often unable to supply sufficient rolling stock to cater for seasonal demand without compromising their profits, and often, like some railways in the pampas or the Peruvian Corporation in the early 1900s, were forced into reinvesting only by the threatened construction of competing lines.

A final problem arising from the railways' concessions related to import duties and employment. The privileges on imports limited the backward linkages between the railways and the economy, since the companies had little incentive to seek local suppliers, and this impeded the growth of metals and engineering industries which railway systems the size of Brazil's or Argentina's might have stimulated. Moreover, foreign railway companies persisted in employing large numbers of expatriates and using English in offices and workshops down to quite junior levels. In part this was due to prejudice, in part because company directors believed that three-year contracts gave them a means of control over their employees, but the effect was to discourage local engineers and restrict the diffusion of technical and managerial skills into local economies.

Without the privileges offered in the original concessions, governments could not have obtained British finance for railways as quickly. However, they seem to have made little real attempt to tighten their control once the initial investment had been secured and companies had become profitable. Even in the case of the guarantees the renegotiations seem to have left the companies with substantial benefits. In Argentina the railways received approximately £10 million in bonds in the 1890s to commute them.[21] Out of fear that new railway construction would cease, governments seem to have done relatively little to tighten their control over tariffs, the taxation of the companies (for example by limiting their concessions on imports) or their employment policies. Using foreign capital to construct railways more quickly thus created considerable problems in the longer term.

Public utilities

The dilemma of providing sufficient rewards to attract investment while maximising the returns to the economy was equally acute for urban utilities. Local entrepreneurs or the municipal authorities had often taken the initiative in developing water, gas, electricity and tramway services, but then sold out to foreign companies. The complaints about them resembled those concerning the railways: abuse of monopoly, high tariffs and poor service, and the disregard of the terms of their concessions. Like the railways these companies entered into direct everyday contact with the public and this gave them a high degree of political exposure. The rapid growth of most Latin American cities during the export boom placed great strains on them, since local demands for the reinvestment of profits to improve and extend services inevitably conflicted with the payment of dividends and loan interest.

British investors had interests in large numbers of utility companies, as noted earlier, but very few historians have analysed them in any depth. The most detailed studies are confined to Rio de Janeiro, São

Paulo, Montevideo and Rosario. One obvious problem was that the resident of a single Latin American city might use the services of several British companies. This seems to have been most acute in Montevideo, where many utilities were under British control and even diplomats complained of the 'costly and deficient' service of all except the gas company.[22] Both the telephone and water companies there paid good dividends but lagged behind the demand for service. In São Paulo, too, where rapid urban growth would have made it impossible for any entrepreneur, official or private, to keep pace with the demand for services, both the gas and electricity companies came under the control of British and Canadian investors, and the council found it impossible, for long periods, to persuade either to improve the city's lighting.

CONSEQUENCES AND PROBLEMS OF INVESTMENT

British investment in Latin America inevitably had profound economic effects. Latin American countries in the 1870s and 1880s were still short of capital, and it was difficult to mobilise large sums for long-term investments. The taxation base of governments was also limited. Those countries which could attract British investment were able to respond more quickly to the increasing demand for exports, and the wealth derived from this then helped to bring down local interest rates and to provide governments with greater resources. Over the longer term, however, there were serious costs involved in dependence on inflows of foreign finance. Not only did it create problems in managing the economy, but it also had unforeseen political and social consequences.

Financial and economic implications

It is important to determine the returns on British capital in Latin America. If they were excessive, this might have cancelled out the value of the initial investment relatively quickly. However, research on rates of return is complex, and even the two most exhaustive studies of British investment overseas use a sampling method to analyse them which so restricts the database referring specifically to Latin America that their results may seriously distort the reality. Michael Edelstein's figures, the more reliable, suggest that for Latin

137

America loans to governments and railway company debentures both gave relatively high returns in comparison with other overseas investments, and that the rewards on ordinary shares in companies were also substantial (investments in the banks were exceptionally profitable).[23] Much more research on financial flows is required for a full analysis of the economic value to Latin American countries of British investment, but it seems likely that two processes were occurring. First, returns were quite high overall, and, except for the early 1870s, when investment shifted towards Latin America, and the subsequent boom years of 1885–89 and 1905–13, the outflow of interest and dividend remittances exceeded the inflow of new capital. Second, the returns received from earlier investments were indirectly recycled away from the poorer countries towards those the British favoured, Argentina especially.

This seriously affected governments' abilities to manage their economies. The growth of public debt put pressure on both government finances and the balance of payments, especially as commercial recessions coincided with falls in new investment. As direct investments grew, the problem became worse. Governments could not control the repatriation of profits (exchange controls did not become common until the 1930s), even if, in the last resort, they could still default or reschedule their own obligations. The popularity of fixed-interest paper (debentures and government bonds) exacerbated the difficulties. Unless a country did default, the demand for foreign exchange in a commercial crisis would scarcely fall. Moreover, the depreciation of local currencies caused by sudden adverse movements in the balance of payments brought enormous problems for governments unable to expand their tax revenues but liable for interest payments in sterling. Thus by 1890, when the Baring crisis occurred, Argentina's liabilities for debt service, as a result of the large fixed-interest component due to public borrowing and the railway guarantees, exceeded 60 per cent of export earnings, and the premium the government paid for sterling was increasing rapidly.[24]

Why, then, did governments and elites seek foreign capital? In part it was due to the imperfections and inefficiencies of capital markets in Latin America, which put constraints on the mobilisation of local resources. Foreign funds provided the means to finance expensive public works projects more quickly and at an apparently reasonable level of interest. Moreover, both governments and businessmen in Latin America worked with restricted time horizons. Most constitutions prohibited the re-election of a president, making it likely that the burdens of adjustment would fall on his successor. With a few exceptions Latin American entrepreneurs had little long-term interest in public works projects which offered lower returns than investments in urban real estate, agricultural land or short-term loans. Their involvement more often lay in using their political influence to obtain concessions which they could then sell at a profit to a foreign entrepreneur.

There was no technological imperative that made foreign ownership of advanced enterprises essential. Latin American entrepreneurs and governments showed themselves perfectly capable of introducing modern technologies. In the early stages of railway and utility construction they contracted foreign expertise quite effectively, showing that these activities could have developed under local ownership, even if some loan finance might have been needed from overseas. But instead they tended to sell out to foreign companies, particularly the British, who had long experience of such investments at home and abroad.

In the case of Latin American governments the pressures for selling enterprises were both ideological (a growing acceptance of the idea that private enterprise would operate utilities more efficiently than the public sector) and practical (a fiscal deficit and the opportunity to sell at a profit). Local capitalists who constructed railways and utilities only to sell them to foreign companies some years later probably ran into problems raising funds for further expansion. They found it more difficult than governments to secure loan finance in Britain without relinquishing control. There may have been political reasons for selling, too, especially in the case of public utilities, which needed much smaller amounts of capital than railways. Here local businessmen may have sold out simply because they received a good price which they could reinvest to get better returns elsewhere, in urban real estate for example. If they retained a minority shareholding they might continue to receive a good income without being exposed to the hostility the public utilities inevitably provoked from consumers and municipalities.

Technology and techniques

These arguments have implications for Furtado's comment that one effect of foreign investment was to enhance Latin America's technological dependence (see p. 20). In the sense that Latin America relied more heavily on imports of capital goods from Britain, this was true. However, unlike the later era of multinational investment, technology in the late nineteenth century was not usually embodied in the firm. The growth of textile industries using British technicians but under local ownership, and of the early state railways which recruited foreign engineers, both suggest that the acquisition of technology and foreign capital did not have to be so closely related.

The problem was rather that governments, in their desire to attract foreign capital, were frequently too lax, and made few attempts to recover control in areas like supplies and staffing. The concession of duty-free imports was normally wide ranging and long term instead of being targeted on essential items of equipment for a limited period. Moreover, while concessions might contain provisions about employing a high percentage of local staff, they did not normally differentiate among workers. The result was that most railways, utilities and mining companies developed an ethnically differentiated hierarchy of employees in which technical, managerial and supervisory staff, and even some skilled workers, were English, while the unskilled workforce was recruited locally. This was encouraged by conservative directors in London who regarded the contracting of expatriate staff as some guarantee against defalcations and also as a means of labour discipline. In the railway companies large numbers of expatriates remained in senior management and technical positions in Argentina, Uruguay, Chile and Peru until well into the twentieth century. Control from London thus limited the opportunities open to Latin American managers and engineers in foreign-owned enterprises, and consequently the spread effects of innovations in business organisation and technology (in this respect, those countries which maintained state operation of their railways probably did better). The lack of opportunities for local personnel which these policies created also reinforced the bias against technical education, a key feature of many countries' development. James Street compares Argentine attitudes towards imports of foreign capital and technology adversely with those of the United States and Japan, where much greater efforts were made to assimilate and build upon the foreigners' skills.[25]

The political influence of British companies

Research on the equation of power between British companies and their host governments proliferated after the early 1970s, as business archives became available. However, it often focused on specific negotiations or confrontations and was not particularly conclusive. Negotiating strength was rarely one-sided or, indeed, constant over time.

Despite the evidence that states were frequently slow in tightening their control over the activities of foreign firms, it is clear that governments and elites in Latin America were not simply submissive collaborators of British firms. Administrations, at both the national and provincial level, were frequently constrained by opposition in Congress from conceding too much to British interests. Once a company possessed fixed investments the state had the potential to use threats to revoke or revise concessions to make life difficult for it, although at the cost of perhaps deterring it from reinvesting. If there was no prospect of the firm raising new capital, the government's power to exercise greater control was increased. Moreover, British companies were usually acting on their own in this period. Except over an issue like taxation or labour relations, which had wider implications, they could rarely expect much support from other British firms, even in the same economic sector. Unless a company could prove that it had suffered illegal treatment it could also expect little diplomatic help. Unlike bondholders, who frequently blocked new loan issues for countries with which they were in dispute, individual companies found it difficult to persuade others not to invest. Furthermore, the scope for government action was enhanced by the increasing frequency with which British companies came into conflict with one another, for example in Chile in the late 1880s when Gibbs and Campbell Outram were fighting against the monopoly position of Colonel North's Nitrate Railways Company.

The key variables in any negotiations seem to have been the possibilities of new investment, the strength of opposition to an administration, the attitudes of local business elites represented by interest-group associations, and the governments' own changing perceptions of the costs and benefits of foreign investment. Evidence from a variety of activities indicates that British companies did not always have the freedom to act that nationalist critics have supposed. Peru passed radical legislation concerning insurance-company deposits and investments in 1901 which caused the withdrawal of the British, while ten years later Uruguay established a state insurance bank which largely excluded British companies from the fire and life business. Nationalist opposition in Argentina delayed the full amalgamation of the Buenos Ayres & Rosario and Central Argentine Railways from 1901 to 1908, and prevented the merger of the Buenos Ayres Great Southern and Western Railways in 1912. In the case of the St John d'El Rey gold mining company in Brazil Marshall Eakin finds that although it had good political connexions it never achieved the permanent concessions on export taxes, import duties and mining legislation that it desired.[26] However, by concentrating on specific issues and conflicts, the research on business imperialism and control has tended to obscure the longer-term political and social consequences of direct investment.

The growth of British firms greatly increased the opportunities for Latin American lawyers and politicians, areas into which expatriates could not venture (the two occupations were, of course, closely linked). All companies needed local lawyers since they operated, for the most part, under specific concessions and legal codes, and it made sense to retain those with political influence. The Santiago manager of the Anglo-South American Bank commented candidly of one adviser in 1907 that 'it was as an ex-diplomat and as personal friend of the president that his services were of value to us, far more than as a lawyer'.[27] In Argentina the River Plate Trust used a former minister and an old schoolfriend of the president as legal advisers. Obtaining ministerial or congressional approval of new concessions or alterations to old ones needed considerable public relations work, involving constant lobbying, the distribution of favours, and the cultivation of friendly politicians. All a company's efforts could be undone by a sudden change of ministry, so a range of contacts covering the entire political spectrum was often vital. Besides employing lawyers and 'political advisers' on retainers, in some cases it also became customary to appoint local boards comprising influential businessmen and political figures, especially for the railway and public utility companies in the Plate. In a crisis, such as the footplatemen's national strike in Argentina in 1911–12, these boards became an important channel for political influence.

The expansion of British companies, therefore, meant that increasing numbers of Latin American politicians developed contacts with them, and these links may provide a further reason why governments apparently often disregarded the more profound problems of British investment and their countries' long-term interests. Frequently the ministers who made key decisions had developed close connexions with British companies earlier in their careers. For example, the Minister of Public Works who finally approved the sale of an Argentine state railway to British interests in 1909, against bitter opposition, had been a lawyer for several railway companies. To a large extent the oligarchic political systems of Latin America already contained a strong element of clientelism rather than ideological cleavages, in which congressmen were the key intermediaries and personal contacts with ministers essential. The means which the

British companies used to promote and defend their interests were formed by the prior existence of such customs of brokerage, but they strongly reinforced them.

It is important not to confine the focus to the national level. For many companies access to local sources of power – garrison commanders, police chiefs, prefects and intendants – was of much greater everyday importance. This might mean making use of political connexions to ensure the appointment of sympathetic officials, paying them retainers, or using the voting influence of the firm's employees in local elections to obtain the right result, a process which Harold Blakemore discusses for congressional elections in the Chilean nitrate region in 1890.[28] Eakin, having described the St John d'El Rey's connexions with lawyers and politicians in the state capital, concludes that its political and economic power was 'enormous at the local level' but 'its influence diminished with distance'.[29]

Political conditions became more difficult for British companies in the decade before 1914, just as investment was reaching its peak, for three reasons: the increasing remoteness of directors; the growth of nationalism; and the greater intensity of labour protest. After the mid 1870s the revolution in communications had made it practicable for the first time to manage companies' everyday affairs from London, but for some years leading firms were still headed by men with considerable experience in Latin America. Gradually, however, they became more closely associated with City financiers and their attitudes. Even directors with past experience in Latin America became more remote and prejudiced and less sensitive to changes in the region. 'Personally I never trust the word of any South American,' Lord Forres, the senior partner of Balfour Williamson and later chairman of both Lobitos Oilfields and the Central Argentine Railway, wrote privately, 'and I always ask myself what is his motive or object in conveying the information, or the answer he has given.'[30] Another railway company chairman publicly disparaged 'the Peruvian Government, Congress, Press, and People [as] the typical defaulting republic of South America' at his annual general meeting in London while the firm was in the midst of difficult negotiations in Peru.[31] The British companies' pursuit of immediate profits and their insensitivity to local feelings evoked many complaints from British diplomats. The chargé d'affaires in Buenos Aires was writing of the 'foolishness and greed' of the railways as early as 1888, while the minister in Uruguay criticised the 'narrow and parochial-minded policy' of the Central Uruguay Railway in 1911.[32] 'Providence has gifted us,' his successor in Montevideo wrote in 1914 out of frustration with the British banks, 'with the singular power of being able to live all our lives among foreigners without being able to see their side. . . . We English must possess admirable qualities to carry us over the obstacles which our stupidity erects in our way.'[33]

This insensitivity, together with the increasing visibility of British firms and their expatriate managers, made it difficult for them to cope with both nationalism and labour demands. For all opposition politicians nationalism was a useful weapon with which to attack governments, as the railway companies in Argentina trying to rationalise their interests had found just before 1914. Its impact increased as British investment grew, and in the cases of Balmaceda in Chile and Batlle in Uruguay politicians who were more sceptical of the value of foreign investment and determined to control it actually achieved power. A particular fear, shared by elite politicians and the popular press alike, was that a foreign trust would come to control a crucial sector of the economy. This showed itself in the unpopularity of firms like the Peruvian Corporation and Colonel North's nitrate enterprises around 1890, or, at the very time that US courts were taking their most famous antitrust decision by breaking up Standard Oil in 1911, in apprehensions that the 'Big Four' railway companies in Argentina would merge or that Percival Farquhar's Brazil Railway Company, supported by British capital, would achieve dominance over transport there. British businessmen, however, found it difficult to understand nationalist attacks, whether they came from elite politicians or from popular protests focusing on foreign property as a symbol of oppression. The railways, tramway companies, gas works and power plants became increasingly vulnerable to attack in popular riots, and strikes could also expand into more widespread disturbances in which company property was damaged.

The growth of trade-union activity increased the companies' problems, for in many countries they were among the largest employers. The first Argentine railway union, La Fraternidad, was founded in 1887, and both the Buenos Ayres Western and Great Southern faced strikes in the 1890s. The first major protest in the Chilean nitrate zone occurred in 1890, at the peak of British ownership of the *oficinas*. While British companies (with the marked exception of the nitrate firms) were often quite paternalistic towards their workers, providing housing, hospitals and social clubs as well as relatively good wages, labour militancy was something they found it difficult to comprehend. Frequently managers rationalised it in terms of loyal workers being led astray by outside agitators, although some showed themselves as prejudiced as their less understanding directors in London. 'It has been assumed,' the new manager of the Chilean Electric Tramway Company wrote in 1919, 'that all the members of the lower grade staff, i.e. conductors, conductresses, drivers, car cleaners, and workshop employees, are thieves, drunkards, and evilly disposed towards the company'.[34] In many industries and countries the reluctance of British companies to employ local managers meant that confrontations with labour became ethnic as well as class conflicts and at times British managers were physically attacked by strikers.

British companies were not slow to defend their interests by appealing to elite fears of working–class militancy, a tactic made more effective by the fact that stoppages in export production or transportation would quickly affect government revenues. Increasingly they paid retainers to officials and police and military commanders to ensure their loyalty. In Antofagasta the railway company, after major strikes in 1906 and 1907, actually constructed a new cavalry barracks in the hope of maintaining order. Such measures led, on occasion, to British complicity in state violence against their employees, for example in separate incidents in Chile in 1903, 1906 and 1907. However, they possessed other methods of controlling labour militancy: eviction from housing, dismissal, blacklisting for future employment, and the use of blackleg labour to break strikes. In both Brazil and Chile British firms encouraged national and ethnic rivalries within their workforces in order to hinder labour organisation. In Argentina and Peru separate unions developed among railway workers divided by craft and skill, just as they had in Britain. Moreover, labour problems were one sphere in which British firms did have mutual interests and combined to defend them. In Chile the Association of Nitrate Producers organised labour recruitment in common after 1901, and also consulted regularly on wage payments and labour discipline. In Argentina, according to the British minister, the railway companies took the lead in the formation of the Free Labour Society, the institution responsible for the collapse of the Buenos Aires dock strike in 1911–12.[35]

CONCLUSION

The massive growth in British investment which occurred after the 1860s totally redefined the nature of Britain's relations with Latin America. For the British both the government loans and the direct investments provided substantial profits over the years to 1914, but the direct investments particularly put them into an exposed position in Latin American societies as the threats of nationalist opposition and labour militancy grew. The political methods they had developed when gaining concessions, the formation of close ties with politicians and government officials, became less useful and indeed counter-productive as they became identified with conservative elites or found themselves ignored by politicians whenever an alliance with popular feelings against foreign firms appeared more expedient. As long as the British economy could provide more investment, they could maintain their influence. If that were to cease their vulnerability would be greater.

The Latin American countries whose elites welcomed British investment also made themselves vulnerable to its cessation. The long prewar boom diminished politicians' memories of earlier financial crises. Key sectors of the economy came to be controlled by firms based in London whose primary interests lay in profit remittances from Latin America. Both the external loans and the direct investments thus created enormous problems of economic management which would become evident as soon as commerce declined and credit was curtailed. British and other foreign investment helped governments to put off much-needed reforms to taxation structures and financial institutions, and probably also undermined local political institutions as more deputies and senators, even ministers and presidents, became beholden to their links with the British companies.

REFERENCES

1. Cain and Hopkins, 'Gentlemanly Capitalism, II', 2–5.
2. US Federal Trade Commission, *Report on Cooperation*, II, 537–74.
3. Cain and Hopkins, 'Gentlemanly Capitalism, II', 11.
4. Platt, *Britain's Investments Overseas*; but see Feinstein, 'Britain's Overseas Investments', for a critique of Platt.
5. These are late twentieth-century definitions. Before 1914 all investment which passed through the Stock Exchange was classified as 'portfolio', that which did not as 'direct'.
6. Stone, 'British Direct and Portfolio Investment', 693; Svedberg, 'Portfolio-Direct Composition', 771.
7. Marichal, *Century of Debt Crises*, pp. 243–50.
8. Harvey and Press, 'Overseas Investment', 67.
9. Marichal, *Century of Debt Crises*, pp. 243–5.
10. Burk, *Morgan Grenfell*, p. 33.
11. 'Report from the Select Committee on Loans to Foreign States', *PP* 1875, XI, xxiv and xlv.

12. Graham, *Britain and the Onset*, p. 104.
13. Wilkins, 'Free-Standing Company', 259–82.
14. Huxley to Norman, 19 September 1910, FO 371/970/A34235 (PRO).
15. Rippy, *British Investments*, p. 60.
16. Armstrong and Nelles, 'Curious Capital Flow', 195–7.
17. Joslin, *Century of Banking*, pp. 109–10.
18. Quoted in Joslin, *Century of Banking*, p. 193.
19. Jones, 'State and Business Practice', 191–2.
20. Platt, 'Economic Imperialism', 300.
21. Marichal, *Century of Debt Crises*, p. 169.
22. Finch, 'British Imperialism', 257–8.
23. Edelstein, *Overseas Investment*, pp. 111–59; Davis and Huttenback, *Mammon and the Pursuit of Empire*, pp. 111–14. Edelstein's calculations also include capital gains and losses as well as dividends and interest.
24. Ford, 'British Investment and Argentine Economic Development', 25–7.
25. Street, 'Platt-Stein Controversy', 178.
26. Eakin, *British Enterprise*, pp. 106–7.
27. Quoted in Fernández, 'Merchants and Bankers', 326.
28. Blakemore, *British Nitrates*, p. 183.
29. Eakin, 'Business Imperialism', 740.
30. Lord Forres to Archie Balfour, 14 May 1929, private letter-book (1929–31), BWA (UCL).
31. Quoted in Miller, 'Grace Contract', 333.
32. Ferns, *Britain and Argentina*, p. 412; Finch, *Political Economy of Uruguay*, p. 199.
33. Mitchell Innes to Foreign Office, 17 July 1914, FO 371/2156/A37696 (PRO).
34. Quoted in deShazo, *Urban Workers*, p. 49.
35. Sir Reginald Tower, 'Annual Report for 1912', FO 371/1573/F5066 (PRO).

CHAPTER SEVEN

Three Perspectives on the Links with Britain before 1914: Argentina, Brazil and Chile

In each of the principal Latin American countries debates about the British role in trade and investment have centred on issues arising from the literature on informal imperialism and dependency: the degree to which export trades depended on the British market and the role of British intermediaries in them; the economic impact and political influence of individual British firms; and the extent to which British interests collectively moulded Latin American economies and societies to their own advantage. What varies is the context within which these questions are analysed; in one country British participation in a key export sector appears crucial, while elsewhere government finance or the railway companies dominate discussion.

The profile of British business was distinct in each republic. Its growth depended on the opportunities available and the responses of local entrepreneurs and the state. The British role in individual export trades, for example, varied according to the technological, financial and marketing requirements of each. The need for railways and the expense of constructing them differed from one region to another. Some countries looked for British capital largely to finance the economic activities of the state; elsewhere ideological preferences or pragmatic reactions to past problems created a predilection for direct foreign investment. National policies on fiscal and monetary questions, on protection for industry and on the constitutional relationship between different levels of government varied enormously.

Lack of space precludes a consideration of these questions for each country. This chapter is confined to a comparison of these problems in Argentina, Brazil and Chile. One point which becomes very clear is that despite a well-developed historiography for each of these countries, enormous imbalances remain. Literature on subjects like the railways or the public debt is abundant in one case but virtually non-existent in another, making a comparative analysis more difficult.

ARGENTINA

In 1895, even before the twenty-year boom which preceded the First World War, M.G. Mulhall estimated that income per head in Argentina equalled that of most contemporary European countries.[1] Through massive imports of foreign capital and immigrant labour and the incorporation of formerly Indian land on the pampas, Argentina was able to produce a series of valuable agricultural exports: hides, wool, arable products (wheat, maize, linseed) and meat (initially preserved meat and later frozen mutton, live cattle, and frozen and chilled beef). Total exports grew from an annual average of £18 million in 1885–89 to £39 million in 1900–04, and £85 million between 1909 and 1913.[2] This in turn increased Argentina's importance as a market; Britain's exports there surpassed those to Brazil in 1899 and then more than trebled between 1900 and 1913.[3]

Argentine exports

Britain's significance for Argentina's exporters increased between 1880 and 1914, in contrast to most other Latin American countries (see Table 5.4). As new products replaced wool, which had gone largely to Belgium and France, the United Kingdom became the country's leading market, a position it retained, with the occasional exceptional year, from 1895 until 1950. Initially, as Table 7.1 shows, the growth was centred on wheat and maize, especially in the 1890s, but in the decade before the First World War the most dynamic element of the export trade was meat.

Britain purchased a considerable share of Argentina's agricultural surplus by the early twentieth century: about two-fifths of its maize exports, one-third of its wheat, and half its oats.[4] However, British intermediaries exercised very little control over marketing and prices in these trades. In 1913 the two indisputably British grain merchants in Buenos Aires handled only 9 per cent of exports; the trade was dominated by four large international dealers of continental European origin.[5] Argentine producers did not depend solely on British demand, and world grain markets conformed more closely to liberal ideals of perfect competition than most primary products, although market imperfections increased significantly within Argentina.

149

Table 7.1 British imports from Argentina, 1860–1913 (annual averages, £000)

	Total	Wool	Hides	Tallow	Wheat	Maize	Linseed	Oats	Frozen mutton	Live cattle & sheep	Chilled & frozen beef	Other
1860–64	1226	242	438	215	—	—	—	—	—	—	—	331
1865–69	1153	133	308	420	—	—	—	—	—	—	—	292
1870–74	1851	237	335	589	—	—	—	—	—	—	—	690[b]
1875–79	1330	116	233	298	20	—	—	—	—	—	—	633[b]
1880–84	962	58	106	172	32	54	52	—	22	—	—	466
1885–89	2075	115	90	107	250	380	296	—	496	—	—	341
1890–94	4625	152	109	72	1854	608	243	—	880	79	28	593
1895–99	8509	348	68	139	2056	1443	816	—	1219	1641	116	663
1900–04	16339	600	86	416	4489	3541	1649	—	2202	155	1629	1572
1905–09	28942	1412	311	550	9083	5707	1832	682	2360	—	5002	2003
1910–13	34898	1894	712	687	6454	6373	1454	1747	2475	—	10440	2662

a   Until the 1880s some proportion of Argentina's exports, especially in the late 1860s and early 1870s, was entered by British customs as having come from Uruguay.

b   Over half the 'other' imports in the 1870s consisted of sheep-skins.

Source: 'Annual Statements of Trade and Navigation'

The most significant contact many farmers had with the British was through the railways, about which they complained incessantly on account of their tariffs and shortages of rolling stock and storage facilities. However, the most important determinants of the grain farmers' income were probably the state of world markets and the incidence of poor weather, disease and pests.

The meat trade was very different. As the United States' export surplus fell, Britain turned to Argentina for beef; Argentina also supplied mutton and lamb in competition with Uruguay and New Zealand. Developments in farming and transport technology, beginning with the introduction of fencing and pedigree livestock and the improvement of pasture in the 1860s, gradually raised the quality of Argentina's meat and its ability to supply Britain's growing demand. In 1882 George Drabble founded the first *frigorífico* (refrigerating plant) in Argentina. However, technical limitations meant that initially the *frigoríficos* concentrated on sheep rather than cattle. Until foot-and-mouth disease closed the British market in 1900, the beef trade consisted mainly of shipments of live animals. But by then the *frigoríficos* had learned to process cattle successfully, and soon further technical advances permitted them to produce higher-quality chilled beef. Beef exports to Britain increased from 1.2 million hundredweight in 1903 to 4.9 million in 1909 and 7.0 million, over half of which was chilled, in 1913.[6] The United Kingdom began to depend on Argentina, which accounted for over 80 per cent of its beef imports between 1911 and 1924, and despite periodic attempts to find alternative outlets in North America Argentine producers also relied increasingly on Britain. In 1929–31 the UK took 99 per cent of Argentina's chilled and 56 per cent of its frozen beef exports, 90 per cent of its frozen mutton and lamb, and 56 per cent of its preserved meat.[7]

While most cattle producers were Argentine, foreigners dominated the processing and shipment of beef. The trade became extremely specialised. It demanded large investments in processing plants in Argentina, refrigerated shipping and cold storage facilities in Britain, and close coordination between all of these so that *frigoríficos* could operate at optimum capacity. The potential for vertical integration was obvious, and the large meat companies came under criticism on both sides of the Atlantic for their pricing and trading methods. Both governments feared a loss of control. The British took the threat of oligopoly seriously enough to investigate the trade officially in 1909, while Argentine criticisms of the meat-packers rose to a peak after the war.

In comparison with Australia and New Zealand there was a relatively small number of *frigoríficos* in the River Plate, and this made cooperation easier. During the sheep era, from the mid 1880s, three firms dominated production, Drabble's River Plate Fresh Meat Company, Sansinena (an Argentine firm) and Nelsons. They planned strategy jointly and even acquired and closed a minor competitor in 1898 in order to restrict production and maintain prices. The beginning of frozen beef exports attracted two new British firms in 1902–03 (La Plata Cold Storage Co., and the Smithfield & Argentine). By 1905 British companies controlled two-thirds of freezing capacity and were making large profits, using them both to pay dividends and to expand production. But their success, which coincided with the decline of US exports to Britain, tempted the large Chicago meat-packers into Argentina. Swifts bought La Plata in 1907, and the National Packing Company the Argentine plant at La Blanca in 1909. In response, a majority of the remaining British interests combined into the British and Argentine Meat Company in 1914 (which was later acquired by the Vestey family in 1922).

By the 1920s meat-packing in Argentina was controlled by a few oligopolistic firms which possessed close associations with shipping lines, cold storage companies and retail chains in Britain. Before 1914, however, the adverse effects of this consolidation were not so clear. Initially producers gained from the higher prices paid for cattle for chilling. While control was disputed between the British and US firms there were some rewards for Argentine interests. Although the meat companies concluded a market-sharing agreement in 1911, giving the British firms a 40.2 per cent quota, Argentines 18.5 per cent and the North Americans 41.4 per cent, it lasted only until April 1913, and the struggle which followed provided producers of chilling cattle with good rewards as the packers fought for access to supplies. However, in June 1914 a new and more permanent agreement gave the British 29.6 per cent, Argentines 11.9 per cent and US firms 58.5 per cent.[8] The latter had been able to use their enormous reserves and the cushion of their position in Chicago to overcome the British and Argentine firms confined to the River Plate trade. The long-term implications for Argentine *estancieros*, who had thus far tended to profit from the foreign firms' competition for their livestock, were, however, obscured by the war.

Public debt and the Baring crisis

British investment entered Argentina in two waves: during the

1880s and between 1900 and 1913. The first cycle was abruptly terminated in 1890 by a financial crisis in Argentina and the collapse of Barings in London. Yet by the end of the 1890s the earlier railway investments had begun to show results, world prices were rising, and Argentina's trade was growing rapidly. In 1897 the government resumed full interest payments on its foreign debt for the first time since 1891, and two years later it made the paper peso fully convertible into gold at a fixed rate, primarily to prevent a rise in its value. These measures, together with the continued growth in trade, made investment in Argentina even more attractive than in the 1880s. British capital flowed into a wide variety of enterprises, including the rural sector (directly through *estancia* companies and indirectly through mortgages). However, for historians the principal controversies about British investment have focused on government loans and railways.

While Argentina attracted huge amounts of foreign, largely British, capital, every recession brought problems for the state. In 1875–76 it avoided default only by negotiating a short-term loan with Barings. It also experienced difficulties in the mid 1880s, partly due to the failure of a loan in 1884. However, a successful issue of £8.3 million in 1886 initiated a recovery, and over the next three years a speculative mania developed in both Argentina and Europe which culminated in the Baring crisis.

There were three significant areas of investment during this boom, all of which contributed to the subsequent crisis. First, the national government borrowed extensively, primarily for public works projects like railways and port facilities but also for a national bank. Between 1886 and 1890 it issued bonds with a face value of £31 million (£14 million of which was for refinancing). Second, during the 1880s provincial governments issued bonds totalling £32 million in London and other European centres (and there was little refinancing in this borrowing), partly to establish provincial banks of issue but also for public works.[9] The national government had little control over provincial finances, and corruption and maladministration were widespread. Third, the government approved an enormous number of new railway guarantees. This led to a doubling of mileage between 1886 and 1891 but placed a heavy burden on the Treasury until sufficient traffic developed.[10]

There is little evidence that ministers considered the implications of these decisions. The government continued to collect import duties, on which it depended for revenue, in paper rather than gold, while it relied on continued inflows of new capital for the foreign exchange to meet interest payments. Financial problems were inevitable once this ceased, for it would force the gold premium upwards and make it impossible for the government to meet payments on its debt. A banking crisis in neighbouring Uruguay early in 1890 drained gold from Buenos Aires and ignited the flames. The Argentine banks ran into difficulties and had to be supported by the government. In August 1890 President Juárez Celmán was overthrown. The new administration increased taxes and sent an emissary to Europe for discussions with merchant banks, but shortly after his arrival Barings, the house most closely associated with Argentine finance, informed the Bank of England that it could no longer meet its liabilities. The reaction of many in Britain was to blame Argentina for the crisis.

Analysis of the 1890 crisis has been hindered by the lengthy closure of Barings' and the Bank of England's archives. It is doubtful, however, that the Argentine government's mismanagement was the primary cause of the broader crisis, although ministers should have anticipated many of the problems. There was a panic in Europe in 1890 for reasons totally unconnected with Argentina: the failure of de Lesseps' Panama Canal scheme and the near-collapse of the Comptoir National d'Escompte after an attempt to corner world copper supplies. This inevitably affected confidence, making it more difficult to raise finance for countries like Argentina. Barings themselves made fatal errors: injudiciously attempting to monopolise concessions in Argentina; refusing to syndicate or underwrite capital issues; and floating projects too quickly. The house's acceptance business, which should have carried little risk, was also overstretched. Stanley Chapman believes that mismanagement would probably have caused the collapse of Barings even without Argentina.[11] The partners in London also had little understanding of Argentine conditions in the 1880s, relying on cooperation with a local financier, C.H. Sanford, in whom they had already expressed distrust. 'The bribery and corruption is really quite awful,' John Baring wrote home in amazement when he was finally sent to Buenos Aires in February 1890, adding of the Buenos Ayres Water Supply and Drainage Co, the crucial concession which Barings had tried to monopolise, 'you have no idea, I am sure, of the scale it is on'.[12]

As Argentine finances deteriorated both sides sought to avoid outright default, the British bankers because they needed to dispose of Barings' unsold Argentine securities, the Argentines because they wished to retain access to foreign capital. 'Rather than suspend service on the debt, I would renounce the presidency,' President Pellegrini stated.[13] In negotiations with the Rothschild Committee, which was overseeing the restructuring of Barings, the Argentine government therefore agreed to capitalise its interest liabilities by issuing new bonds. This arrangement was deeply unpopular in Argentina, and it was replaced in 1893 by the Arreglo Romero, under which the national government suspended amortisation payments for ten years and reduced interest payments for five. In many ways the new agreement represented a skilful piece of negotiation by the Argentines, but although it resolved the problem of the national government's loans the total foreign debt still continued to increase due to the issuing of new bonds to convert the provincial and municipal loans and to compensate the railway companies for the abrogation of the guarantees, on which payments had been suspended in 1891. On the former Argentina managed to obtain a fair degree of interest forgiveness, at the cost of adding to the national debt, but assessing the terms on which the railway guarantees were ended is more problematic. The Rothschild Committee had given them a lower status than the other debts, and most guarantees involved small and inefficient companies rather than the large railways on which Argentina relied for further investment. Even so, the guaranteed railways obtained £10 million in bonds.[14]

By 1900 Argentine exports were growing rapidly and the country's finances were sound. A renewed spate of government borrowing and direct investment followed. But the longer-term problems inherent in this dependence on foreign capital, which the Baring crisis had demonstrated, persisted. Argentina relied on a continuing inflow of foreign exchange, either through more loans or through rising exports. Financial stringency in Europe or difficulties in overseas markets would put pressure both on the balance of payments and on government revenues (since a decline in trade would reduce import duties). The government would then have to choose whether to abandon the Gold Standard (which would stimulate domestic inflation), introduce exchange controls (which would alarm investors) or reduce levels of consumption and investment within Argentina. The ratio of interest and dividend outflows to export earnings, which had exceeded 60 per cent in the 1890 crisis, had risen to 35 per cent in 1911–14, making Argentina again vulnerable to any downturn in foreign trade.[15]

The British-owned railways

By 1914 Argentina's railway network had grown to 20,857 miles, 70 per cent of it under British ownership. Four large regional companies, the Buenos Ayres Great Southern (BAGSR), Buenos Ayres Western (BAWR), Buenos Ayres and Pacific (BAPR), and the Central Argentine Railway (CAR) together controlled 12,017 miles.[16] This, for many Argentines, was the real symbol of the British economic presence. One of the leading nationalist writers of the 1930s, Raúl Scalabrini, talked of Argentina as an 'immense fly trapped and immobilised in the web of English railway domination'.[17] Criticisms of the British firms began from the moment the first concessions were awarded, and they covered several issues: the relative roles of state and foreign companies; the guarantee system; the Mitre Law of 1907; the amalgamations which created the 'Big Four'; and the railways' tariffs and services.

British dominance of Argentina's railways was not inevitable. From 1862 until 1889 the provincially owned Ferrocarril Oeste in Buenos Aires was one of the most efficient and extensive networks in the country, but in the late 1880s this, along with lines in Entre Ríos, was sold to British investors in order to salvage provincial finances. The national government also sold several important railways to the British at times when the stock market was favourable to Argentine securities, again to obtain relief from the debts arising from construction. The outcome, however, was increasing British control over the national network.

The extent of private ownership placed the government in a continual dilemma: how to ensure that the companies received sufficient profits to stimulate investment while offering good services at low tariffs. It was impossible to reconcile these objectives. Only the threat of expropriation forced the BAGSR into reducing tariffs, improving services and constructing extensions in 1880–81, while the CAR remained content with its original length of track for twenty years. In May 1888 the British chargé d'affaires endorsed the president's complaint that some of the guaranteed railways had 'converted the protection of the State into an iniquitous and criminal exaction', and also criticised the large companies, which no longer received guarantees, for their lack of enterprise and poor services.[18] The Mitre Law of 1907, agreed when the national government was under pressure from landowners to secure railway extensions and the companies were concerned about the imminent expiry of import duty and tax concessions, was a further attempt to harmonise both sides' interests. Temporarily it did provide a framework under which the British companies invested considerable sums in new equipment and extensions. However, new construction largely ceased with the First World War. Meanwhile, the government had limited its right to tax the railways and its powers to intervene in the setting of freight rates for forty years. The amalgamation of railways into regional companies, which also reached a climax in the first decade of the century, reflected the same central dilemma. Mergers would permit the railways to operate more efficiently, increasing their revenues, reducing their expenses, and thus encouraging investment, but they also raised the threat of regional monopolies which might use the absence of competition to resist innovation and raise tariffs as far as possible. They thus met with a hostile reaction in Argentina, especially in the provinces.

It would always have been difficult to fulfil the demands for railway services in a country growing as quickly as Argentina. Traffic was seasonal and grain shipments fluctuated enormously from one year to the next. In retrospect, however, it seems that the state, under short-term pressures to reduce its expenditure and expand railway capacity, persistently conceded too much to the large British companies. Services probably reached their best level just before the First World War, when the Mitre Law and the amalgamations were both encouraging new investment, and freight tariffs, due to Argentina's adhesion to the Gold Standard, were stable. At the same time opposition politicians prevented the fusion of the BAGSR and BAWR and obtained the introduction of pension funds and accident insurance for employees. However, long-term problems remained. The outflow of profits to pay interest and dividends was less significant when exports and investment were growing. Trade stagnation, depreciation of the *peso* and wage inflation would, however, inevitably provoke demands from the companies to raise tariffs, just when the domestic economy hit difficulties. Such a situation would also highlight the strain which the British-owned railways' purchases and remittances placed on the balance of payments.

An assessment of the Anglo-Argentine relationship

How much influence did British businessmen possess in Argentina before 1914? In David Rock's view the British had 'a highly extensive system of semi-institutionalised direct linkages with the elite' through influential politicians and the press. 'The British lobby,' he affirms, 'ranked with the cattlemen's association as the most powerful in the country.'[19] However, distinctions must be drawn, first, between a collective lobby and the influence which individual companies exercised through their Argentine advocates, and then between them applying pressure and successfully obtaining their demands. The instances on which the British combined together before 1914 were few. Cooperation was most obvious over labour questions where their interests normally coincided with those of the Argentine government and elite. On other issues there is less evidence of effective combination. 'The British railway companies,' Colin Lewis asserts, 'did not act in concert until the 1930s.'[20] There are more signs of concerted action by the British meat companies, but their complaints about the US threat in 1909–10 failed to elicit any sympathy from the Argentine government, probably because landowners were benefiting. Whether companies or investors obtained their objectives on particular issues depended on the precise combination of circumstances at the time – in particular the financial situation of the national or provincial governments and the political pressures upon them. The negotiating skill of individual ministers also varied enormously. The Arreglo Romero, for example, is regarded by Carlos Marichal as a particularly successful bargain which saved the national government large amounts of interest.[21]

In the crucial areas of monetary and fiscal policy there is little evidence of British pressure succeeding except in the immediate aftermath of the Baring crisis, when the Rothschild Committee negotiated short-term payments in return for the 1891 Funding Loan. Even then the British commercial banks hardly cooperated since their speculation in exchange and the defensive measures they took against the crisis hindered the government's attempts to achieve the stabilisation other British investors desired. In periods of growth Argentina had almost unlimited freedom to 'shop around' for loans, playing off merchant banks and capital markets against one another, and to determine policy. In the 1880s the government adopted a paper currency regime which was financed largely by foreign loans, and while the decision to return to the Gold Standard in 1899 undoubtedly suited British merchant bankers and investors it was primarily a response to the interests of Argentine exporters, who feared an appreciation of the *peso* as a result of increasing exports and new foreign investment.

However, the Golden Years of the Anglo-Argentine connexion just before 1914 obscured longer-term problems. Argentine exports increasingly depended on the United Kingdom and its commitment to free trade in food. Protected markets elsewhere in Europe and North America were much more difficult to penetrate, and in Britain the Tariff Reform movement, which aimed to give preference to imperial producers like Australia, was emerging. Argentina's balance of payments relied on continued foreign investment and hence the health of European capital markets. The British companies' control of railways was also a time-bomb which threatened to place the Argentine government in an uncomfortable position between consumers and workers on the one hand (demanding lower tariffs and higher wages respectively) and remote and ageing British financiers on the other. Any halt in investment or deterioration in the Argentine economy would set it ticking.

Economic growth in Argentina also appears to have reinforced the elite's desire to protect their own status and interests, rather than revolutionising their attitudes. Creole political structures based on clientelism and favours were little altered. Very few leading politicians took a critical view of the process of Argentine development. The principles of comparative advantage and the benefits of foreign investment were rarely questioned. Indeed, the experience of the 1880s and 1890s reinforced the elite's preference for liberal orthodoxies and opposition to state enterprise. Governments seem to have been quite willing, often for short-term reasons, to relinquish public property and permit foreign investors quite extensive privileges. Thus while Anglo-Argentine relations were relatively harmonious and their economic interests complementary in the Golden Years just before 1914, there were potentially serious difficulties for both sides.

BRAZIL

There were significant differences between Brazil and Argentina: in the composition of exports; the relative importance of markets in Britain, continental Europe and the United States; industrial development; fiscal and monetary policies; and political systems. Whereas Argentina's growth depended on its capacity to produce a range of exports, coffee remained Brazil's most important product for most of the century before 1914, although at its peak in 1910 the rubber trade almost equalled it. In both these trades Brazil held a dominant position in world markets (at least until the Malayan rubber plantations emerged in 1910, causing the rapid collapse of the Amazon trade). Immediately before 1914 Brazil accounted for over 70 per cent of world coffee exports.[22] Yet in neither coffee nor rubber was Britain a large consumer. Coffee went primarily to the United States and continental Europe, and although large quantities of rubber arrived in Britain most was re-exported. Other contrasts with Argentina are apparent. Manufacturing industry had advanced much further by 1914, to the point where local factories produced about 80 per cent of Brazil's demand for goods like cotton cloth, shoes, hats and beer.[23] Despite a broad acceptance of liberal economic ideas by the exporting elites, the national government played an interventionist role under both the empire (which collapsed in 1889) and the First Republic (1889–1930). Monetary policies were more unorthodox for longer periods than in Argentina, leading to a particularly steep decline in the Brazilian currency's value in the 1890s, when the *milreis* fell from 26.4 (old) pence in 1889 to 7.2 pence in 1898.[24] There was also a move towards political decentralisation after 1889. The principal states (São Paulo, Minas Gerais, Rio de Janeiro and Rio Grande do Sul) acquired considerable autonomy in policy-making, including the ability to impose export duties and float foreign loans.

The British and Brazil's coffee trade

Although they did own some *fazendas* (plantations), British interests in coffee were generally restricted to an intermediary role. British lines became dominant in shipping. After 1895 the stability and management techniques of the 'conference' which controlled the Brazil – New York route using devices like deferred rebates appear to have been among the most highly developed of those which affected South America. In the view of the (US) Alexander Committee in 1914 coffee freights were 'fixed at the highest possible level'.[25] Coffee growers in São Paulo also faced the monopoly of the British-owned San Paulo Railway (SPR) which controlled the route to the port of Santos.

British merchants, however, did not dominate the commercialisation of coffee, partly because of the weakness of Britain as a market. Naumann Gepp and Johnstons, the two leading British houses, handled only 20 per cent of shipments from Rio and Santos between 1895/96 and 1910/11, and before 1914 the most important exporter was probably a German, Theodor Wille.[26] Nevertheless, in their attempts to retain a share of the trade, British houses made significant innovations. Johnstons began to bypass Brazilian and Portuguese middlemen (*comissários*) and negotiate directly with landowners. They also invested in processing machinery and warehousing with the aid of a ten year profits guarantee from the state government of São Paulo. Having consolidated their interests into the Brazilian Warrant Company (BWC) in 1909, Johnstons began to offer planters loans against coffee stocks, charging 9 per cent interest. The rewards came first in the form of good profits (the BWC returned 15 per cent on capital in 1918), and then when they were awarded control over the buffer stocks established under the Third Valorisation Scheme in 1921.[27] Yet while the British played a significant, though not a dominant role in coffee, it is doubtful whether they had much control over the prices paid to *fazendeiros*. The merchants competed fiercely for business, and also faced an oligopsony of importers in New York. It was this struggle which led them towards vertical integration in Brazil. While they brought more transactions under their control, this occurred at the cost of Brazilian commercial intermediaries rather than the large planters for whom interest rates and commissions were reduced.

The planters' real problems lay in the combination of a long time-lag between planting and harvesting (normally five years) and the relative inelasticity of demand for coffee. These factors made it vulnerable to periodic crises of over–supply and a consequent collapse of prices. However, Brazil's dominant position in world production, together with the fact that the crop did not deteriorate, also gave it some potential to manipulate markets. In 1906, after an unsuccessful attempt to cooperate with Minas Gerais and Rio de Janeiro, São Paulo went ahead with the First Valorisation Scheme (which involved buying coffee to hold it off world markets). Although the state found it necessary to use both foreign finance (culminating in a £15 million loan organised by Schroders in 1908) and foreign merchanting expertise (led by Wille) to organise the scheme, it proved successful in stabilising markets and prices. The state was able to offload its valorisation stocks and repay its debt by 1915. Moreover, São Paulo succeeded in financing valorisation despite the opposition of the US Justice Department, which considered pursuing an anti-trust suit over coffee, and Rothschilds, the federal government's financial agents, who doubted whether Brazil had the resources to undertake it.

Historians have often suggested that São Paulo paid a high price for the 1908 loan, emphasising in particular the loss of autonomy inherent in Schroders' dominance of the committee which controlled coffee stocks, the appointment of the Bank of England to arbitrate disputes, and the bankers' veto over coffee legislation and the export surtax which guaranteed the loan. Robert Greenhill terms the measures 'draconian' and believes that the scheme earned large profits for both financiers and merchants.[28] Certainly, in view of their control of stocks and the federal government's guarantee for the loan, they took little risk. However, the loan was raised on relatively good terms (an issue price of 92.5 and an interest rate of 5 per cent) and was easily repaid from the sale of coffee stocks when the price rose after 1911. What is not known is the level of the bankers' and merchants' commissions, and these may have been above normal.

To evaluate fully the benefits accruing to British firms from coffee valorisation it is necessary to distinguish between British and other foreign interests, and between the potential for exploitation and the actual outcome. The primary interest for the British was the 1908 loan rather than the commercial arrangements for the sale of valorised coffee, which were dominated by US and continental European houses. Even so, London institutions underwrote only one-third of the issue.[29] As coffee prices first stabilised and then rose, the bankers had no need to invoke the guarantee clauses in the agreement, and the constraints on São Paulo's freedom of action were relatively short-lived. In retrospect the scheme does appear to have been remarkably successful at stabilising markets, to the benefit of planters, the state government, and merchant and financial intermediaries alike. The losses São Paulo did incur were caused by the wartime confiscation of its assets in Germany rather than the scheme itself. The principal criticism of the episode may well be that the state did not grasp the opportunity to undertake a more fundamental restructuring of the trade by retaining controls on planting and establishing a proper coffee exchange in Brazil.

Britain and other Brazilian exports

Rather than coffee, Brazil's direct exports to Britain, as Table 7.2 shows, centred on cotton and sugar until the 1880s, and then on rubber. The stimulus to the cotton trade came from rising prices due to the US Civil War, deliberate attempts by Manchester businessmen to develop alternative supplies, and the initiatives of the SPR superintendent, but it did not last. By the end of the century Brazilian planters were mainly supplying domestic factories. Sugar producers also turned to local outlets after a steep fall in world prices in the 1880s. There were some British attempts to invest in modern refineries in Pernambuco and Bahia but they seem to have failed completely, principally because of the companies' own short-sightedness and incompetence. British credit for the industry does not seem particularly important. Capital for the modernisation of sugar tended to come from domestic sources, while the technology was French. The main stimulus the British offered was through railway construction in the north-east.

The wild rubber trade of the Amazon involved the British

in several respects, but primarily as intermediaries, especially in shipping. Whether Britain's significance as an entrepôt allowed importers to manipulate prices, as Brazilian producers charged, is impossible to say. In her study of Pará's trade Barbara Weinstein repeats these complaints but does not provide quantitative evidence on price changes in different commercial centres which might substantiate them.[30] Some British merchants in Brazil had interests in rubber exports, but they were a minority among the Pará merchant community which was dominated by Brazilian and Portuguese traders. They may have been more influential upriver in Manáus (in the state of Amazonas) where the local commercial elite was weaker than in Pará, and they certainly invested in rubber enterprises higher up the Amazon in Peru and Bolivia.

Table 7.2   British imports from Brazil, 1860–1913 (annual averages, £000)

	Cotton	Coffee	Sugar	Rubber	Others	Total
Total imports						
1860–64	1877	272	1032	268	716	4165
1865–69	4219	365	1253	425	679	6941
1870–74	3223	589	1796	869	857	7334
1875–79	1254	852	1831	969	762	5668
1880–84	1112	810	1679	1470	714	5785
1885–89	995	807	722	1510	607	4641
1890–94	727	583	270	1891	667	4138
1895–99	190	224	179	2912	488	3993
1900–04	717	311	93	4154	742	6017
1905–09	907	451	220	6427	1090	9093
1910–13	1158	691	242	8776	1065	11932
Retained imports*						
1905–09	752	−119	217	1992	832	3674
1910–13	1046	−59	241	2373	860	4461

*Figures for retained imports are available only from 1905. 'Total imports' includes goods later re-exported from the United Kingdom.

Sources: Graham, *Britain and the Onset*, p. 75; 'Annual Statements of Trade and Navigation'

The British did play a leading role in shipping, through the Amazon River Steam Navigation Co., which controlled the river trade after the 1870s, and in international shipments through the Liverpool-based Booth and Red Cross Lines, which received subsidies from the states of Amazonas and Pará and eventually amalgamated in 1901. These companies also controlled lighterage facilities at the main ports. Following the merger Booths negotiated a pooling agreement with the Hamburg-Amerika Line, thus maintaining freight rates and excluding other firms from the Amazon trade. Although this control may have been less burdensome when rubber prices were rising, the British shipping lines, which sailed up to Iquitos in Peru, certainly provided a highly visible sign of the region's dependence on foreign markets and companies. This was to become all too evident when rubber prices collapsed in 1910 due to competition from plantations in the British empire, leaving the Amazon a commercial backwater.

The Brazilian public debt

Brazil ranked second only to Argentina in Latin America as a destination for British investment, but the balance between the public debt and direct investments was quite different, due to the Brazilian state's more active role, especially in railways. Moreover, Brazil, which used Rothschilds as its financial agents throughout the period, seems to have been more dependent on the City of London, whereas Argentina moved its business around. The problems created by British investment in Brazil nevertheless resembled those in Argentina: the inevitable complaints about the tariffs and services of railways and public utilities and, for the government, balance of payments difficulties whenever exports or new investment diminished. As in Argentina, speculation by the British commercial banks could exacerbate short-term financial instability, since they possessed considerable scope to manipulate the exchange market whenever the state needed sterling to remit funds for interest and amortisation payments in Europe.

In the late 1880s Brazil took advantage of Latin America's popularity in the London capital market to refinance existing loans and raise new ones, using them to expand domestic liquidity, provide credit for landowners, and therefore ease the transition from slavery after its abolition in 1888. Early in the 1890s, however, economic problems intensified. The inflow of funds declined following the Baring crisis, while an uncontrolled increase in paper money, partly due to budget deficits caused by a serious civil war, induced high rates of inflation. Initially the exchange rate bore the brunt of the necessary adjustment: as noted already, the value of the *milreis* fell by more than two-thirds in the 1890s. Yet while this benefited coffee planters, who gained because the *milreis* value of coffee increased faster than their costs, the government began to face serious problems in servicing its debts. A 40 per cent fall in world coffee prices in the late 1890s due to over-supply placed further pressures on the balance of payments and (because of the reduced volume of imports) on government revenues, compelling it to seek an accommodation with foreign bankers.

The result was the notorious 1898 Funding Loan organised by Rothschilds and later termed by Richard Graham 'the nineteenth-[century] equivalent of an IMF imposition'.[31] It provided for the funding (payment in new bonds rather than cash) of interest payments and railway guarantees for three years, and suspended the amortisation of the external debt for thirteen. In return the federal government gave a written commitment to introduce policies of austerity and partially to withdraw paper money. President Campos Salles, who negotiated the agreement, claimed in his memoirs ten years later that Rothschilds had threatened that 'beyond the total loss of credit of the country, [default] could gravely affect national sovereignty itself, provoking claims that would perhaps end in foreign intervention'.[32] If Campos Salles took this seriously, it illustrates the gulf between the Foreign Office's policy and Latin American perceptions of it and raises the possibility that Rothschilds, in view of Salisbury's statements in 1891, were deliberately misleading the Brazilians (see pp. 62–3). Although the Funding Loan may have saved Brazil from default, it was extremely unpopular and the deflationary policies on which it was conditional led to an intense three-year recession. Campos Salles did not manage to obtain the reduction in interest payments which the Argentines had negotiated with Barings in 1893, and he was also forced to accept much stricter constraints on policy. The principal beneficiaries were certainly Rothschilds and the other banks in the syndicate they led. As the *Economist* warned, any such renegotiations involved 'handsome commissions for the loan agents and the syndicates which are always ready to undertake business of this kind'.[33]

Nevertheless, the Brazilian government maintained its credit. In 1901 it raised £16.5 million to expropriate twelve railways and thus reduce the burden of guarantee payments, and this was followed by further loans to finance port works and urban reconstruction in Rio, Lloyd Brasileiro (the semi-official shipping line), and the state railways. The credit of the federal government was also essential for São Paulo's successful negotiation of its valorisation loan in 1908, even though Rothschilds rejected the business. Besides allowing the national government to refinance its outstanding debt and raise new money, the country's good reputation thus permitted individual states and municipalities to draw on the London capital market. São Paulo, for example, besides its valorisation operations, borrowed a further

£11.7 million through Schroders in 1913–14 to refinance its debt.[34]

The lack of control over the provinces' external obligations, however, exacerbated the problems the national government would face if a crisis in trade, and hence in revenue, coincided with a halt to new loans. Overall, Brazil's borrowings were huge. The ratio of public foreign debt to export earnings in 1914 reached 3.51, compared with 1.91 for Argentina and 1.45 for Chile.[35] Brazil's vulnerability was again highlighted in 1913–14. As the European crisis deepened, Brazil tried desperately to search for new financing, but because of the onerous conditions which Rothschilds were demanding talks had not been concluded when war broke out. Only in October 1914 did Rothschild agree to a bond issue of £15 million to fund interest payments for the next three years as well as a further suspension of amortisation until 1927.

It is difficult to escape the conclusion that Brazil over-borrowed and thus became liable to problematic renegotiations and severe constraints on policy whenever a crisis occurred. Both in 1898 and in 1914 the capitalisation of interest liabilities continued the steady increase in the public external debt, which was made worse by the lengthy suspensions of amortisation payments.

British investment in Brazilian railways

Whereas Brazil's policy on the external debt appears more poorly considered than Argentina's after 1890, its attitude towards foreign-owned railways seems much stricter. There were exceptions. Planters and merchants justifiably complained about the monopoly concession, lack of expansion, and high profits of the SPR, which paid annual dividends averaging over 10 per cent in the 1880s and 12 per cent between 1902 and 1913.[36] Generally, however, Brazil kept tighter control.

The state seems to have learned quickly from the generosity of early concessions like the one given to the SPR, and limited the periods and zones for which monopolies were granted. The national government offered guarantees of 5 or 6 per cent on capital invested but only in return for some control over the level of equipment, freight rates, and the right to repurchase the company. It also retained control of the key railway serving Rio de Janeiro, the Dom Pedro II (after 1889 the Central), though partly because on two occasions when it attempted to lease it, in 1891 and 1896, it met with angry protests from the workforce. Nevertheless, the Brazilian government faced increasing problems with the guaranteed lines as the *milreis* declined in the 1890s, since it was using its leverage over the railway companies' tariffs to help landowners at the cost of paying greater sums in guarantees. In 1893 the foreign guaranteed railways, excluding the SPR, yielded only 0.3 per cent on capital, and by 1898 a third of the federal budget was going on railway guarantees.[37] Campos Salles' solution was to raise a loan in 1901 to provide the funds to expropriate twelve companies, thereby saving the difference between the interest on the loan and the guarantee payments. By 1914 the federal government owned 53 per cent of the country's track. However, it operated only 18 per cent and permitted two large British companies, the Leopoldina, which ran northwards out of Rio, and the Great Western of Brazil (GWBR), which dominated the north-east, to assemble extensive networks by absorbing smaller companies and leasing track from the state.[38]

Both before and after the 1901 reorganisation the British railways, like their counterparts in Argentina, engaged in continuous battles with politicians and clients over freight rates and the standard of service they offered. The Recife and San Francisco (RSF) faced perpetual complaints about its tariffs, its lack of rolling stock and storage facilities, and the problems of trans–shipping cargoes from its terminus to the docks. The manager of the GWBR, which leased the RSF after its expropriation, later became known in Recife as 'the British dictator'.[39] The British ambassador in the 1920s commented of the Leopoldina that its managers 'in years of prosperity did little to win the favour of their public or to assist in the development of the country'.[40] However, their power was circumscribed. In order to aid landowners the Brazilian government continued to restrain tariff increases and this created serious difficulties for the companies at times of falling exchange rates. Overall, the greater control exercised by the national government, the diversification of the economy, and wider opportunities for Brazilians to obtain managerial and technical experience, especially on the railways operated by the state or Brazilian capitalists, made the developmental impact of railways in Brazil more broadly based than in Argentina.

Brazilian elites and the British connexion

The relationship of provincial elites and governments with British interests varied according to their contacts with the London capital market and the presence of British companies in particular regions. Many states, including Minas Gerais, preferred to seek loans in continental Europe rather than London. Others could not afford overseas borrowing at all. While it was often at this (and the municipal level) that the greatest complaints about the British railway and public utility companies arose, the national government had to confront the most serious problems arising from the growth in British investment.

Historians like Steven Topik have tended to refute the assumption that the national government was simply the tool of the large coffee planters of São Paulo and Minas Gerais, even though together they supplied all but two of the federal presidents between 1894 and 1930.[41] Because of its own borrowing requirements and its obligation to manage the country's balance of payments, exchange rate and monetary policy, the national government's objectives often conflicted with the landowners' desires. While coffee-growers welcomed currency depreciation in the 1890s, the federal government saw its liabilities for debt service becoming more difficult to fulfil. Thereafter presidents and finance ministers worried constantly about maintaining Brazil's image and credit abroad. Both Campos Salles and Rodrigues Alves, his successor, favoured a tight monetary policy and a revaluation of the *milreis*. This eventually resulted in the establishment of the Caixa de Conversão and adhesion to the Gold Standard in 1906, but only because many coffee exporters now feared that due to the capital inflow arising from the valorisation loans the *milreis* would appreciate too much. As in Argentina, therefore, adhesion to the Gold Standard was not just an acceptance of the orthodox economic liberalism espoused by foreign financiers. In both cases it occurred when the national government's desire for respectability and exchange rate stability coincided with exporters' fears of a rising currency due to the success of exports and foreign investment.

Yet while paying lip-service to monetary stability after the late 1890s Brazilian governments departed from laissez-faire principles in many other respects: their ownership of railways and ships, frequent budget deficits (at both national and provincial levels), tariff protection for industry, and the provision of federal guarantees for São Paulo's coffee valorisation. Gradually and somewhat reluctantly, the state became more interventionist, while foreign financiers tried, not very successfully, to halt or reverse this trend.

There were clear limitations on foreign control. Although Rothschilds did eventually influence monetary policy directly in 1898, they had exercised little power in the preceding inflationary decade. The government refused in 1892 to accept earlier plans they proposed to stabilise Brazilian finances. The temporary surrender of control over the coffee trade by São Paulo in 1908 must be judged against its ability to obtain foreign finance for valorisation, despite the opposition of

Rothschilds and the London financial press. While Rothschilds and Schroders did apparently exert pressure to defend the SPR against the threat of a competing concession in 1909, the merchant banks never succeeded in persuading the federal government to lease out the Central Railway, even in 1914 when Rothschilds also wanted the government to relinquish its control of Lloyd Brasileiro and accept British administration of the Banco do Brasil. While they did not consistently reflect the coffee planters' views, Brazilian governments were more responsive to the demands of local interests than those of foreigners, although the balance could temporarily swing in a crisis. In the long term their main problem lay in the massive external public debt which they incurred, for this made them extremely vulnerable to a curtailment of credit in London, and led to serious constraints on policy in the interwar period.

CHILE

There were two significant differences between the role of British business in Chile after the Pacific War (1879–83) and the part it played in Argentina and Brazil. First, large British merchant houses, like Gibbs, Balfour Williamson, Duncan Fox, Graham Rowe and Locketts, remained important. Besides the import–export trade and the ownership and management of nitrate production companies, these firms had many other interests, ranging from sheep farms in Patagonia and Tierra del Fuego to flour mills and sugar refineries in the centre of the country. Second, whereas the Chilean elite generally continued to control agriculture, finance and manufacturing, and the state operated most of the country's railways, except for those in the north and the link with Bolivia, foreigners, particularly the British, dominated the nitrate industry, the main source of export earnings after the capture of the Bolivian and Peruvian deposits in 1879–80. They thus had a much more direct role in a key export sector than in Argentina or Brazil.

There has been very little study either of the non-nitrate activities of British merchants after the Pacific War or of the Chilean government's relations with foreign financiers, particularly Rothschilds. Interest in Chile's ties with Britain between 1880 and 1914 has focused almost entirely on nitrate, exports of which grew from 224,000 tons in 1880 to 1,454,000 in 1900 and 2,336,000 in 1910.[42] The expansion of the industry was essential not only to the country's supply of foreign exchange but also to government revenues. From the late 1880s until the First World War export duties on nitrate provided approximately half the government's income (and much of the remainder came from duties on imports made possible by the foreign exchange nitrate provided).[43] The British role in nitrate raises a number of issues: the reasons why they gained control; their role in the 1891 Civil War; the extent to which the nitrate 'combinations' which they led harmed Chile's interests; and the idea that nitrate was a classic enclave which provided few benefits to the country as a whole.

Like the coffee trade, nitrate suffered from cyclical crises. Although demand in Europe rose steadily, it was not price-elastic and investment in new plants could quickly create a situation of excess capacity and severe over-production. The first collapse had occurred in the mid-1870s, when most *oficinas* (processing plants) were in the Peruvian department of Tarapacá. It had culminated in a partial expropriation of nitrate enterprises by the Peruvian state and the bankruptcy of many smaller firms. This left the private sector dominated by three large European companies, two of which were English and one German. Once they had captured Tarapacá the Chileans reprivatised the industry, but the foreigners increased their share of ownership. By 1890 twenty-three British *oficinas* produced 69 per cent of output.[44] This was the peak. After 1900, when the industry's focus moved southwards to Antofagasta and a new wave of company formation occurred, the British participation declined. By 1913 about half the output came from Chilean companies, and 36 per cent from British.[45] However, the British also invested in companies which serviced the industry. Colonel North took control of the Tarapacá Waterworks Company (1888), the Nitrate Railways Company (NRC), bought from Peruvian entrepreneurs in 1887, and the Bank of Tarapacá and London (established in 1888 and renamed the Anglo-South American Bank in 1905). North also owned a shipping line. Behind his extensive interests in production and services lay a personal ambition to control the market for nitrate, of which Chile was the principal producer.

Why did the British achieve this dominance? Having captured the nitrate *oficinas*, in 1880, the Chileans, under pressure from Peru's creditors, which included British bondholders, Gibbs, and the London Bank of Mexico and South America (LBMSA), had quickly to decide how to increase revenue from nitrate and resolve the tangled ownership problems which had resulted from Peru's partial nationalisation. Both Gibbs and the LBMSA had purchased considerable quantities of the certificates issued by the Peruvian government in exchange for expropriated *oficinas*, and threatened Chile's credit in

Europe if their claims were not satisfied. Thus the decision was taken in June 1881 to return the *oficinas* to private hands in return for 75 per cent of the certificates on each (reduced to 50 per cent three months later), with the balance in cash. This permitted European partnerships like Gibbs, North and Harvey, and Campbell Outram, who possessed expert knowledge and access to capital and credit, to purchase nitrate concessions which they knew had good potential. Colonel North, in particular, used his skills as a company promoter to raise capital for both *oficinas* and many peripheral services, with the result that he became the leading figure in the industry. Output increased rapidly, and a sharp fall in prices eliminated smaller producers, further enhancing concentration. By 1890 many Chileans, from President Balmaceda downwards, feared a monopoly of nitrate in one foreigner's hands, while other British interests, in bitter dispute with North over the NRC's tariffs and monopoly in Tarapacá, were attempting to obtain competing railway concessions from the Chilean government.

These events lay behind the alleged involvement of British firms in the 1891 Civil War. Supporters of Balmaceda charged that British capitalists were closely allied with the opposition in Congress, many of whom they employed as lawyers, and that they organised and paid for the defeat of the president. Nationalist historians later repeated these assertions, explaining the supposed British conflict with Balmaceda in terms of the president's attempts to use nitrate revenues for a programme of national development, his opposition to a second nitrate combination which would diminish the Chilean government's income (a combination had been mooted in 1889–90), and the abrogation of the NRC's monopoly. Research during the 1970s and 1980s generally undermined these interpretations. There is no doubt, as noted earlier (p. 65), that many British merchants actively sympathised with the rebels. Nor is there any doubt that foreign firms made payments to politicians on both sides before 1891, often as lawyers but occasionally simply for support in a crucial vote. But whether the British companies conspired to initiate the revolution is a different question.

The British were not united. In the principal dispute between Balmaceda and North, the NRC's monopoly, two British companies, Gibbs and Campbell Outram, strongly opposed North. The private letters of three major merchant houses, including Gibbs, have survived for the key year, and they demonstrate their lack of partisan involvement in Chilean internal politics. Colonel North's business archives, in contrast, have largely disappeared, but there is strong circumstantial evidence that politicians whom North probably financed formed the backbone of the Congressionalist opposition. Overall, therefore, British involvement in the 1891 Civil War was much more complex than conspiracy theories which blame British capital as a whole would suggest. Moreover, the domestic reasons for conflict appear much more significant. Political controversies over the relative powers of Congress and the executive had deepened in the final years of Balmaceda's presidency. The sudden influx of nitrate revenues, which gave the president the funds for extensive patronage and the opportunity to reverse the trend towards increasing Congressional power, placed immense strains on the political system. While British companies had close associates among politicians on both sides, the real problem lay in the acute factionalisation which occurred in Congress over a range of issues, now that the pecuniary rewards of political power were so much greater.

The recurrent crises of over-supply in the nitrate industry also created tensions between the state and British companies. Despite its partial nationalisation of the industry in 1875, the Peruvian government had been unable to stabilise the market, partly because of competition from Bolivia and Chile. Once the war had given Chile a monopoly of nitrate, the producers were in a stronger position. When the next crisis arrived, in 1884, they responded by limiting output in an attempt to maintain prices. This affected both employment (since the *oficinas* laid off workers) and government revenues (because duties were levied on the volume rather than the value of exports). The combination lasted until 1887 when price levels recovered due to the steady growth in European demand.

Within two years the industry faced a renewed crisis, and producers ran into their most serious conflict with the government, due partly to its greater dependence on nitrate duties but also Balmaceda's fear that North's purchase of peripheral services together with his increased share of production represented an attempt to monopolise exports, a move which would greatly reduce Santiago's power to bargain with producers. The administration probably underestimated the degree to which other British firms shared the government's antagonism towards North, illustrated by their attacks on the NRC monopoly in 1889–90, but the producers formed a new combination to control output in 1891, again reducing employment and tax revenues while stabilising prices. It lasted until 1894 when North himself withdrew because he needed to increase his own companies' output to maintain their share prices.

In the long term ministers found that they could control the expansion of the industry through their power to auction un-developed nitrate deposits. Gradually the state and the companies recognised a common interest in attempting to even out fluctuations and maintain stable price, income and employment levels. The first three combinations (the third was in 1896–97) had incurred criticism because the foreign companies organised them without worrying about the effects on employment, investment and consumption in Chile. But after the turn of the century, as the industry expanded southwards and Chilean ownership grew, the government supported combinations by withholding the release of new nitrate lands and lobbying reluctant producers to join.

Because of the high degree of British ownership, it has often been assumed that nitrate was a foreign-owned enclave which extracted high returns and contributed little to the domestic economy. Certainly some of the nitrate companies were extremely profitable. The Liverpool returned an average dividend of 50 per cent for forty-five years, while the London gave its ordinary shareholders an average 35 per cent annually for thirty-eight years.[46] However, Markos Mamalakis estimates that between 1880 and 1924 export proceeds were divided roughly equally among the Chilean government, profits for the owners of the *oficinas*, and local expenditure (which included labour costs).[47] Some of the latter, in the form of commissions and payments for peripheral services, leaked abroad, as did the majority of the owners' profits. Nevertheless, the share of nitrate income remaining in Chile far exceeds that from other 'classic' enclaves like copper or oil in the twentieth century. Nitrate provided some stimulus for agricultural and consumer goods production in central Chile, but its most important contribution to economic growth came through government expenditure financed largely by nitrate revenue.

Two other aspects of British direct investment in the north of Chile should be noted. First, their activities, because they depended on concessions of nitrate grounds, railways and water rights, required strong connexions with lawyers and politicians at both national and local levels. As in Argentina, it is difficult to talk of a united British lobby except for the combinations and in labour disputes, but it is clear that individual British firms created extensive channels through which they could influence ministers and local officials, usually through highly placed Chilean advocates. Harold Blakemore's study of the Antofagasta (Chili) and Bolivia Railway Company suggests that expatriate managers also spent a fair proportion of their time on 'public relations'.[48]

Second, the north was a crucible of Chile's working-class movement, although it was often dock and transport workers in the ports, rather than nitrate miners, who participated in strikes and protests. The nitrate companies seem to have been some of the worst British employers in Latin America. They did little to provide their local employees with social benefits like hospitals or educational facilities. Although monetary wages were higher than in central Chile the increased cost of living ate up much of the difference. Particular complaints about the profiteering attitudes of the British companies arose over their continued use of *fichas* (tokens) to pay wages, even though such payments had been illegal since 1852, and the monopolies of the firms' *pulperías* (shops), where, according to one estimate in 1904, the companies recovered three-quarters of their wage bill.[49] There was a wide gulf between expatriate managers and migrant workers, and techniques of labour discipline were primitive. The companies consciously exploited the antagonisms among Chilean, Peruvian and Bolivian employees, formed an employers' association to recruit workers and blacklist labour leaders, and resorted frequently to appeals to the local political and military authorities to use force, one of which resulted in the infamous massacre of over 1000 men, women and children at Santa María de Iquique in 1907.

The Chilean elite and Britain

As in Brazil, the Chilean elite seems far from being the compliant creature of British financiers, meekly pursuing liberal economic models in order to attract foreign investment. Governments followed distinctly unorthodox policies. Even before the Pacific War the state participated extensively in the construction and operation of railways, ran increasing budget deficits, and instituted deliberately protectionist tariffs. The growing resources which the government obtained from the nitrate trade further enhanced its power to intervene, and it went far beyond the traditional functions of national defence and civil administration by consciously devoting funds to public works and education. The state's construction and operation of railways aided the elite by offering landowners cheap transport facilities and opportunities for employment for their relations and dependants. Congress took measures to stimulate industrial growth, and after the Pacific War the Sociedad Nacional de Agricultura joined the Sociedad de Fomento Fabril in demanding tariff protection. The use of inconvertible paper money, reversed only briefly when Chile attempted to adhere to the Gold Standard between 1895 and 1898, aided both landowners and industrialists. It is difficult to find evidence that foreign interests seriously opposed such unorthodox policies. Indeed, the brief attempt to stabilise the currency in the late 1890s was undermined by both the commercial banks' exchange operations and Rothschilds' refusal to countenance further loans (in contrast to its attitude in Brazil the following year).

Chilean economic policy, therefore, hardly conformed to laissez-faire, free-trade ideals. Yet although policies on tariffs and monetary policy were very different in Chile from those in Argentina, the social consequences of export growth and foreign investment seem to have been similar: to reinforce the power of the landowning elite, to provide considerable opportunities for lawyers and politicians to benefit from the foreign presence, but in the long term to raise the threat of a nationalist and militant working class which had been, at least in part, nurtured by the structures and strategies of the British companies.

CONCLUSION

It is clear that the profile of British interests in each Latin American country diverged more and more in the half-century before 1914. As a result historians have focused on different questions: the increasing dependence on the British market and on railways in Argentina; on government loans and the coffee trade in Brazil; and on British firms' dominance of the nitrate industry in Chile. The relationship between Britain and the other Latin American countries involves similar questions to those discussed here, but with unique features in each. In Peru, for example, the government had little contact with British merchant banks between 1890 and the 1920s; controversy focuses on the railways, petroleum and the merchants. In Uruguay the problems resemble those of Argentina: increasing dependence on the British market and the role of British firms in banking, railways and public utilities. The centre of attention in Mexico is British participation in the oil industry, still in its early stages when the revolution commenced there in 1910.

A comparative analysis therefore highlights some important differences. Argentina and Uruguay were almost alone in their *growing* dependence on British markets and the degree to which British companies controlled extensive railway systems. Brazil and Chile, in contrast, both confronted the problems of dependence on a single export which ran into periodic crises of over-production and in

175

which British firms were important actors. Yet in Brazil they were intermediaries and market stabilisation was the responsibility of local elites aided by British finance; in Chile the British were the producers and, at least initially, they undertook stabilisation without consulting the government.

Of the countries discussed here only Argentina conformed at all closely to the liberal ideal of the state in areas like tariff and monetary policy. Even that came late in the period, after the Baring crisis. Until then Argentine monetary policy was expansionary and there was much greater acceptance of the principle of state enterprise in areas like railway construction and banking. Brazil and Chile followed distinctly unorthodox monetary policies (although Brazil became more orthodox after 1898), as well as developing a high degree of state intervention in the economy. Both in Argentina and in Brazil the stabilisation of exchange rates and adhesion to the Gold Standard, while benefiting foreign commercial and financial interests, was as much a response to the domestic elite's fears of exchange appreciation as a simple desire to conform to the orthodox economic models which foreign investors preferred. Only in crises do British financiers appear to have exercised any serious constraints over economic policies. For long periods the leading Latin American countries could negotiate loans on favourable terms and without conceding control over policy.

The growth of exports and foreign investment was not the zero-sum game which some later writers believed. The elites in all these countries obtained substantial increments to their wealth and power. The problems were rather that the benefits were concentrated among certain social groups and regions within each country and tended to consolidate the power of the landowners. Moreover, the costs of the export model became fully evident only after 1914.

With hindsight, it seems clear that elites overlooked four points. First, external borrowing offered governments access to cheaper funds than they could obtain domestically, but at the cost of making them vulnerable to crises in London. If the export sector ran into difficulties at the same time as foreign lending ceased, it would immediately threaten government revenues and the exchange rate, as imports fell and the ratio of external liabilities to foreign exchange earnings rose. These problems affected all the countries discussed at some point before 1900, but the long prewar boom then masked them until they reappeared, with increasing vehemence, in the early months of the First World War. Second, no government satisfactorily resolved the central dilemma of attracting direct investment without relinquishing control over the level of reinvestment, staffing, tariffs, services and taxation. Of the countries discussed here Brazil came closest, but at the cost of a massive foreign debt and continuing fiscal deficits. Third, no country could fully control the ownership of direct investments. Local capitalists sold out to foreigners, and in some industries such as nitrate or meat there was a move towards the consolidation of oligopolies beyond the control of governments. The Argentine public's opposition to the further merger of railway companies once they had become consolidated into the Big Four was a rare example of a Latin American country halting the movement towards trusts; in Brazil at the same time British investors partially financed (though they did not organise) the amalgamations which formed the Brazilian Traction, Light and Power Company and the Brazil Railway Company. Finally, the scale of British direct investments stimulated both nationalism and labour movements. Governments found it more difficult to negotiate with the British firms as a result, and in the end both helped to undermine the control of the domestic elites in the 1920s and 1930s.

REFERENCES

1. Street, 'Platt-Stein Controversy', 174.
2. Calculated from Mitchell, *International Historical Statistics*, pp. 550–2.
3. Platt, *Latin America and British Trade*, pp. 316–19; Gravil, *Anglo-Argentine Connection*, pp. 97–8.
4. Gravil, *Anglo-Argentine Connection*, p. 37.
5. Gravil, *Anglo-Argentine Connection*, pp. 37–41.
6. Gravil, *Anglo-Argentine Connection*, pp. 64 and 226.
7. Crossley and Greenhill, 'River Plate Beef Trade', 306; República Argentina, Dirección General de Estadística, *Anuario del comercio exterior, 1931*.
8. Smith, *Politics and Beef*, pp. 60–8.
9. Marichal, *Century of Debt Crises*, pp. 247–8.
10. Lewis, *British Railways*, pp. 67–71.
11. Chapman, *Rise of Merchant Banking*, pp. 77–80.
12. John Baring, writing to his father, Lord Revelstoke, quoted in Ziegler, *Sixth Great Power*, p. 241.
13. Quoted in Cuccorese, 'La versión histórica argentina', 290.
14. Marichal, *Century of Debt Crises*, p. 169.
15. Ford, 'British Investment', 13 and 33.
16. Lewis, *British Railways*, p. 197.
17. Quoted in Falcoff, 'Raúl Scalabrini Ortiz', 93.
18. George Jenner to Marquess of Salisbury, 27 May 1888, FO 6/399 (PRO).
19. Rock, *Politics in Argentina*, p. 6.

20. Lewis, 'British Railway Companies', 402.
21. Marichal, *Century of Debt Crises*, pp. 162–3.
22. Greenhill, 'Brazilian Coffee Trade', 198.
23. Albert, *South America and the First World War*, pp. 185–6.
24. Normano, *Brazil*, p. 200.
25. Quoted in Greenhill, 'Shipping', 131.
26. Calculated from Greenhill, 'Brazilian Coffee Trade', 208.
27. Topik, *Political Economy*, p. 76.
28. Greenhill, 'Brazilian Coffee Trade', 223; see also Holloway, *Brazilian Coffee Valorization*, pp. 67–8 and 80–2; Love, *São Paulo*, pp. 46–7.
29. *Economist*, 12 December 1908.
30. Weinstein, *Amazon Rubber Boom*, p. 20.
31. Graham, 'Sepoys and Imperialists', 34.
32. Quoted both in Love, *São Paulo*, p. 208, and Topik, 'The Evolution', 331.
33. *Economist*, 4 and 18 June 1898.
34. Holloway, *Brazilian Coffee Valorization*, p. 74.
35. Albert, *South America and the First World War*, p. 156.
36. Love, *São Paulo*, p. 65.
37. Topik, *Political Economy*, p. 95.
38. Topik, 'The Evolution', 337.
39. Quoted in Levine, *Pernambuco*, p. 41.
40. Quoted in Wirth, *Minas Gerais*, p. 181.
41. Topik, *Political Economy*, p. 164; Font, 'Coffee Planters', makes a parallel argument for São Paulo in the 1920s.
42. Sunkel, *Un siglo de historia económica*, p. 126.
43. Mamalakis, 'Role of Government', 184.
44. O'Brien, *Nitrate Industry*, p. 111.
45. Couyoumdjian, 'El mercado de salitre', 50.
46. Rippy, *British Investments*, p. 62.
47. Mamalakis, 'Role of Government', 192–5.
48. Blakemore, *From the Pacific*, pp. 67 and 83–6.
49. Fernández, 'British Nitrate Companies', 57–9.

CHAPTER EIGHT
The First World War and its Aftermath

The growth of Britain's links with Latin America before 1914 depended on the unhindered flow of trade and finance across frontiers, Britain's ability to export capital, and the unwillingness of the major powers to seek zones of exclusive influence in the region. Together these factors permitted the British government to play a passive role. Other countries, especially Germany and the United States, offered competition in trade and finance, but Latin America was not an area of such strategic or economic significance that the government needed to devote resources to defending and promoting British interests there.

While these assumptions were finally undermined by the Depression of the 1930s and the Second World War, the First World War brought them seriously into question. The adjustment mechanisms of the Gold Standard, to which the major countries (except for Chile) had adhered, could not withstand the outbreak of war. London's dominance of long-term investment finance and short-term commercial credit ended. The British government, because of its need for supplies and shortage of shipping, could not now avoid involvement. International economic rivalries in Latin America became more intense. While the British sought to cripple German interests, the United States made strong inroads into the Europeans' position in South America and began to seek exclusive privileges in areas like telecommunications, oil and government finance. Within Latin America itself the economic disruption caused by the war accelerated the growth of nationalist ideologies and labour protest, with potentially serious implications for the many British firms operating there.

To some extent the immediate postwar boom of 1919–20 obscured the changes which had occurred. Although many expected to return to prewar conditions, this proved impossible. The United States, a major producer of both primary exports and industrial goods, played a very different role as the world's leading creditor from Britain before 1914, for Britain was a significant importer of foodstuffs and raw materials and had consistently run a deficit on visible trade. Britain itself now faced enormous financial problems. Meanwhile, demand for Latin America's exports faltered during the 1920s, and over-production of commodities like coffee, sugar and petroleum weakened prices. For both sides of the Anglo-Latin American relationship, therefore, the postwar decade was effectively one of crisis management. Neither fully comprehended how impossible a return to the pre-1914 world had become. British attempts to recover their hegemony and Latin Americans' failure to realise how quickly it was disintegrating created enormous difficulties for both.

THE FIRST WORLD WAR

The problems confronting Latin American economies began to increase in 1913 as the European political situation deteriorated and capital markets tightened, bringing foreign investment to a standstill. Both Argentina and Brazil, which depended heavily on capital inflows, found it impossible to raise long-term loans in London early in 1914. The outbreak of war in August then brought a temporary but almost total collapse of the financial and commercial infrastructures of Latin America. In Bill Albert's words, 'shipping and insurance became scarce and expensive, banks shut their doors, capital and credit completely dried up, and sterling bills disappeared.'[1] Most countries made their currencies inconvertible in order to stem the outflow of gold, and announced moratoria on commercial debts. Government revenues fell alarmingly because of the decline in imports.

Commercial credit became available again, at a price, by the end of 1914, but the disruption of trade remained serious. Even when an improvement began the following year, it was uneven and Latin American producers and governments still faced considerable difficulties. Some imports were virtually unobtainable. Some markets had disappeared, while others were strictly regulated by the British government. The cost of shipping and insurance had increased enormously. The British, moreover, made continued efforts to restrict German commercial activities. Early in the war their ownership of the transatlantic cables allowed them to stop the transmission of ciphered messages, seriously hampering the operations of German firms, while their naval dominance resulted in the internment of German merchant ships in Latin American ports. Later, in February 1916, the British government blacklisted many German firms and prohibited trade with them.

Latin American trade during the war

Britain, which before the war had imported 60 per cent of its food, including much of its meat, 80 per cent of its wheat and all its sugar, regarded Latin America primarily as a source of necessary foodstuffs and raw materials, especially now that supplies from central Europe were cut off.[2] The government introduced some controls over imports almost immediately. The newly established Royal Commission for Sugar Supplies bought one million tons in August 1914, and then suspended purchases, hoping for a short war. Producers in countries like Peru, therefore, quickly found their Liverpool markets closed.

The experience of Argentina, the most important of Britain's South American suppliers, illustrates some of the problems producers faced. Initially they made some gains as the Allies, with the help of British loans, forced up wheat prices by bidding against one another. As the war progressed, however, Britain began to purchase supplies on behalf of its partners, thus holding prices below their true level. From early 1915 the Board of Trade bought frozen meat for France and Italy as well as itself, and within eighteen months 80 per cent of Argentina's meat exports were subject to such contracts.[3] By the end of 1916 the European Allies were coordinating orders and shipping for wheat, which was becoming scarce, while Argentina's maize and linseed sales suffered since they were not considered essential for the war. The 1917 wheat harvest was small, and the Yrigoyen government placed restrictions on exports, probably to preserve stocks for domestic consumption, but in a normal year the British market was vital and concern was increasing about other areas of Argentine trade. In January 1918, therefore, Yrigoyen agreed to sell the Allies 2.5 million tons of cereals in return for assurances about shipping space and coal supplies.[4] The Allies also prevented the Argentines from selling wheat elsewhere, blocking a deal with Mexico later that year.

The entry of the United States into the war in April 1917 reinforced British controls on Latin American trade, as it joined Allied purchasing boards for grain, sugar and meat. Exports of Chilean nitrate, essential for the manufacture of explosives, also came under foreign influence. From February 1915 Antony Gibbs & Sons acted as sole agents for the British and French governments' purchases; by 1917 they bought about a third of the industry's output with another third going to two US companies.[5] In December 1917 the British and US governments further enhanced their control by forming the Nitrate of Soda Executive, with Gibbs acting for all the Allies except the United States. Nitrate prices then fell, in contrast to the rise in other commodities, and this was reversed (temporarily) only when the Chilean government belatedly established state controls over sales just before the war ended.

Shipping shortages also created enormous problems. German ships could no longer sail, and by December 1915 almost a third of the British merchant fleet had been lost due to submarine attacks and military requisitions.[6] Cargo space was limited, even for essential foodstuffs, and British controls over its allocation gradually became more effective. From February 1917 the Tonnage Priority Committee began to reserve shipping for key raw materials and supplies. Exports like Peruvian cotton and Brazilian coffee which the British considered inessential piled up on quaysides. When ships did arrive, the cost of freight and insurance was enormous in comparison with the prewar years.

The introduction of the Black List (naming German firms with which trade was prohibited) also extended Britain's influence, even though it aroused considerable resentment throughout Latin America, since it clearly infringed sovereignty and disrupted particular trades, like nitrate, coffee, grain and sugar, where German merchants and producers had become well established. While it was possible for such firms to evade it, by working through Latin American nominees for example, the US entry into the war brought more effective enforcement and increased discontent. The British also used their control of coal and oil fuel, and jute supplies from India, which were needed for sacks, to hinder German firms' operations. These measures had a hidden objective besides that of aiding the war effort, for British officials were consciously attempting to make Germany's recovery more difficult.

Despite all these impediments to Latin Americans' freedom to trade, the value of exports did increase after the crisis of 1914–15, in some cases quite significantly. There was, however, an enormous variation in each country's experience, depending on the significance of particular commodities to the war effort and the degree of monopsonistic power Britain and its allies could exercise. Argentina (exporting grain and meat) and Peru (sugar, cotton, minerals and oil) gained more than their neighbours from wartime demand and the subsequent boom. Mexico's oil shipments also grew rapidly as navies converted from coal. Brazil benefited less, partly because the Allies considered coffee supplies dispensable when allocating shipping. While Chile profited from increased nitrate and copper sales, especially in the final two years of the war, the nitrate trade collapsed suddenly late in 1918, when demand for explosives ceased, whereas other producers in Latin America gained from a massive boom in commodity prices in 1919–20.

The significance of the war for Anglo-Latin American relations

Does the wartime experience support those who have interpreted the relationship between Britain and Latin America as 'imperialistic' or 'dependent'? In many respects it does. Although their control was not complete, the British role in trade and its infrastructure gave them many sources of leverage. Monopsonistic purchasing, especially later in the war, clearly reduced export prices below 'free market' levels. In 1919 one Argentine commentator estimated the loss of export earnings due to Allied controls at over £70 million.[7] Dependence on British shipping caused exporters serious problems, and gave Britain a further means of control, for example in its negotiations with Argentina.

The war also exposed Latin America's dependence on imported goods rather than, as authors like Frank and Véliz have suggested, aiding the growth of manufacturing.[8] Commentators in Argentina and Peru deplored the lack of expansion in manufacturing there during the war.[9] Even in Brazil, where industrial production did increase, it was due more to the intensive use of existing capacity than to new investment. Many countries suffered serious shortages of fuel and capital goods, and initially the United States took as much advantage as local industrialists from the decline in imports from Europe. In 1917–18 the shortage of imports from all sources caused balance of trade surpluses and exchange rate appreciation, while the pace of inflation accelerated. Although some exporters may have profited later in the war, on balance these years underlined the vulnerability of those countries which depended most on Britain. The war highlighted the influence London might exercise over prices, commerce, communications and shipping, especially if reinforced by the United States.

In the longer term the war had important consequences for Britain's position in Latin America, although it took some years for its true significance to be appreciated. In South America, at least, many officials and businessmen remained obsessed with Germany's commercial rivalry. One diplomat commented in June 1918 on Brazil, where over 500 'enemy' firms had been blacklisted, 'What we are after is . . . destroying German trade not only for the present but for the future.'[10] Yet the more serious threat came from the United States, which had begun a drive for trade just before the opening of the Panama Canal in August 1914. The Wilson administration established the Bureau of Foreign and Domestic Commerce, created a system of permanent commercial attachés in South America, and permitted US banks to open branches overseas. US officials then fought hard to reduce British participation in activities which they believed crucial to their own future, in particular radio and cable communications and oil. They also attempted to gain influence over Latin American government finance.

Towards the end of the war serious differences arose between Britain and the United States over a number of issues: the competition for oil concessions; the role of the two countries in Brazil's coffee trade and finances; and cable and telegraph concessions in Argentina, Brazil and Peru. The British resented US attempts to hinder the De Bunsen Mission, which was despatched in 1918 to rebuild Britain's commercial relations with South America. They were also at odds with President Wilson over Carranza's regime in Mexico, which they regarded as a serious threat to Allied interests due to his attacks on the oil companies and seizure of British-owned railways.

While tensions with the United States eased in the early 1920s, these conflicts have a broader significance as an indication of Britain's growing inability to support fully its financial and commercial interests in the region. The funds for costly schemes to maintain British influence in Latin America were simply not available. The Treasury refused to support either the Foreign Office's grandiose attempt, at the time of the Second Valorisation in 1917–18, to wrest control of Brazil's coffee trade from Wille or its backing for Marconi's efforts to resist US domination of radio networks in the western hemisphere.

Britain emerged from the war severely weakened. Its prewar prosperity had depended in part on using its invisible earnings, including the dividends and interest on overseas investment, to finance new loans and companies and pay for imports. By 1918, however, Britain's foreign investment had fallen by about a quarter, largely through the disposal of assets in the United States, and its wartime debt to the USA totalled $4.1 billion.[11] Trade had also suffered. The attempt to use the Black List to destroy German competition and the despatch of the De Bunsen Mission during 1918 reflected official unease about Britain's ability to compete commercially. These fears were justified by events. Although exports to Central and South America grew during the 1920s, in real terms they never regained their 1913 level throughout the interwar period (see Table 8.1).

Table 8.1 British exports to Latin America, 1920–1938

	£ million (current prices)	Index of volume (1913 = 100)
1913	55.4	100
1920	114.4	57
1921	59.6	40
1922	52.4	47
1923	64.4	61
1924	66.5	63
1925	73.4	71
1926	60.7	63
1927	65.2	71
1928	71.4	80
1929	72.2	82
1930	54.3	64
1931	29.1	39
1932	24.1	35
1933	29.9	43
1934	30.7	43
1935	31.6	44
1936	32.6	44
1937	42.6	53
1938	35.9	44

Source: 'Annual Statements of Trade and Navigation'. Adjusted to constant prices using the export price index for Britain's global exports in Mitchell, *British Historical Statistics*, p. 527

Nevertheless, even though resources were lacking, the war had shown the British government that it could no longer neglect Latin America to the extent it had before 1914. Latin American countries had been too important as suppliers of raw materials and foodstuffs, and the growth of exports to the region was seen as vital to Britain's commercial recovery. In 1918–19, as competition for the world's oil supplies intensified, the government stopped British companies in Mexico and Peru from selling out to US firms, and it also persuaded Lord Cowdray to purchase German-owned public utilities in Chile. Although the wartime controls over purchasing and shipping were quickly dismantled, new government institutions like the Petroleum Department and the Department of Overseas Trade developed a strong interest in Latin America and eroded the Foreign Office monopoly of negotiations and information. The Treasury and the Bank of England, which attempted to retain some control over new investment in order to uphold the value of sterling, also became deeply involved in Latin American affairs.

THE POSTWAR DECADE: THE BRITISH VIEWPOINT

British investment during the 1920s

The bedrock of Britain's international economic policy after the First World War was the re-establishment of the Gold Standard with the pound at its prewar parity of $4.86, something it eventually achieved in 1925. This held back British investment in Latin America in the early 1920s, since in order to protect sterling the Bank of England generally discouraged merchant banks from issuing loans until after the return to gold. The bar was not complete. Argentina (£2.5 million in 1923), Chile (£1.6 million in 1922), Peru (£1.25 million in 1922) and Brazil (£9 million in a joint London – New York issue in 1922) all floated bonds in London.[12] However, except for a few months in 1924, the market was fully open only from November 1925 until July 1929. Between 1924 and 1930 new capital issues for Latin America led by merchant banks in the City totalled about £132 million, less than a third of the amount issued in Latin American government bonds alone in New York.[13]

Apart from the 'polite blackmail against foreign issues' operated by the Bank, borrowing in the City of London also became unattractive for other reasons: interest rates often exceeded those in New York and the British government levied a 2 per cent stamp duty on new issues.[14] This was retained after 1926 as an informal means of deterring lending, and it prevented Barings from leading Argentine loans in 1926–27. However, City institutions frequently bought substantial blocks of the bonds issued in New York. Thus the barriers to lending diminished British influence (and commissions and export orders) less than they reduced the flow of capital. In Peru the impossibility of borrowing in London prevented British participation in public works projects, including railway construction and the development of Callao docks; US firms monopolised the civil engineering contracts financed by the New York loans.

The Bank's discouragement of new issues also applied to companies operating in Latin America, although there is little evidence that large concerns like the railways were much affected. The expansion of their networks had almost ceased, and they seemed generally content with the income from the increasing traffic on their existing lines. In fact towards the end of the 1920s British investors began to relinquish their interests in some free-standing companies, especially in mining and utilities. The Guggenheims, using new processing methods, began to purchase nitrate *oficinas*. US firms acquired control of the principal telephone and electricity companies in Chile, telephone companies in Bogotá, Caracas, Montevideo and Buenos Aires, and the Atlas Light and Power Company, which controlled tramway and electricity undertakings in Argentina and Uruguay. US investors even threatened to purchase control of British-owned railways in Argentina, forcing the Pacific and then the other three principal companies to alter their statutes so that only British or Argentine citizens could hold voting stock.

The two most important prewar channels for new investment in Latin America, government loans and free-standing companies, thus became much less significant after 1918. A new departure, however, was much greater medium-term lending by the Anglo-Latin American banks, over which the Bank of England had no control. Both the Bank of London and South America, a subsidiary of Lloyds formed in 1923 by an amalgamation of British banks in the River Plate and Brazil, and the Anglo–South American Bank, which remained independent until 1936, lent substantial sums to British and US enterprises in Latin America. The railways in Argentina, for example, financed modernisation projects in the late 1920s with bank loans. The ASAB also supported Guggenheims' nitrate schemes in Chile, a venture which eventually brought it down.

The other area of growth came through multinational groups which did not need the Stock Exchange (and hence Bank of England permission) to raise finance for ventures in Latin America, particularly in manufacturing and petroleum. Several leading industrial companies established factories, especially in Argentina and Brazil. Their motives were normally to escape the effect of rising tariffs, but some were also encouraged by the availability of local raw materials or the potential of a market. British companies with factories operating in Latin America by 1930 included ICI in chemicals, Dorman Long in steel, Gourock Ropework, J. & P. Coats (sewing thread), British American Tobacco (BAT), Reckitt & Sons and Lever Brothers (household products),

Bryant & May (matches), Glaxo (pharmaceuticals) and Columbia Records (later part of EMI).

Investment in petroleum was much more significant due to its scale, its strategic importance, and the problems which arose between companies and host governments. British entrepreneurs sought oil concessions throughout Latin America from the late nineteenth century, but production became concentrated in three countries, in Peru from 1890, Mexico from 1904 and Venezuela from 1919. Peru remained a small exporter. Output, led by two small British companies, rose to over 2 million barrels annually by 1913, when the bigger firm was sold to Standard Oil of New Jersey.[15] In Mexico both the local market and the oilfields were much larger. Output rose to 33 million barrels in 1915 and peaked at 193 million in 1921.[16] The Mexican Eagle company, founded by Weetman Pearson (Lord Cowdray) and actively assisted by the government of Porfirio Díaz, played a key role. In 1908 Pearson captured about half the domestic market following a bitter price war with the distributor of Standard Oil's products, and in 1910 he made his first major oil strike near Tampico. However, in the 1920s the emphasis shifted from Mexico to Venezuela. In Mexico the existing oilfields suffered from salt-water intrusion and new exploration was disappointing, but Venezuela was found to possess large, easily recoverable reserves. While Mexico's output fell to less than 40 million barrels in 1930, in Venezuela it rose from less than 1 million in 1920 to 136 million in 1929.[17]

During the 1920s the organisation of the industry changed as firms integrated under the pressure of falling prices, forming a small group of 'oil majors' dominated by Anglo-Persian, Royal Dutch-Shell, and Standard Oil of New Jersey. The intense rivalry in which British and US firms, supported by their governments, had engaged immediately after the end of the war was replaced by market-sharing and price-fixing agreements. Of the two leading 'British' firms Anglo-Persian took little interest in Latin America, in part because the Venezuelans would not accept investment from a company controlled by a foreign government. British oil interests in Latin America thus came mainly to be represented by Royal Dutch-Shell (despite its majority Dutch ownership), which purchased a minority share in Mexican Eagle in 1919 and took over its management and distribution networks. Shell also acquired important concessions in Venezuela before the First World War, and remained the leading producer there until Jersey Standard surpassed it in 1934.

These changes, particularly the shift towards investment which did not pass through the Stock Exchange, make it impossible to quantify

British investment in Latin America in the 1920s. Estimates range from Lord Kindersley's total of £832 million for December 1930 to the *South American Journal*'s figure of £1213 million for 1929, but they are simply untrustworthy.[18] Besides the usual problems of measuring British investment in government loans and free-standing companies (particularly amortisation payments and foreign purchases of stocks, bonds and debentures denominated in sterling and issued in London), they neglect British holdings of loans issued in New York, the direct investments of the multinational manufacturing companies (which were not particularly large in value), and Royal Dutch–Shell (whose investments, in Venezuela particularly but also in marketing and distribution facilities elsewhere, were extensive).

These changes also altered the geographical distribution of British investment. The west coast of South America became less significant as US companies strengthened their position in copper (in Chile and Peru), petroleum (in Peru) and nitrate. Venezuela and Mexico became important to the British for oil, although in the latter production fell after 1921. Apart from this there was little new investment in Mexico due to the Revolution and its associated nationalist rhetoric; the two most important British manufacturing companies there, Coats and BAT, had both entered before 1910. The concentration of British interests in Brazil and the River Plate persisted, despite the difficulties of the government loan business and the sale of some free-standing companies.

British trade

The problems of British investment in the 1920s had a serious, though unquantifiable, effect on British exports. The restrictions on new loans caused the loss of contracts, hindering sales of iron and steel products, machinery and transport equipment, and the sterling–dollar exchange rate after 1925 made other products uncompetitive. Prices were the factor which members of the British Chamber of Commerce in Buenos Aires mentioned most often in explaining the loss of British competitiveness. The newer enterprises could not replace the loss of dynamism in the older types of investment. Branch factories often used local inputs (tobacco, timber, fibres, oils), and the petroleum firms purchased much of their equipment from the United States as well as seriously harming coal exports.

The 1920s were thus extremely difficult for British trade in Latin America. As Table 8.1 shows, exports never regained more than about four-fifths of their 1913 volume. Britain's dependence on the

Argentine market also became more marked (see Table 8.2). Yet even there its share of imports fell from 31 per cent in 1913 to 18 per cent in 1929, while in Brazil it dropped from 25 to 19 per cent, and in Chile from 30 to 18 per cent.[19] Some of the reasons for this decline were apparent before 1914 (see pp. 112–16). They became more acute after the war as a result of changes in Latin American demand and Britain's loss of its position as the major source of investment finance and commercial credit.

Table 8.2 Direction of British exports to Latin America, 1920–1938 (£000)

	1920	1925	1928	1930	1935	1938
Argentina	42921	29145	31210	25234	15257	19338
	(37.5%)	(39.9%)	(43.7%)	(46.5%)	(48.2%)	(53.9%)
Brazil	24289	16155	16034	7970	4757	5185
	(21.2%)	(22.1%)	(22.4%)	(14.7%)	(15.0%)	(14.4%)
Chile	9662	6029	5128	5963	2051	1641
	(8.4%)	(8.3%)	(7.2%)	(11.0%)	(6.5%)	(4.6%)
Peru	4733	2381	1954	1443	1101	1033
	(4.1%)	(3.3%)	(2.7%)	(2.7%)	(3.5%)	(2.9%)
Uruguay	5916	3179	3106	3578	1516	2187
	(5.2%)	(4.4%)	(4.3%)	(6.6%)	(4.8%)	(6.1%)
Bolivia & Paraguay	916	716	639	495	206	278
	(0.8%)	(1.0%)	(0.9%)	(0.9%)	(0.7%)	(0.8%)
Colombia, Venezuela,	10919	7043	6316	3589	3280	3339
Ecuador	(9.5%)	(9.7%)	(8.8%)	(6.6%)	(10.4%)	(9.3%)
Central America	3465	2660	2202	2011	1077	1026
	(3.0%)	(3.6%)	(3.1%)	(3.7%)	(3.4%)	(2.9%)
Spanish Caribbean	7267	2957	2046	1539	1070	1025
	(6.4%)	(4.1%)	(2.9%)	(2.8%)	(3.4%)	(2.9%)
Mexico	4344	3136	2800	2433	1386	854
	(3.8%)	(4.3%)	(3.9%)	(4.4%)	(4.4%)	(4.4%)
Total	**114432**	**72968**	**71435**	**54244**	**31630**	**35906**

Note: These are current values, and thus they take no account either of changes in prices or of the fluctuating value of sterling.

Source: 'Annual Statements of Trade and Navigation'

Manufacturing grew quickly in Latin America in the 1920s, especially in textiles, which displaced British products from traditional markets. Compared with the 700 million yards of cloth sold to Latin America in 1913, British cotton exports hovered around 400 million yards throughout the 1920s.[20] Oil replaced coal as a fuel, even on the British-owned railways in Argentina. Motor transport spread. The

United States monopolised the trade connected with the growing radio and film industries. Thus while Britain's older exports lost their dynamism the import schedules of the principal Latin American countries became orientated towards new products in which Britain lagged behind the United States and Germany. One commercial attaché in the mid 1920s ascribed the decline in Britain's share of Brazilian imports simply to the growing demand for cars, gasoline and electrical goods.[21] Britain performed particularly badly in the motor trade, in which Argentina was one of the largest markets in the world. 'The Department of Overseas Trade,' one frustrated official minuted, 'cannot supply initiative to British business houses. British [motor] firms *will* not display business initiative, they will not push local *agencies*, nor establish local spares depots, nor take pains to meet local demand.'[22]

The new products frequently demanded different methods of sales and financing. One enquiry found in 1925 that Germany had won large electrical contracts in Argentina and Brazil because of Siemens' effective network of representatives and their links with the German banks which enabled them to offer good credit terms.[23] A decade later the Royal Institute of International Affairs complained that the British financial system was not equipped to offer the medium–term credits (three or four years) required for many new exports, especially machinery.[24] Large North American and German companies tended to employ their own sales staff rather than using merchants, and introduced more advanced marketing techniques such as sophisticated advertising campaigns and hire-purchase schemes. Selling through merchant houses, the customary British practice, had disadvantages. Lever Brothers, one of the most dynamic manufacturing companies, found it difficult to develop markets for branded consumer products through merchants, complaining of the 'lack of push' shown by its agents in Rio and Santos.[25] Sales offices in Buenos Aires, a frequent answer to the merchants' inefficiency, might work for Argentina but could not cover the whole continent. Other British firms simply ignored the problems. The Sheffield steel companies admitted in 1930 to their 'serious neglect of the Latin American market [where] no Director or Works' Representatives of any . . . cutlery firms [had] made a proper business tour . . . since 1914'.[26] The difficulties of the British export trade were summarised in the scathing comments of the d'Abernon Mission at the end of the 1920s: 'Our methods of production, representation, advertisement, marketing and sales require thorough revision. . . . A considerable volume of British trade is lost owing to old methods and inadequate representation'.[27]

191

The British government and Latin America

After the First World War the British government could not return to its passive policies towards business in Latin America, and it became more active in controlling, encouraging and protecting trade and investment. However, it was handicapped by difficulties and contradictions within Whitehall. The multiplicity of departments now involved made policy formulation more complex; the interests of the Foreign Office, Board of Trade, Treasury and Bank of England frequently differed. Resources were lacking; Latin America had a lower priority than Europe and the empire. Many officials retained the view that business should look after itself and that diplomats should confine themselves to reporting. Others, having discovered the importance of British business interests, meekly followed their bidding. Generally there was little understanding of Latin American viewpoints, especially over issues like nationalism or labour protest, although a few exceptional diplomats were becoming more critical of the railways and public utility companies' attitudes.

Shortly after the war, in surveying the prospects for commercial recovery, the Department of Overseas Trade had equated South America with India and the Dominions as 'the quarter of the Globe to which we can most hopefully look'.[28] The results were disappointing. As exports failed to regain their prewar levels, some officials began to complain bitterly about the inability of British businessmen to grasp opportunities or build on Britain's prestige in Latin America. Yet Treasury and Bank of England policies over sterling did little to ease the path for British exports, and fiscal retrenchment also led to reduced commercial representation in South America. The Department of Overseas Trade complained in 1922 that only two commercial attachés remained in the region, in Buenos Aires and Rio. In addition government cuts had led to the withdrawal of all the service attachés.[29] Britain's early influence in civil and military aviation, together with the potential trade in aircraft and spares, thus collapsed. Moreover, many diplomats trained in the laissez-faire approach of the prewar period were reluctant to give active support to British entrepreneurs, in contrast to US diplomats who often lobbied against British companies on the instructions of the State Department. In Peru, for example, they held up a concession for Marconi to operate domestic postal and telegraph services and later in the decade protested successfully against an armaments contract with Vickers. D'Abernon again was scathing. 'With some brilliant exceptions,' he commented, 'our diplomatic representation is chosen rather with a view to dignity and correctness than to active economic development.'[30]

The petroleum industry, where British diplomacy was much more active, showed up different problems. Before 1914 the government had ignored the oil companies' operations. After 1916, however, when the country came close to a complete breakdown of oil supplies, Whitehall attempted to ensure continued British access to Latin American deposits. It thus prevented the sale of Mexican Eagle and Lobitos Oilfields to US interests. As the competition with the United States for oil concessions subsided, policy focused more on the protection of British interests against host governments, and diplomats took a hard line towards nationalist governments and labour disputes. On oil, Louis Turner claims, the British government rarely deviated from a policy of 'backing British companies whatever the merit of the dispute'.[31] While it had failed to bring Royal Dutch-Shell under majority British control, the government considered it British enough to offer Shell fairly consistent support. Again resources were a problem, but in petroleum this meant that officials rarely queried the companies' claims. The Petroleum Department had only three permanent staff in the early 1930s, relied on the companies for information, and tended to act as a mouthpiece for Shell's interests in Whitehall. Diplomats overseas also often depended on local managers for information, and transmitted their requests to Whitehall without question. Foreign Office archives are thus littered with references to Mexican presidents using terms like 'Bolsheviks', for both diplomats and businessmen had enormous problems in evaluating and coping with Latin American nationalism.

THE POSTWAR DECADE: THE LATIN AMERICAN VIEWPOINT

While most Latin American exports experienced some years of good prices in the 1920s, producers and governments who had anticipated a prolonged return to the golden years before 1914 were disappointed. In western Europe population growth slowed down, while food production recovered rapidly, often with government support in the form of protection or bounties. Even Britain retained its wartime duty on sugar and began to grow its own beet. By the end of the decade the terms of trade for all the major Latin American commodities had fallen below their 1913 level.[32] Generally the British market became less important for Latin American exporters, although Argentina and Uruguay were becoming much more dependent on free access to it. As the United States and continental European countries protected their own farmers against imports it made them more vulnerable to any changes in British policy (see Table 8.3). In other countries particular sectors or regions, like the Peruvian sugar producers, faced similar threats.

Table 8.3 British share of Latin American countries' exports, 1900–1940 (%)

	Argentina	Brazil	Chile	Peru	Uruguay
1910	21.7	24.8	35.3	35.2	8.3
1915	29.6	12.0	33.4	31.3	17.7
1920	26.8	8.0	20.4	36.2	22.2
1925	23.9	5.0	33.9	34.6	24.2
1930	36.5	8.2	14.5	20.1	33.7
1935	34.3	9.2	18.1	21.4	31.2
1940	38.2	17.3	5.8	12.3	34.8

Note: Latin American export statistics are notoriously unreliable. These figures are intended only as a guide to trends and relative proportions.

Source: Mitchell, *International Historical Statistics*, pp. 593–609

The major Latin American countries also faced difficulties due to the scale of Britain's existing investments and the shortage of new funds from London. This meant that they frequently had to rely on export earnings and capital from the United States to provide the foreign exchange necessary for remittances on British investments. In countries like Argentina and Brazil the burden of interest and dividend payments to Britain was substantial. Railways and public utilities were introducing little new capital but reached the peak of their earnings in the 1920s, and their demands for foreign exchange to repatriate profits thus grew. Pedro Skupch estimates that in Argentina the profits on British-owned railways alone averaged £12.8 million annually between 1923 and 1930, about 8 per cent of export earnings.[33]

A further problem for Latin American governments was that the political burden of control from London, already evident before 1914, was increasing, especially as railway and public utility companies often seemed more interested in paying dividends than reinvesting profits in improved services. British company directors appeared incapable of understanding the demands of consumers and the threat posed to them by the rising tide of economic nationalism. In Pernambuco, for example, the GWBR and the tramways company had been able to rely in 1922 on the authorities' repression of a serious labour dispute, but by the end of the decade they were under severe attack from the opposition press, and the state government was unwilling to help them. The intransigence of the public utility companies dismayed the more perceptive British diplomats who believed it necessary to compromise with nationalist politicians rather than perpetually fighting them. 'We shall begin to get a move on', the ambassador in Buenos Aires wrote in frustration in 1929, 'when directors are forced by law to travel annually to the parts of the world where their companies are interested. It seems incredible, but I know of directors, chairmen, even general managers, of some of the greatest companies connected with Argentina, who have never been to South America'.[34]

The oil companies presented particular difficulties for Latin American governments, although they almost certainly offered substantial pecuniary advantages to unscrupulous politicians (Louis Turner comments that Latin America accounted for the bulk of the 'unusual payments' made by oil companies to politicians before 1939).[35] Mexican Eagle had certainly possessed close connexions with leading officials of the Díaz regime. Shell was suspected of contributing financially towards Leguía's coup in Peru in 1919, while Venezuela under Gómez was a byword for corruption. Such stories, however intriguing, are symptoms of a much greater problem: how could governments lacking technical expertise deal with a complex industry dominated by large international firms?

In many respects the pattern in oil resembled earlier problems with railways (see pp. 134–6): generous concessions, delays in revising them, and growing nationalist criticisms of the foreign role. This created bitter disputes between Latin American politicians and British firms. Most governments had conceded too much before the potential of oil became clear. In 1889 the Peruvian government provided enormous tax concessions on the Negritos oilfield, which turned out to be the principal one in the country. Eventually, after 1913, this brought Peru into conflict with a Standard Oil subsidiary registered in Canada and hence able to call on the British government for support. In Mexico Porfirio Díaz offered the oil companies extensive privileges which gave rise to major disputes over concessions, taxes and production levels following the Revolution. In Venezuela British firms acquired many concessions before the government tightened up its oil legislation between 1918 and 1922. Royal Dutch-Shell consequently accounted for 43 per cent of total output between 1922 and 1935 but contributed only 34 per cent of the taxes paid by the industry.[36] Although the Gómez government extracted money from Shell in 1922 and 1925 in return for confirming their concessions, in the main the administration failed to control the industry. The 1922 law (drafted mainly by the foreign oil companies at President Gómez's invitation) permitted them to import almost anything free of duty by claiming it as 'equipment'. Until 1930 the government accepted the oil firms' production statistics rather than verifying them itself. The benefits Venezuela derived from the industry were further diluted by the companies' decision, unopposed by the government, to site the refineries treating Venezuelan oil offshore on the Dutch islands of Curaçao and Aruba.

The oil firms compounded the potential for nationalist attacks on their interests with their own behaviour. 'It would be difficult,' George Philip comments, 'to find anything good to say about the behaviour in Mexico of the oil companies, whose arrogance was legendary and whose attitudes made their eventual loss of position almost inevitable.'[37] A Foreign Office minute concerning Mexico commented in 1926 that their 'main idea of negotiation appears to be bluff, with graft if bluff fails'.[38] A Mexican Eagle manager later complained that Sir Henri Deterding, the head of Royal Dutch-Shell, 'was incapable of conceiving Mexico as anything but a Colonial Government to which you simply dictated orders'.[39] The companies' local workers faced job insecurity, the danger of accident and sickness, and low wages compared with foreign employees in the industry. In Mexico they formed an important element of the organised working class after 1916, and a potentially powerful ally for nationalist politicians.

A further problem for governments was that the successful British oil companies made good profits, while paying little in taxes to the host government and purchasing few supplies locally. The Mexican Eagle dividend reached a peak of 60 per cent in 1920 before production declined, while in Peru Lobitos Oilfields paid over 10 per cent for all but one year between 1912 and 1933.[40] Royal Dutch-Shell, which paid over 30 per cent throughout the 1920s, except for 1929, obtained enormous benefits from both its Mexican interests and its Venezuelan holdings. Deterding once described Venezuela as 'our most colossal deal'.[41] Latin American countries lacked the knowledge to police such a technologically specialised industry, and could never control the transfer of concessions from one company to another or the extent of competition or collusion among them. If they imposed laws which appeared to be too harsh or encouraged high wage settlements, they simply diverted new investment towards other countries where tax and wage regimes were easier. Increasingly they confronted a common front of large international firms which refused to compete with each other and, in the case of Shell at least, could almost always persuade the British government of the justice of their claims.

ARGENTINA, BRAZIL AND THE BRITISH CONNEXION IN THE 1920s

The economic difficulties of Argentina were growing in the 1920s, although relatively few contemporary observers perceived them clearly. The area under cultivation increased by scarcely 10 per cent between 1914 and 1930.[42] Four products, wheat, maize, linseed and beef, accounted for two-thirds of the country's exports.[43] They were vulnerable to any North American or European attempt to protect their own farmers. The meat trade was dominated by a small number of North American and British packing houses and, by the end of the 1920s, almost entirely dependent on the British market. The 'Big Four' British companies controlled much of the railway system.

The First World War hit the British-owned railways badly. Their expenses rose from 63 per cent of gross receipts in 1913 to 75 per cent in 1917, due to increasing costs, particularly for coal, and declining revenues caused by poor harvests. By 1918 dividends on ordinary shares had fallen to nominal levels.[44] New construction virtually ceased, and during the 1920s the railways brought little fresh capital into Argentina. However, their dividends recovered, and the cost to Argentina of British ownership of the railways thus increased. Moreover, the companies imported over 80 per cent of their supplies under the duty-free concessions of the Mitre Law, causing a further drain on foreign exchange and a loss of income to the government.[45] Similar problems occurred with other public utilities, leading to much greater questioning of the value of British capital. The tramways, which in 1926 carried 89 per cent of passenger traffic in Buenos Aires, were particularly criticised as 'slow, uncomfortable, and noisy'.[46] Few Argentines had much reason to show them sympathy when they came into competition with buses and cars at the end of the decade. Antagonism towards the railways was also increasing, making it more difficult for Argentine politicians to negotiate with them without being attacked for selling out to foreign interests.

During the First World War and the 1920s two issues dominated the railways' relationship with the government: labour demands and passenger and freight tariffs. They were, of course, interlinked. Higher wages or social security contributions would raise operating costs and place upward pressure on tariffs. For the companies the political climate became more difficult since the policies of the Radical administrations of Yrigoyen and Alvear which ruled Argentina between 1916 and 1930 were often framed with federal and provincial elections in mind. A further drawback was that many of the railways' lawyers and local directors were identified politically with the conservative opposition.

These problems began to become evident after 1915, when an arbitrary tariff increase and the companies' refusal to implement a new pensions law caused resentment. From mid-1917 the railways faced a series of violent strikes, and with elections approaching Yrigoyen showed some sympathy with the protests. However, the companies succeeded in dividing the unions and obtained the support of domestic business interests harmed by the stoppages and the British government, which threatened to cancel its wheat purchases from Argentina. Yrigoyen bowed to their pressure, used troops and the police to quell unrest, and permitted the railways to dismiss union leaders. Later in the 1920s, however, a reformed and powerful national union, the Unión Ferroviaria, was able to use the threat of disruption to pressurise the Alvear government into forcing the companies to recognise it and grant employment contracts and wage increases to their workers.

Problems over passenger and freight tariffs, which the railway companies regarded as insufficient to counteract the inflation of prices and wages, were also common, and the railways' strategic position in Argentina made this a central political issue. The outcome frequently depended on the stage of the electoral cycle and the possibilities of access to finance in London. In 1921 a demand for tariff increases coincided with the approach of elections. The companies did not gain official sanction for it until June 1922, shortly before Yrigoyen left office, and then probably because he hoped for a loan from London. Further difficulties arose in 1926–27 when the railways were pressurised into granting tariff rebates as grain prices fell, but Yrigoyen, when he returned to office in 1928, reversed some of the reductions in the hope of obtaining a loan in London for public works construction. Negotiating was becoming much more difficult for both sides. The railways had little to offer Argentina (their main weapon was the Argentine government's perception that they could influence loan issues), while governments could not afford either to permit disruptive strikes or to concede too much to the railways over tariffs.

There was also considerable potential for conflict in the meat trade, which the Radical governments failed to control whether for their own or the landowners' benefit. The companies customarily used techniques like transfer pricing and under-invoicing to evade taxation, as Raúl Prebisch demonstrated in 1928 in a report for the Sociedad Rural (the association of large landowners) in showing the great discrepancy between the value of exports in the Argentine statistics and that for meat imports from Argentina declared to the British authorities. He also argued that the *frigoríficos* had tended to benefit from price rises while transferring falls to the producers.[47] Argentine discontent with the packers over prices and grading had first come to a head five years before, when landowners threatened to stop cattle deliveries to the *frigoríficos*, and demanded the establishment of a national packing-house and shipping line to compete with and hence control the companies. However, the meat firms proved the stronger. By halting cattle purchases they compelled the government to abandon attempts at reform (except a minor one permitting producers to be paid according to the live weight of cattle rather than dead weight, 'the most innocuous of all' in Peter Smith's words).[48] Even the temporary breakdown of the packers' cartel in 1925–27 did not bring higher prices for the landowners, in contrast to the 1913–14 meat war. The Argentines' position then weakened further. Three companies withdrew from the export trade, further increasing the degree of monopsony. Some firms acquired plants in Uruguay, obtaining additional independence from Argentine supplies. Markets contracted. In 1926 the United States closed its ports to Argentine beef to guard against foot-and-mouth disease, and continental European countries raised import duties to protect their own farmers. Thus Argentina's dependence on free access to the British market increased.

One response to these problems was a 'Buy from those who buy from us' campaign, promoted by the Sociedad Rural and welcomed by the British, who had their own anxieties about trade. When Viscount d'Abernon led his commercial mission to Argentina, Brazil, Chile and Uruguay in 1929, in an attempt to take advantage of growing concern that Britain would introduce Imperial Preference and discriminate against South American exports, he obtained his warmest reception in Buenos Aires. D'Abernon and Yrigoyen agreed that the two countries should purchase £8.7 million of goods from each other, and that British firms should receive preferential treatment in the allocation of government contracts. Argentina was committing itself to new purchases, while the British were merely guaranteeing existing Argentine trade. Hardly surprisingly d'Abernon thought the results 'astonishing', while the British ambassador, Sir Malcolm Robertson, believed the agreement made 'a present of £8 or £9 million sterling to our industries', 'something for nothing' in his words.[49]

The d'Abernon agreement is not worth the attention historians have paid to it. It was not a straightforward sign of British strength and Argentine weakness. The British showed an amazing capacity for self-delusion. They appear to have made no realistic assessment of Yrigoyen's ability to guide the agreement through the Argentine Senate, which he did not control; of the response of other countries, like France, which could claim 'most-favoured nation' treatment; or of the ability of British manufacturers to meet the orders. British steel firms, for example, were barred from selling rails to Argentina under international cartel arrangements. The one concrete outcome was that Yrigoyen succeeded in raising a short-term loan of £5 million in London.[50] When Uriburu overthrew Yrigoyen in 1930 he simply abandoned the d'Abernon agreement, leaving the British with no concrete benefits.

Overall, therefore, the problems of the Anglo-Argentine relationship were increasing as the British economy failed to recover and Argentine criticism of British firms grew. The potential for friction with companies which had ceased to invest and whose services were deteriorating was enormous, although the continued possibilities of borrowing in London gave British interests some bargaining counters. The Argentine experience also suggests that the prewar model of growth was becoming more difficult to follow in the 1920s. Argentina did not restore the convertibility of the *peso* until 1927, and gold outflows forced its suspension in December 1929. The British relationship with Brazil in the 1920s, although centred on different issues, coffee and public finance, confirms these points.

While New York became a significant source of finance for Brazil in the 1920s, London remained more important than it did for Argentina because the US Commerce Department opposed loans to support coffee valorisation on the grounds that they contravened antitrust legislation. However, borrowing in London was nothing like as straightforward as it had been before 1914, partly due to the Bank of England's restrictions, but also because Rothschilds, the Brazilian government's traditional bankers, distrusted intervention in the coffee market and the apparent laxity of monetary and fiscal policy in Brazil. Only between 1926 and 1929, after two years of strongly deflationary policies, did Brazilians obtain reasonable access to the London capital market, and then because coffee intervention had become the responsibility of the state of São Paulo rather than the federal government and Lazards were prepared to conduct this business. At other times Brazil could borrow only by relinquishing some control over policy-making, and for different reasons both London and New York barred individual loan issues.

This potential loss of autonomy had already become clear in the 1908 Valorisation Scheme and the 1898 and 1914 Funding Loans (see pp. 161–2 and 165–6). For the Third Valorisation Scheme, in 1921–22, the federal government borrowed £9 million through a consortium of Rothschilds, Schroders and Barings, who floated the loan in London and New York and again assumed control over coffee stocks. Topik describes the terms as 'onerous' on account of the storage and commission charges the government paid and the restrictions placed on its use of receipts from coffee, which prevented it from redeeming some of its earlier loans.[51] A request to Rothschilds in 1923 for £25 million to convert the floating debt and strengthen the Banco do Brasil resulted in the despatch of the Montagu Mission to advise on financial reorganisation in Brazil. Yet by the time Montagu reported on Brazil's good faith in reforming the budget, selling public companies, and making the Banco do Brasil independent of government, the Bank of England prohibition on foreign lending was in full force. Two years later the Foreign Office stopped Rothschilds issuing a loan because of a conflict with Brazil at the League of Nations (though Brazil managed to raise the money in New York). Finally, in 1929 Lazards pulled out from financing São Paulo's Institute for the Permanent Defence of Coffee and coffee prices collapsed. Although São Paulo raised a nominal £20 million through Rothschilds and Schroders in April 1930 (£8 million of which was placed in London), the loan was poorly subscribed and undertaken only on condition that Brazil would abandon attempts to support coffee prices.[52] As in Argentina, therefore, the export economy was already deep in trouble before the Wall Street Crash, in part because of the difficulties of obtaining the foreign capital on which it had come to depend. Moreover, the Brazilian experience in the 1920s had also shown the extent to which the London merchant banks would demand greater rights to intervene in policy-making.

CONCLUSION

In retrospect it is clear that contemporaries did not fully appreciate the problems which the First World War exposed or accelerated. Yet these had enormous implications for the relationship between Britain and Latin America. British trade with Latin America exhibited to an even greater degree the problems of dependence on older technologies, the uncompetitiveness of exports, and the failures of marketing which had become evident before 1914. In addition London had lost its position as the world's premier financial centre, a serious development in view of the extent to which Britain's economic role in Latin America had come to depend on its ability to invest. In Latin America itself the war exposed the disadvantages of dependence on foreign commercial credit, on long-term loans, on foreign shipping and on foreign imports, all of which were either supplied by Britain or open to disruption by Britain.

By 1929 the decline of British influence in Latin America was evident: the United States had captured markets and become the principal source of foreign investment. In Mexico, Central America and the west coast of South America the United States seemed clearly dominant by 1929. Yet the British did not regard their position as totally irretrievable, and they certainly did not see the extension of US hegemony to Argentina and Brazil, where their role remained substantial, as inevitable. British officials, while frequently critical of businessmen, still had some confidence in a recovery. City financiers railed against the Bank of England's restrictions on lending, which deprived them of commissions while having (in their view) little effect on the British balance of payments, and they tried to maintain their contacts with Latin America through the early years of the Depression. The returns on investment were still relatively high at the end of the 1920s; many railways and public utilities were recording record profits, and both the commercial banks and oil interests were also returning impressive dividends. Moreover, many Latin Americans, especially in Argentina and Brazil, had begun to show some fear about increasing US penetration of their economies, and welcomed British investment as a potential counterweight (this is perhaps the main explanation for Yrigoyen's attitude to d'Abernon). Both Argentina and Brazil also turned to Sir Otto Niemeyer, a senior Bank of England official, for financial advice in the early 1930s.

With hindsight, however, it seems clear that the problems arising from the British presence became more acute for Latin America in the 1920s. Brazil, in particular, had found that its need for the merchant bankers' goodwill imposed constraints on policy-making. Argentina and Uruguay were concerned about their growing dependence on the British market. Governments were squeezed between London capitalists and the domestic opposition over issues like the labour and tariff policies of railways, public utilities, oil and mining companies, and the conditions attached to loans. The growth of nationalism, together with British investors' almost total incomprehension of the reasons for it, created the potential for major conflicts as the world economic situation became more difficult and Britain's relative decline more terminal.

REFERENCES

1. Albert, *South America and the First World War*, p. 37.
2. Barnett, *British Food Policy*, pp. xiv and 3.
3. Barnett, *British Food Policy*, pp. 33–4; Gravil, *Anglo-Argentine Connection*, p. 130.
4. Albert, *South America and the First World War*, p. 67; Gravil, *Anglo-Argentine Connection*, pp. 124–6.
5. Couyoumdjian, 'El mercado de salitre', 22.
6. Barnett, *British Food Policy*, pp. 69–71.
7. Gravil, *Anglo-Argentine Connection*, p. 134.
8. Frank, *Latin America*, pp. 9–10; Véliz, *Centralist Tradition*, p. 256.
9. Bunge, *Los problemas económicos*, p. 341; Lavalle, *La Gran Guerra*, pp. 33–4.
10. Sir Francis Elliott, quoted in Albert, *South America and the First World War*, p. 82.
11. Kindleberger, *Financial History*, p. 296.
12. Ziegler, *Sixth Great Power*, p. 349; Marichal, *Century of Debt Crises*, pp. 251–6; Wynne, *State Insolvency*, pp. 183–4; Fritsch, *External Constraints*, p. 67.
13. RIIA, *Problem of International Investment*, p. 146; Marichal, *Century of Debt Crises*, p. 182.
14. Sir Otto Niemeyer, quoted in Moggridge, 'British Controls', 121.
15. Thorp and Bertram, *Peru, 1890–1977*, p. 97.
16. Philip, *Oil and Politics*, pp. 16–17; Brown, 'Why Foreign Oil Companies', 365–71.
17. Philip, *Oil and Politics*, p. 17; McBeth, *British Oil Policy*, p. 87.
18. RIIA, *Problem of International Investment*, pp. 142 and 303.
19. Mitchell, *International Historical Statistics*, pp. 552 and 593–6.
20. Redford, *Manchester Merchants*, p. 226.
21. Manchester, *British Pre-Eminence*, p. 335.
22. Minute by W. Burbury on Bentinck to Chamberlain, 28 February 1929, FO 371/13507/A2406 (PRO). Emphasis in original.
23. DOT Advisory Committee, 'German Credits Abroad', Paper 130A, BT 90/22 (PRO).

24. RIIA, *Problem of International Investment*, p. 93.
25. 'Report on the Visit to Brazil of Mr Chipperfield, September–October 1930', Overseas Committee Papers, Brazil no. 5, Unilever archives.
26. Overseas Trade Development Council, *Report of the Sheffield Industrial Mission*, p. 14.
27. DOT, *Report of the British Economic Mission*, p. 6.
28. DOT Advisory Committee, 'British Naval, Military and Air Representation in South America', Paper 102, BT 90/19 (PRO).
29. DOT Advisory Committee, 'Measures for Promoting British Trade', Paper 88, BT 90/18 (PRO); 'British Naval, Military and Air Representation', Paper 102, BT 90/19 (PRO).
30. DOT, *Report of the British Economic Mission*, p. 7.
31. Turner, *Oil Companies*, p. 31.
32. Thorp (ed.), *Latin America in the 1930s*, pp. 4–6; O'Connell, 'Argentina into the Depression', 190.
33. Skupch, 'El deterioro y fin', 73.
34. Sir Malcolm Robertson quoted in García Heras, 'Hostage Private Companies', 57.
35. Turner, *Oil Companies*, p. 86.
36. Philip, *Oil and Politics*, p. 23.
37. Philip, *Oil and Politics*, p. 224.
38. Quoted in Philip, *Oil and Politics*, p. 225.
39. Quoted in Philip, *Oil and Politics*, p. 207.
40. Philip, *Oil and Politics*, p. 16; Miller, 'Small Business', 404.
41. Philip, *Oil and Politics*, p. 12.
42. Skupch, 'Las consecuencias', 121.
43. O'Connell, 'Free Trade', p. 76.
44. Rock, *Politics in Argentina*, pp. 135–6.
45. Skupch, 'Las consecuencias', 124–5.
46. Skupch, 'Las consecuencias', 134.
47. O'Connell, 'Argentina into the Depression', 190 and 214.
48. Smith, *Politics and Beef*, p. 103; Gravil, 'State Intervention', 159–61.
49. D'Abernon quoted in Villanueva, 'Economic Development', 61; Robertson quoted in both Gravil, 'Anglo-US Trade Rivalry', 59–60, and Goodwin, 'Anglo-Argentine Commercial Relations', 38–9.
50. Gravil, 'Anglo-US Trade Rivalry', 62.
51. Topik, *Political Economy*, p. 75; Fritsch, *External Constraints*, pp. 67–8.
52. Fritsch, *External Constraints*, pp. 155–7.

CHAPTER NINE

The Loss of British Influence: the Great Depression and the Second World War

When the Wall Street Crash occurred in October 1929 many Latin American countries were already facing problems due to falling export prices and difficulties in obtaining foreign loans. Most governments responded to the crash by pursuing orthodox deflationary policies, in the hope that after a short recession investment and trade would soon resume their normal pattern, but the depression became much deeper than anyone expected. A financial crisis spread through Europe, culminating in Britain's decision to abandon the Gold Standard in September 1931. Trade declined further. In Chile, the worst-hit country, the value of exports had fallen to one-sixth of the 1929 level by 1932; Argentina's exports fell by over 60 per cent in the same period.[1]

On both sides of the Atlantic governments began to introduce less orthodox policies. Britain abandoned free trade and moved towards Imperial Preference. The Ottawa agreements of 1932 gave the Dominions priority in supplying the British market for foodstuffs, especially meat. In Latin America the burden of interest payments on the foreign debt increased as export income and government revenues both declined. Between 1931 and 1934 every government except for Argentina, Cuba, Honduras and Venezuela defaulted at least partially on its sterling loans. Import duties were raised, and many countries also began to take control over the allocation of the foreign exchange their exports earned. These changes finally undermined the unhindered flows of trade and finance on which Britain's links with Latin America had depended for over a century, forcing the British government to restructure its relationship with the leading Latin American countries.

While Latin America's trade revived later in the 1930s, there was little reason for optimism in London. Exports remained depressed. They had lost ground to the United States, Germany, Italy and Japan in every country except Argentina. Commercial intermediaries like the merchant houses and shipping lines were struggling, while the Bank of England had had to mount an expensive rescue operation for the Anglo-South American Bank, which had over-committed itself to the support of the Chilean nitrate industry. As road transport increased, the railway and tramway companies were losing what remained of their profitability.

The problems for Britain became even more acute in the two years before war broke out in September 1939. Brazil suspended payments on its external debt in November 1937. Four months later, Mexico expropriated the foreign oil companies, stimulating fears that Venezuela might do likewise. Relationships between the Argentine government and the railway and utility companies deteriorated sharply. Throughout the region, it seemed, a wave of nationalism threatened to engulf British interests in bitter conflicts. The Second World War inevitably accelerated the demise of British influence, despite some desperate attempts to limit the long-term damage. Paradoxically, though, developments during the war did permit the British to withdraw from the region in the late 1940s with considerably less acrimony than had appeared likely in 1938–39.

For Latin American governments the legacies of the position the British had built up before 1914 created enormous problems in the 1930s and 1940s. The nineteenth-century commercial treaties, which effectively prevented them negotiating bilateral trading concessions with other countries, were no longer viable, yet replacing them was difficult. Uncertainties about the future role of the City as a source of finance complicated decisions about the external debt. The railways and utilities still offered vital services, but they were not reinvesting and acted in a quite recalcitrant manner on issues like tariffs, taxation, access to foreign exchange, employment and social security policies. Many still had a mainly British managerial staff (creating potential problems if they were nationalised) and often paid more in taxes in Britain than in Latin America. Export sales to Britain during the 1940s appeared simply to create more problems, since Britain could not afford to pay in convertible currency or supply the capital goods and industrial inputs Latin American countries needed. By the early 1950s, however, trade and investment links with Britain had become insignificant, and the policies of British companies and governments had for the most part become marginal to Latin American affairs.

TRADE AND INVESTMENT IN THE 1930s

British trade with Latin America

The policies adopted on each side of the Atlantic in the early 1930s placed new obstacles in the way of trade. The British decisions to float the pound, abandon free trade, and offer preferential treatment to imperial producers had serious implications for countries like Argentina, Uruguay and Peru, which still sold a significant proportion of their exports to the United Kingdom (see Table 8.3). The agreements made at the Imperial Conference in Ottawa in 1932, where the Board of Trade came under enormous pressure from the Dominions, particularly, threatened access to the British market for Latin American products. While the meat trade, where Britain was forced to impose quotas on supplies from outside the empire, was the immediate problem, there were fears that products like wool, wheat, maize and sugar might also soon face restrictions.

Policy changes in Latin America also threatened British exporters. Tariff increases, import substitution and exchange controls all undermined trade. In Chile, for example, import duties were increased by 20 to 35 per cent in March 1931. This helped textile output to grow by 30 per cent annually in the early 1930s; by 1935 Chilean factories were supplying 77 per cent of the textiles consumed in the country and 60 per cent of demand for metal products, machinery and transport equipment.[2] In Argentina the government introduced exchange controls, which discriminated against non-essential imports, in October 1931, and imposed a 10 per cent surcharge on import duties in November 1932. Brazil announced exchange controls in September 1931, and under pressure from domestic industrial interests began to restrict imports by the use of quotas.

The measures taken to deal with the crisis thus undermined the system of trade and payments which had been dominant before 1930. British investors could no longer be certain of being able to repatriate profits, while exporters might face problems in obtaining payment. The introduction of Imperial Preference threatened Latin American countries' willingness to retain commercial treaties based on the 'most favoured nation' (MFN) clause, which had formed the foundation for commercial relations since the mid nineteenth century. Under pressure from domestic agricultural and industrial interests, many governments sought the freedom to negotiate reciprocal agreements with others. During the 1930s Peru, Colombia and Venezuela all demanded the abrogation of the existing treaties. Britain, on the

Britain and Latin America in the Nineteenth and Twentieth Centuries

other hand, needed to maintain MFN access for its own exports to these countries as far as possible. Brazil, which remained a significant market, presented a slightly different problem, for it had had no commercial treaty with Britain since 1844 (see p. 53). Yet while Britain obtained from Brazil a guarantee of MFN status in September 1931 (reaffirmed in August 1936), Britain's exports there still declined. Successful trade depended also on the ability to secure payment relatively quickly, and this in turn varied according to Britain's ability to offer a market to Latin American producers.

Table 9.1 British balance of visible trade with individual Latin American countries, 1928–1933 (£000)

	1928	*1929*	*1930*	*1931*	*1932*	*1933*
Argentina	−42884	−51130	−29480	−35828	−38006	−27484
Brazil	+11892	+6592	+456	−1316	+993	+1725
Chile	−2317	+491	+221	−1347	−2518	−1581
Uruguay	−3605	−1674	−3524	−2958	−1301	−1632
Peru	−4207	−3875	−2526	−2648	−3484	−3588
Venezuela	+1945	+2124	+894	+315	+633	+743
Colombia	+1488	+1268	+256	+668	+1267	+1312
Mexico	+505	−34	−316	−1340	−1195	−1035

Notes: These figures are subject to the normal reservations about customs authorities' ability to identify the direction of trade accurately.

Since these are figures for 'visible' trade, they do not include 'invisibles' such as freight and insurance charges, the repatriated profits of British companies, and the interest payments on Latin American public debt. These would reduce the negative balances and increase the positive ones.

The Venezuelan figures do not take account of British imports of Venezuelan oil refined in the Dutch West Indies.

Source: 'Annual Statements of Trade and Navigation'

This is probably the key to explaining commercial trends in the 1930s. The overall importance of the British market, its significance to particular groups of influential producers, and the balance of trade with individual countries (shown in Table 9.1) all became critical. In general, Britain possessed little leverage where its balance of trade was positive, and it depended on Latin American governments not pushing matters to a climax. In such cases British diplomats tried to maintain MFN status while prevaricating, often quite successfully, on negotiations for a new treaty. Where Britain offered one of the few markets which remained open to exporters, such as cattle producers in Argentina and Uruguay or sugar planters in Peru, its potential leverage was greater. In such instances Imperial Preference permitted the British to obtain guarantees about the level of import duties, commitments to purchase in the United Kingdom, and assurances about the equitable treatment of British companies and the supply of foreign exchange.

There are several indications that Latin American exports to Britain diminished in significance for both sides in the 1930s. First, the proportion of Britain's imports supplied by Latin America fell, from 11 per cent in 1929 to less than 8 per cent in 1938.[3] Second, the total value of Britain's imports from Latin America, as Table 9.2 shows, dropped in the 1930s. Third, the share of exports taken by Britain was either stagnant, in the cases of Argentina and Uruguay, or in decline, in Chile and Peru (see Table 8.3). Statistics for Brazil are difficult due to the problems of valuing its compensation trade with Germany, but the crude figures suggest that the proportion of Brazil's exports taken by Britain hovered around 9 per cent until the war.[4]

Britain's own export performance was disappointing. The volume rarely rose much above half its 1928–29 level (see Table 8.1), and dependence on the Argentine market grew (Table 8.2). By 1938 Britain supplied only 13 per cent of Latin America's imports, compared with about a quarter in 1913.[5] An official report in March 1939 complained that Britain had not obtained its proper share of 'an expanding market', despite the huge investments it still possessed in Latin America.[6] Competition was intense, particularly from the United States, Germany, Italy and Japan. The United States gained from its more modern and efficient industries and the support of the Export-Import Bank. German trade benefited from government subsidies and the system of bilateral trade adopted in 1934, under which Latin American countries sold exports to Germany for inconvertible *askimarks* which were then used to purchase industrial goods. This guaranteed prompt payment for German exporters and made it easier for them to offer credit to Latin American importers. It particularly harmed British trade with Brazil. By 1938 Germany was supplying 20 per cent of Brazil's imports, Britain only 11 per cent.[7] Italy's trade also increased, while Japanese textiles made inroads into markets like Peru's which the British had formerly shared with domestic firms.

British exporters faced enormous problems. Wherever Britain did not offer a good market for Latin American products, shortages of sterling caused delays in payment. Exporters often had to wait

Table 9.2 British imports from Latin America, 1920–1938 (£000)

£000	1920	1925	1928	1930	1932	1935	1938
Argentina	121918 (59.4%)	64687 (52.4%)	74094 (58.6%)	54714 (55.6%)	48666 (63.9%)	42282 (57.6%)	37004 (52.3%)
Brazil	8064 (3.9%)	4768 (3.9%)	4142 (3.3%)	7514 (7.6%)	3686 (4.8%)	6758 (9.2%)	7421 (10.5%)
Chile	10345 (5.0%)	10980 (8.9%)	7445 (5.9%)	5742 (5.8%)	3181 (4.2%)	3994 (5.4%)	5254 (7.4%)
Peru	14230 (6.9%)	7979 (6.5%)	6161 (4.9%)	3969 (4.0%)	4212 (5.5%)	3427 (4.7%)	3285 (4.6%)
Uruguay	6029 (2.9%)	4731 (3.8%)	6711 (5.3%)	7102 (7.2%)	2802 (3.7%)	3332 (4.5%)	3852 (5.4%)
Bolivia and Paraguay	1671 (0.8%)	5449 (4.4%)	7349 (5.8%)	3491 (3.5%)	1887 (2.5%)	3547 (4.8%)	3257 (4.6%)
Colombia, Venezuela, Ecuador	4138 (2.0%)	3009 (2.4%)	2519 (2.0%)	2191 (2.2%)	710 (0.9%)	1109 (1.5%)	1752 (2.5%)
Central America	1110 (0.5%)	3260 (2.6%)	2878 (2.3%)	2223 (2.3%)	1709 (2.2%)	689 (0.9%)	715 (1.0%)
Hispanic Caribbean	26073 (12.7%)	13661 (11.1%)	12791 (10.1%)	8711 (8.9%)	7046 (9.2%)	5222 (7.1%)	6249 (8.8%)
Mexico	11779 (5.7%)	4958 (4.0%)	2295 (1.8%)	2749 (2.8%)	2284 (3.0%)	2990 (4.1%)	1954 (2.8%)
Total	**205357**	**123482**	**126385**	**98406**	**76183**	**73350**	**70743**

Notes: These are figures for *retained* imports only.

These figures are subject to the usual provisos about customs officials' ability to identify accurately the source of imports. Particular problems arise in the case of imports of Venezuelan oil, since this was normally refined in the Dutch West Indies and entered in the British statistics as originating there.

Source: 'Annual Statements of Trade and Navigation'

months for the Brazilian government, for example, to sanction foreign exchange remittances. The scale of British investments actually became a hindrance. In Uruguay and Argentina company remittances took priority over non-essential imports in the allocation of foreign exchange. Underlying these problems, however, were the old ones of high prices, inadequate credit, inefficient marketing and unsuitable products. Manufacturing firms seemed unable to take advantage even in those countries where Britain managed to negotiate favourable concessions on exchange or tariffs. 'The attitude of British exporters is apathetic,' the 1939 report concluded with regard to Peru.[8] In Brazil, where the loss of British influence in the 1930s was particularly acute, the prevailing gloom was summarised by Rothschilds' representative in May 1939: 'What are we, the British, doing? Nothing! Just sitting back with inertia allowing our prestige and past performance in all affairs here to fade away.'[9]

Investment in the 1930s

The defaults on existing government loans would have stopped much British lending to Latin America even without the informal controls which the British authorities reintroduced in 1930. After 1934 there was some relaxation: the Treasury permitted foreign governments to refund debts at lower rates of interest, and to issue new loans if they would benefit British industry. The major Latin American beneficiary was Argentina, which converted £13 million of debt between June and December 1934.[10] New British investment came not through the Stock Exchange but from the reinvestment of earnings by multinational companies, and like the 1920s this was concentrated in petroleum and manufacturing. Mexican Eagle discovered a major new oilfield at Poza Rica in 1932, which helped to reverse the decline in the country's petroleum output, and in Venezuela Royal Dutch-Shell cooperated with Jersey Standard to purchase Gulf Oil's operations in 1937–38. Several leading industrial companies, including Pilkington, ICI, Unilever and Glaxo, established or substantially expanded manufacturing operations, especially in Argentina and Brazil.

Returns on the older investments fell off. By the end of 1934 almost 60 per cent of the South American securities quoted on the Stock Exchange were receiving no interest, and the average return had fallen to only 1.6 per cent.[11] One reason for this was default by national, state and municipal governments, and attempts to persuade them to recommence payments became a priority in negotiations.

211

The profitability of the transport companies, especially the railways, also collapsed. Pedro Skupch estimates that the proportion of the stocks and debentures of the British-owned railways in Argentina not receiving dividends or interest rose from an average of 2 per cent in 1925–29 to 41 per cent in 1930–34 and 57 per cent in 1935–39. Average returns on these investments fell from 5.3 per cent in the late 1920s to 1.7 per cent a decade later.[12]

The transport companies faced numerous economic and political problems. Apart from the depression of trade in the early 1930s, road construction, often encouraged by governments anxious to relieve unemployment, seriously eroded their business. On long journeys trucks tended to cream off the more valuable traffic, which the railways had previously used to cross-subsidise bulk freights like fuel, minerals or grain. In the cities competition from buses ate into the profitability of suburban railways and tramways. Disputes with governments grew in intensity. Many companies requested increases in fares and freight rates to counteract the depreciation of Latin American currencies which eroded the sterling value of their income, but governments found it politically difficult to accede to their demands during a recession. They often also prevented the companies from cutting wages or dismissing staff to reduce costs; indeed, new social security legislation increased them. Exchange controls further hindered the transport firms' ability to repatriate the profits they did make, creating problems with debenture-holders, bankers and the British tax authorities.

Political attacks on the railway and tramway companies mounted. Their attempts to surcharge tariffs always aroused antagonism, and their financial problems led them into conflicts with their workforces over wage levels and social security payments. At a time of growing nationalism they became symbols of the foreign presence and vulnerable to physical attack. In Buenos Aires a bus-drivers' strike in 1936 began with bombs outside the British embassy and main railway stations and continued with attacks on trams and trains. Often the companies themselves exacerbated the tensions. The psychological distance between directors in London and their customers and workers in Latin America, together with their employment of powerful members of the oligarchy as advisors, antagonised the press and public. Injudicious remarks – a director of the Buenos Ayres and Pacific complained publicly in 1935 that President Justo was 'disloyal' to his 'British friends' – alienated governments while providing further fuel for the opposition.[13]

Because of their uncompromising and insensitive attitude the transport companies found themselves isolated from other British interests. 'Local managers or directors . . .,' the *Buenos Aires Herald* complained in 1936 with the Anglo–Argentine Tramways in mind, 'have engaged in manipulations which have not deceived Argentine onlookers, but which have provided centavos of profit today, and a wagon-load of mischief for tomorrow.'[14] They also failed to attract much practical support from the Foreign Office, which charged them with making peremptory and unrealistic demands, and marginalised them from more important negotiations over trade and the public debt. 'It is essential,' one minister commented in 1938 with regard to the railways, 'not to create in the Argentine that feeling of extreme hostility to foreign interests which has produced so disastrous a position in Mexico.'[15]

While several diplomats had been sceptical of some of the activities of British companies operating in Latin America for a long time, it was Mexico's expropriation of the oil firms in March 1938 which really brought home the threat posed by the failure to understand economic and political nationalism in Latin America. Disputes between the British and US oil firms and successive Mexican administrations over the companies' concessions, taxation and labour relations had begun during the revolutionary decade of the 1910s. Then, in the mid 1920s, the oil companies had taken a hard line towards President Calles' attempts to implement Article 27 of the 1917 constitution, which vested ownership of the subsoil in the Mexican state, and to renegotiate their concessions. This dispute was settled only by US Ambassador Morrow's refusal to support their intransigent attitude. Yet it was not a conflict over concessions or taxation which finally led to expropriation, for Mexican Eagle had successfully concluded negotiations to exploit the Poza Rica field in November 1937, just four months before. The nationalisation decree was precipitated instead by the oil companies' refusal to accept the award of wage increases by the official commission arbitrating a long-running labour dispute. Again, the distancing of London businessmen from events in Latin America played an important part. British diplomats and local managers in Mexico City had both urged Mexican Eagle and Shell to compromise, but without success.

The Mexican expropriation came at a critical moment in the deteriorating international situation. Britain broke off diplomatic relations with Mexico, which, faced with a boycott by the major companies, began to export oil to Germany. The real fear, though, was that Mexico would offer an example to Venezuela, which accounted for about one-third of Shell's global production and supplied about 40 per cent of Britain's oil.[16] The growth of economic nationalism after the death of President Gómez in 1935, opposition attacks, and the government's desire to increase taxes on the industry all threatened British interests there, and the companies' response, in the eyes of the Foreign Office, was a potentially disastrous one: a tendency to 'haggle and bicker' with the government, and continual attempts to defer problems by making advance payments of taxes. The Venezuelans, with a massive output, few refining facilities and a tiny local market, would have found expropriation more difficult than Mexico, but they did eventually succeed in increasing taxation as the British and US governments, fearful of antagonising them, pressurised Shell and Standard Oil to accept a settlement. The Foreign Secretary, for example, urged Shell in 1942 to 'accept additional burdens with good grace'.[17] A further incentive for agreement was that Shell's concessions, which predated the laws of the 1920s and 1930s, were shortly due to expire. In 1943, therefore, the companies agreed in principle to an equal division of profits between themselves and the Venezuelan government.

All these cases suggest that the problems for those British firms most exposed to the growth of nationalism were becoming acute. As pressure from both their workers and host governments increased, they found that the traditional methods of deflecting criticism, particularly their alliances with influential local politicians, lost their usefulness and might indeed further damage their interests. Much to the companies' surprise, too, many British officials were unwilling to offer them much support, since they began to regard firms like the railways and public utilities as impediments to Britain's future relations with Latin America.

British government policy in the 1930s

The restructuring of trade, defaults on government loans, and the problems of British companies all forced the government into a much-enhanced role in Latin American affairs in the 1930s. Essentially, however, its response was pragmatic and short term. In part this was due to the rapidity of change, but it was also because several different departments, each with their own priorities, had interests in Latin America. Besides the Foreign Office, all negotiations involved the Treasury and Board of Trade, and some the Dominions Office, Petroleum Department and Ministry of Agriculture as well. Yet while there was little sense of a long-term strategy regarding relations with

Latin America in the 1930s there were some fairly consistent features underlying the British government's response.

First, Latin America became subservient to imperial considerations. As Joseph Tulchin rightly states with regard to the Ottawa Conference: 'Sentiments of loyalty to the informal empire and a long tradition of responsibility, even several hundred millions of investment, did not keep Great Britain from sacrificing Argentine interests on the altar of imperial preference.'[18] Second, within Latin America Argentina took precedence, to the detriment of interests elsewhere. Third, British priorities were headed by financial rather than commercial considerations, in particular the need for interest payments on loans and profit remittances. However, this did not extend, except perhaps in oil, to an unquestioning defence of British firms. If the host government's actions were legitimate and the companies had acted unilaterally, appealing for diplomatic aid only as a last resort, they attracted little sympathy. Complaints about the underhand and ill-considered behaviour of the transport and meat companies are scattered through Foreign Office archives. The belief began to grow that it might be better to sacrifice some investment interests. 'The Americans have long adopted,' Victor Perowne, the head of the South American department in the Foreign Office, stated in 1942, 'the principle of sacrificing US vested interests abroad whenever they conflicted with trading, and I think that they are right. From the political point of view we have, I think, practically everything to gain by freeing ourselves from the inconveniences which these public utility companies represent.'[19] The intransigence of the oil companies also clearly annoyed the Foreign Office in the 1930s, but they attracted more support. What made them different was their strategic importance and the fact that in both Mexico and Venezuela they were the principal British interests rather than part of a more complex mosaic.

Outside the River Plate Britain retained relatively little political influence by 1939. Stanley Hilton notes that Britain could do little about German compensation trade in Brazil without US support (which for strategic reasons was not forthcoming) and talks of 'the political indispensability [for London] of maintaining Washington's goodwill'.[20] The same applied to British policy in Mexico. The rupture of diplomatic relations in 1938 proved an empty gesture without US participation. Almost certainly Mexican Eagle misjudged the backing Washington would give to its own oil firms. Everywhere, except the River Plate, British interests attempted to shelter behind Roosevelt's 'Good Neighbor' policy, without fully realising that it depended in part on a distancing between the US administration and business which was reflected in Washington's distrust of financial interests and oil companies. Moreover, the maintenance of British interests in Latin America ran counter to the long-term objectives of US policy, in particular the desire to restore multilateral trading arrangements (which Britain's agreements with Argentina impeded), and to limit European interests in the western hemisphere and bring it more fully under US hegemony.

ARGENTINA, BRAZIL AND BRITAIN IN THE 1930s

Argentina

Argentina, the d'Abernon Mission's report in 1930 had stated, 'has a special position in relation to Great Britain for which no exact parallel exists outside the British empire. . . . The two countries are economically bound to each other in a quite peculiar fashion.'[21] It identified three elements in this relationship: Argentine dependence on the British consumer; British dependence on Argentine foodstuffs and raw materials; and the scale of British investment in Argentina. It might have added that for many exporters Argentina was one of their largest markets. Both sides considered the relationship unique. Comments like that of Sir Malcolm Robertson, the British ambassador, that 'Argentina must be regarded as an essential part of the British Empire' found echoes within the country's elite, even though many were critical of the precise terms of the links with Britain.[22]

The problem for Argentina was that within the empire power lay with the Dominions, supported by a considerable part of the British press. Australia, Canada, South Africa and New Zealand all saw Argentine exports as a threat to their own. Although the British delegates at the Ottawa Conference in 1932 did succeed in defeating the Australians' demand for duties on 'foreign' (Argentine) meat, they could not appease Australia, which the Treasury feared might default on its debt, without agreeing to quotas on imports from outside the empire. The priorities of other government departments prevailed over the Foreign Office's fears for the future of the Anglo-Argentine relationship.

These developments spurred the Argentines into the negotiations which culminated in the Roca-Runciman Pact of 1933. Britain was the only major meat importer in the world, its market was saturated, the Argentines had failed to regain access to the US market, and the prevailing pessimism about the spread of protectionism led many to believe that British import controls might be extended to wheat, maize and wool. For their part the British sought some guarantees about export markets and the relaxation of exchange controls to permit companies and exporters to make remittances. The Board of Trade also hoped to defend the British meat-packing companies against their North American rivals. While the Ottawa agreements seemed to have given the British the upper hand in dealing with the Argentines, the Foreign Office warned against pushing them too far for fear that this might might result in 'a revolution, the collapse of the currency, hostility towards [British] firms, the imposition of a state monopoly of the meat trade, and the expropriation of British property'.[23]

Daniel Drosdoff comments perceptively that 'the Roca-Runciman treaty, for many people, has been turned into a symbol of the faults of the Argentine economy and society, but not everyone is agreed why'.[24] There are two major problems in evaluating the Roca-Runciman Pact and its related agreements: the range of topics they covered, and the difficulties of isolating and quantifying their effects. Six major issues were involved. First, on meat imports, Britain guaranteed annual purchases of at least 90 per cent of the 390,000 tons of chilled beef shipped from Argentina in the 'Ottawa base year' (July 1931–June 1932).[25] The Dominions would be permitted to make experimental shipments, but Argentina obtained guarantees against further reductions in the quota. Shipments of frozen beef, mutton and lamb were restricted to 65 per cent of the Ottawa year. Britain also undertook not to impose duties on meat imports for three years (the expected duration of the agreement), and not to restrict the entry of wheat, maize and wool. Second, the meat-packers themselves, rather than the Argentines, would control the distribution of the quota; the Board of Trade wished to protect the British firms which had suffered when the cartel had broken down on earlier occasions. Third, Argentina agreed to reduce import duties on 235 widely differentiated articles, and guaranteed that all imports currently free of duties would remain so. However, it retained the 10 per cent tariff surcharge imposed in November 1932 which the Board of Trade had hoped to eliminate. Fourth, the foreign exchange earned by Argentina's exports to Britain, after a reasonable reduction for servicing Argentine bonds (many of which were denominated in dollars), would be placed at the disposal of British interests. Fifth, Argentina promised 'benevolent treatment' for British companies.

Finally, the blocked balances which British firms wished to remit would be freed by a new issue of 4 per cent sterling bonds.[26]

The agreements evoked contrasting reactions. Argentine officials claimed to have achieved important concessions over meat and foreign exchange. If Britain wanted remittances on its investments it would have to provide Argentina with markets. One of them, Raúl Prebisch, stated fifty years later that he could find no evidence that Roca-Runciman had damaged the Argentine economy. The closure of US markets, he argued, left few alternatives. 'What else could have been done. . . ?', he asked his critics. 'Nothing, except to complain and keep complaining.'[27] However, opponents of the Argentine regime criticised the failure to gain control of the meat quotas and the promise of 'benevolent treatment' for British firms. Rodolfo Ghioldi, the Communist leader, spoke for many in claiming that the cattle-breeding oligarchy had betrayed the country.[28]

Historians are also in bitter disagreement. Tulchin, for example, believes that Argentina could not have reversed the British move towards Imperial Preference and that the treaty prevented further restrictions on exports. The tariff and exchange provisions, in his view, did not dilute the Argentine government's power, and the agreement bought time for it to adjust to a changed world.[29] More radical historians, however, have seen the pact as reinforcing British control over the Argentine economy. Pedro Skupch, for example, considered the clauses which limited Argentina's rights to dispose freely of foreign exchange and to distribute the meat quota the most draconian.[30] Roger Gravil and Timothy Rooth claim that the Argentine government adopted an 'abject posture towards Britain', serving the interests of the oligarchy rather than the nation as a whole. As a consequence, they argue, manufacturing industry in Argentina suffered a major setback.[31]

Evaluation of Roca-Runciman thus depends on which aspects each historian chooses to emphasise. On meat, the central issue for the Argentine negotiators, they bought three years' grace for their exports but did little to resolve longer-term problems. The meat-packers had escaped from the control of both governments. An investigation by the Argentine Senate failed to gain access to their books (some of the Anglo's accounts were discovered on board a ship in November 1934 packed and labelled as 'corned beef'). The joint Anglo-Argentine commission on the meat trade established under the Roca-Runciman pact also complained later that the companies had refused to supply it with information. It clearly suspected, though, that the meat-packers had engaged in a considerable degree of transfer pricing, especially in

1932–34, to conceal their income from both governments, and claimed that during the depression they had maintained their profits at the expense of Argentine cattlemen.[32] Moreover, the British government had certainly known in 1933 that the Australians could produce much more chilled beef than the 'experimental shipments' permitted under the treaty, and that they had no mechanism to control meat exports.

On tariffs the Argentine concessions certainly covered an extensive range of goods, but they would have to be granted to other countries under MFN agreements. They probably affected government revenues more than industrial growth. Gravil and Rooth, who make much of the adverse effects of these clauses, themselves present figures showing a near 40 per cent increase in manufacturing output between 1933 and 1938.[33] For British businessmen the more important concessions were those which gave them preference in the allocation of foreign exchange, since this ensured that as long as Britain remained the principal market for Argentine exports they could expect reasonably prompt payment. However, the pact did not prevent Argentina from establishing differential rates for buying and selling sterling, a practice which British interests condemned as 'nothing less than a tax on trade' but which provided the government with the resources to guarantee minimum prices for farmers.[34]

The clauses on 'benevolent treatment' for companies, despite the political storm they aroused, were so vague as to be meaningless. While the transport firms gained marginally from the exchange rate at which their blocked balances were converted, the 'Roca Funding Loan' which permitted them to do so was essential for the stabilisation of the Argentine economy. Without this Argentina could not have controlled foreign exchange markets, converted its internal debt and established its agricultural price support system. Both Peter Alhadeff and Carlos Marichal consider these operations indisputably successful, although in Marichal's view the cost was increased dependence on Britain.[35]

The Roca–Runciman Pact was only a three-year agreement, buying time for both countries without solving the fundamental problems of their relationship. During the 1936 renegotiations Argentina obtained some concessions, including control over the distribution of the meat quota, but at a price. It had to accept further small cuts in exports (5 per cent of the chilled beef quota and 10 per cent of frozen mutton and lamb by 1939) and a $3/4$d per pound import duty.[36] In one sense this was a victory, for the Argentines had known eighteen months earlier that Australia wanted Britain to renounce Roca–Runciman and impose a differential duty of at least one penny per pound immediately. However, the British believed that the new duty would fall on Argentine producers rather than British consumers, and Runciman himself claimed after the 1936 negotiations that he had driven 'a very hard bargain' with Argentina.[37]

These agreements did not resolve all the questions at issue. They largely ignored the transport companies, which wanted greater coordination of transport provision to help them meet the threat of road competition. Superficially the tramways achieved greater concessions on this than the railways. In September 1936 Congress approved an extremely controversial measure to coordinate transport in Buenos Aires under the direction of Anglo-Argentine Tramways, though it remained unimplemented for over two years. The railways obtained little except for some concessions over exchange rates in 1939. The Argentine government continued its road construction programme. Although a National Transport Coordination Act passed Congress in 1937, the British-owned railways obtained only one seat on the seven-member commission, and it did not even begin work until August 1938. The rising level of nationalist protest made it politically impossible for Presidents Justo and Ortiz to offer these firms overt support, even though Ortiz had been a lawyer for the railways. The British government also provided them with little aid and began to favour an agreed nationalisation as a potential solution to the railways' problems.

The history of Anglo-Argentine relations underlines several points about the 1930s. First, as Tulchin states, 'the Foreign Office counted for very little'.[38] The Board of Trade, Dominions Office and Ministry of Agriculture possessed more influence. Second, British objectives were short term. They concentrated on maintaining access to the Argentine market and to the foreign exchange which would permit companies and exporters to repatriate profits. Third, British officials became more wary of supporting unpopular companies. They deliberately marginalised the railways, despite their persistent complaints, in both 1933 and 1936. Finally, in trying to preserve the Anglo-Argentine connexion, which remained vital to Britain's food supplies, the government sacrificed interests everywhere else, except perhaps in Uruguay, which was also dependent on the British market and which signed a trade and payments agreement giving Britain concessions over the allocation of foreign exchange in 1935. However, agreements like Roca-Runciman could not solve the structural weaknesses of British exports, even if they provided some temporary relief. Nor could they resolve the future of the railway and tramway companies.

Brazil

Two central points distinguished Britain's relationship with Brazil from that with Argentina: the insignificance of British markets for Brazil's exports, and the much greater British interest in Brazil's public debt (see pp. 164–6 and 200–1). For most of the interwar period Brazil maintained close connexions with the London merchant banks. Although the Montagu Mission of 1924 did not provide Brazil immediately with the loans it desired, it illustrated Brazil's willingness to listen to British advisors and helped to reinforce the policies of monetary orthodoxy which became dominant in the mid-1920s. After the Wall Street Crash Brazil again obtained short-term finance from Rothschilds and turned to British advisors. Sir Otto Niemeyer, a senior Bank of England official, headed a new financial mission which spent the first half of 1931 there.

Accounts of Anglo-Brazilian relations in the 1930s are dominated by the public debt. While President Vargas, who came to power in October 1930, quietly ignored many of Niemeyer's highly orthodox recommendations, which included balancing the budget and establishing a proper central bank, the hope that London financiers might consider further loans probably secured for the British a greater income from their investments in Brazil than appears justified now. When Vargas suspended amortisation and interest payments on much of the foreign debt in September 1931, he excluded the Funding Loans of 1898 and 1914 and gave those bondholders a gold guarantee (which protected them against the devaluation of sterling) in return for their agreement to further funding operations. In 1934, in another renegotiation with the bankers, Brazil accepted a new plan, apparently conceived by Niemeyer who was returning via Rio from a mission to establish a central bank in Argentina. This involved categorising the foreign debt into seven classes, with the 1898 and 1914 Funding Loans and the São Paulo coffee loans, which were mostly held in Britain, in the top two categories. British fears that the Roca-Runciman agreements and Britain's insignificance as a market might persuade the Brazilian government to give US creditors preference in the payment of blocked commercial balances also proved unfounded. A further agreement in March 1935 guaranteed British interests equal access to foreign exchange.

Niemeyer attracted criticism for several reasons. The British ambassador complained in 1932 that the bankers were not concerned about other British interests. 'Both they [Rothschilds' representatives] and Niemeyer,' he stated, 'have their eyes solely on finance, not on trade.'[39] The City criticised him in 1934 for favouring Rothschilds over Lazards, the bankers for the São Paulo coffee loans. In essence, though, the British position was weakening. Even in the early 1930s it depended on the United States not using its leverage as Brazil's leading export market to demand concessions, in contrast to Britain's own policy in Argentina. Then, as Germany offered a market for cacao, cotton and fruit after 1934, Britain lost more influence. In 1937 Brazil correctly deduced that the United States would not take reprisals against default for fear of pushing Brazil towards Germany and that Britain could no longer offer new finance. It therefore suspended all debt payments while revising exchange controls to give a lower priority to the private remittances of foreign companies, leaving the British with little.

The Brazilian experience illustrates several points. Under Treasury and Bank of England influence, the British government gave financial returns a higher priority than trade, but even those had disappeared by the end of the decade. Britain was weak in countries like Brazil where it did not offer much of a market, unless there was the possibility of further loans. It also relied upon the forbearance of the United States. While the US government's lack of support for its financial interests initially helped the British to obtain returns on their loans, in the end the lack of US support harmed them, since they were quite unable to apply pressure by themselves.

THE SECOND WORLD WAR

Economic relations during the war

The British government acted rapidly to assert its authority in September 1939. It quickly established exchange controls, a Black List, shipping regulations and purchasing boards. It persuaded the oil companies to finance Venezuelan coastal defence works in order to protect its most important source of petroleum and sent ships to defend vital sea lanes. Funds were allocated to propaganda and publicity campaigns, while the intelligence services took counter-measures against German espionage networks in Latin America and commenced subversive activities of their own.

Latin America's fundamental importance to Britain was again as a supplier of foodstuffs and essential raw materials, but besides securing their own needs the British had to make some pre-emptive purchases to prevent strategic commodities reaching the Axis powers.

Almost immediately the war began they negotiated contracts for the supply of meat and grain with Argentina. Other countries, however, suffered from the suspension of British purchases of their exports, since the government did not perceive any immediate need (either for themselves or for the Axis) for the nitrates, copper and wool that countries like Chile and Uruguay normally supplied. This had significant implications. Without sterling from export sales Latin American countries had less capacity to pay interest on their debts. It also threatened Britain's future trade and investment in the region. 'We may well wake up,' Perowne warned, 'to find our whole position in South America so affected by this concatenation of circumstances that it will never recover.'[40]

Britain's attitude towards Latin America during the war was dominated by pragmatic considerations, the need to obtain supplies and defer payment for them, and later maintaining and strengthening the Anglo-American alliance. However, the decisions taken for short-term reasons had significant consequences in the longer term, both for the Latin American countries themselves and for Britain's role in the region. Britain could not permit the unrestricted conversion of sterling into dollars or pay high interest on sterling deposits in London. During 1939–40 the Bank of England therefore negotiated new payments agreements with many Latin American central banks, under which the sterling earned from exports to Britain would accumulate in 'Special Accounts' in London, from which it could be drawn to pay for British goods, interest payments and company remittances. In effect the Special Accounts (which paid little or no interest) meant that Latin Americans were subsidising the British war effort by not claiming the surpluses on their sales there and forgoing both the market interest rate on them and the right to convert pounds into dollars. At the same time they were expected by Britain to pay the full interest on their own sterling loans. However, deferred payments might be better than no sales at all, and in order to receive some income on its investments Britain would have to ensure that it purchased some Latin American exports. Moreover, the fall of France in May 1940 strengthened the Bank of England's bargaining position, for it left Britain as the only major *European* outlet with the shipping to buy Latin American goods. This permitted the Bank severely to limit the power of Argentina, the most important of Britain's Latin American suppliers, to convert sterling to service its dollar bonds. It also replaced the setting aside of gold reserves to back Argentina's balances with a straightforward guarantee against devaluation.

A further problem for Latin Americans was the increasing shortage of imports from Britain, especially coal and machinery. Events had quickly confirmed Perowne's premonitions about British exports. Initially, because of British purchasing restrictions, most Latin American countries were desperately short of foreign exchange and unable to pay for British goods. The despatch of a commercial mission led by Lord Willingdon late in 1940 to promote trade in South America was purely for cosmetic reasons. Moreover, Britain could not afford to allocate production facilities or shipping for exports to Latin America, unless it was essential to the maintenance of good relations or to Britain's own import requirements. In February 1941 the government introduced export licensing for Brazil, Chile, Colombia and Peru. In May the Board of Trade openly admitted to the United States that, except for Argentina where the railways needed coal and the *frigoríficos* tinplate (for canning meat), 'we are now using the fruit of our investments to pay for necessary imports. . . . [We] only . . . stimulate exports when there is a balance which cannot be made up otherwise.' This would of course also lead to the depreciation of British assets in Latin America, as companies would be unable to purchase new equipment. 'It is scarcely too much to say,' the Board of Trade continued, 'that we have abandoned, for the time being, almost the whole of our pre-war objectives. It is now entirely a question of securing indispensable imports, if necessary by sacrificing our investments and even our post-war prospects.'[41]

In the London winter of 1941–42 the situation changed again. Several countries began to accumulate surpluses on their Special Accounts, raising the question of how they might eventually be used. The British obviously wished to restrict their own postwar debts and took the decision to pay for their growing imports if possible by realising investments. This offered some advantages to Latin American countries, especially as they were securing little interest on their own deposits. As Marcelo Abreu explains in the case of Brazil, acquiring British companies and holdings of loans would release the foreign exchange otherwise used for interest payments for essential imports after the war.[42] In 1943 Vargas agreed to redeem Brazil's sterling debt and begin repurchasing railways and other British-owned assets. In Argentina, where the Foreign Office had been attempting since 1940 to persuade the government to use sterling balances to redeem its debt and purchase a share in the railways, negotiations were more difficult. As the war continued the balances mounted. Despite its expenditure Brazil's frozen deposits in London had reached £50 million by mid-1945, while Argentina's exceeded £100 million.[43]

With hindsight it seems doubtful whether the leading Latin American countries bargained as effectively as they might. Jorge Fodor criticises Argentina for permitting British advisors in the Banco Central to pass information to London about its negotiating position. He argues strongly that the Argentine authorities did not complain sufficiently about the conditions imposed on them by the Bank of England. They might have used their leverage as a key supplier of foodstuffs to begin acquiring dollar bonds held in Britain and obtain either more British exports or some payments in hard currency. Britain, after all, received dollars for the meat it purchased for US forces in Europe, yet paid the Argentines in Special Account sterling. The result of their passivity was that Argentina found itself in 1945 with massive sterling balances which, though guaranteed against devaluation, paid little interest and could be converted into dollars only when the Bank of England wished.[44] Marcelo Abreu likewise criticises Brazil's failure to obtain higher interest payments or 'gold set-aside' guarantees on its Special Accounts, and questions the level of compensation paid for companies like the Southern São Paulo and Sorocabana railways.[45]

The United States contributed to the weakening of Britain's overall position. Government and business interests there perceived the war as an ideal opportunity to eradicate European influence in South America. Early in the war the administration offered loans and purchasing agreements to stabilise Latin American economies and thus buy influence. Washington also attempted to undercut Britain's remaining exports, using the opposition which existed in the United States towards Lend-Lease to extract a commitment from Britain to restrict its sales to Latin America. Britain was barred from exporting goods similar to those it was obtaining from the United States, and this included key items like textiles and transport equipment. The signs that US officials saw no future role for Britain in Latin America were unmistakeable. At the conference of American states which Washington called in February 1942, after its entry into the war, Britain was politely ignored, even though it might have helped to mediate between Washington and Buenos Aires when the US–Argentine relationship collapsed due to the Argentines' refusal to declare war on the Axis.

The question of Argentina

British views on Argentina diverged sharply from those of the US government. The United States distrusted both President Castillo, who had succeeded Ortiz in 1940, and the military regime which overthrew him in 1943, taking Argentina's continued neutrality as a sign of pro-Axis sympathies. In British eyes, however, Washington persistently misread the Argentine situation and meddled unnecessarily in the country's internal affairs, a process which culminated in Braden's counter-productive intervention against Perón in the 1946 election campaign.

The extent of Anglo-US rivalry over Argentina and its implications has been the subject of intense debate in all three countries. R.A. Humphreys, who worked in the Foreign Office during the war, plays it down, dismissing as myth the idea that Britain actively encouraged Argentine neutrality.[46] But while the Foreign Office made occasional statements deploring Buenos Aires' attitude, it carefully ensured that nothing disturbed the flow of goods from Argentine ports, for which neutrality, since it protected Argentine shipping from attack, offered positive advantages. Perowne made the point, early in 1943, that Argentina's position had 'certain charms for us', having warned a month earlier that 'we must not let the State Department stampede us into anti-Argentine action contrary to our present and long-term interests. We must distinguish between form and substance.'[47] Generally Britain tried to retain its independence of action. When US–Argentine relations reached a crisis at the end of 1943, due to suspected Argentine interference in Bolivia, the United States pressed Britain to join it in imposing economic sanctions. The Foreign Office pointed out that in 1944 Argentina would supply 14 per cent of Britain's wheat imports, 70 per cent of its linseed, 40 per cent of its carcass meat, 29 per cent of its canned meat and 35 per cent of its hides, and that the invasion of France would be impossible without them.[48] The actions which the British did occasionally take for the sake of its alliance with the United States (token condemnations of Argentine neutrality in January and September 1943, the withdrawal of its ambassador in July 1944, and a refusal to sign a *long-term* meat contract in October 1944) did not seriously harm their interests. They consistently refused to follow the United States into economic sanctions against the military regime dominated by Perón, both during and immediately after the war.

While US policy towards Argentina irritated the British, therefore, it probably gave them greater opportunities to defend their interests. In private statements to Argentine officials the British distanced themselves from Washington, and this brought some rewards. Leading nationalists like General Mosconi publicly drew distinctions between US and British imperialism, and the railways were permitted to increase tariffs to meet higher wage settlements. However, these differences between Britain and the United States, coupled with the continued economic interdependence of Britain and Argentina, left a legacy of serious problems for resolution after the war.

THE POSTWAR YEARS

In 1945 Britain's future in Latin America was uncertain. Six years before, when the war had begun, the position had already been serious: trade was stagnating, a large proportion of Britain's investments were earning no returns, and many companies were exposed to attacks from nationalist governments and politicians. In the Second, as in the First World War, the disappearance of German competition was outweighed by the rapid growth of US power. Some still hoped that Britain might retain some influence in Argentina, which, according to the ambassador in Rio, contained 'about the only overseas investments of any value left', and that in the absence of German competition in the immediate postwar years trade might recover, but generally a lack of confidence about the future prevailed.[49] Few observers, however, anticipated the speed with which the position Britain had established in Latin America in the nineteenth century would finally disintegrate.

Britain was now dependent on the United States. With its export production in tatters and in need of imports of foodstuffs and raw materials, Britain could not survive the immediate postwar years without financial assistance from Washington, but the price was a commitment to the restoration of the multilateral system of trade and payments desired by the United States. Thus the credit of $3750 million (£933 million) to which the United States agreed in December 1945 was conditional upon the pound becoming convertible again within twelve months of Britain's ratification of the agreement. This was eventually achieved in July 1947. However, within seven weeks convertibility had to be suspended and exchange controls reimposed, bringing an end to hopes of the rapid resumption of multilateral arrangements. Two years later, in September 1949, Britain devalued the pound from $4.02, where it had been fixed in September 1939, to $2.80. Both these measures had serious consequences for Latin American countries, especially those which conducted a significant part of their trade with the Sterling Area or possessed substantial balances in their Special Accounts in London.

These balances were a particular obstacle to the multilateral system which the United States desired. Britain could not afford either to make them convertible or to release them immediately for purchases from the Sterling Area, for there was little to export. Thus the government was forced either to search for some means of eliminating them or to persuade its creditors to defer reclaiming them. This meant engaging in some difficult negotiations with Argentina and Brazil, the leading creditors in Latin America. Other issues also had to be taken into account: the future of Britain's investments; its export trade, which had fallen to one-quarter of its 1937 value by 1944; and its continued need for foodstuffs and raw materials from Latin America.[50] The failure to maintain the convertibility of sterling in 1947 raised further problems. British industry was unlikely to be able to supply Latin American countries' requirements for imports, and inconvertibility meant that if they continued to export to Britain they would not be able to obtain dollars to purchase essential US products like machinery.

The key negotiations were those with Argentina, since Britain still hoped to retain some influence there and US officials viewed Britain's policy towards Buenos Aires as a test of its intentions to revert to a multilateral system. Furthermore, Argentina epitomised the doubts which many Latin American governments now had about the benefits of an international division of labour and foreign investment. Perón's administration aimed to bring vital infrastructure like the railways under national control and to industrialise quickly, though this would require large imports of machinery and manufacturing inputs. Argentina therefore had to find means of using the sterling balances to achieve these objectives. For Britain the Argentine problem was acute: its sterling balances were substantial, the largest in Latin America; the tax concessions the railways held under the Mitre Law were due to expire in 1947; and imports of meat and grain were essential to the British food supply. Other governments which held large sterling balances, especially India and Egypt, were also watching the Argentine negotiations closely. Yet if the problems could be resolved Argentina might still offer a good market for British exports and provide a model for others.

The railways were central to the negotiations. The suggestion that the Argentine state might purchase a stake in them dated back to 1936 and it had gained strength from the growth of sterling balances during the war. The British government began to encourage a settlement in which Argentina might use the Special Accounts either to carry out a full-scale nationalisation or to establish a mixed Anglo-Argentine holding company. By mid-1942 all the departments involved had agreed that Britain should dispose of the railways, but they had been unable to negotiate terms with Buenos Aires or persuade the railway boards to agree. Four years later the problem had become even more urgent, partly because of the growth in the sterling balances, which the Argentines wanted to convert into hard currency or an interest-bearing loan, but also due to the impending expiry of the Mitre Law, which would further weaken the companies' financial position.

After considerable difficulties the two countries concluded the Eady-Miranda agreement in September 1946. This involved a four-year meat contract, the convertibility of all Argentina's future sterling receipts, the release of £20 million of the blocked balances over four years, a gold guarantee and 0.5 per cent interest on the remainder, and the formation of a mixed company to acquire the railways. In February 1947, however, for reasons which remain obscure, Perón decided on the complete nationalisation of the railways for £135.5 million, the minimum the companies considered acceptable, together with another £14.6 million for some associated companies. Most historians have criticised the price as too high, in view of the obsolescence of the railways' equipment and the Stock Exchange valuation of the companies, although Skupch considers that factors like the acquisition of railway-owned land in Buenos Aires made it a reasonable bargain.[51] In fact, though, without knowing how the Argentine government would have replaced the Mitre Law, it is impossible to value the railways in 1947 with any accuracy.

The 1946 agreement did not solve the problems of the Anglo-Argentine relationship, because, as Fodor comments, 'sterling's collapse in August 1947 destroyed the whole of Argentina's international economic strategy', by undermining the assumption that Argentina would be able to convert the income from its future meat and cereal sales to Britain into dollars.[52] For Argentina to receive payment for its exports in inconvertible sterling was an unattractive proposition, for Britain could not supply the capital goods it needed and imports of consumer goods like textiles and whisky would compete with Argentine producers. Another series of complex negotiations therefore took place, resulting in the Andes Pact of February 1948. This contained a new meat contract and arranged for the railway compensation to come from an advance on 1948 meat sales, since the Argentines, rightly fearing a devaluation of sterling, wished to preserve the accumulated wartime balances, which had a gold guarantee, whereas current earnings from Britain did not.

Argentina now began a deliberate policy of selling grain and meat to other European countries rather than a Britain which could pay only with sterling, although a further five-year agreement, mainly trading meat for coal, was signed in 1949. Declining export surpluses in Argentina soon undermined the relationship. Early in 1950 the Bank of England began to realise that '1920/40 assumptions', namely that Argentina would always have a surplus of grain and meat, were no longer valid.[53] The Anglo–Argentine relationship thus disintegrated because neither side could sustain the level of exports, food or industrial inputs and fuel, which the other expected.

Other agreements followed a similar pattern. Brazil had drawn on its Special Accounts to repurchase bonds and other assets since 1943, but even so balances continued to accumulate, reaching a peak of £68 million early in 1947.[54] It then finally became clear to the Brazilians that Britain would not permit the wholesale release of these balances to purchase goods like transport equipment. Some torrid negotiations ensued in which Britain limited releases to £6 million over four years and suggested (unsuccessfully) that Brazil write down Britain's debts as a contribution to the war effort. While using some of the balances to repurchase railways, Brazilian negotiators failed to guarantee their current earnings against devaluation, thus suffering serious losses in 1949. Moreover, they also delayed using the balances to redeem the public debt fully, adding to the errors they had already made, and when they finally did so paid considerably above the market value of the bonds.

Negotiations with other countries have been less intensively researched than those with Argentina, but they appear to have enhanced the process of withdrawal from the old investments while attempting also to defuse possible conflicts over those which remained. In July 1947 Britain agreed with Uruguay to release 10 per cent of its blocked wartime balances to purchase imports, earmarking the remainder for the nationalisation of the tramways, railways and other public utilities and the repatriation of the sterling debt.[55] The government resolved the dispute over Mexican Eagle's expropriated properties in 1947, while the following year Shell's concessions in Venezuela were placed on a firmer basis by a new agreement for the companies and government to share profits on a fifty-fifty basis.[56] As a result of all these negotiations the stock of British capital in Latin America is estimated to have halved between 1939 and 1949.[57] Some railway and public utility companies remained (the former principally in northern Chile, Bolivia and Peru), as well as a few small oil and mining firms. However, the only real investments of any value left were BOLSA's commercial banking network, Shell's production and distribution facilities, and the subsidiaries of a few manufacturing firms.

CONCLUSION

British businessmen generally found it difficult to come to terms with nationalism and labour militancy after 1930. Marshall Eakin's criticisms of the St John d'El Rey Mining Company in Brazil – that they failed to Brazilianise their staff and that they obtained a poor reputation from their confrontation tactics over wage levels, labour conditions and social security legislation – have a much wider application.[58] Businessmen still tried to rely on the methods of securing influence and maintaining control which had served them well before 1914. Yet, as the problems of the Argentine railways showed, sympathetic politicians often could not afford to appear too friendly towards British companies, and techniques such as the infiltration of labour unions with informers became less effective as union organisation progressed, often with the support of populist governments. Many companies thus suffered bitter and violent strikes, as well as becoming targets for nationalist politicians.

These attitudes dismayed many in the British government, for the companies' behaviour undermined their attempts to withdraw from the old investments and restructure commercial relations on a fresh basis. It was difficult, for example, to persuade the directors of the British-owned railway companies in Argentina of the need to relinquish control. The parsimonious attitude of Shell, while supported by the Petroleum Department, did little to help the Foreign Office's attempts to resolve complex disagreements in Venezuela. The government's specialists in Latin American affairs were also constrained by the broader belief that Britain should safeguard its position in the empire at the expense of interests elsewhere, and by the financial problems facing the country after 1914, which stimulated the search for short-term policies to defend the pound and Britain's remaining investment income at the expense of a longer-term vision.

That is not to say that British officials did not bargain skilfully (and Latin American countries suffered losses as a result). In retrospect Britain obtained more than its own vulnerability in supplies and its financial weakness warranted. There are, perhaps, two explanations for this. First, throughout the period from 1914 to 1950 events were unpredictable. No-one could forecast with any accuracy the state of the world economy or Britain's role within it five years hence, and this made policy-making and negotiation difficult for both sides. Second, most Latin American officials remained under the spell of Britain's reputation as the world's leading trading nation and financial centre, and they did not fully perceive how the weakness of Britain's economy was affecting its relations with Latin America. It was even more difficult if, like Argentina, they still depended on British markets. Only at the end of the 1930s, after almost four decades of attempts to conform to the City's views on policy, did Brazil discover that, at least for a time, it could default on its debt with impunity, a solution which the Argentines never seriously considered in the 1930s. The war changed the outlook again. With hindsight both Argentina and Brazil appear to have been unnecessarily unwilling to bargain hard with Britain over the guarantees and interest on the Special Accounts during the Second World War and to redeem loans on which the interest rate was higher. In Brazil, moreover, these failures of policy-making carried over to cause the country quite substantial losses in the postwar period. After the war several countries faced serious problems, for Britain could no longer offer new investment, an adequate market or the goods they needed, and yet it still retained control of significant assets in the region and of the Latin American Special Accounts. These in fact provided the solution, since they permitted the repatriation of many of Britain's investments. Once these negotiations had been completed Britain had little basis left for a continued financial and commercial relationship with Latin America and retreated further towards the apparent security of the empire.

REFERENCES

1. Mitchell, *International Historical Statistics*, p. 552; Palma, 'External Disequilibrium', 327–8.
2. Palma, 'External Disequilibrium', 328 and 334–5.
3. Mitchell, *Abstract of British Historical Statistics*, pp. 284 and 323.
4. Mitchell, *International Historical Statistics*, pp. 554 and 604.
5. Humphreys, *Latin America and the Second World War*, I, 7; Miller, 'British Trade'.
6. 'Memo on German Competition in South and Central America, 21.3.39', T 160/1160/F18151/018/1 (PRO).
7. Abreu, 'Brazil and the World Economy', 101–4 and 122.
8. 'Memo on German Competition'.
9. Quoted in Hilton, *Brazil and the Great Powers*, p. 215.
10. RIIA, *Problem of International Investment*, p. 314.
11. RIIA, *Problem of International Investment*, p. 23.
12. Skupch, 'El deterioro y fin', 34–6.
13. Wright, *British-Owned Railways*, p. 161.
14. Quoted in Wright, *British-Owned Railways*, p. 186.
15. Quoted in García Heras, 'Hostage Private Companies', 66.
16. Perowne's minute on Stirling to Balfour, 12 August 1939, FO 371/22851/A5540/480/47 (PRO); Philip, *Oil and Politics*, p. 45.
17. Quoted in Philip, *Oil and Politics*, pp. 510–11.
18. Tulchin, 'Decolonizing an Informal Empire', 137.

19. Quoted in García Heras, 'Las compañías ferroviarias británicas', 478.
20. Hilton, *Brazil and the Great Powers*, pp. 135–6 and 214.
21. DOT, *Report of the British Economic Mission*, pp. 12–13.
22. Quoted in Wright, *British-Owned Railways*, p. 135.
23. Foreign Office memorandum of November 1932, quoted in Skupch, 'El deterioro y fin', 38.
24. Drosdoff, *El gobierno de las vacas*, p. 150.
25. Shipments at the peak of the trade in 1927 had been 463,239 tons: Drosdoff, *El gobierno de las vacas*, p. 15.
26. Drosdoff, *El gobierno de las vacas*, pp. 15–34; Alhadeff, 'Dependency, Historiography and Objections', 371–3.
27. Prebisch, 'Argentine Economic Policies', 142–3.
28. Ghioldi, *¿Qué significa el pacto Roca?*, p. 32.
29. Tulchin, 'Decolonizing an Informal Empire', 130–2; 'Foreign Policy', 97–100.
30. Skupch, 'El deterioro y fin', 37.
31. Gravil and Rooth, 'Time of Acute Dependence', 376.
32. BOT, 'Report of Joint Committee', 805, 816, 854–7, 862, 867, 870.
33. Gravil and Rooth, 'Time of Acute Dependence', 370.
34. President of the British Chamber of Commerce in Buenos Aires, quoted in Goodwin, 'Anglo-Argentine Commercial Relations', 47.
35. Alhadeff, 'Economic Formulae', 109–16; Marichal, *Century of Debt Crises*, p. 215.
36. Drummond, *Imperial Economic Policy*, p. 377.
37. Quoted in Gravil and Rooth, 'Time of Acute Dependence', 368.
38. Tulchin, 'Decolonizing an Informal Empire', 133.
39. Sir William Seeds, quoted in Abreu, 'La deuda externa brasileña', 207.
40. Perowne to Stirling, 15 November 1939, T 160/1159/F18151/010 (PRO).
41. 'UK Trade Policy in Latin America', memorandum by R. Fraser, May 1941, OV 6/17 (Bank of England).
42. Abreu, 'La deuda externa brasileña', 219.
43. Skupch, 'El deterioro y fin', 56; Abreu, 'Anglo-Brazilian Economic Relations', 393.
44. Fodor, 'Origins of Argentina's Sterling Balances', 154–79.
45. Abreu, 'Brazil and the World Economy', 190–1 and 214; Abreu, 'Brazil as a Creditor', 451.
46. Humphreys, *Latin America and the Second World War*, II, p. 140.
47. Quoted in Stemplowski, 'Castillo's Argentina', 812–13.
48. Humphreys, *Latin America and the Second World War*, II, pp. 159 and 167.
49. Quoted in Bowen, 'End of British Economic Hegemony', 6.
50. Humphreys, *Latin America and the Second World War*, II, p. 223.
51. Skupch, 'El deterioro y fin', 61–6.
52. Fodor, 'Perón's Policies', 146.
53. 'Argentina', memo by F.F. Powell, 11 February 1950, OV 102/28 (Bank of England).
54. Abreu, 'Brazil as a Creditor', 450.
55. Finch, *Political Economy of Uruguay*, p. 218.
56. Philip, *Oil and Politics*, pp. 64–6.
57. Rippy, *British Investments*, pp. 84–6.
58. Eakin, 'Business Imperialism', 731–3.

The Relationship between Britain and Latin America in Retrospect

Academic interest in Britain's historic links with Latin America began to grow in the early 1950s, just when the commercial and financial relationship which had developed over the previous century and a half was entering its final stages of disintegration. Since then some impetus to research has come from sporadic attempts by the British government, often in association with academic specialists on Latin America, to reappraise the past in order to identify a basis on which closer relations with the leading countries in the region might be rebuilt. The need to understand and explain Britain's relative economic decline, which has been thrown into sharp relief by events since the Second World War, has also raised questions among historians about its past 'performance' in Latin America. However, the great majority of the research which has been undertaken on different aspects of the subject, whether in Britain, the United States or the Latin American countries themselves, has been concerned with the long-term consequences of the British connexion for the region's development. It has thus generally been located within the context of broader controversies over imperialism and dependency. From this corpus of literature historians can now derive a much clearer image of the development of Britain's interests in the region, and from that basis make some more meaningful comments about the theoretical issues which stimulated the empirical research.

THE DYNAMICS OF THE RELATIONSHIP

Until around 1870 Britain's priorities in Latin America were focused primarily on trade. The strategic objectives of the British government were limited to preventing any other major power from securing exclusive privileges following the collapse of the Spanish and Portuguese empires. British commercial interests changed considerably, however, between the mid eighteenth and the mid nineteenth centuries. Initially, during the period of Spanish and Portuguese domination, Latin America was seen primarily as the principal region where, through plunder, contraband or legitimate trade, Britain could acquire gold and silver bullion and other products like dyestuffs. In the early stages of the Industrial Revolution, and particularly during the Napoleonic Wars, the emphasis shifted. Latin America became more significant as an outlet for the production of Britain's growing industries as markets elsewhere were closed. Merchants flocked to ports on the Atlantic coast, and in smaller numbers to the Pacific, in order to sell manufactures. Many of these ventures failed. There were some brief periods of boom after Latin American ports were opened (with a peak in 1825 when there was also a short-lived surge in British investment), but generally the demand for British goods proved disappointing. It soon became clear to the merchants who survived the recession of the late 1820s that an import trade which was often dependent on payment in silver had limited potential. They therefore began to interest themselves in other activities, particularly the development of exports from Latin America which, besides offering opportunities for speculation or commissions, might also provide return cargoes for vessels arriving with imports from Britain.

As the export boom gathered pace in the middle of the nineteenth century the few commercial houses which remained from the independence era were joined by new merchant partnerships and by other firms from Britain which offered vital intermediary services, especially in shipping and banking. Economic growth also attracted many other European and North American traders who settled in the ports and competed intensely with the British. In several countries the role of British merchants therefore became rather less significant. By the end of the nineteenth century they had almost vanished from some parts of Latin America. In Chile, Peru and Brazil, though, they remained influential in certain export trades (nitrate, sugar and coffee particularly), despite the fact that most sales were made to markets other than Britain. Many British commercial houses also remained in business in Argentina and Uruguay, but with very diffuse functions and a much smaller role in these countries' export trades than on the west coast.

There were other important developments in the final third of the nineteenth century which contributed to the growth in Latin

American exports while transforming the profile of British business there. A far-reaching revolution in communications occurred within a very short period. Innovations in transport (railways and steamships) together with submarine cables and overland telegraphs were introduced through much of the region. These improvements transformed the basis on which foreign merchants had conducted business since before independence, while also making it possible for Latin American countries to export new products. Together they contributed to a shift in Britain's economic interests in Latin America away from an emphasis on trade alone towards investment and finance.

Just as Britain's commercial connexions with Latin America had evolved in several stages, its financial interests also developed through a number of overlapping phases. At first investors concentrated on loans to national and provincial governments. Then, as confidence improved, especially in those countries which survived the crisis of the mid 1870s without defaulting, the small investments which had already been channelled through 'free-standing companies' operating railways, public utilities and, to a much lesser extent, mines, factories and landholdings, were greatly expanded. Between 1875 and 1914 hundreds of such enterprises were formed. Slightly later, but particularly after the turn of the century, multinational firms also began to appear, initially in services like banking but then, after the First World War, in the 'classic' multinational sectors, manufacturing and petroleum (though rarely, in contrast to US interests in Latin America, in plantations or, except for nitrate, in mining). This growing focus on investment had certain implications. British interests became more concentrated into a small number of countries (Mexico and the larger South American republics); a significant portion of Britain's export trade became dependent on the companies already operating in Latin America and on the City's ability to finance new investment; and, particularly as a result of the improvements in communications, the locus of strategic decision-making in British firms became even more firmly centred in London.

In retrospect it is clear that, overall, British interests in Latin America entered a period of slow decline during the First World War, and that the process accelerated from the 1930s, reflecting Britain's global economic difficulties and its growing preference for its own empire. However, it was some time before this process became fully evident to contemporaries, whether in Britain, its principal rivals in the developed world (the United States and Germany), or in Latin America itself. Britain's investments in the region were still considerable and, until the Depression, reasonably profitable, while it remained a significant commercial partner for many South American republics. One of the leading historians of the British connexion with Brazil, Alan Manchester, wrote of Britain as 'still a decisive factor in the life of Portuguese America' in 1933.[1] It was only later the same decade that Britain began, somewhat unwillingly, to surrender its influence there. At about the same time, in 1938, the Cárdenas government expropriated the oil interests in Mexico, the major investments remaining there. Yet in the case of Argentina, the most important destination for British trade and investment, it was not until the early 1950s that British officials resigned themselves to the loss of primacy; US policy-makers continued to regard Britain's extensive interests there as a significant obstacle to the establishment of their own hegemony in the whole hemisphere until the nationalisation of the railways in the late 1940s. The relinquishing of British economic influence, especially in the larger republics of South America, should therefore not be seen, as historians like Platt have suggested, as an inevitable and obvious process in which the British began deliberately to withdraw from the whole region (except perhaps for Argentina) before 1914 in the face of the greater political and economic power of the United States.[2]

To do so greatly oversimplifies the issues. Such an interpretation ignores the possibility that other countries, in particular Germany and Japan, might have replaced British interests and stalled the US advance. More significantly it also overlooks the internal dynamics and long-term weaknesses of the links which Britain had constructed with Latin America, as well as discounting the attempts which officials and businessmen in the United Kingdom made to preserve some influence. In fact the changes which became evident in the last third of the nineteenth century, the shift of emphasis from trade to finance, the decisions to invest in particular activities (especially services such as railways, public utilities and banking), and the concentration of interest in a few countries, eventually led Britain into a cul-de-sac in Latin America. However rational and profitable they were for those who invested before 1914, their cumulative effect was to make much of Britain's export trade and the maintenance of its influence in the countries on which attention had focused dependent on its continued ability to finance new investment. Moreover, many British firms came to occupy a vulnerable position within the principal Latin American countries, since they controlled crucial services, frequently as monopolies, and consequently often became the targets of political discontent.

These problems began to become apparent when Britain found

after the First World War that it could no longer invest on the pre-1914 scale. In real terms its exports to Latin America never recovered their 1910–13 level during the whole of the inter-war period. The leading firms, many of which were dependent on old technologies, became more vulnerable to nationalist attacks and lost ground to competitors using more modern innovations. The protection of returns on the pre-1914 investments became critical to Britain's overall balance of payments while new investment in Latin America was officially discouraged. In the 1930s, for the first time in a century, British officials were thus forced to make fundamental decisions about their future role in Latin America. They chose to protect financial interests (especially in government loans) and to give priority to the relationship with Argentina. In the short term such policies offered some relief, for example in the temporary recovery of exports to Argentina after 1933, but in the longer term, even without the intervention of the Second World War, they could not have provided a foundation for the maintenance of the relationship between Britain and Latin America. The effect of the war was to exacerbate the financial weakness of the United Kingdom, bringing its influence in Latin America rapidly to an end as many of the older investments were repatriated. The war also reversed the spread of German and Japanese economic influence, both of which had been growing rapidly in the 1930s. It was the combination of all these factors which gave the United States the dominant and largely unchallenged position it possessed in Latin America from the late 1940s until the 1970s.

QUESTIONS OF IMPERIALISM AND DEPENDENCY

An understanding of the dynamics of Britain's interests in Latin America is fundamental to discussions of imperialism and dependency. Early theoretical writers on these subjects often simply assumed that British commercial interests were dominant throughout nineteenth-century Latin America before being quickly replaced by the United States after 1914. A further problem was that although these debates provided the context for much of the research undertaken after the 1960s, the literature rapidly became extremely diffuse due to the enormous quantity of empirical studies which were published. As these accumulated, 'dependency' interpretations, like 'structuralist' theories before them, became much less fashionable, for many historians found the assumptions theorists had made about the activities of British officials and businessmen in nineteenth-century Latin America undermined by the more detailed research.

Generalising about the consequences of Britain's role in Latin American history has therefore become extraordinarily difficult, since there is no widely accepted theoretical paradigm. Four other obstacles are also apparent. First, all historians surveying a long sweep of history face the problems of isolating elements of continuity, distinguishing the principal changes which occurred, and balancing the significance of both. In this instance it is quite clear that, while some continuities in attitudes remained, the nature of British government interest in Latin America, like that of British businessmen, was quite different in 1900 even compared with 1870. Second, all historians writing about Latin America face the problem of balancing the factors which give the region some unity with the need to explain the diverse historical experiences of individual countries and the regions within them.[3] Third, there are obvious problems of definition. 'Dependency' could be defined so broadly as to become analytically meaningless. 'Imperialism', similarly, could be defined so narrowly by more conservative writers, many of whom confined their focus to intergovernmental relations and used little more than the Foreign Office papers available in the Public Record Office, that it became simple, within the terms they themselves set, for them to 'prove' that no imperial or neo-colonial relationship had existed between Britain and Latin America. Finally, historians find it difficult to be always conscious of their own assumptions, with the result that they may distort some facts and ignore others in order to make them match preconceived interpretations. Many in Britain have found it difficult to perceive events from a Latin American viewpoint, but on the other hand many of the interpretations originally proposed by nationalist historians in Latin America have remained remarkably persistent in the face of more sophisticated and critical archival research.

Some of the assumptions made by nationalist and radical writers are indeed difficult to uphold. The growing integration of Latin America into an international economy dominated by Britain was not a 'zero-sum game' in which profits for one side inevitably meant losses for the other. British and Latin American interests both secured substantial benefits from the growth of trade and investment. Latin Americans generally retained control of internal trade, much of the domestic banking sector and, until the growth of modern mining and petroleum industries, of export production, leaving the British in an intermediary role in the service sectors. Much of the research suggests that, rather than being due primarily to the extraction of excessive profits by foreign interests, headed by the British, many of the development problems arising from the export boom may lie instead in the way in which elites and states in Latin America distributed and utilised the surpluses which they acquired.

There is also little evidence of a conspiracy in which British governments and businessmen acted together as a bloc to enhance their collective influence in Latin America. British interests were much more complex. The actions of governments and businessmen were frequently unsynchronised; they often criticised one another; and the interests of individual firms generally diverged and often conflicted. Thus the view of authors writing in the 1960s and drawing on the nationalist tradition, such as Frank, who believed that the British government persistently intervened in Latin American political conflicts in the interests of British businessmen, was greatly overdrawn.

Examples of decisive and long-term British intervention in crucial areas of economic policy, such as tariffs and monetary regimes, are also infrequent. While the British clearly desired low import tariffs, it took them a considerable part of the nineteenth century to persuade Latin American policy-makers of their value. Even at the height of 'free trade', in the 1850s and 1860s, advocates of protection remained vocal and they recovered much of their influence in the final quarter of the nineteenth century as countries like Mexico, Brazil and Chile supported industrial and agricultural producers. Money supply, similarly, was normally a subject of intense debate among political economists in Latin America. While strong currencies and stable exchange rates obviously favoured British investors, achieving them was difficult. Exchange rates often fluctuated wildly, metallic currencies were debased, and paper money issued without adequate backing. The Gold Standard, which became a prime objective of liberal thinking towards the end of the nineteenth century, prevailed in the major countries of Latin America only for two short periods, just before the First World War and, in modified form, during the late 1920s. Latin Americans also proved reluctant to overturn completely the long-standing Iberian tradition of state involvement in the economy. Nineteenth-century governments constructed railways and other public works, intervened in financial markets and the export trades, and often tried, at least in principle, to regulate the entry and activities of British investors.

To reject the nationalists' assumptions, however, does not make

240

it necessary to adopt the position taken by the more conservative historians. At the extreme such writers often view the general lack of interest which the Foreign Office showed in Latin America, its publicly stated policy of non-intervention in internal and international conflicts, and the apparent limits to the political influence of businessmen as sufficient to disprove allegations of 'imperialism'. For D.C.M. Platt, the absence of British planning with regard to Latin America, the discontinuities he found in the post-independence period, the enormous benefits which countries like Argentina derived from their integration into the international economy, and the autonomy of Latin American governments in central areas of decision-making seemed enough also to destroy the usefulness of 'dependency' theories.[4] In fact both the extreme nationalist and the more conservative interpretations of Britain's relations with Latin America, by focusing their attacks on the oversimplifications and misleading assumptions of each other, distort and overlook the complexities of the subject.

Though often now ignored, some of the arguments developed by 'structuralist' writers remain important in understanding the consequences of the relationship with Britain for Latin America. First, the connexions established in the independence era meant that commercial and financial crises originating in Britain were easily transmitted to the region, initially in the mid 1820s and then, after the revival of British investment, in the mid 1870s, the early 1890s, 1914–15 and 1929–32. Those Latin American countries most closely tied to Britain could not avoid, in such instances, a precipitate decline in trade, foreign capital inflows, government revenues and economic activity. Second, the relationship with Britain, especially once investment began to grow after 1870, complicated economic policy-making in the major countries. The balance of payments and the management of the exchange rate became crucial. In a crisis governments were forced to adopt short-term corrective measures, the burden of which fell on the mass of the population, if they wished to continue interest payments on loans and therefore maintain their credit. Over the longer term dependence on foreign investment, which for most South American countries before 1914 meant the City of London, placed greater constraints on policy-making. This was partly due to the presence of established British firms whose investment decisions were crucial to future growth, but also because London bankers issuing loans for foreign governments gradually developed a clearer perception of orthodox policies in such areas as monetary emission and state intervention in the economy and began to emphasise such factors when negotiating new loans at

241

times of crisis. Third, Latin American nations remained dependent on Britain and other developed countries for much of the technology on which the export boom relied. Where structuralists perhaps erred was in assuming that 'technological' dependence on Britain in the late nineteenth century took a similar form to the 1960s, when much modern technology had become embodied in the individual multinational firm. The situation before 1914 was quite distinct. The knowledge and equipment required to build railways, improve agriculture or exploit oil or mining deposits were widely available internationally. The significant question, therefore, as James Street argues in his commentary on Platt's critique of 'dependency' theorists, is why Latin American elites and governments were content to employ foreign firms over the long term rather than making greater efforts to assimilate new technologies.[5]

Writers within the 'dependency' tradition in the late 1960s and 1970s also made several important points about the consequences for Latin American countries of their relationship with Britain. From the late eighteenth century imports of manufactured goods, especially of British textiles, did undermine traditional production (though more slowly than many commentators claimed), and make it difficult for new factories in Latin America to compete except under the stimulus of protectionist tariffs. The rhythm of economic life in Latin America was increasingly determined by the oscillations of commodity and capital markets in the developed world, particularly Britain, where the principal trading exchanges for many exports, including cotton, sugar, wool, minerals and rubber, were located. In some cases Latin American producers enhanced their dependence by specialising in accordance with the particular requirements of the British market, most notably in the River Plate meat trade. International finance was dominated by the City of London, and as British investment in the major countries grew, more of the key decisions affecting the direction of economic change were made there. The spread of British interests in the service sectors of Latin American economies, especially in the financing of international trade, commercial banking and transport, made them extremely vulnerable to a curtailment of credit or shipping facilities, as the events of the First World War demonstrated.

Two other points emphasised by Cardoso and Faletto in the 1960s remain important, although critics of 'dependency' theories often overlooked the fact that they had made them. First, each country's relationship with the British economy and with British businessmen differed and evolved over time. In some, such as

Colombia, the absence of British merchants, of exports dependent on British markets, and of large-scale British investment meant that the relationship with Britain was much more marginal to the republic's development and took a very different form from that which developed in Argentina, Brazil or Chile. Even in those three countries there were enormous differences in the role Britain played. Second, Latin American governments remained the essential mediators in the relationship with Britain. In some countries, such as Argentina after the late 1880s, those controlling the state decided to relinquish some influence over important sectors of the economy and to adopt more orthodox policies in the desire for further foreign investment. Others were more circumspect about loosening all controls over foreign companies, for example in Mexico after the Revolution of 1910 or in Brazil (at least in certain sectors of the economy).

Overall, the impression is that Latin American governments and elites did not maximise the benefits they obtained from their commercial and financial links with Britain. In part this may have been due to the greater bargaining abilities of British firms and, after 1914, of the British government, but it also raises questions about the capacity of Latin American elites to learn from previous experiences, their investment and consumption preferences, and the extent to which, in the light of the information available to them, they correctly evaluated trends within the global and British economies. In certain areas, in ensuring, for example, that new technology or management techniques were assimilated, monitoring the ownership of firms operating in their countries, or tightening regulations or taxation policies regarding existing firms, some governments appear to have been extraordinarily lax.

Writers like Platt tended to define imperialism in terms of *conscious* political or economic control and the extraction of excessive profits, and to pose autonomy as the antonym to dependence. By confining the debate to the period before 1914 and to the question of institutional relationships and behaviour, they were able to argue that Latin American governments did normally possess the final word in their relationship with the British government and British businessmen, and to discount many of the points their critics raised about the structures of the relationship which developed between Britain and Latin America. Yet even at the institutional level the evidence is nowhere near as clear cut as more conservative writers assume. The assumption that the British government maintained a consistent policy of non-intervention in Latin American affairs throughout the century after Castlereagh falls down on two counts: the more aggressive attitudes adopted in Whitehall between the late 1830s and the late 1860s towards the political instability and apparently arbitrary actions of Latin American governments, and the freedom to act on their own initiative which diplomatic representatives and naval officers enjoyed until the advent of the cable. Research in business archives, especially concerning Brazil, has also shown that merchant banks did try to exercise some influence over policy (the events of 1914–30 are probably more significant in this than those of 1898 and 1908 on which historians used to focus). Other companies operating in Latin America, while rarely acting, as nationalist writers often supposed, as a British bloc, also developed important channels through which they might attempt, not always successfully, to exert political influence. The problem is that nationalist writers focused on the 'big' events like wars and revolutions, and more conservative historians were able to attack them on the same ground. In fact the techniques which individual companies adopted to try to secure their everyday influence in Latin America were much more subtle: the establishment of networks of lawyers and politicians at the national level, and the development of close relationships with government officials in the provinces and municipalities where they operated.

Research in government records, business archives, official publications and the press has therefore clarified many of the details of British influence at the institutional level, as well as the structural problems of Latin America's relationship with Britain, although knowledge about individual topics and countries remains very uneven. Two other issues have attracted much less interest. First, while more is known about the everyday realities of British influence, there has been relatively little study of the mentalities either of the British officials and businessmen who were primarily concerned with Latin America, or of the Latin American elites and politicians who dealt with them. Much of the evidence in government and business archives would suggest that many of the British adopted an attitude towards Latin Americans which bordered on the arrogant. In the long term this made it extremely difficult for them to come to terms with political and social change, especially after 1930. And what effect did the reality of British naval power in the early nineteenth century, its economic influence after the middle of the century, and the pecuniary opportunities offered by British investors have on Latin American attitudes towards the British, and hence on policy-making? Research using modern techniques of linguistic analysis would throw considerable light on the changes in mentalities which occurred on both sides as a result of the long connexion between Britain and Latin America.

Second, while there was much research during the 1970s and 1980s on the development of labour movements and, to a lesser extent, the growth of nationalism in Latin America, it is still difficult to isolate the social impact of British investment. In some countries the British companies played an important role as employers and as suppliers of services. The actions of British managers and directors thus had potentially far-reaching consequences for working-class organisation and the growth of popular nationalism, both of which contributed to the political support and populist discourse of leaders like Batlle in Uruguay early in the century, or Perón in Argentina and Vargas in Brazil in the 1940s. Part of the appeal of these politicians, particularly to the urban residents who formed a critical part of their constituency, may have been derived from the experience which many possessed as the regular customers of British railway and utility companies.

EPILOGUE: BRITAIN AND LATIN AMERICA SINCE 1950

As nationalist and reformist governments spread in Latin America in the 1940s Victor Perowne, the head of the South American department of the Foreign Office, called for a reappraisal of Britain's relationship with the region in the light of its potential as a source of raw materials and as a market, and its apparently growing significance in world affairs (Latin American countries formed a significant bloc within the early United Nations, before the decolonisation of the European empires in Africa and Asia). In 1942 Perowne had brought seriously into question accepted ideas about the value of Britain's investments in railways and public utilities, calling them 'just the kind of irritant . . . likely to produce . . . a deleterious effect' on its image in the region (he even cast doubt on the value of Shell's continued presence in Venezuela in view of its disastrous behaviour in Mexico). In the future, he began to argue, the emphasis should be 'on trade, rather than, as hitherto, on safeguarding our historical position as owners of invested capital'.[6] To this end he advised that the British government should encourage trade through the provision of better credit facilities, work to eliminate the territorial disputes affecting British Honduras (now Belize), British Guiana and the Falklands/ Malvinas, and make extensive use of cultural diplomacy in order to enhance British prestige in Latin America.[7]

One part of this prescription was quickly fulfilled. The process of disinvestment, especially from holdings of government bonds and the railway companies and public utilities in Argentina, Brazil and Uruguay, which occurred immediately after the Second World War, soon reduced the role of Britain's financial interests. However, few new ties between Britain and Latin America developed in place of the old. The trading links, rather than reviving, continued to diminish in relative significance. Latin America took 7 per cent of Britain's total exports in 1950 but only 1.2 per cent in 1988. Britain's share of the Latin American import market fell over the same period from 6.8 per cent to 2.2 per cent. Parallel trends were evident in the Latin American export trade. By 1988 Latin American countries supplied only 1.4 per cent of Britain's imports (in 1950 it had been almost 8 per cent).[8] Britain continued to provide some markets for foodstuffs and petroleum and, in the case of Brazil, manufactured goods, but in global terms these were not important to Latin American producers.

The reasons for this continued decline of the commercial relationship, which had still possessed some significance even after the repatriation of investments in the late 1940s, lie on both sides. In Latin America the postwar years saw an accelerated growth in manufacturing industry, under the stimulus of protectionist tariffs and exchange and import controls, and this deprived many British consumer goods of their old outlets. Moreover, some of the traditional suppliers of the British market, particularly Argentine and Uruguayan farmers, were unable to maintain the level of their exports as production stagnated and domestic demand grew. In Britain, meanwhile, the emphasis in trade shifted first towards the Commonwealth and then, after Britain's entry to the European Community (EC) in 1973, towards the continent. This seriously harmed trade with Latin America. The Community's Common Agricultural Policy (CAP), coupled with successive Lomé Conventions (which gave preferences in the supply of tropical products to the former British and French colonies in Africa and the Caribbean), closed outlets for Latin American producers of foodstuffs. The CAP further harmed them through the dumping of excess European production on the world market. Measures to protect EC industry, such as the Multi-Fibre Arrangement, hindered Latin American attempts to develop non-traditional exports to Britain. Some British firms were successful in selling electrical generating equipment, chemicals and arms in Latin American markets, but on the whole Britain's own exports suffered from the persistent failings of British trade and industry. A mission led by the London Chamber of Commerce in 1971 complained in much the same terms as nineteenth-century consuls, or Viscount d'Abernon forty years before: 'The British image is not always what it should be, owing to failure to keep delivery dates, failure to supply spare parts quickly enough, failure to provide adequate servicing, and failure to back up sales efforts by imaginative literature in Spanish and making use of metric unit'.[9]

British direct investment in Latin America also continued to decline in significance after 1950. Many of the remaining investments (a few railway and utility companies, the Bank of London and South America's branch network, and the oil firms) were extremely vulnerable to nationalist attacks and faced enormous financial problems. Most of the transport and utility companies found it almost impossible to maintain profits and secure funds for reinvestment, especially in periods of rapid inflation. The Bank of London and South America's ability to obtain deposits was restricted by new legislation favouring domestic competitors as well as the liquidation of many of the older British companies. There were pressures on both sides, therefore, for a continuing process of disinvestment, which further reduced the railway, utility, banking and oil interests, and culminated in the agreed nationalisation of Royal Dutch-Shell's Venezuelan holdings in 1975.

Manufacturing provided the only real area of growth in direct investment. Many leading firms, such as Unilever, ICI, Pilkington, Reckitt & Colman, J. & P. Coats, BAT, and the pharmaceutical companies, expanded their operations in Latin America, both in the larger industrial countries such as Argentina, Mexico and Brazil on which they had concentrated before 1939, and in intermediate economies like Uruguay, Chile and Peru. Generally, however, interest in overseas expansion among manufacturing firms tended to focus on other areas of the world, particularly on the Dominions and later on the United States. The Bank of England's exchange controls, which lasted until 1979, almost certainly made it more difficult for companies which perceived opportunities in Latin America to invest there. Other firms, for example in the motor industry, were for the most part ignorant of markets in the region. The book value of British investment in Latin America by the end of the 1960s thus totalled only £252 million, less than it had been in 1945, despite inflation.[10] In the early 1980s Latin America as a whole accounted for only 6 per cent of Britain's direct foreign investments, and much of this was in one country, Brazil.[11]

Alongside this continuing decline in the commercial relationship and direct investment, the British government's interest in Latin America also faltered. Between 1945 and 1982 only two foreign secretaries visited Latin America. Perowne's advocacy of cultural diplomacy soon turned into cutbacks in the budgets of the British Council and the BBC's World Service and a marginalisation of their Latin American operations. An effort to promote Latin American studies in higher education between 1965 and 1975 stagnated thereafter as research grants were slashed and posts 'frozen'. A simultaneous attempt to promote British exports to the region by targeting certain markets (Argentina, Brazil, Mexico and Venezuela) also petered out as entry to the EC approached. British policy was dominated by the relationship with the United States, the Cold War, the Middle East and (from 1973) western Europe, and Latin America played only a marginal role. Although individual government departments employed officials who possessed considerable knowledge and experience of the region, senior politicians showed little interest. As a consequence no coherent strategy on Latin America, as opposed to policies reacting to specific problems, was ever adopted, or even, apparently, debated. It is thus hardly surprising that two major crises concerning Latin America both appeared out of the blue, at least to the highest levels of government, within a few months of each other in 1982.

One problem which Perowne had identified at the end of the Second World War had been the continuation of three territorial disputes affecting Britain's colonies in the region. These were never satisfactorily concluded, although independence for Guyana in 1966 absolved the British government of continuing responsibility for its latent boundary problem with Venezuela. The independence of Belize (formerly British Honduras) in 1981 presented more difficulties, for the threat of conflict with Guatemala remained serious. The immediate outcome was a break in diplomatic relations (which had already been reduced to consular level), the closure of the frontier, and the conclusion of the UK–Belize Defence Agreement under which a detachment of British troops was stationed in the newly independent country. However, it was the third territorial problem, the dispute with Argentina over the Falklands/Malvinas, which gripped the attention of the world early in 1982.

British forces occupied the Falkland Islands in 1833, ejecting the Argentine garrison which had been there since 1829. Subsequently a small population of British extraction developed in the colony, primarily as sheep-farmers. Argentina continued to claim sovereignty over the islands, but the dispute was of only marginal significance to Anglo-Argentine relations in the nineteenth century and did nothing to impede the rapid growth of investment in Argentina.

The growth of nationalism and increasing criticisms of the British role in Argentina in the 1920s then began to make it more salient. In 1927–28 Buenos Aires raised the question of postal jurisdiction in the light of its own claim to the islands. Further problems arose over the centenary of the British occupation in 1933, and Argentine complaints continued through the 1930s and 1940s. Although research on the development of the dispute is hampered by the continued closure of many of the crucial Foreign Office files, Peter Beck makes it clear that in the 1930s some officials began to express their own doubts about the validity of Britain's claims to the islands and to consider possible solutions to a dispute which threatened the relationship with Argentina, its most important ally in Latin America. This more conciliatory approach met with considerable resistance from other departments, especially the Colonial Office.[12]

The lines which eventually led to war in 1982 were therefore already being drawn: on the one hand the Argentines' claim to sovereignty (strengthened after 1945 by the decolonisation of the old European empires and increasing support for its stand within the United Nations), and on the other the political difficulties that a compromise deal with Argentina would create in Britain. The Foreign Office was unable to carry other departments and senior politicians with it. Whenever the idea of relinquishing sovereignty was mooted there was an outcry in the press and Parliament. Successive governments thus had little alternative but to implement a policy best described as prevarication. This persisted through a further crisis in the mid 1960s, in the course of which, under pressure in Parliament, the Wilson government withdrew from a Memorandum of Understanding it had agreed with Argentina and took the crucial decision to give priority to the islanders' views on any transfer of sovereignty. Pressure from Argentina mounted during the 1970s, and a series of minor naval incidents occurred, exacerbating tension. Attempts, after the Conservatives had regained power in 1979, to negotiate a 'leaseback' arrangement in exchange for British recognition of Argentine sovereignty again met a hostile reaction in the Commons and in the islands, making negotiations with Buenos Aires yet more difficult.

The crisis came to a head with the Argentine *junta*'s invasion of the islands on 2 April 1982. This brought to the surface the miscalculations in London which had resulted from the lack of attention given to Latin American affairs and the failure of coordination within the British government. Through 1981 British intelligence reports continued to suggest that the prospect of a military invasion was minimal, and in June the Defence Secretary announced proposals to retire HMS *Endurance*, the only Royal Navy ship permanently stationed in the area, without considering seriously the inferences which the Argentine government might draw from this. While opinion in the islands hardened against negotiations with Argentina, giving the British government, once it had taken the decision to make the islanders' views 'paramount', little alternative but to stall, impatience in Buenos Aires with the delays in negotiations grew, especially after the replacement of President Viola by General Galtieri in December 1981.

The Franks Committee, which reported early in 1983 on the origins of the war, criticised several aspects of the Conservative government's behaviour: the misleading signals, such as the withdrawal of the *Endurance*, which it had given to Buenos Aires; the fact that policy towards Argentina was never discussed at inter-departmental or cabinet level from January 1981 until a week before the invasion; and ministers' lack of appreciation of the domestic pressures on the new Galtieri government and the changes in its policy.[13] However, the handling of the Falklands/Malvinas dispute by successive governments, whatever their political complexion, illustrated several of the problems apparent in British policy towards Latin America throughout the twentieth century, in particular a poor appreciation of Latin American nationalism, and a tendency to prevaricate and react rather than develop long-term strategies on which all government departments could cooperate.

The principal implications of the Falklands crisis for Britain were political: the likely outfall, if British forces had proved unsuccessful in recovering the islands, would have been the resignation of the prime minister and the collapse of the Conservative administration. Trade with the remainder of Latin America was now so marginal that the economic consequences of a deterioration of relations with countries sympathetic to Argentina were insignificant. The dispute with Argentina primarily endangered Britain's political image in the region. However, just two months after the war had ended a second crisis, over Latin American debt, began to become evident. This had much more far-reaching implications, for it directly threatened the stability of the major international banks, including two of the four leading clearing banks in Britain.

The City of London was involved in the enormous growth of lending to Latin American governments and official bodies (such as state development banks and public enterprises) which had occurred during the 1970s in two principal ways. First, the City was the centre of the Eurocurrency markets which had emerged in the 1960s to handle offshore deposits in US dollars and other currencies. After the Arab – Israeli conflict of 1973 and the resulting rise in world oil prices it therefore became one of the major conduits through which the earnings of Middle Eastern countries were recycled through the banking system towards other areas of the world, in particular Latin America. Second, British banks themselves lent quite considerable amounts to Latin American countries, especially towards the peak of the cycle in 1980–82. Two of the 'Big Four', Lloyds and Midland, were particularly heavily exposed. At the end of 1982 Lloyds had loans of $5.8 billion outstanding to Latin America, Midland $5.2 billion.[14] These figures far exceeded their capital base and were surpassed only by four large banks in the United States.

Like the Falklands War, the debt crisis also illustrated the persistence of some of the features which had characterised Britain's relations with Latin America during the twentieth century. One of the attractions of the City of London for foreign banks and borrowers was the Bank of England's unwillingness to regulate their transactions. While the government preserved quite severe restrictions on outward industrial investment between 1947 and 1979, it permitted much greater freedom to financial institutions operating in Britain. The Bank had also clearly failed to regulate, even if it had monitored, the Latin American exposure of the leading British banks. In the previous debt crisis, during the 1930s, official policy towards Latin America had explicitly favoured the short-term interests of the City of London at the expense of industrial exporters, and this preference reappeared in the 1980s as the government and Bank of England attempted to find solutions to the debt problem. 'The commercial banks', Robert Graham comments, 'ensured their interests remained paramount in government thinking, at the expense of a more sympathetic attitude towards the [Latin American] debtor countries.'[15] In contrast to its policies towards the poorest African countries the British government took no initiative over Latin American debt, despite evidence that the burden of repayments and the recession which affected many countries during the 1980s was hindering British manufacturing exports to Latin America.

After the mid 1980s both the debt crisis and the dispute over the Falklands/Malvinas diminished in importance. The immediate threat to the banks was overcome by coordinated action on the part of the international financial community, at the cost of the worst recession Latin America had experienced since the early 1930s. While partial defaults did occur, the most serious did not come until later in the decade, after the banks had restructured their balance sheets to ensure that Latin American debt no longer threatened their future. The British recapture and subsequent fortification of the Falkland/Malvinas Islands, coupled with the advent of constitutional regimes in Argentina wishing to improve relations with Britain, removed that problem from the political agenda. While British forces remained stationed in Belize, the advent of civilian governments in Guatemala also reduced the dangers of conflict in Central America. The one serious problem complicating relations between Britain and Latin American countries was the drugs trade, and that was unlikely to lead to a major confrontation. As a result Latin American issues again sank in the consciousness of British politicians and officials. The recession in Latin America, the opportunities offered by Europe and the United States, and vivid memories of the debt crisis also demoted the region in the perceptions of businessmen, although, ironically, popular interest in Britain in the developmental and environmental problems and cultural achievements of Latin America increased significantly during the 1980s.

'Well into the early part of this century, Britain was by far the largest foreign investor in Latin America,' the British Foreign Secretary, Sir Geoffrey Howe, stated in December 1988. 'It was British capital that developed agriculture and industry *across* Latin America. And the question I always asked myself is what happened? What took place to diminish that relationship?'[16] The half-truths and misunderstandings inherent in this comment show the extent to which knowledge about the history of Britain's relationship with Latin America had faded by the end of the 1980s. As this book has shown, Britain's involvement in developing Latin American agriculture and 'industry' had been largely an indirect one, through the provision of merchant expertise and contacts, and later in the nineteenth century loans to governments and investments in shipping, banks, railways and public utilities. By the time of the First World War Britain's interests had become concentrated in certain republics rather than stretching across the region, and the maintenance of its influence in countries like Argentina, Brazil and Chile depended on the City of London's continued ability to export finance. This diminished after the First World War and then largely ceased in the 1930s, leaving a host of problems and little basis for the reconstruction of the relationship, particularly as Britain's competitiveness as a manufacturer and significance as a market for raw materials were also declining.

Howe's statement also illustrates how senior politicians and other opinion-formers in London like to muse about the bonds of friendship which they believe ought to exist between Britain and Latin America as a result of the nineteenth-century ties. Few people in Britain fully realise that there is in fact considerable ambivalence among Latin Americans about the historical links between their own countries and the United Kingdom. Although British expertise and capital undoubtedly contributed to economic growth, and British governments, at least after the mid nineteenth century, often seemed much less oppressive than the United States later became, over the long term Britain's influence exacerbated the problems of development as well as creating many points of political friction. It is hardly surprising that the nationalist interpretation of the relationship, which was founded on contemporary distrust and criticism of British firms and bankers in the inter war period and of which most people in Britain know nothing, continues to exert a powerful popular appeal in Latin America itself.

REFERENCES

1. Manchester, *British Pre-Eminence*, p. 341
2. Platt, *Latin America and British Trade*, pp. 305–9.
3. On this see especially Roxborough, 'Unity and Diversity'.
4. Platt, 'Dependency in Nineteenth-Century Latin America'.
5. Street, 'Platt-Stein Controversy', 174–8.
6. The first quotation comes from a 1942 minute quoted in García Heras, 'World War II', 154; the subsequent one is from a 1947 memorandum cited in MacDonald, 'United States', 185.
7. On Perowne's 1945 memorandum see Graham, 'British Policy', 55–6.
8. International Monetary Fund, *Direction of Trade Statistics, 1990*; Atkinson, 'Trade, Aid and Investment', 104–5.
9. Quoted in Marett, *Latin America*, p. 135.
10. Marett, *Latin America*, p. 93.
11. Atkinson, 'Trade, Aid and Investment', 104–5. These figures for investment exclude oil, branch banking and insurance.
12. Beck, 'Research Problems', 7–11.
13. *Falkland Islands Review* [Franks Committee], pp. 73–89. The evidence in the body of the Franks Report is at odds with its rather bland final paragraph absolving the Conservative government of responsibility.
14. Griffith-Jones, 'Financial Relations', 127.
15. Graham, 'British Policy', 64.
16. Quoted in Bulmer-Thomas, 'British Relations', 237. My emphasis.

Appendix: Chronological Table

LATIN AMERICA FROM INDEPENDENCE TO 1950

1806   RIVER PLATE: British expedition under Commodore Home Popham occupies Buenos Aires.

1807   RIVER PLATE: British forces driven from Buenos Aires and Montevideo.

1808   BRAZIL: Portuguese Royal Family arrives in Brazil on British warships.

1809   After the deposition of Ferdinand VII of Spain by Napoleon patriotic *juntas* organised in several Latin American cities.

1810   ARGENTINA: *Junta* in Buenos Aires deposes Viceroy.

BRAZIL: Anglo-Portuguese Treaty gives British merchants concessions in the Brazilian market.

1811   VENEZUELA: *Junta* in Caracas declares independence.

PARAGUAY: *Junta* in Asunción declares independence both from Spain and from Buenos Aires.

1814   Ferdinand VII restored to the Spanish throne.

1814–15 VENEZUELA: royalist forces recapture control.

1816   ARGENTINA: 'United Provinces of South America' declare independence at a congress dominated by representatives from Buenos Aires.

1818   CHILE: José de San Martín's victory at Maipo secures Chile's independence.

1819   NEW GRANADA (COLOMBIA): Simón Bolívar's victory at Boyacá secures independence of New Granada.

1821   VENEZUELA: Bolívar's victory at Carabobo secures independence of Venezuela.

PERU: San Martín declares Peruvian independence in Lima.

MEXICO: *Junta* led by Agustín de Iturbide declares Mexican independence.

1822   MEXICO: Iturbide proclaimed as Emperor Agustín I.

BRAZIL: Dom Pedro, son of Portuguese monarch, declares independence, and becomes first Emperor of Brazil.

1824   MEXICO: After two years of internal conflict Iturbide, who had abdicated as emperor the previous year, is executed.

CENTRAL AMERICA: Formation of Confederation comprising Guatemala, El Salvador, Nicaragua, Honduras and Costa Rica.

PERU: Independence secured by Antonio José de Sucre's victory at Ayacucho.

1828   URUGUAY: Three-year war between Argentina and Brazil over the Banda Oriental (east bank of the River Plate) is ended by agreement to create the Republic of Uruguay.

1829   ARGENTINA: After a series of civil wars Juan Manuel de Rosas becomes Governor of Buenos Aires for the first time.

MEXICO: Spanish expeditionary force defeated at Tampico by Antonio López de Santa Anna.

1829–30 COLOMBIA/VENEZUELA/ECUADOR: Disintegration of Federation of Gran Colombia into three separate states.

1830   CHILE: Conservatives establish themselves in power after defeating Liberals at Lircay.

1831   BRAZIL: Pedro I abdicates as emperor. Council of Regency established.

1833   ARGENTINA: British forces expel Argentine garrison from Falkland/Malvinas Islands.

1835   ARGENTINA: Rosas elected governor of Buenos Aires with absolute powers, confirmed by plebiscite.

1836   MEXICO: Texas declares independence.

PERU/BOLIVIA: Andrés Santa Cruz establishes Peru–Bolivia Confederation.

1838   MEXICO: French occupation of Vera Cruz over unpaid claims arising from civil conflicts.

1838–39 CENTRAL AMERICA: Disintegration of Central American Federation into five separate states.

1838–40 ARGENTINA: French blockade of Buenos Aires.

1839   PERU/BOLIVIA: Confederation disintegrates as a result of civil wars and Chilean opposition.

1840   PARAGUAY: Death of Francia, ruler of Paraguay since 1814; succeeded by Carlos Antonio López who begins technological modernisation of Paraguay using foreign experts.

BRAZIL: Pedro II assumes full powers as emperor.

PERU: First guano export contract.

1845　United States' annexation of Texas.

PERU: Ramón Castilla becomes president.

1845–48 ARGENTINA: Anglo-French blockade of Buenos Aires.

1846–48 MEXICO: US-Mexican War. Ended by Treaty of Guadelupe Hidalgo under which Texas, California, New Mexico and Arizona ceded to United States.

1850　BRAZIL: Government takes effective action to end the transatlantic slave trade under British pressure.

CENTRAL AMERICA: Clayton–Bulwer Treaty between Britain and the United States limits rights of each nation over future canal and over stationing of forces in region.

1852　ARGENTINA: Rosas defeated by Justo José de Urquiza, Governor of Entre Ríos, in alliance with Brazilian and Uruguayan forces. Buenos Aires then rebels against Urquiza's Argentine Confederation.

1854　PERU: After victory in civil war against José Rufino Echenique, who had succeeded him in 1851, Castilla becomes president for the second time.

1855　COLOMBIA: Completion of Panama Railway.

MEXICO: Liberal rebels succeed in gaining power and inaugurate period of *La Reforma*.

1858　MEXICO: Civil war between Conservatives and Liberals recommences.

1861　ARGENTINA: Buenos Aires forces defeat Confederation army at Pavón, thus effectively reunifying country.

1861–62 MEXICO: Spanish, French and British troops land at Vera Cruz to enforce claims for unpaid debts.

1862　ARGENTINA: Bartolomé Mitre inaugurated as Argentine President.

PARAGUAY: Death of Carlos Antonio López, ruler of Paraguay since 1840; succeeded by his son, Francisco Solano López.

1863　MEXICO: After withdrawal of British and Spanish forces, Napoleon III, in alliance with Mexican Conservatives, imposes Maximilian as emperor.

1864　PARAGUAY/URUGUAY: López government offers aid to Blancos in Uruguay in their conflict with the Colorados (who were supported by Brazil).

1864–66 PERU: Spanish attempt to seize guano deposits on Chincha Islands defeated by Peruvian and Chilean naval forces.
1865 PARAGUAY/URUGUAY: Defeat of Uruguayan Blancos. Argentina joins the victorious Colorados and the Brazilians to form the Triple Alliance after Paraguayan troops had crossed its territory.
1867 MEXICO: After withdrawal of French troops Maximilian defeated by Liberals and executed. Diplomatic relations with Britain broken.
1868–72 PERU: Under President José Balta Peruvian state embarks on extensive railway-building schemes financed by foreign loans.
1870 PARAGUAY: Death of Francisco Solano López ends the war with the Triple Alliance, leaving Paraguay devastated.
1872 PERU: Despite a revolt in Lima Manuel Pardo becomes first civilian President of Peru.
1875 PERU: Government given power by Congress to take control of nitrate oficinas, compensating owners with 'nitrate certificates'.
1876 MEXICO: Former Liberal general, Porfirio Díaz, leads revolt and secures presidency.
1879 PERU/BOLIVIA/CHILE: Bolivia declares war on Chile after dispute over taxes in Antofagasta; Chile declares war on Peru, justifying the step on the grounds of the secret treaty signed between Peru and Bolivia in 1873.
1880 ARGENTINA: 'Indian' threat to pampas settlement eliminated by campaign led by General Julio A. Roca, who is then elected president; Buenos Aires 'federalised' as national capital.
1881 CHILE: Former Peruvian state nitrate deposits in Tarapacá returned to private ownership.
1884 MEXICO: After four-year break Porfirio Díaz becomes President of Mexico for the second time.
1886 CHILE: José Manuel Balmaceda elected as president.
URUGUAY: Restoration of civilian government.
1888 BRAZIL: Slavery ended by law.
1889 BRAZIL: Empire overthrown by military revolt led by Marshal Deodoro da Fonseca.
PERU: President Cáceres signs Grace Contract with foreign (largely British) bondholders to settle Peruvian external debt dating from 1870–72
1890 ARGENTINA: Miguel Juárez Celmán resigns as president

after demonstrations against him; Vice-President Carlos Pellegrini replaces him. Onset of Baring crisis.

1891 CHILE: Eight-month civil war ends with the suicide of Balmaceda.

BRAZIL: Floriano Peixoto replaces Deodoro as president. New federal and decentralised constitution introduced.

1894 BRAZIL: Prudente de Morais elected as first civilian president.

1895–96 VENEZUELA: Boundary dispute with British Guiana. US President, Grover Cleveland, presents ultimatum to both sides demanding the submission of the dispute to arbitration.

1898 BRAZIL: Campos Salles elected president. Funding Loan organised by Rothschilds, accompanied by strongly deflationary policies.

1898 CUBA: United States intervenes in Cuban War of Independence against Spain.

1899 VENEZUELA: General Cipriano Castro becomes president.

1901 CENTRAL AMERICA: Hay-Pauncefote Treaty between the United States and Britain permits the United States to establish control over a trans–isthmian canal.

1902–03 VENEZUELA: Anglo-German naval demonstrations, largely over unpaid claims arising from civil wars.

1903 COLOMBIA/CENTRAL AMERICA: Panama, with US support, secedes from Colombia.

URUGUAY: José Batlle y Ordóñez, leader of the Colorados, becomes president.

1906 BRAZIL: State government of São Paulo initiates first coffee valorisation scheme.

1907 CHILE: Chilean troops massacre workers and their families at Iquique in the nitrate zone.

1908 VENEZUELA: Vice-President Juan Vicente Gómez leads a coup during President Castro's absence in Europe.

1911 MEXICO: Revolt led by Francisco Madero succeeds in overthrowing Porfirio Díaz.

URUGUAY: Batlle commences his second four-year term as president.

1913 MEXICO: Huerta's revolt against President Madero precipitates civil war.

1914 Opening of Panama Canal.

VENEZUELA: Commercial production of oil begins.

1916   ARGENTINA: Hipólito Yrigoyen, leader of Radical Party, wins power in presidential elections.

1917   MEXICO: Agreement on new constitution, which includes provisions for state to arbitrate in conflicts between employers and labour and to recover ownership of mineral and petroleum deposits.

1917–20 Wave of labour and student agitation, fuelled by wartime inflation, throughout major countries of Latin America.

1919   URUGUAY: New constitution introduces collegiate executive and consolidates control of Colorado and Blanco parties over the state.
PERU: Augusto B. Leguía, previously president 1908–12, takes power in a coup d'état.

1920   MEXICO: Alvaro Obregón becomes president, and begins to re-establish power of Mexican state.
CHILE: Arturo Alessandri wins presidential elections with substantial working–class support.

1922   ARGENTINA: Marcelo T. de Alvear replaces Yrigoyen as president.

1923   MEXICO: Bucareli agreements provide Obregón with US recognition in return for acceptance of oil companies' rights to concessions on which they had begun work before 1917.

1924   MEXICO: Plutarco Elías Calles succeeds Obregón as president.
CHILE: Military coup pushes social legislation through Congress.

1928   ARGENTINA: Yrigoyen elected as president for the second time.

1930   ARGENTINA: Yrigoyen overthrown by military revolt.
BRAZIL: After disputed elections President Washington Luis overthrown by revolt of junior officers and dissident civilians headed by Getúlio Vargas, former Governor of Rio Grande do Sul.
PERU: After eleven years in power Leguía overthrown in revolt led by Colonel Luis M. Sánchez Cerro.

1931   CHILE: Overthrow of President Carlos Ibáñez leads to a year of political uncertainty. Anglo-South American Bank seeks help from Bank of England because of its over-exposure in nitrate industry.

1932   ARGENTINA: Agustín P. Justo inaugurated as president after fraudulent elections.

BRAZIL: São Paulo rebellion against Vargas government defeated by the national government after two months' fighting.

1932–35 BOLIVIA/PARAGUAY: Chaco War, ending in defeat of Bolivia.

1933 ARGENTINA: Negotiation of Roca–Runciman Pact in London.

PERU: Assassination of Sánchez Cerro. General Oscar Benavides becomes president.

URUGUAY: Gabriel Terra leads coup against *batllistas*.

1934 MEXICO: Lázaro Cárdenas becomes president.

1935 VENEZUELA: Death of Gómez, president for all but two years since 1908. Succeeded by General Eleazar López Contreras, but increasing civil turmoil and labour militancy.

1937 BRAZIL: Vargas closes Congress and with the support of the military proclaims the Estado Nôvo.

1938 MEXICO: Cárdenas nationalises the major foreign oil companies.

ARGENTINA: Roberto M. Ortiz elected as president.

1940 ARGENTINA: Ortiz resigns presidency due to ill-health: Ramón S. Castillo succeeds.

1943 ARGENTINA: Military revolt overthrows Castillo government.

VENEZUELA: New Hydrocarbons Law imposed on petroleum companies with consent of US and British governments.

1944 ARGENTINA: Internal coup within the military; Juan Domingo Perón becomes vice-president.

1945 BRAZIL: Vargas resigns presidency.

VENEZUELA: Acción Democrática under Rómulo Betancourt takes power. New *junta* decrees a new tax on oil company earnings to ensure a fifty-fifty profits split between companies and government.

1946 BRAZIL: General Eurico Dutra elected as president.

1946 ARGENTINA: Perón elected president.

Bibliographical Essay

(This essay concentrates on works published in English and apart from the first two sections the headings within it correspond to the chapters of the book itself. Shortened titles for each work mentioned are provided here; for full details refer to the Select Bibliography. At the end of the essay a final section provides some more information about the principal primary sources that historians have used for this subject.)

GENERAL

The fullest history of Latin America in English is Bethell (ed.), *Cambridge History of Latin America (CHLA)*. This contains both thematic surveys (for example on international relations or economic change) and chapters on individual countries, but most were written during the 1970s and many are becoming outdated. For a one-volume introduction see Keen and Wasserman, *Short History of Latin America*. Bushnell and Macaulay, *Emergence of Latin America*, is an excellent survey of the nineteenth century, but the companion volume on the twentieth century, Skidmore and Smith, *Modern Latin America*, was designed primarily for readers in the United States and is somewhat uneven in its coverage.

The standard of one-volume histories in English on individual countries is patchy. Rock, *Argentina, 1516–1987*, is thorough and reliable, although Scobie, *Argentina, a City and a Nation*, can still be read with profit. In contrast Brazil is very poorly served. The best survey, Bethell (ed.), *Brazil: Empire and Republic*, consists of chapters extracted from *CHLA* but it runs only to 1930. Loveman,

Chile, Lombardi, *Venezuela*, and Klein, *Bolivia*, all in the generally excellent Oxford University Press series, are the best introductions to those countries. For Mexico see Meyer and Sherman, *Course of Mexican History*, and Bazant, *Concise History of Mexico*. There is no good general history of Peru in English. The least poor is still Pike, *Modern History of Peru*; Mörner, *Andean Past*, is also useful since it encompasses Bolivia and Ecuador as well as Peru.

A good English-language economic history of Latin America since independence is also lacking. For the period of the export boom, though, Albert, *South America and the World Economy*, provides a concise introduction, and those who read Spanish should consult Cardoso and Pérez Brignoli, *Historia económica de América Latina*. Díaz Alejandro, *Essays on the Economic History*, is still worth reading on Argentina; see also Randall, *Economic History of Argentina*. Sunkel, *Un siglo de historia económica*, provides some suggestive ideas about Chilean economic history. Thorp and Bertram, *Peru, 1890–1977*, and Finch, *Political Economy of Uruguay*, are both excellent studies by historically minded economists.

The literature on both British and US imperialism in the nineteenth and twentieth centuries is surveyed by Smith, *Pattern of Imperialism*. On Britain alone see Cain, *Economic Foundations*, for a concise overview of the debates. Following this Cain and Hopkins developed the concept of 'gentlemanly capitalism' to analyse Britain's relationship with the overseas world, initially in a series of articles ('Political Economy'; 'Gentlemanly Capitalism'). This new and controversial interpretation of British expansion culminates in their two volumes, *British Imperialism: Innovation and Expansion 1688–1914* and *British Imperialism: Crisis and Deconstruction 1914–1990*, which contain sections on Latin America. Other modern historians of British imperialism have tended to ignore Latin America because of the lack of formal colonies. While Davis and Huttenback, *Mammon and the Pursuit of Empire*, resist this tendency and incorporate the region more fully into their analysis, much of what they say about it is inaccurate. Weaver, 'American Underdevelopment', and Pregger Román, 'Dependence, Underdevelopment and Imperialism', both provide readable interpretations of nineteenth-century imperialism from a more radical perspective.

Apart from this volume there are no other books surveying the British role in Latin America, although Bethell, 'Britain and Latin America', does provide a useful short survey. Much can also be gained from two collections of papers, Platt (ed.), *Business Imperialism*, and Abel and Lewis (eds), *Latin America, Economic Imperialism, and the*

State, both of which contain several good empirical studies. Lewis and Miller (eds), *British Business in Latin America*, will include both sectoral and country studies. Useful comparative material on German interests in Latin America can be found in Forbes, 'German Informal Imperialism', and Herwig, *Germany's Vision of Empire*. The literature on US interests in Latin America is enormous, though much of it is of a rather conventional diplomatic history genre. The most useful items on US economic expansion are Wilkins, *Emergence of Multinational Enterprise* and *Maturing of Multinational Enterprise*, and Frieden, 'Economics of Intervention'.

There are several important thematic or country studies of the British role in Latin America, even though there is no full survey. Rippy, *British Investments*, is a standard source, although his statistical material is dubious. For British investments in government loans before 1900 see Marichal's marvellous *Century of Debt Crises*. On commerce Platt, *Latin America and British Trade*, is wide ranging but controversial in its conclusions. The standard work on British interests in nineteenth-century Argentina is Ferns, *Britain and Argentina*; this provides, though, a more conservative interpretation than Ferns' earlier articles, particularly 'Britain's Informal Empire'. Fodor and O'Connell, 'La Argentina y la economía atlántica', Gravil, *Anglo-Argentine Connection*, and Skupch, 'El deterioro y fin', take the story from 1900, where Ferns stopped, and offer a much more critical viewpoint. On Anglo–Brazilian relations Manchester, *British Pre-Eminence*, is still worth reading some sixty years after it was published, but see also Graham, *Britain and the Onset of Modernisation*, and Ridings, 'Business, Nationality, and Dependency', both of which reflect the informal imperialism/dependency paradigm of the late 1960s and 1970s. Leff, *Underdevelopment and Development*, in contrast, relies on a strongly neo-classical approach, and, like Peláez, 'Theory and Reality', is critical of the application of theories of informal imperialism to the Brazilian experience. For discussion of Chile in the light of these same debates see Mayo, 'Britain and Chile' and *British Merchants and Chilean Development*, for the pre-1880 period, and then Monteón, 'British in the Atacama Desert' and *Chile in the Nitrate Era*. Carl, *First among Equals*, sketches the history of British interests in nineteenth-century Venezuela. On Mexico Tischendorf, *Great Britain and Mexico*, contains a mine of information about British investment there.

THEORETICAL DEBATES

The majority of the early critiques of the British and the problems which they seemed to create for Latin American development remain untranslated. Encina, *Nuestra inferioridad económica*, and Bunge, *Los problemas económicos*, were the most important dissenting pieces produced in the early years of this century. The conservative reaction to the British probably went furthest in Argentina. See especially Scalabrini Ortíz, *Política británica* and *Historia de los ferrocarriles argentinos*, and Irazusta, *Influencia económica británica*, and for a commentary on this school Falcoff, 'Raúl Scalabrini Ortíz'. Mariátegui, *Seven Interpretive Essays*, is the most important early Marxist critique. Later works in the same tradition sold widely and were crucial in establishing the popularity of nationalist interpretations; see Ramírez, *Historia del imperialismo*, for Chile, and Prado, *História econômica do Brasil*, for Brazil. Yepes, *Perú, 1820–1920*, provides a similar appraisal of British interests there. Brewer, *Marxist Theories of Imperialism*, is an extremely useful survey, even though he pays little attention to Latin American writers.

The British debate over Latin America developed separately from this literature. The seminal article was Gallagher and Robinson, 'Imperialism of Free Trade'. Louis (ed.), *Imperialism*, provides a good overview of the controversy which followed and includes one paper, Graham, 'Robinson and Gallagher', specifically on Latin America. Graham, 'Sepoys and Imperialists', and Winn, 'Britain's Informal Empire', show the strong influence of Robinson and Gallagher in discussing Brazil and Uruguay respectively. In contrast, Mathew, 'Imperialism of Free Trade', rejects the hypothesis of informal imperialism for mid nineteenth-century Peru. The most sustained attack on Robinson and Gallagher, though, came from Platt, in *Finance, Trade, and Politics* and several shorter articles: 'Imperialism of Free Trade', 'Economic Factors' and 'Further Objections'. The papers in Owen and Sutcliffe (eds), *Studies in the Theory*, provide an excellent impression of how the debate over various strands of imperialism stood in the early 1970s. This includes important articles by Robinson on the 'collaborating elite' and Platt on the limitations of 'business imperialism'.

The evolution of Latin American development theories after 1945 is analysed in both Kay, *Latin American Theories*, and an older work, Roxborough, *Theories of Underdevelopment*. Love, 'Raúl Prebisch', explains the origins of structuralist thought, and Furtado, *Economic Development*, is an economic history based upon these ideas. By

1970, however, more radical dependency analyses were beginning to dominate. The most important early interpretations for historians were Frank, *Capitalism and Underdevelopment*, Cardoso and Faletto, *Dependency and Development*, and Stein and Stein, *Colonial Heritage*. Cardoso himself, though, in 'Consumption of Dependency Theory', questioned the enthusiasm shown by many US scholars for these ideas, and a leading Latin American historian, Halperín Donghi, '"Dependency Theory"', also expressed doubts. Platt again vehemently opposed the use of such theory to analyse the British role in Latin America; see his 'Dependency in Nineteenth-Century Latin America' and 'Dependency and the Historian', the first of which resulted in a bitter debate with the Steins.

THE COLONIAL AND INDEPENDENCE ERAS

Apart from Bethell (ed.), *CHLA*, I and II, the best histories of the colonial period are Lockhart and Schwartz, *Early Latin America*, and Burkholder and Johnson, *Colonial Latin America*. Liss, *Atlantic Empires*, is also a useful comparative study. On Spain's trade with its colonies in the eighteenth century see Walker, *Spanish Politics*. The official and contraband trade of the English in Spanish America has been analysed by several historians. Zahedieh, 'Trade, Plunder, and Economic Development', and Fortune, *Merchants and Jews*, deal with the seventeenth-century Caribbean, while Palmer, *Human Cargoes*, considers the use the British made of their privileged position in the slave trade after 1713 to smuggle other cargoes. Older articles like Christelow, 'Great Britain and the Trades', Nettels, 'England and the Spanish American Trade', Nelson, 'Contraband Trade', and Brown, 'Contraband Trade', are still useful but are being superseded by more careful local studies. The pioneer, in many ways, was Villalobos, *El comercio y la crisis colonial* and *Comercio y contrabando*, which concentrate on the River Plate and Chile. Grahn, 'An Irresoluble Dilemma', is also an important contribution on the Caribbean coast of South America. Much less has been published on British trade with Brazil before 1770, but Boxer, 'Brazilian Gold', and H. Fisher, 'Anglo-Portuguese Trade', provide an outline. The trade of the Spanish empire after the commercial reforms of the late eighteenth century has attracted much more attention. J. Fisher, *Commercial Relations*, and Cuenca Esteban, 'Statistics of Spain's Colonial Trade', are fundamental, while Barbier, 'Commercial Reform', considers the

265

significant case of Cartagena. Goebel, 'British Trade', is still worth consulting on the later period.

Lynch, *Spanish-American Revolutions*, provides an excellent survey of the independence era, while Costeloe, *Response to Revolution*, says much about attitudes towards Britain in Madrid. The basic British documents of the era were reprinted, with an excellent introduction, in Webster (ed.), *Britain and the Independence*. Kaufmann, *British Policy*, added little to Webster's work. Much better are Lynch's succinct surveys of British official thinking, 'British Policy and Spanish America' and 'Great Britain and Spanish American Independence'. Street, 'Lord Strangford', and Waddell, 'British Relations with Venezuela', add important regional studies to the overviews provided by Webster and Lynch. Waddell also reinterprets particular periods of crisis in London's relations with Madrid in 'British Neutrality' and 'Anglo-Spanish Relations'. Graham and Humphreys (eds), *The Navy*, examine one important aspect of British power. For Canning's attitude towards Latin America, Temperley, *Foreign Policy of Canning*, still has much to offer, while Macaulay, *Dom Pedro*, provides essential background on Portugal and Brazil.

There is no overview of Britain's commercial relations with Latin America in the independence era, but local studies provide much basic information. See especially Williams, 'Establishment of British Commerce', Segreti, 'La política económica porteña', and Brown, *Socioeconomic History of Argentina*, on the Plate; Centner, 'Relaciones comerciales', Kinsbruner, 'Political Influence', Goebel, 'British – American Rivalry', on Chile. Empirical studies of British trade in other regions during the independence wars are more difficult to find, and future research may undermine many of the preconceptions about the influence of British merchants which are apparent in the 'dependency' literature. It is clear, for example, that US traders, supported by officials, were also present in large numbers; for their role in Peru immediately after independence see Gootenberg, *Tejidos y harinas*.

THE BRITISH GOVERNMENT AND LATIN AMERICA FROM INDEPENDENCE TO 1914

Platt, *Finance, Trade, and Politics*, claims a limited role for the British government in nineteenth-century Latin America, and sets the parameters of debate. For the institutional background see Jones, *Nineteenth-*

Century Foreign Office and *British Diplomatic Service*, and also Cromwell and Steiner, 'Foreign Office before 1914'. Williams, *British Commercial Policy*, is an excellent survey of the earlier phase of commercial expansion, while Gaston, 'Trade and the Late Victorian Foreign Office', takes the story further. Kennedy, *Strategy and Diplomacy*, provides some stimulating ideas about the place of Latin America in Britain's strategic thinking before the Great War.

Most studies of the British government concentrate on particular regions of Latin America or incidents of conflict. On the River Plate see Pratt, 'Anglo–American Commercial and Political Rivalry', and particularly Cady, *Foreign Intervention*, as well as Lynch's excellent biography of Rosas, *Argentine Dictator*. Morgan, 'French Policy' and 'Orleanist Diplomacy', throws more light on the French dimension to British policy. On Brazil Bethell, *Abolition of the Brazilian Slave Trade*, is fundamental. It should be supplemented with Eltis, *Economic Growth*, a wide-ranging and impressive study. The essential work on Central America is Rodríguez, *Palmerstonian Diplomat*. Other important items about this area are the debate between Naylor, 'British Role', and van Aken, 'British Policy Considerations', Dozier, *Nicaragua's Mosquito Shore*, and Waddell, 'Great Britain and the Bay Islands'. Some studies of other countries also undermine Platt's claim for non-interventionist and disinterested British officials in the first half-century after independence; see Wu, *Generals and Diplomats*, Mayo, '"The Impatient Lion"', and Scobie, 'Los representantes británicos'. Smith, 'New World Diplomacy', in contrast, follows the Platt interpretation more closely.

On the later nineteenth century Smith, *Illusions of Conflict*, is a good guide to Anglo-US 'rivalries' and the general lines of British policy. There are many items on the background to the Paraguayan War of 1865–70 and the war itself, for the precise nature of Paraguayan policy and the extent of its isolationism have been the subject of much debate. Apart from Kiernan, 'Britain's First Contacts', contrast the views of Williams, 'Paraguayan Isolation' and *Rise and Fall of the Paraguayan Republic*, with White, 'The Denied Revolution' and *Paraguay's Autonomous Revolution*. Tate, 'Britain and Latin America', summarises Foreign Office papers on the subject, and Plá, *The British in Paraguay*, concentrates on the British technicians employed there immediately before the war. On the war itself Fornos Peñalba, 'Draft Dodgers', epitomises the nationalist view that Britain was to blame; McLynn, 'Causes of the War', and Abente, 'War of the Triple Alliance', are both much more sober analyses emphasising the internal dynamics of developments within Latin American states.

Archival research has also undermined nationalist assumptions about Britain's role in the Pacific War between Chile, Peru and Bolivia. On Chile's decision to go to war see especially Mayo, 'La Compañía de Salitres', O'Brien, 'Antofagasta Company', and Ortega, 'Nitrates', all of which use business archives. Kiernan, 'Foreign Interests', is an older study based on Foreign Office documents. The Venezuelan crisis of 1902–03, in contrast to both these wars, remains an area of polemic rather than research. While offering valuable information on late nineteenth-century Venezuela neither Carl, *First among Equals*, nor Hood, *Gunboat Diplomacy*, contains any archival research on the crisis itself; the most reliable studies are Platt, 'Allied Coercion of Venezuela', and Herwig, *Germany's Vision of Empire*. Mexican history, in contrast, is much better studied, and there are several good analyses of the British reaction to the revolution which followed the overthrow of Porfirio Díaz in 1910; see Calvert, *Mexican Revolution*, Durán, *Guerra y revolución*, and especially Katz, *Secret War in Mexico*.

LATIN AMERICA AND BRITISH BUSINESS IN THE FIRST HALF-CENTURY AFTER INDEPENDENCE

The best surveys of the period are Halperín Donghi, *Aftermath of Revolution* and the essays by him and Safford in *CHLA*, IV. One problem which has plagued research has been the unreliability of both Latin American and British commercial statistics. On this see Platt, 'Problems in the Interpretation'. Davis, *Industrial Revolution*, however, later reworked some of the British figures for trade with Latin America before the 1860s. Of the vast literature on Britain's overseas trade generally during the Industrial Revolution the main items worth consulting for Latin America are Crouzet, 'Toward an Export Economy', and Farnie, *English Cotton Industry*.

For Latin America itself the early chapters of Platt, *Latin America and British Trade*, survey Britain's commercial activities before 1860. Ridings, 'Foreign Predominance', views the influence of foreign merchants as much more pervasive than Platt, but he fails to distinguish 'expatriates' and 'immigrants', a crucial shortcoming of the analysis. Clapp, *John Owens*, is an interesting case study. For British merchants in the River Plate see both Reber, *British Mercantile Houses*, and Robinson's succinct 'Merchants of Post-Independence Buenos Aires'. Other local studies include Berglund, 'Mercantile Credit', on Venezuela, and Mayo, 'Before the Nitrate Era', on Chile. Mathew,

Antony Gibbs & Sons, examines that firm's role in the Peruvian guano trade, while Walker, *Kinship, Business, and Politics*, and Tenenbaum, 'Straightening out some of the Lumpen' and *Politics of Penury*, include material on British merchants in Mexico City. The contraband activities of the separate merchant community on the west coast of Mexico form the subject for Mayo, 'Consuls and Silver Contraband', and Gough, 'Specie Conveyance'.

Interpretations which stressed the overwhelming power of British businessmen vis-à-vis local states and entrepreneurs in the half-century after independence have come under much questioning. On Argentina see especially Brown, 'Dynamics of Autonomy', which should be read alongside Burgin's older *Economic Aspects*, and on Peru Hunt, 'Guano y crecimiento', and Gootenberg, 'Social Origins of Protectionism' and *Between Silver and Guano*. Mexican tariff policy and industrialisation, a central area of debate, is examined in Thomson, 'Protectionism and Industrialization' and 'Continuity and Change', Bernecker, 'Foreign Interests', and Córdova, 'Proteccionismo y librecambio'. Will, 'La política económica', and Ortega, 'Economic Policy and Growth', also question the extent to which Chileans fully accepted the principles of free trade.

The spurt of British investment immediately after independence has attracted a lot of attention. The informative analysis of Dawson, *First Latin American Debt Crisis*, depends heavily on the contemporary press, and complements Marichal, *Century of Debt Crises*, and an older classic, Jenks, *Migration of British Capital*. Again there is a whole series of country studies of government debt. On Mexico see Platt, 'British Finance', Bazant, *Historia de la deuda exterior*, Carmagnani, 'Finanzas y estado', and Liehr, 'La deuda exterior de México'. Liehr has also written 'La deuda exterior de la Gran Colombia'. Platt's 'Foreign Finance' deals with Argentina, although the most important work on the controversial Buenos Aires loan of 1824 is Amaral, 'El empréstito de Londres'. On Chile see Veliz, 'Irisarri Loan', and on Peru Mathew, 'First Anglo-Peruvian Debt', and Palacios, *La deuda anglo-peruana*. The investment in mining has been much less studied, but there are some useful works. Eakin, *British Enterprise in Brazil*, analyses an unusually successful gold-mining firm, and Randall, *Real del Monte* and 'British Company and Mexican Community', the most important silver-mining venture in early nineteenth-century Mexico. Veliz, 'Egaña, Lambert', explains why British mining firms were not successful in the expanding Chilean industry, though Mayo, 'Commerce, Credit and Control', stresses the merchants' role in providing finance.

MERCHANTS AND TRADE, 1870–1914

Many of the works noted earlier, in particular Platt and Ridings, are relevant to the later nineteenth century, but for an excellent survey see also Greenhill, 'Merchants'. Jones, *International Business*, offers a stimulating interpretation of the changing activities of foreign merchants, emphasising Latin America. The shift of emphasis from purely commercial functions also lies at the core of Chapman's *Rise of Merchant Banking* and 'British-based Investment Groups'. Such arguments, as Jones explains in '"Business Imperialism"', have important implications for an understanding of imperialism.

Case studies of merchants for this period are relatively few, and they depend on the haphazard survival of business archives. Greenhill and Miller, 'Peruvian Government', and O'Brien, *Nitrate Industry*, provide information on Gibbs' participation in nitrate. Pregger Román, 'Role of the Banking and Insurance Sector', and Albert, 'External Forces', draw rather different conclusions about the west-coast merchants' impact on the economies of Chile and Peru. Burga and Reátegui, *Lanas y capital mercantil*, is an important regional study of southern Peru. There is much less on the east-coast firms. Shipping has also suffered from some neglect due to archival problems, but Albion, 'British Shipping', Greenhill, 'Shipping' and 'Latin America's Export Trades', and Oribe Stemmer, 'Freight Rates', are all worth consulting.

There is no space here to detail the extensive literature on the problems of Britain's export trades after 1880, but for a good insight into the debate see Pollard, *Britain's Rise and Britain's Decline*. For Latin America there is a sharp contrast between those who play down the problem (Platt, *Latin America and British Trade*, and Nicholas, 'Overseas Marketing Performance') and those who are much more critical of the abilities of British manufacturers and traders: Saul, *Studies in British Overseas Trade*, and more recently Gravil, *Anglo-Argentine Connection*, and Miller, 'British Trade with Latin America'.

THE INVESTMENT BOOM, 1870–1914

There are many more studies of investment in the late nineteenth century. The traditional starting points are Feis, *Europe, the World's Banker*, and Rippy, *British Investments*, together with the studies of Stone, 'British Long-Term Investment' and 'British Direct and

Portfolio Investment'. Since 1980, however, the statistics have been subject to much criticism, most importantly by Platt, 'British Portfolio Investment' and *Britain's Investment Overseas*, though his estimates have in turn been disputed by Feinstein, 'Britain's Overseas Investments'. Other quantitative studies, relating returns on investment to the outflow of capital, have come from Davis and Huttenback, 'Export of British Finance', and, most impressively, Edelstein, *Overseas Investment*. Pollard, 'Capital Exports, 1870–1914', provides an excellent summary of the debate over the consequences of foreign investment for Britain.

The institutional changes which occurred in British financial markets and the impact of crises in the City of London on Latin America itself have also attracted research. For background see Kindleberger, *Financial History*, and Born, *International Banking*. On government loans the most important item is Marichal, *Century of Debt Crises* but Chapman, *Rise of Merchant Banking*, and two company histories, Burk, *Morgan Grenfell*, and Ziegler's more anecdotal *Sixth Great Power* (on Barings), are vital to understanding the incentives and mechanisms for British lending. Both Felix, 'Alternative Outcomes', and Fishlow, 'Lessons from the Past', like Marichal, draw long-term conclusions about Latin American government indebtedness from the literature on the nineteenth century. For more detailed analyses of the problems incurred by Argentina, Brazil, and Chile as a result of their borrowing, see the section below. On Peru, one of the most important examples of debt reconstruction, Miller, 'The Making of the Grace Contract' and 'The Grace Contract', builds on the earlier work of Wynne, *State Insolvency*.

The mechanisms of investment in companies are less well studied. The crucial theoretical article is Wilkins, 'The Free-Standing Company', complemented by Chapman's research. There are, however, several important sectoral studies. Lewis, 'Financing of Railway Development', takes issue with the belief that foreign capital was always dominant, and also argues, in 'Railways and Industrialization', that their economic impact was more positive for Latin American development than many writers assume. (For studies of railways in individual countries see the following section.) Much less has been written on public utilities; the most significant items are Jones and Greenhill, 'Public Utility Companies', Finch, 'British Imperialism', and Greenfield, 'Dependency and the Urban Experience'. García Heras' forthcoming work on Anglo–Argentine Tramways will add another important case study. The history of British commercial banking in Latin America has passed through three clearly defined stages: first, Joslin's company biography, *Century of Banking*, then C. Jones' work on the River Plate, 'Commercial Banks', and finally G. Jones, 'Competitive Advantages', which, together with his forthcoming book, places the British experience in Latin America in a much broader framework. C. Jones' unique work on 'Insurance Companies', an area of much greater importance for British interests than historians' lack of attention to it would indicate, is also significant. Mining, with the exception of Eakin, *British Enterprise*, and the various works on nitrate, has also been neglected. Harvey and Press, 'Overseas Investment', suggest that Latin America was not that important to British metal-mining firms, but this still leaves open the question of why not, as well as the experience of those which did invest. On the growth of British oil interests in Mexico before 1911, Brown, 'Domestic Politics', is essential.

The unevenness of research on investment is, in part, due to the availability of archives, but it also depends on the significance of a particular activity to contemporary political developments. Both factors explain why so much has been written on nitrate, for this sector was crucial in the formation of Chilean working-class movements. On this see Monteón, 'The Enganche', and Fernández, 'British Nitrate Companies'. DeShazo, *Urban Workers*, dissents from the common assumption that nitrate miners were the dominant force behind worker militancy. Bergquist, *Labor in Latin America*, compares workers in different export sectors, and makes an important contribution not only to the understanding of British firms' activities in nitrate but also in the Argentine meat industry and Venezuelan oil. On railway workers in Argentina see Thompson, 'Limitations of Ideology', Stang, 'Entrepreneurs and Managers' and 'Aspectos de la política de personal', and Horowitz, 'Occupational Community'. On other countries Blanchard, *Origins of the Peruvian Labor Movement*, is a sound analysis with some information about British firms, and Brown, 'Foreign Oil Companies' (on Mexico), contains some important ideas about the diverging expectations of British employers and Latin American workers which might be applied elsewhere.

ARGENTINA, BRAZIL AND CHILE BEFORE 1914

Just as they received the majority of British investment before 1914, so Argentina, Brazil and Chile have been the focus of most foreign research on the British role in Latin America. The strong academic traditions of these three countries have also contributed enormously to knowledge about their history.

Rock, *Politics in Argentina*, and Scobie, *Revolution on the Pampas*, remain important for a basic understanding of Argentina after 1880, while Di Tella and Platt (eds), *Political Economy of Argentina*, and Rock (ed.), *Argentina in the Twentieth Century*, are valuable collections of essays on the same period. Denoon, *Settler Capitalism*, considers Argentina in a comparative study of 'areas of recent settlement'. On trade after 1880 see Williams, *Argentine International Trade*, and on investment various works by Ford, in particular *Gold Standard*, 'British Investment in Argentina' and 'British Investment in Argentine Economic Development', as well as Platt, 'Canada and Argentina'. Ford's 'Argentina and the Baring Crisis' is still valuable on the events of 1890, together with Cuccorese, 'La versión histórica argentina' and Hodge, 'Carlos Pellegrini'. Jones, 'State and Business Practice' and 'Personalism, Indebtedness and Venality', also examines the political environment within which British investors operated. In Argentina, as elsewhere, nationalist or 'dependency' interpretations, emphasising the control exercised by the British and denying the autonomy of local politicians, have come under criticism for their simplistic assumptions; see, for example, Guy, 'Dependency, the Credit Market, and Argentine Industrialization' and 'Carlos Pellegrini'. However, the most useful single item on the Argentine elite, which stresses the socially and politically conservative attitudes which many leaders of the elite retained despite the growth of the economy, is Brown, 'Bondage of Old Habits'.

The railways, not surprisingly, have attracted much research. Lewis, *British Railways in Argentina*, is sceptical of many of the attacks made on them, and in 'British Railway Companies' he argues that their influence, individually and collectively, was more circumscribed than normally assumed. Wright, 'Foreign-Owned Railways' and *British-Owned Railways*, also provides a useful survey of their development, and Regalsky, 'Foreign Capital', shows how French investment affected the British. On the British role in agricultural exports see Sábato, 'Wool Trade', Crossley and Greenhill, 'River Plate Beef Trade', and most importantly Smith, *Politics and Beef*. Perren, *Meat Trade*, provides some background on the British market for Argentina's exports.

Two works published at the end of the 1980s are crucial for understanding Britain's role in Brazil, a subject which has been much less exhaustively researched than the Anglo-Argentine relationship. One was Topik's *Political Economy of the Brazilian State*, which consolidated his earlier articles while also providing one of the first modern analyses of Brazilian railway policy, the other Fritsch, *External Constraints*. The earlier regional studies of Love, *São Paulo*, Levine, *Pernambuco*, and Wirth, *Minas Gerais*, remain useful, however, as do Eisenberg, *Sugar Industry in Pernambuco*, and Pang, 'Modernization and Slavocracy' (on Bahia), for delineating British interests in Brazil. See also Fonseca, 'Os investimentos ingleses', on the Great Western Railway in the north-east. On rubber Weinstein, *Amazon Rubber Boom*, suggests a more limited role for British interests than many have assumed, but John's study of the Booth Shipping Line, *Liverpool Merchant House*, should not be neglected. The other important area of research in Brazil's export sectors is the coffee trade. Greenhill, 'Brazilian Coffee Trade', provides a survey, to be supplemented by his forthcoming company history of Johnston's. The role played by British merchants and financiers in coffee price support schemes is particularly significant. On this see Holloway, *Brazilian Coffee Valorization*, and Krasner, 'Manipulating International Commodity Markets'. Nevertheless, much research remains to be done on the British role in Brazil, particularly regarding the activities of merchants, industrial firms and railway companies, and the relationship between federal and state governments in Brazil and merchant bankers in London (two-thirds of Fritsch's fine book is devoted to the period between 1914 and 1930).

Both in Argentina and in Brazil the research has tended to question the assumption that the British exercised overwhelming power. Much more attention is now paid to the local elites and their use of the state to further their interests. A similar change of emphasis is apparent in Chile; see particularly Bauer, 'Industry and the Missing Bourgeoisie', and Sater, 'Economic Nationalism and Tax Reform' and 'Chile and the World Depression'. The trend is especially marked in studies of nitrate, the best of which are O'Brien's sophisticated *Nitrate Industry*, Mamalakis, 'Role of Government', and Blakemore's influential interpretation of the 1891 Civil War, *British Nitrates and Chilean Politics*. On this and earlier conflicts see also Zeitlin, *Civil Wars in Chile*. Apart from Fernández, 'Merchants and Bankers' and the work on labour noted earlier, there has, however, been relatively little research on British interests in Chile between 1891 and 1914, although some material appears in Blakemore, *From the Pacific*, a useful biography of the leading British railway company in northern Chile.

On the development of British interests in other countries much less has been published than in these three, even for Mexico where investment interests also grew quite significantly during the Por-

274

firiato. González Deluca, 'Los intereses británicos', surveys the growth of investment in Venezuela (see the following section for more material on oil). For Paraguay after the war see Warren, *Paraguay and the Triple Alliance, Rebirth of the Paraguayan Republic* and 'Golden Fleecing', as well as Abente, 'Foreign Capital'. Nahum and Barrán's multi-volume *Historia rural del Uruguay moderno* and *Batlle, los estancieros, y el imperio británico* provide an important supplement to the work of Finch and Winn on Uruguay.

THE FIRST WORLD WAR AND ITS AFTERMATH

Barnett, *British Food Policy*, provides essential background to the study of Latin American exports during the First World War, but the literature on the period is headed by an excellent analysis of finance, trade, industry and labour: Albert, *South America and the First World War*. This draws on the earlier work of Albert and Henderson, 'Latin America and the Great War', and on Henderson's PhD thesis on Peru and Chile. Like Albert, Miller, 'Latin American Manufacturing', is sceptical of the claims of 'dependency' writers about the extent of Latin America's industrial progress during the war, a view also questioned by Gravil, 'Argentina and the First World War'. Couyoumdjian, 'El mercado del salitre', concentrates on the strategically important Chilean nitrate industry. The war exacerbated rivalries between Britain and the United States, as Rosenberg explains in two studies, 'Anglo–American Economic Rivalry' and 'Economic Pressures'. Gerhardt, 'Inglaterra y el petroleo mexicano', looks at policy-making in a key sector for British interests, while Tulchin incorporates the rivalry over oil into a much broader study, *Aftermath of War*, which also contains a discussion of US attempts to erode Britain's monopoly of the Atlantic cables and its dominance of Latin American government finance.

The impact of Britain's postwar financial problems on lending to Latin America are well explained in both Moggridge, 'British Controls', and Atkin, 'Official Regulation'. Sayers, *Bank of England*, and RIIA, *Problem of International Investment*, are also essential for an understanding of Britain's inter war policies on capital exports. Very few historians, however, have considered in detail why British enterprise in Latin America seems to have declined so markedly after 1914. An exception is O'Brien, '"Rich Beyond the Dreams of Avarice"', but, in contrast to his own conclusions about British failure, his evidence could also be interpreted as suggesting that Gibbs were justified in withdrawing from Chilean nitrate when they did. The problems of the Anglo-South American Bank, which over-committed itself in the same industry, can be followed in Joslin, *Century of Banking*, and Sayers.

There is a growing literature on the petroleum industry, headed by Philip's impressive *Oil and Politics*. Turner, *Oil Companies*, and Venn, *Oil Diplomacy*, are also useful but concerned primarily with international political and business rivalries. McBeth, *British Oil Policy*, is a useful summary of the interwar period but lacking in analysis. Meyer, *The Mexican Revolution*, is a neat discussion of the problems faced by the Mexican Eagle oil company and other British interests there in the 1920s. In 'Why Foreign Oil Companies', however, Brown reinterprets the shift of interest from Mexico to Venezuela as a consequence of technical rather than political problems. McBeth, *Juan Vicente Gómez*, is the basic work on the Venezuelan industry, but he again provides a lot of information without much analysis. The Venezuelan story after the death of Gómez in 1935 can be followed in Singh, 'Oil Politics'. On British oil companies in Peru Thorp and Bertram, *Peru, 1890 – 1977*, and Miller, 'Small Business', are the principal sources.

Manufacturing was the other significant area in which British direct investment expanded between the wars, but the story must be assembled from company histories. Traditionally British industrial firms were thought to lack dynamism, a view epitomised in Chandler, 'Growth of the Transnational Industrial Firm'. This interpretation has been revised by a number of studies: Stopford, 'Origins of British-based Multinational Manufacturing Enterprises'; Wilkins, 'History of European Multinationals' and 'European and North American Multinationals'; Jones, 'Expansion of British Multinational Manufacturing', 'Origins, Management and Performance' and 'Performance of British Multinational Enterprise'; and Nicholas, 'British Multinational Investment'. These authors disagree, however, on the significance of Latin America, and it is only by piecing together information in company histories that a picture of growth, principally in Argentina and Brazil, begins to emerge. The most important of these are Wilson, *History of Unilever* and *Unilever, 1945 – 1965* (but note that Fieldhouse, *Unilever Overseas*, explicitly excludes the company's activities in Latin America), Barker, *Glassmakers* and 'Pilkington', Reader, *Imperial Chemical Industries*, Reckitt, *History of Reckitt and Sons*, Cox, 'Growth and Ownership' (on British American Tobacco), and Davenport-

Hines, 'Glaxo'. Greenhill and Miller, 'Merchants, Industrialists', draw together these examples into a broader survey.

The experience of the 1920s was crucial to Britain's links with Argentina. The background to the growing trade problems of both countries is well explained in a series of papers by O'Connell, 'Argentina into the Depression', 'Free Trade in One (Primary Producing) Country' and 'La fiebre aftosa', all of which reflect the strong feeling among some Argentine historians that the country diversified too late and became too dependent on the British market. Goodwin, 'Anglo-Argentine Commercial Relations', shows how growth in manufacturing was beginning to divide the British Chamber of Commerce, while Gravil, 'Anglo-US Trade Rivalry', studies the ill-fated d'Abernon trade mission. The problems of the railway companies are investigated in Goodwin, 'Politics of Rate-Making', Skupch, 'Las consecuencias de la competencia', and García Heras, *Automotores Norteamericanos*, which also covers urban transport. In contrast to this effort on Argentina, however, Britain's economic interests in other countries in the 1920s are somewhat neglected. Fritsch, *External Constraints*, provides a detailed analysis of financial relations with Brazil, but there are few other studies apart from the literature on oil.

THE GREAT DEPRESSION AND THE SECOND WORLD WAR

The imbalance of effort is also apparent for the 1930s and 1940s, where the literature on Argentina dwarfs the rest. The basic survey of the prewar decade is Thorp (ed.), *Latin America in the 1930s*; Falcoff and Dolkart (eds), *Prologue to Perón*, provides a useful introduction to Argentina. On British economic policy towards the region Drummond, *British Economic Policy* and *Imperial Economic Policy*, are essential. The specialised literature on the 1930s concentrates on the Roca-Runciman pact of 1933 between Britain and Argentina, on which there is enormous debate. Writing from an imperial perspective Drummond argues that the Argentines achieved more than the British Dominions like Australia expected London to concede, a view partly shared by Tulchin, 'Decolonizing an Informal Empire'. This contrasts with nationalists who view the pact as a sellout of Argentine interests by the cattle producers, an interpretation best reflected in Gravil and Rooth, 'Time of Acute Dependence'. The most balanced view comes from Drosdoff, *El gobierno de las vacas*, one of the few historians to use Argentine government archives, but Alhadeff's articles on the financial aspects of the agreement, 'Economic Formulae of the 1930s' and 'Dependency, Historiography and Objections', are also vital to any assessment. It is worth noting, too, the strong defence of the agreement made by Prebisch in 'Argentine Economic Policies'.

On other aspects of the 1930s the deteriorating situation of the British–owned railways in Argentina is analysed by García Heras, 'Las compañías ferroviarias británicas' and 'Hostage Private Companies', which update the work of Skupch by using British sources more intensively. British attempts to maintain some influence in Argentina contrast with the eventual abandonment of their interests in Brazil. On this comparison see especially Abreu, 'Anglo-Brazilian Economic Relations' and 'Argentina and Brazil', which draw on 'Brazil and the World Economy', his PhD thesis. Hilton, *Brazil and the Great Powers*, also neatly dissects Britain's deteriorating influence there, contrasting it with the United States and Germany. Outside Argentina and Brazil, however, there is little on the retreat of British interests in the 1930s with the exception of Albert, 'Sugar and Anglo-Peruvian Trade Negotiations'.

The starting-point for the study of Anglo–Latin American relations in the Second World War must be Humphreys' two-volume *Latin America and the Second World War*, which makes extensive use of British diplomatic archives. Fodor, 'The Origin of Argentina's Sterling Balances', and Abreu, 'Brazil as a Creditor', draw on Treasury and Bank of England papers to provide excellent discussions of the wartime financial arrangements which Britain made with its chief trading partners. Hillman, 'Bolivia and British Tin Policy', and Dobson, 'Export White Paper', are also useful. Both emphasise US pressure on Britain, a theme which also emerges strongly in Knape, 'British Foreign Policy'. There is a large literature on the disagreement between Britain and the United States over Argentine neutrality; on this see particularly Stemplowski, 'Las potencias anglosajones' and 'Castillo's Argentina', Rapoport, 'La política británica' and *Gran Bretaña, Estados Unidos, y las clases dirigentes argentinas*, and MacDonald, 'Politics of Intervention'. García Heras, 'World War II', investigates the problems British officials faced in persuading the railway companies to negotiate sensibly with Argentina.

Bethell and Roxborough, 'Latin America', summarises events in the immediate postwar period, but most of the research on Britain again concentrates on conflicts with the United States and on the retreat from Argentina. On the former see Knape, 'Anglo-

American Rivalry', which analyses policy on arms sales, and on the latter MacDonald, 'United States, Britain and Argentina', Escudé, 'Las restricciones internacionales', and Bowen, 'End of British Economic Hegemony'. Fodor, 'Perón's Policies', like Escudé, spells out the constraints imposed on Peron's ministers by the international situation. For the constraints on British policy see Pressnell, *External Economic Policy*, and for the continuing retreat from Brazil the articles and thesis by Abreu. Overall, however, there is still plenty of work to be done on the period since the First World War, especially on countries other than Argentina. There is virtually nothing published, for example, on the British withdrawal from Chile, Peru and Uruguay, nor on the expropriation of the Mexican Eagle oil company.

BRITAIN AND LATIN AMERICA SINCE 1950

This period has been almost totally neglected. The one item of any real significance is Bulmer-Thomas (ed.), *Britain and Latin America*, which contains especially important articles by Martin (cultural relations), Thomas (the relationship with the United States) and Griffith-Jones (financial relations). Before this there were a few articles and books on Anglo-Latin American relations, including Lewis, 'Anglo-Argentine Trade', Nove, 'Great Britain and Latin American Economic Development', and Marett, *Latin America*, all of which regretted the loss of interest in Latin America, but pleas for the reconstruction of Britain's relations with the region generally vanished in the face of economic and political realities. The only other topic on which much was published was on the background to the Falklands/Malvinas War. Tulchin, 'Malvinas War of 1982', provides an able review of the literature which appeared immediately after the conflict, while Beck, *Falkland Islands*, is a dispassionate historian's view of the development of the dispute.

A NOTE ON BIBLIOGRAPHIES AND PRIMARY SOURCES

There are many bibliographies dealing with different aspects of Latin American history. For this subject the most useful is probably Cortes Conde and Stein (eds), *Latin America*, published in 1977. To update it see later volumes of *Handbook of Latin American Studies*, which has an impressively wide coverage, and *Hispanic American Periodicals Index*, now available on-line. For British economic history the best guide to new literature is the comprehensive listing which appears annually in *Economic History Review*.

The principal primary sources used by historians of Britain's relationship with Latin America can be subdivided into travellers' accounts, government publications, the press and archival sources. British travellers produced an enormous number of books about their experiences from the time of independence onwards, and many contain valuable information about British interests in Latin America. For a guide to this literature see Naylor, *Accounts of Nineteenth-Century South America*. Historians have also relied heavily on British government publications, particularly statistics published in 'Annual Statement of Trade and Navigation', the annual reports of British consuls and ministers posted to Latin America, and the reports of bodies like Royal Commissions and Select Committees. For the century before 1919 all these were normally published in *Parliamentary Papers*; thereafter they generally appear as separate booklets. Official publications of other developed countries, the reports of US consuls and the Bureau of Foreign and Domestic Commerce for example, can also provide much information, not all of it accurate, about the British. Latin American official sources have suffered an unjustifiable neglect. The statistical abstracts, annual presidential messages and, even more, the annual *memorias* of ministers, especially those of the treasuries, departments of foreign affairs and departments of public works, offer much information. Congressional debates are more difficult to use since they are largely unindexed, but on key issues they can provide important insights into elite and popular attitudes towards British interests.

Apart from standard British press sources such as *The Times*, specialist weeklies like the *Economist* and *South American Journal* provide a wealth of information, especially on the countries in which the British were most interested. The indebtedness of the poorer nations resulted in the accumulation of press cuttings on them by the Corporation of Foreign Bondholders; these are now in the Guildhall Library in London. On other aspects of business, specialist journals, for example on shipping, mining or railways, are vital. There was also a thriving daily press in Latin America from early in the nineteenth century, and most countries with British communities of any size possessed weekly English-language journals which offer a mine of information on business. The regular publications of interest-group associations such as Chambers of Commerce or mining societies have also been profitably used by Latin American historians.

Archival sources can be subdivided into official and business sources. Probably the most heavily used archive is that of the British Foreign Office (in the Public Record Office). Yet while this provides a wealth of information not only on British relations with each country but also on internal developments, too many historians have confined themselves to correspondence between London and the Latin American capitals. In fact the internal correspondence of legations and consulates in Latin America was often not transmitted to London, and historians like Rodríguez have used it to illustrate more clearly the role played by individual officials within Latin American societies. Moreover, other British government departments possessed interests in Latin America, and their documents have hardly been exploited. The papers of the Admiralty could tell us much more about British policy and trade in Latin America in the early nineteenth century, while those of the Treasury, Board of Trade and Bank of England are vital for the period after 1914 (the latter retains its own archive at its headquarters). Business archives are scattered throughout the United Kingdom and Latin America, although many are concentrated in two repositories in London, the Guildhall Library and University College. For information on such archives see Platt, 'Business Archives', Pressnell and Orbell (eds), *Guide to Historical Records of British Banking*, Richmond and Turton (eds), *Directory of Corporate Archives*, and Richmond and Stockford (eds), *Company Archives*. For want of organisation Latin American government and business documents, though normally deposited in national archives, have been much less heavily used. Where they have been, they have frequently provided the material for a complete reappraisal of a particular subject. Yet many papers remain to be discovered or catalogued. One of the great excitements of research in Latin America on this subject is the probability of discovering sources unknown to earlier historians.

Select Bibliography

ABBREVIATIONS

AHR	*American Historical Review*
BELAC	*Boletín de Estudios Latinoamericanos y del Caribe*
BLAR	*Bulletin of Latin American Research*
BH	*Business History*
BHR	*Business History Review*
CHLA	*Cambridge History of Latin America*
CLAS	Centre for Latin American Studies
CSSH	*Comparative Studies in Society and History*
CUP	Cambridge University Press
EcHR	*Economic History Review*
EEH	*Explorations in Economic History*
HAHR	*Hispanic American Historical Review*
HJ	*Historical Journal*
IAA	*Ibero-Amerikanisches Archiv*
IAEA	*Inter-American Economic Affairs*
IEP	Instituto de Estudios Peruanos
JEcH	*Journal of Economic History*
JEEH	*Journal of European Economic History*
JIASWA	*Journal of Inter-American Studies and World Affairs*
JICH	*Journal of Imperial and Commonwealth History*
JLAS	*Journal of Latin American Studies*
LAP	*Latin American Perspectives*
LARR	*Latin American Research Review*
NY	New York
OUP	Oxford University Press
PP	*Parliamentary Papers*

282

RChHG *Revista Chilena de Historia y Geografía*
RIIA   Royal Institute of International Affairs
TAm   *The Americas*
UCP   University of California Press
UP   . . . University Press
UTP   University of Texas Press

PRIMARY SOURCES

Manuscripts

This book is based primarily on secondary sources, but some research was conducted in the following archives open to the public:

Bank of England
Guildhall Library: Antony Gibbs & Sons
Public Record Office (Board of Trade, Foreign Office, Department of Overseas Trade, Treasury archives)
University College, London (Balfour Williamson and Peruvian Corporation papers)

The following companies also granted permission to use their archives:

Antofagasta (Chili) and Bolivia Railway Co.
British Steel Corporation (for Dorman Long papers)
Burmah Oil plc (for Lobitos Oilfields Ltd papers)
Unilever plc

Published material

International Monetary Fund, *Direction of Trade Statistics*.
República Argentina, Direccion General de Estadística, *Anuario del comercio exterior de la República Argentina, 1931*.
United Kingdom, 'Annual Statement of Trade and Navigation' (published in *PP* until 1920, separately by the Board of Customs and Excise thereafter).
United Kingdom 1983, *Falklands Island Review* (Franks Committee).
United Kingdom, 'Report of the Departmental Committee appointed to inquire into Combinations in the Meat Trade', *PP* 1909, XV.
United Kingdom, Board Of Trade, 'Report of Joint Committee

of Enquiry into the Anglo-Argentine Meat Trade', *PP* 1937–38, VIII.

United Kingdom, Department of Overseas Trade, 1930, *Report of the British Economic Mission to Argentina, Brazil, and Uruguay*, London: HMSO.

United Kingdom, House of Commons, 'Report from the Select Committee on Loans to Foreign States', *PP* 1875, XI.

United Kingdom, Overseas Trade Development Council, 1931, *Report of the Sheffield Industrial Mission to South America, August – November 1930*, London: HMSO.

United States, Federal Trade Commission, 1916, *Report on Cooperation in American Export Trade*, Washington: GPO.

BOOKS AND ARTICLES

Abel, C. and Lewis, C.M. (eds), 1985, *Latin America, Economic Imperialism and the State: the political economy of the external connexion from independence to the present*, London: Athlone Press.

Abente, D., 1987, 'The War of the Triple Alliance: three explanatory models', *LARR* **22**:2, 47–69.

Abente, D., 1989, 'Foreign Capital, Economic Elites, and the State in Paraguay during the Liberal Republic, 1870–1936', *JLAS* **21**, 61–88.

Abreu, M. de P., 1984, 'Argentina and Brazil during the 1930s: the impact of British and American international economic policies' in Thorp (ed.), *Latin America in the 1930s*, pp. 144–62.

Abreu, M. de P., 1985, 'Anglo-Brazilian Economic Relations and the Consolidation of American Pre-Eminence in Brazil, 1930–1945' in Abel and Lewis (eds), *Latin America, Economic Imperialism and the State*, pp. 379–93.

Abreu, M. de P., 1989, 'La deuda externa brasileña, 1824–1943', *Trimestre Económico* **56**, 193–237.

Abreu, M. de P., 1990, 'Brazil as a Creditor: sterling balances, 1940–1952', *EcHR* **43**, 450–69.

AHILA, 1983, *Capitales, empresarios y obreros en América Latina*, 2 vols, Stockholm: Instituto de Estudios Latinoamericanos.

Albert, B., 1982, 'Sugar and Anglo-Peruvian Trade Negotiations in the 1930s', *JLAS* **14**, 121–42.

Albert, B., 1983, *South America and the World Economy from Independence to 1930*, London: Macmillan.

Albert, B., 1985, 'External Forces and the Transformation of Peruvian Coastal Agriculture' in Abel and Lewis (eds), *Latin America, Economic Imperialism and the State*, pp. 231–49.

Albert, B., 1988, *South America and the First World War: the impact of war on Brazil, Argentina, Peru, and Chile*, Cambridge: CUP.

Albert, B. and Henderson, P., 1981, 'Latin America and the Great War: a preliminary survey of developments in Chile, Peru, Argentina and Brazil', *World Development* **9**, 717–34.

Albion, R.G., 1951, 'British Shipping and Latin America, 1806–1914', *JEcH* **11**, 361–74.

Alden, D., 1984, 'Late Colonial Brazil, 1750–1808' in Bethell (ed.), *CHLA*, II, 601–60.

Alhadeff, P., 1985, 'Dependency, Historiography, and Objections to the Roca Pact' in Abel and Lewis (eds), *Latin America, Economic Imperialism and the State*, pp. 367–78.

Alhadeff, P., 1986, 'The Economic Formulae of the 1930s: a reassessment' in Di Tella and Platt (eds), *Political Economy of Argentina*, pp. 95–119.

Amaral, S., 1984, 'El empréstito de Londres de 1824', *Desarrollo Económico* **23**, 559–88.

Armstrong, C. and Nelles, H.V., 1984, 'A Curious Capital Flow: Canadian investment in Mexico, 1902–1910', *BHR* **58**, 178–203.

Atkin, J., 1970, 'Official Regulation of British Overseas Investment, 1914–1931', *EcHR* **23**, 324–35.

Atkinson, D., 1989, 'Trade, Aid and Investment since 1950' in Bulmer-Thomas (ed.), *Britain and Latin America*, pp. 103–20.

Barbier, J.A., 1990, 'Commercial Reform and *comercio neutral* in Cartagena de Indias, 1788–1808' in Fisher *et al.* (eds), *Reform and Insurrection*, pp. 96–120.

Barker, T.C., 1977, *The Glassmakers: Pilkington, the rise of an international company, 1826–1976*, London: Weidenfeld and Nicolson.

Barker, T.C., 1986, 'Pilkington, the Reluctant Multinational' in Jones (ed.), *British Multinationals*, pp. 184–201.

Barnett, L.M., 1985, *British Food Policy during the First World War*, Boston: George Allen and Unwin.

Barrán, J.P. and Nahum, B., 1967–1978, *Historia rural del Uruguay moderno*, 7 vols, Montevideo: Banda Oriental.

Barrán, J.P. and Nahum, B., 1985– . *Batlle, los estancieros y el imperio británico*, 8 vols, Montevideo: Banda Oriental.

Bauer, A.J., 1990, 'Industry and the Missing Bourgeoisie: consumption and development in Chile, 1850–1950', *HAHR* **70**, 227–53.

Bazant, J., 1968, *Historia de la deuda exterior de México, 1823–1946*, Mexico City: Colegio de México.

Bazant, J., 1977, *A Concise History of Mexico from Hidalgo to Cárdenas, 1805–1940*, Cambridge: CUP.

Beck, P.J., 1983, 'Research Problems in Studying Britain's Latin American Past: the case of the Falkland Islands, 1920–1950', *BLAR* 2:2, 3–16.

Beck, P.J., 1988, *The Falkland Islands as an International Problem*, London: Routledge.

Berglund, S., 1985, 'Mercantile Credit and Financing in Venezuela, 1830–1870', *JLAS* **17**, 371–96.

Bergquist, C., 1986, *Labor in Latin America: comparative essays on Chile, Argentina, Venezuela and Colombia*, Stanford: Stanford UP.

Bernecker, W.L., 1988, 'Foreign Interests, Tariff Policy and Early Industrialization in Mexico, 1821–1848', *IAA* **14**, 61–102.

Bethell, L., 1970, *The Abolition of the Brazilian Slave Trade: Britain, Brazil, and the slave trade question, 1807–1869*, Cambridge: CUP.

Bethell, L. (ed.), 1984– , *Cambridge History of Latin America*, Cambridge: CUP.

Bethell, L., 1984, 'The Independence of Brazil' in Bethell (ed.), *CHLA*, III, 157–96.

Bethell, L. (ed.), 1989, *Brazil: empire and republic, 1822–1930*, Cambridge: CUP.

Bethell, L., 1989, 'Britain and Latin America in Historical Perspective' in Bulmer-Thomas (ed.), *Britain and Latin America*, pp. 1–24.

Bethell, L. and Roxborough, I., 1988, 'Latin America between the Second World War and the Cold War: some reflections on the 1945–1948 conjuncture', *JLAS* **20**, 167–89.

Blakemore, H., 1974, *British Nitrates and Chilean Politics, 1886–1896: Balmaceda and North*, London: Athlone Press.

Blakemore, H., 1990, *From the Pacific to La Paz: the Antofagasta (Chili) and Bolivia Railway Company, 1888–1988*, London: Lester Crook.

Blanchard, P., 1982, *The Origins of the Peruvian Labor Movement, 1883–1919*, Pittsburgh: Pittsburgh UP.

Bonilla, H., 1974, *Guano y burguesía en el Perú*, Lima: IEP.

Born, K.E., 1983, *International Banking in the 19th and 20th Centuries*, Leamington Spa: Berg.

Bowen, N., 1975, 'The End of British Economic Hegemony in Argentina: Messersmith and the Eady-Miranda agreement', *IAEA* **28**:4, 3–24.

Boxer, C.R., 1969, 'Brazilian Gold and British Traders in the First Half of the Eighteenth Century', *HAHR* **49**, 454–72.

Brewer, A., 1980, *Marxist Theories of Imperialism: a critical survey*, London: Routledge and Kegan Paul.

Brown, J.C., 1976, 'Dynamics and Autonomy of a Traditional Marketing System: Buenos Aires, 1810–1860', *HAHR* **56**, 605–29.

Brown, J.C., 1979, *A Socioeconomic History of Argentina, 1776–1860*, Cambridge: CUP.

Brown, J.C., 1985, 'Why Foreign Oil Companies Shifted their Production from Mexico to Venezuela during the 1920s', *AHR* **90**, 362–85.

Brown, J.C., 1986, 'The Bondage of Old Habits in Nineteenth-Century Argentina', *LARR* **21**:2, 3–32.

Brown, J.C., 1986, 'Foreign Oil Companies, Oil Workers, and the Mexican Revolutionary State in the 1920s' in Teichova *et al.* (eds), *Multinational Enterprise*, pp. 257–69.

Brown, J.C., 1987, 'Domestic Politics and Foreign Investment: British development of Mexican petroleum, 1889–1911', *BHR* **61**, 387–416.

Brown, V.L., 1928, 'Contraband Trade: a factor in the decline of Spain's empire in America', *HAHR* **8**, 178–89.

Bulmer-Thomas, V., 1989, 'British Relations with Latin America into the 1990s' in Bulmer-Thomas (ed.), *Britain and Latin America*, pp. 205–28.

Bulmer-Thomas, V. (ed.), 1989, *Britain and Latin America: a changing relationship*, Cambridge: CUP/RIIA.

Bunge, A., 1920, *Los Problemas económicos del presente*, Buenos Aires.

Burga, M. and Reátegui, W., 1981, *Lanas y capital mercantil en el sur: la casa Ricketts*, Lima: IEP.

Burgin, M., 1971 [1946], *The Economic Aspects of Argentine Federalism, 1820–1852*, NY: Russell & Russell.

Burk, K., 1989, *Morgan Grenfell, 1838–1988: the biography of a merchant bank*, Oxford: OUP.

Burkholder, M.A. and Johnson, L.L., 1990, *Colonial Latin America*, NY: OUP.

Bushnell, D. and Macaulay, N., 1988, *The Emergence of Latin America in the Nineteenth Century*, NY: OUP.

Cady, J.F., 1969 [1929], *Foreign Intervention in the Río de la Plata, 1838–1850*, NY: AMS Press.

Cain, P.J., 1980, *Economic Foundations of British Overseas Expansion, 1815–1914*, London: Macmillan.

Cain, P.J. and Hopkins, A.G., 1980, 'The Political Economy of British Expansion Overseas, 1750–1914', *EcHR* **33**, 463–90.

Cain, P.J. and Hopkins, A.G., 1986, 'Gentlemanly Capitalism and

British Expansion Overseas. I: the old colonial system, 1688–1850', *EcHR* **39**, 501–25.

Cain, P.J. and Hopkins, A.G., 1987, 'Gentlemanly Capitalism and British Expansion Overseas. II: new imperialism, 1850–1945', *EcHR* **40**, 1–26.

Cain, P.J. and Hopkins, A.G., 1993, *British Imperialism: innovation and expansion 1688–1914,* London: Longman.

Cain, P.J. and Hopkins, A.G., 1993, *British Imperialism: crisis and deconstruction 1914–1990,* London: Longman.

Calvert, P., 1968, *The Mexican Revolution, 1910–1914: the diplomacy of Anglo-American conflict,* Cambridge: CUP.

Cardoso, C.F.S. and Pérez Brignoli, H., 1979, *Historia económica de América Latina,* 2 vols, Barcelona: Crítica.

Cardoso, F.H., 1977, 'The Consumption of Dependency Theory in the United States', *LARR* **12**:3, 7–24.

Cardoso, F.H. and Faletto, E., 1979, *Dependency and Development in Latin America,* Berkeley: UCP.

Carl, G.E., 1980, *First among Equals: Great Britain and Venezuela, 1810–1910,* Syracuse: Dept of Geography.

Carmagnani, M., 1983, 'Finanzas y estado en México, 1820–1880', *IAA* **9**, 279–318.

Centner, C.W., 1943, 'Relaciones comerciales de Gran Bretaña con Chile, 1810–1830', *RChHG* **95**, 96–107.

Chandler, A.D., 1980, 'The Growth of the Transnational Industrial Firm in the United States and the United Kingdom: a comparative analysis', *EcHR* **33**, 396–410.

Chapman, S.D., 1984, *The Rise of Merchant Banking,* London: George Allen & Unwin.

Chapman, S.D., 1985, 'British-Based Investment Groups before 1914', *EcHR* **38**, 230–51.

Christelow, A., 1947, 'Great Britain and the Trades from Cadiz and Lisbon to Spanish America and Brazil, 1759–1783', *HAHR* **27**, 2–29.

Clapp, B.W., 1965, *John Owens, Manchester Merchant,* Manchester: Manchester UP.

Córdova, L., 1970, 'Proteccionismo y librecambio en el México independiente, 1821–1847', *Cuadernos Americanos* **29**, 135–57.

Cortes Conde, R. and Stein, S.J. (eds), 1977, *Latin America, 1830–1930: a guide to the economic history,* Berkeley: UCP.

Costeloe, M.P., 1986, *Response to Revolution: Imperial Spain and the Spanish American revolutions, 1810–1840,* Cambridge: CUP.

Couyoumdjian, R., 1974–75, 'El mercado de salitre durante la primera guerra mundial y la posguerra, 1914–1921: notas para su estudio', *Historia* (Santiago) **12**, 13–55.

Cox, H., 1989, 'Growth and Ownership in the International Tobacco Industry: BAT, 1902–1927', *BH* **31**, 44–67.

Cromwell, V. and Steiner, Z.S., 1972, 'The Foreign Office before 1914: a study in resistance' in G. Sutherland (ed.), *Studies in the Growth of Nineteenth-Century Government*, London: Routledge & Kegan Paul.

Crossley, J.C. and Greenhill, R.G., 1977, 'The River Plate Beef Trade' in Platt (ed.), *Business Imperialism*, pp. 284–334.

Crouzet, F., 1980, 'Toward an Export Economy: British exports during the industrial revolution', *EEH* **17**, 48–93.

Cuccorese, H.J., 1976, 'La versión histórica argentina sobre la crisis de Baring Brothers & Co. en 1890', *Investigaciones y ensayos* **20**, 265–321.

Cuenca Esteban, J., 1981, 'Statistics of Spain's Colonial Trade, 1792–1820: consular duties, cargo inventories, and balances of trade', *HAHR* **61**, 381–428.

Culver, W.W. and Greaves, T.C. (eds), 1985, *Miners and Mining in the Americas*, Manchester: Manchester UP.

Dahl, V.C., 1961, 'Business Influence in the Anglo-Mexican Reconciliation of 1884', *IAEA* **15**, 33–51.

Davenport-Hines, R.P.T., 1986, 'Glaxo as a Multinational before 1963' in Jones (ed.), *British Multinationals*, pp. 137–63.

Davis, L.E. and Huttenback, R.A., 1985, 'The Export of British Finance, 1865–1914', *JICH* **13**, 28–76.

Davis, L.E. and Huttenback, R.A., 1986, *Mammon and the Pursuit of Empire: the political economy of British imperialism, 1860–1912*, Cambridge: CUP.

Davis, R., 1979, *The Industrial Revolution and British Overseas Trade*, Leicester: Leicester UP.

Dawson, F.G., 1990, *The First Latin American Debt Crisis: the City of London and the 1822–25 loan bubble*, New Haven: Yale UP.

Denoon, D., 1983, *Settler Capitalism: the dynamics of dependent development in the Southern Hemisphere*, Oxford: Clarendon Press.

DeShazo, P., 1983, *Urban Workers and Labor Unions in Chile, 1902–1927*, Madison: Wisconsin UP.

Díaz Alejandro, C.F., 1970, *Essays on the Economic History of the Argentine Republic*, New Haven: Yale UP.

Di Tella, G. and Platt, D.C.M. (eds), 1986, *The Political Economy of Argentina, 1880–1946*, London: Macmillan.

Dobson, A.P., 1986, 'The Export White Paper: 10 September 1941', *EcHR* **39**, 59–76.

Dozier, C.L., 1985, *Nicaragua's Mosquito Shore: the years of British and American presence*, University: Alabama UP.

Drosdoff, D., 1972, *El gobierno de las vacas, 1933–1956: tratado Roca-Runciman*, Buenos Aires: La Bastilla.

Drummond, I.M., 1972, *British Economic Policy and the Empire, 1919–1939*, London: George Allen & Unwin.

Drummond, I.M., 1974, *Imperial Economic Policy, 1917–1939: studies in expansion and protection*, London: George Allen & Unwin.

Durán, E., 1985, *Guerra y revolución: las grandes potencias y México, 1914–1918*, Mexico City: Colegio de México.

Eakin, M.C., 1985, 'The Role of British Capital in the Development of Brazilian Gold Mining' in Culver and Greaves (eds), *Miners and Mining*, pp. 10–28.

Eakin, M.C., 1986, 'Business Imperialism and British Enterprise in Brazil: the St John d'el Rey Mining Company Limited, 1830–1960', *HAHR* **66**, 697–742.

Eakin, M.C., 1989, *British Enterprise in Brazil: the St John d'El Rey Mining Company and the Morro Velho Gold Mine, 1830–1960*, Durham: Duke UP.

Edelstein, M., 1982, *Overseas Investment in the Age of High Imperialism: the United Kingdom, 1850–1914*, London: Methuen.

Eisenberg, P.L., 1974, *The Sugar Industry in Pernambuco, 1840–1910: modernization without change*, Berkeley: UCP.

Eltis, D., 1987, *Economic Growth and the Ending of the Transatlantic Slave Trade*, NY: OUP.

Encina, F., 1955 [1911], *Nuestra inferioridad económica: sus causas, sus consecuencias*, Santiago.

Escudé, C., 1980, 'Las restricciones internacionales de la economía argentina, 1945–1949', *Desarrollo Económico* **20**, 3–40.

Falcoff, M., 1972, 'Raúl Scalabrini Ortíz: the making of an Argentine nationalist', *HAHR* **52**, 74–101.

Falcoff, M. and Dolkart, R.H. (eds), 1975, *Prologue to Perón: Argentina in depression and war, 1930–1943*, Berkeley: UCP.

Farnie, D.A., 1979, *The English Cotton Industry and the World Market, 1815–1896*, Oxford: Clarendon Press.

Feinstein, C., 1990, 'Britain's Overseas Investments in 1913', *EcHR* **43**, 288–95.

Feis, H., 1974 [1930], *Europe, the World's Banker, 1870–1914: an account of European foreign investment and the connection of world finance with diplomacy before the war*, Clifton, NJ: Augustus M. Kelley.

Felix, D., 1987, 'Alternative Outcomes of the Latin American Debt Crisis: lessons from the past', *LARR* **22**:2, 3–46.

Fernández, M.A., 1983, 'Merchants and Bankers: British direct and portfolio investment in Chile during the nineteenth century', *IAA* **9**, 349–80.

Fernández, M.A., 1984, 'British Nitrate Companies and the Emergence of Chile's Proletariat, 1880–1914' in B. Munslow and H. Finch (eds), *Proletarianisation in the Third World*, London: Croom Helm, pp. 42–76.

Ferns, H.S., 1950, 'Investment and Trade between Britain and Argentina in the Nineteenth Century', *EcHR* **3**, 203–18.

Ferns, H.S., 1953, 'Britain's Informal Empire in Argentina, 1806–1914', *Past and Present* **4**, 60–75.

Ferns, H.S., 1960, *Britain and Argentina in the Nineteenth Century*, Oxford: Clarendon Press.

Fieldhouse, D.K., 1978, *Unilever Overseas: the anatomy of a multinational, 1895–1965*, London: Croom Helm.

Finch, M.H.J., 1981, *A Political Economy of Uruguay since 1870*, London: Macmillan.

Finch, M.H.J., 1985, 'British Imperialism in Uruguay: the public utility companies and the *batllista* state, 1900–1930' in Abel and Lewis (eds), *Latin America, Economic Imperialism and the State*, pp. 250–66.

Fisher, H.E.S., 1963, 'Anglo-Portuguese Trade, 1700–1770', *EcHR* **16**, 219–33.

Fisher, J., 1985, *Commercial Relations between Spain and Spanish America in the Era of Free Trade, 1778–1796*, Liverpool: CLAS.

Fisher, J. *et al.* (eds), 1990, *Reform and Insurrection in Bourbon New Granada and Peru*, Baton Rouge: Louisiana State UP.

Fishlow, A., 1985, 'Lessons from the Past: capital markets during the 19th century and the interwar period', *International Organization* **39**, 383–439.

Fodor, J., 1975, 'Perón's Policies for Agricultural Exports, 1946–1948: dogmatism or common sense?' in Rock (ed.), *Argentina in the Twentieth Century*, pp. 135–61.

Fodor, J., 1986. 'The Origin of Argentina's Sterling Balances, 1939–1943', in Di Tella and Platt (eds), *The Political Economy of Argentina*, pp. 154–82.

Fodor, J. and O'Connell, A.A., 1973, 'La Argentina y la economía atlántica en la primera mitad del siglo XX', *Desarrollo Económico* **13**:49, 3–65.

Fonseca, C.F.A., 1983, 'Os investimentos ingleses no nordeste do Brasil e a ferrovia "The Great Western of Brazil Railway Company Limited", 1872–1920' in AHILA, *Capitales, empresarios y obreros europeos*, pp. 694–731.

Forbes, I.L.D., 1978, 'German Informal Imperialism in South America before 1914', *EcHR* **31**, 384–98.

Ford, A.G., 1956, 'Argentina and the Baring Crisis of 1890', *Oxford Econ Papers* **8**, 127–50.

Ford, A.G., 1962, *The Gold Standard, 1880–1914: Britain and Argentina*, Oxford: Clarendon Press.

Ford, A.G., 1971, 'British Investment in Argentina and Long Swings, 1880–1914', *JEcH* **31**, 650–63.

Ford, A.G., 1975, 'British Investment in Argentine Economic Development, 1880–1914' in Rock (ed.), *Argentina in the Twentieth Century*, pp. 12–40.

Fornos Peñalba, J.A., 1982, 'Draft Dodgers, War Resisters, and Turbulent Gauchos: the War of the Triple Alliance against Paraguay', *TAm* **38**, 463–80.

Fortune, S.A., 1984, *Merchants and Jews: the struggle for British West Indian commerce, 1650–1750*, Gainesville: University Presses of Florida.

Frank, A.G., 1971, *Capitalism and Underdevelopment in Latin America: historical studies of Chile and Brazil*, Harmondsworth: Penguin.

Frieden, J.A., 1989, 'The Economics of Intervention: American overseas investment and underdeveloped areas, 1890–1950', *CSSH* **31**, 55–80.

Fritsch, W., 1988, *External Constraints on Economic Policy in Brazil, 1889–1930*, Basingstoke: Macmillan.

Furtado, C., 1970, *Economic Development of Latin America: a survey from colonial times to the Cuban Revolution*, Cambridge: CUP.

Gallagher, J. and Robinson, R., 1953, 'The Imperialism of Free Trade', *EcHR* **6**, 1–15.

García Heras, R., 1985, *Automotores norteamericanos, caminos, y modernización urbana en la Argentina, 1918–1939*, Buenos Aires: Libros de Hispanoamerica.

García Heras, R., 1985, 'World War II and the Frustrated Nationalization of the Argentine British-owned Railways, 1939–1943', *JLAS* **17**, 135–55.

García Heras, R., 1987, 'Hostage Private Companies under Restraint: British railways and transport coordination in Argentina during the 1930s', *JLAS* **19**, 41–67.

García Heras, R., 1990, 'Las compañías ferroviarias británicas y el control de cambios en la Argentina durante la Gran Depresión', *Desarrollo Económico* **29**, 477–505.

Gaston, J.W.T., 1982, 'Trade and the Late Victorian Foreign Office', *International Hist. Rev.* **4**, 317–38.

Gerhardt, R.C., 1975, 'Inglaterra y el petroleo mexicano durante la primera guerra mundial', *Historia Mexicana* **97**, 118–42.

Ghioldi, R., 1974 [1933], *¿Qué significa el pacto Roca?*, Buenos Aires: Anteo.

Goebel, D.B., 1937–38, 'British Trade to the Spanish Colonies, 1796–1823', *AHR* **43**, 288–320.

Goebel, D.B., 1942, 'British–American Rivalry in the Chilean Trade, 1807–1820', *JEcH* **2**, 190–202.

González Deluca, M.E., 1980, 'Los intereses británicos y la política en Venezuela en las últimas décadas del siglo XIX', *Boletín Americanista* (Barcelona) **22**, 89–123.

Goodwin, P.B., 1974, 'The Politics of Rate-Making: the British-owned railways and the Unión Cívica Radical, 1921–1928', *JLAS* **6**, 257–87.

Goodwin, P.B., 1981, 'Anglo-Argentine Commercial Relations: a private sector view, 1922–1943', *HAHR* **61**, 29–51.

Gootenberg, P., 1982, 'The Social Origins of Protectionism and Free Trade in Nineteenth-Century Lima', *JLAS* **14**, 329–58.

Gootenberg, P., 1989, *Tejidos y harinas, corazones y mentes: el imperialismo norteamericano del libre comercio en el Perú, 1825–1840*, Lima: IEP.

Gootenberg, P., 1989, *Between Silver and Guano: commercial policy and the state in postindependence Peru*, Princeton: Princeton UP.

Gootenberg, P., 1991, 'Population and Ethnicity in Early Republican Peru: some revisions', *LARR* **26**:3, 109–152.

Gough, B.M., 1983, 'Specie Conveyance from the West Coast of South America in British Warships, c. 1820–1870: an aspect of the Pax Britannica', *Mariners Mirror* **69**, 419–33.

Graham, G.S. and Humphreys, R.A. (eds), 1962, *The Navy and South America, 1807–1823: correspondence of the commanders-in-chief on the South American station*, London: Navy Records Society.

Graham, Richard, 1969, 'Sepoys and Imperialists: techniques of British power in nineteenth-century Brazil', *IAEA* **23**, 23–37.

Graham, Richard, 1972, *Britain and the Onset of Modernisation in Brazil, 1850–1914*, Cambridge: CUP.

Graham, Richard, 1976, 'Robinson and Gallagher in Latin America: the meaning of informal imperialism' in Louis (ed.), *Imperialism*.

Graham, Robert, 1989, 'British Policy towards Latin America' in

Bulmer-Thomas (ed.), *Britain and Latin America*, pp. 52–67.

Grahn, L.R., 1990, 'An Irresoluble Dilemma: smuggling in New Granada, 1713–1763' in Fisher *et al.* (eds), *Reform and Insurrection*, pp. 123–46.

Gravil, R., 1970, 'State Intervention in Argentina's Export Trade between the Wars', *JLAS* **2**, 147–73.

Gravil, R., 1975, 'Anglo–US Trade Rivalry in Argentina and the d'Abernon Mission of 1929' in Rock (ed.), *Argentina in the Twentieth Century*, pp. 41–65.

Gravil, R., 1977, 'Argentina and the First World War', *JLAS* **9**, 59–89.

Gravil, R., 1985, *The Anglo-Argentine Connection, 1900–1939*, Boulder and London: Westview Press.

Gravil, R., and Rooth, T., 1978, 'A Time of Acute Dependence: Argentina in the 1930s', *JEEH* **7**, 337–78.

Greenfield, G.M., 1978, 'Dependency and the Urban Experience: São Paulo's public service sector, 1885–1913', *JLAS* **10**, 37–59.

Greenhill, R.G., 1977, 'Shipping' in Platt (ed.), *Business Imperialism*, pp. 119–55.

Greenhill, R.G., 1977, 'Merchants and the Latin American Trades: an introduction' in Platt (ed.), *Business Imperialism*, pp. 159–97.

Greenhill, R.G., 1977, 'The Brazilian Coffee Trade' in Platt (ed.), *Business Imperialism*, pp. 198–230.

Greenhill, R.G., 1979, 'Latin America's Export Trades and British Shipping, 1850–1914' in D. Alexander and R. Ommer (eds), *Volumes not Values: Canadian sailing ships and world trades*, St Johns: Memorial University, pp. 247–74.

Greenhill, R.G. and Miller, R.M., 1973, 'The Peruvian Government and the Nitrate Trade, 1873–1879', *JLAS* **5**, 107–31.

Greenhill, R.G. and Miller, R.M., forthcoming, 'Merchants, Industrialists and the Origins of British Multinational Enterprise in Latin America, 1870–1950' in Lewis and Miller (eds), *British Business*.

Griffith-Jones, S., 1989, 'Financial Relations between Britain and Latin America' in Bulmer-Thomas (ed.), *Britain and Latin America*, pp. 121–35.

Guy, D.J., 1979, 'Carlos Pellegrini and the Politics of Early Argentine Industrialisation, 1873–1906', *JLAS* **11**, 123–44.

Guy, D.J., 1984, 'Dependency, the Credit Market, and Argentine Industrialization, 1860–1940', *BHR* **58**, 532–61.

Haitin, M., 1982, 'Urban Market and Agrarian Hinterland: Lima in the late colonial period' in N. Jacobsen and H.-J. Puhle (eds),

*The Economies of Mexico and Peru during the Late Colonial Period,
1760–1810*, Berlin: Colloquium Verlag, pp. 281–98.

Halperín Donghi, T., 1963, 'La expansión ganadera en la campaña de
Buenos Aires, 1810–1852', *Desarrollo Económico* **3**, 57–110.

Halperín Donghi, T., 1973, *The Aftermath of Revolution in Latin
America*, NY: Harper & Row.

Halperín Donghi, T., 1982, '"Dependency Theory" and Latin
American Historiography', *LARR* **17**:1, 115–30.

Halperín Donghi, T., 1985, 'Economy and Society in Post-
Independence Spanish America' in Bethell (ed.), *CHLA*, III,
299–345.

Harvey, C. and Press, J., 1989, 'Overseas Investment and the Pro-
fessional Advance of British Metal-Mining Engineers, 1851–1914',
EcHR **42**, 64–86.

Hertner, P. and Jones, G. (eds), 1986, *Multinationals: theory and history*,
Aldershot: Gower.

Herwig, H.H., 1986, *Germany's Vision of Empire in Venezuela,
1871–1914*, Princeton: Princeton UP.

Hillman, J., 1990, 'Bolivia and British Tin Policy, 1939–1945', *JLAS*
22, 289–315.

Hilton, S.E., 1975, *Brazil and the Great Powers, 1930–1939: the politics
of trade rivalry*, Austin: UTP.

Hodge, J.E., 1970, 'Carlos Pellegrini and the Financial Crisis of 1890',
HAHR **50**, 499–523.

Holloway, T.H., 1975, *The Brazilian Coffee Valorization of 1906:
regional politics and economic dependence*, Madison: State Historical
Society.

Hood, M., 1983, *Gunboat Diplomacy, 1895–1905: great power pressure
in Venezuela*, London: George Allen & Unwin.

Horowitz, J., 1985, 'Occupational Community and the Creation of a
Self-Styled Elite: railroad workers in Argentina', *TAm* **42**, 55–81.

Humphreys, R.A., 1969, *Tradition and Revolt in Latin America and
Other Essays*, London: Weidenfeld & Nicolson.

Humphreys, R.A., 1981 and 1982, *Latin America and the Second World
War*, 2 vols, London: Athlone Press.

Hunt, S.J., 1984, 'Guano y crecimiento en el Perú del siglo XIX',
HISLA **4**, 35–92.

Irazusta, J., 1963, *Influencia económica británica en el Río de la Plata*,
Buenos Aires: EUDEBA.

Irazusta, R. and J., 1934, *La Argentina y el imperialismo británico: los
eslabones de una cadena, 1806–1833*, Buenos Aires: Editorial Tor.

Jenks, L.H., 1963 [1927], *The Migration of British Capital to 1875*, London: Thomas Nelson.

John, A.H., 1959, *A Liverpool Merchant House, being a history of Alfred Booth and Company, 1863–1958*, London: George Allen & Unwin.

Jones, C., 1977, 'Commercial Banks and Mortgage Companies' in Platt (ed.), *Business Imperialism*, pp. 17–52.

Jones, C., 1977, 'Insurance Companies' in Platt (ed.), *Business Imperialism*, pp. 53–74.

Jones, C., 1980, '"Business Imperialism" and Argentina: a theoretical note', *JLAS* **12**, 437–44.

Jones, C., 1983, 'Personalism, Indebtedness and Venality: the political environment of British firms in Santa Fé province, 1865–1900', *IAA* **9**, 381–400.

Jones, C., 1985, 'The State and Business Practice in Argentina, 1862–1914' in Abel and Lewis (eds), *Latin America, Economic Imperialism, and the State*, pp. 184–98.

Jones, C., 1987, *International Business in the Nineteenth Century: the rise and fall of a cosmopolitan bourgeoisie*, Brighton: Wheatsheaf.

Jones, G., 1984, 'The Expansion of British Multinational Manufacturing, 1890–1939' in A. Okochi and T. Inoue (eds), *Overseas Business Activities: proceedings of the Fuji Conference*, Tokyo: University of Tokyo Press.

Jones, G., 1986, 'Origins, Management and Performance' in G. Jones (ed.), *British Multinationals*, pp. 1–23.

Jones, G., 1986, 'The Performance of British Multinational Enterprise, 1890–1945' in Hertner and Jones (eds), *Multinationals*, pp. 96–112.

Jones, G., 1990, 'Competitive Advantages in British Multinational Banking since 1890' in G. Jones (ed.), *Banks as Multinationals*, London: Routledge, pp. 30–61.

Jones, G. (ed.), 1986, *British Multinationals: origins, management and performance*, Aldershot: Gower.

Jones, L., Jones, C. and Greenhill, R., 1977, 'Public Utility Companies' in Platt (ed.), *Business Imperialism*, pp. 77–118.

Jones, R.A., 1969, *The Nineteenth-Century Foreign Office: an administrative history*, London: Weidenfeld & Nicolson.

Jones, R.A., 1983, *The British Diplomatic Service, 1815–1914*, Gerrards Cross: Colin Smythe.

Joslin, D., 1963, *A Century of Banking in Latin America: to commemorate the centenary in 1962 of the Bank of London and South America Ltd*, London: OUP.

Katz, F., 1981, *The Secret War in Mexico: Europe, the United States, and the Mexican Revolution*, Chicago: Chicago UP.

Kaufmann, W.W., 1967 [1951], *British Policy and the Independence of Latin America, 1804–1828*, London: Cass.

Kay, C., 1989, *Latin American Theories of Development and Underdevelopment*, London: Routledge.

Keen, B. and Wasserman, M., 1984, *A Short History of Latin America*, Boston: Houghton Mifflin.

Kennedy, P., 1983, *Strategy and Diplomacy, 1870–1945: eight studies*, London: Allen & Unwin.

Kiernan, V.G., 1955, 'Britain's First Contacts with Paraguay', *Atlante* **3**, 171–91.

Kiernan, V.G., 1955, 'Foreign Interests in the War of the Pacific', *HAHR* **35**, 14–36.

Kindleberger, C.P., 1984, *A Financial History of Western Europe*, London: George Allen & Unwin.

Kinsbruner, J., 1970, 'The Political Influence of the British Merchants Resident in Chile during the O'Higgins Administration, 1817–1823', *TAm* **27**, 26–39.

Klein, H.S., 1982, *Bolivia: the evolution of a multi-ethnic society*, NY: OUP.

Knape, J., 1987, 'British Foreign Policy in the Caribbean Basin, 1938–1945: oil, nationalism and relations with the United States', *JLAS* **19**, 279–94.

Knape, J., 1989, 'Anglo-American Rivalry in Post-War Latin America: the question of arms sales', *IAA* **15**, 319–50.

Krasner, S.D., 1973, 'Manipulating International Commodity Markets: Brazilian coffee policy, 1906 to 1962', *Public Policy* **21**, 493–523.

Lavalle, J.B. de, 1919, *El Perú y la Gran Guerra*, Lima: Imprenta Americana.

Leff, N.H., 1982, *Underdevelopment and Development in Brazil*, 2 vols, London: George Allen & Unwin.

Levine, R.M., 1978, *Pernambuco in the Brazilian Federation, 1889–1937*, Stanford: Stanford UP.

Lewis, C.M., 1975, 'Anglo-Argentine Trade, 1945–1965' in Rock (ed.), *Argentina in the Twentieth Century*, pp. 114–34.

Lewis, C.M., 1977, 'British Railway Companies and the Argentine Government' in Platt (ed.), *Business Imperialism*, pp. 395–427.

Lewis, C.M., 1983, *British Railways in Argentina, 1857–1914*, London: Athlone Press.

Lewis, C.M., 1983, 'The Financing of Railway Development in Latin America, 1850–1914', *IAA* **9**, 255–78.

Lewis, C.M., 1985, 'Railways and Industrialization in Argentina and

Brazil, 1870–1929' in Abel and Lewis (eds), *Latin America, Economic Imperialism and the State*, pp. 199–230.

Lewis, C.M., 1987, 'Immigrant Entrepreneurs, Manufacturing and Industrial Policy in the Argentine, 1922–28', *JICH* **16**, 77–108.

Lewis, C.M. and Miller, R. (eds), forthcoming, *British Business in Latin America, 1850–1950*.

Liehr, R., 1983, 'La deuda exterior de México y los "merchant bankers" británicos, 1821–1860', *IAA* **9**, 415–39.

Liehr, R., 1989, 'La deuda exterior de la Gran Colombia frente a Gran Bretaña, 1820–1860' in Liehr (ed.), *América Latina en la época de Simón Bolívar: la formación de las economías nacionales y los intereses económicos europeos, 1800–1850*, Berlin: Colloquium Verlag.

Liss, P.K., 1983, *Atlantic Empires: the network of trade and revolution, 1713–1826*, Baltimore: Johns Hopkins UP.

Lockhart, J. and Schwartz, S.B., 1983, *Early Latin America: a history of colonial Spanish America and Brazil*, Cambridge: CUP.

Lombardi, J.V., 1982, *Venezuela: the search for order, the dream of progress*, NY: OUP.

Louis, W.R. (ed.), 1976, *Imperialism: the Robinson and Gallagher controversy*, NY: New Viewpoints.

Love, J.L., 1980, *São Paulo in the Brazilian Federation, 1889–1937*, Stanford: Stanford UP.

Love, J.L., 1980, 'Raúl Prebisch and the Origins of the Doctrine of Unequal Exchange', *LARR* **15**:3, 45–72.

Loveman, B., 1988, *Chile: the legacy of Hispanic capitalism*, NY: OUP.

Lynch, J., 1969, 'British Policy and Spanish America, 1783–1808', *JLAS* **1**, 1–30.

Lynch, J., 1981, *Argentine Dictator: Juan Manuel de Rosas, 1829–1852*, Oxford: Clarendon Press.

Lynch, J., 1982, 'Great Britain and Spanish American Independence, 1810–1830' in Lynch (ed.), *Andrés Bello*, pp. 7–24.

Lynch, J., 1986, *The Spanish American Revolutions, 1808–1826*, NY: Norton.

Lynch, J. (ed.), 1982, *Andrés Bello: the London years*, Richmond: Richmond Publishing.

Macaulay, N., 1986, *Dom Pedro: the struggle for liberty in Brazil and Portugal, 1798–1834*, Durham: Duke UP.

McBeth, B.S., 1983, *Juan Vicente Gómez and the Oil Companies in Venezuela, 1908–1935*, Cambridge: CUP.

McBeth, B.S., 1985, *British Oil Policy, 1919–1939*, London: Cass.

MacDonald, C.A., 1980, 'The Politics of Intervention: the United States and Argentina, 1941–1946', *JLAS* **12**, 365–96.

MacDonald, C.A., 1986, 'The United States, Britain, and Argentina in the Years immediately after the Second World War' in Di Tella and Platt (eds), *The Political Economy of Argentina*, pp. 183–200.

McLynn, F.J., 1979, 'The Causes of the War of the Triple Alliance: an interpretation', *IAEA* **33**, 21–43.

Mamalakis, M.J., 1971, 'The Role of Government in the Resource Transfer and Resource Allocation Processes: the Chilean nitrate sector, 1880–1930' in G. Ranis (ed.), *Government and Economic Development*, New Haven: Yale UP, pp. 181–215.

Manchester, A.K., 1972 [1933], *British Pre-Eminence in Brazil: its rise and decline*, NY: Octagon Books.

Marcílio, M.L., 1984, 'The Population of Colonial Brazil' in Bethell (ed.), *CHLA*, II, 37–63.

Marett, Sir R., 1973, *Latin America: British Trade and Investment*, London: Charles Knight.

Mariátegui, J.C., 1974 [1928], *Seven Interpretive Essays on Peruvian Reality*, Austin: UTP.

Marichal, C., 1988, 'Políticas de desarrollo económico y deuda externa en Argentina, 1868–1880', *Siglo XIX* **3**, 89–124.

Marichal, C., 1989, *A Century of Debt Crises in Latin America: from independence to the Great Depression, 1820–1930*, Princeton: Princeton UP.

Martin, G., 1989, 'Britain's Cultural Relations with Latin America' in Bulmer-Thomas (ed.), *Britain and Latin America*, pp. 27–51.

Mathew, W.M., 1968, 'The Imperialism of Free Trade: Peru, 1820–1870', *EcHR* **21**, 562–79.

Mathew, W.M., 1970, 'The First Anglo-Peruvian Debt and its Settlement, 1822–1849', *JLAS* **2**, 81–98.

Mathew, W.M., 1977, 'Antony Gibbs & Sons, the Guano Trade, and the Peruvian Government, 1842–1861' in Platt (ed.), *Business Imperialism*, pp. 337–70.

Mathew, W.M., 1981, *The House of Gibbs and the Peruvian Guano Monopoly*, London: Royal Historical Society.

Mayo, J., 1979, 'La Compañía de Salitres de Antofagasta y la Guerra del Pacífico', *Historia* (Santiago) **14**, 71–102.

Mayo, J., 1979, 'Before the Nitrate Era: British commission houses and the Chilean economy, 1851–1880', *JLAS* **11**, 283–302.

Mayo, J., 1981, 'Britain and Chile, 1851–1886: anatomy of a relationship', *JIASWA* **23**, 95–120.

Mayo, J., 1983, '"The Impatient Lion": Britain's "official mind" and Latin America in the 1850s', *IAA* **9**, 197–223.

Mayo, J., 1985, 'Commerce, Credit and Control in Chilean Copper Mining before 1880' in Culver and Greaves (eds), *Miners and Mining*, pp. 29–46.

Mayo, J., 1987, 'Consuls and Silver Contraband on Mexico's West Coast in the Era of Santa Anna', *JLAS* **19**, 389–415.

Mayo, J., 1987, *British Merchants and Chilean Development, 1851–1886*, Boulder: Westview Press.

Meyer, M.C. and Sherman, W.L., 1987, *The Course of Mexican History*, NY: OUP.

Meyer, L., 1985, *The Mexican Revolution and the Anglo-American Powers: the end of confrontation and the beginning of negotiation*, San Diego: Center for Mexican-American Studies.

Miller, R., 1976, 'The Making of the Grace Contract: British bondholders and the Peruvian government, 1885–1890', *JLAS* **8**, 73–100.

Miller, R., 1977, 'British Firms and the Peruvian Government, 1885–1930' in Platt (ed.), *Business Imperialism*, pp. 371–94.

Miller, R., 1981, 'Latin American Manufacturing and the First World War: an exploratory essay', *World Development* **9**, 707–16.

Miller, R., 1982, 'Small Business in the Peruvian Oil Industry: Lobitos Oilfields Limited before 1934', *BHR* **56**, 400–23.

Miller, R., 1983, 'The Grace Contract, the Peruvian Corporation and Peruvian History', *IAA* **9**, 319–48.

Miller, R., forthcoming, 'British Trade with Latin America, 1870–1950' in J. Davis and P. Mathias (eds), *International Trade and British Economic Growth*, Oxford: Blackwell.

Mitchell, B.R., 1983, *International Historical Statistics: the Americas and Australasia*, London: Macmillan.

Mitchell, B.R., 1988, *British Historical Statistics*, Cambridge: CUP.

Mitchell, B.R. and Deane, P.R., 1962, *Abstract of British Historical Statistics*, Cambridge: CUP.

Moggridge, D.E., 1971, 'British Controls on Long-Term Capital Movements, 1924–1931' in D.N. McCloskey (ed.), *Essays on a Mature Economy: Britain after 1840*, London: Methuen, pp. 113–38.

Monteón, M., 1975, 'The British in the Atacama Desert: the cultural bases of economic imperialism', *JEcH* **35**, 117–33.

Monteón, M., 1979, 'The *Enganche* in the Chilean Nitrate Sector, 1880–1930', *LAP* **6**, 66–79.

Monteón, M., 1982, *Chile in the Nitrate Era: the evolution of economic dependence, 1880–1930*, Madison: University of Wisconsin Press.

Morgan, I., 1978, 'French Policy in Spanish America, 1830–1848', *JLAS* **10**, 309–28.

Morgan, I., 1983, 'Orleanist Diplomacy and the French Colony in Uruguay', *International Hist. Rev.* **5**, 201–28.

Mörner, M., 1985, *The Andean Past: land, societies and conflicts*, NY: Columbia UP.

Naylor, B., 1969, *Accounts of Nineteenth-Century South America: an annotated checklist of works by British and United States observers*, London: Athlone Press.

Naylor, R.A., 1960, 'The British Role in Central America prior to the Clayton–Bulwer Treaty of 1850', *HAHR* **40**, 361–82.

Nelson, G.H., 1945, 'Contraband Trade under the Asiento, 1730–1739', *AHR* **51**, 55–67.

Nettels, C., 1931, 'England and the Spanish American Trade, 1680–1715', *Jnl Modern Hist.* **3**, 1–32.

Newton, R.C., 1986, 'The Neutralization of Fritz Mandl: notes on wartime journalism, the arms trade, and Anglo-American rivalry in Argentina during World War II', *HAHR* **66**, 541–79.

Nicholas, S.J., 1982, 'British Multinational Investment before 1939', *JEEH* **11**, 605–30.

Nicholas, S.J., 1984, 'The Overseas Marketing Performance of British Industry, 1870–1914', *EcHR* **37**, 489–506.

Normano, J.F., 1935, *Brazil: a study of economic types*, Chapel Hill: North Carolina UP.

Nove, A., 1973, 'Great Britain and Latin American Economic Development' in V.L. Urquidi; and R. Thorp (eds), *Latin America and the International Economy*, London: Macmillan, pp. 331–66.

O'Brien, T.F., 1980, 'The Antofagasta Company: a case study of peripheral capitalism', *HAHR* **60**, 1–31.

O'Brien, T.F., 1982, *The Nitrate Industry and Chile's Crucial Transition, 1870–1891*, NY: NYUP.

O'Brien, T.F., 1989, '"Rich beyond the Dreams of Avarice": the Guggenheims in Chile', *BHR* **63**, 122–59.

O'Connell, A.A., 1984, 'Argentina into the Depression: problems of an open economy' in Thorp (ed.), *Latin America in the 1930s*, pp. 188–221.

O'Connell, A.A., 1986, 'La fiebre aftosa, el embargo sanitario norteamericano contra las importaciones de carne y el triángulo Argentina-Gran Bretaña-Estados Unidos en el período entre las dos guerras mundiales', *Desarrollo Económico* **26**, 21–50.

O'Connell, A.A., 1986, 'Free Trade in One (Primary Producing)

Country: the case of Argentina in the 1920s' in Di Tella and Platt (eds), *The Political Economy of Argentina*, pp. 74–94.

Oribe Stemmer, J.E., 1989, 'Freight Rates in the Trade between Europe and South America, 1840–1914', *JLAS* **21**, 23–60.

Ortega, L., 1984, 'Nitrates, Chilean Entrepreneurs, and the Origins of the War of the Pacific', *JLAS* **16**, 337–80.

Ortega, L., 1985, 'Economic Policy and Growth in Chile from Independence to the War of the Pacific' in Abel and Lewis (eds), *Latin America, Economic Imperialism, and the State*, pp. 147–71.

Owen, R. and Sutcliffe, B. (eds), 1972, *Studies in the Theory of Imperialism*, London: Longman.

Palacios Moreyra, C., 1983, *La deuda anglo-peruana, 1822–1890*, Lima: Studium.

Palma, G., 1978, 'Dependency: a formal theory of underdevelopment or a methodology for the analysis of concrete situations of underdevelopment?', *World Development* **6**, 881–924.

Palma, G., 1985, 'External Disequilibrium and Internal Industrialization: Chile, 1904–1935' in Abel and Lewis (eds), *Latin America, Economic Imperialism and the State*, pp. 318–38.

Palmer, C.A., 1981, *Human Cargoes: the British slave trade to Spanish America, 1700–1739*, Urbana: University of Illinois Press.

Pang, Eul-Soo, 1979, 'Modernization and Slavocracy in Nineteenth-Century Brazil', *Jnl Interdisciplinary Hist.* **9**, 667–88.

Peláez, C.M., 1976, 'The Theory and Reality of Imperialism in the Coffee Economy of Nineteenth-Century Brazil', *EcHR* **29**, 276–90.

Pérez Brignoli, H., 1980, 'The Economic Cycle in Latin American Agricultural Export Economies, 1880–1930: a hypothesis for investigation', *LARR* **15**:2, 3–33.

Perren, R., 1978, *The Meat Trade in Britain, 1840–1914*, London: Routledge & Kegan Paul.

Philip, G., 1982, *Oil and Politics in Latin America: nationalist movements and state companies*, Cambridge: CUP.

Pike, F.B., 1967, *The Modern History of Peru*, London: Weidenfeld & Nicolson.

Plá, J., 1976, *The British in Paraguay, 1850–1870*, Richmond: Richmond Publishing.

Platt, D.C.M., 1962, 'The Allied Coercion of Venezuela, 1902–03: a reassessment', *IAEA* **15**, 3–28.

Platt, D.C.M., 1968, *Finance, Trade, and Politics in British Foreign Policy, 1815–1914*, Oxford: Clarendon Press.

Platt, D.C.M., 1968, 'The Imperialism of Free Trade: some reservations', *EcHR* **21**, 296–306.

Platt, D.C.M., 1968, 'Economic Factors in British Policy during the "New Imperialism"', *Past and Present* **39**, 120–38.

Platt, D.C.M., 1971, 'Problems in the Interpretation of Foreign Trade Statistics before 1914', *JLAS* **3**, 119–30.

Platt, D.C.M., 1972, *Latin America and British Trade, 1806–1914*, London: A & C Black.

Platt, D.C.M., 1972, 'Economic Imperialism and the Businessman: Britain and Latin America before 1914' in Owen and Sutcliffe (eds), *Studies in the Theory of Imperialism*, pp. 295–310.

Platt, D.C.M., 1973, 'Further Objections to an Imperialism of Free Trade, 1830–1860', *EcHR* **26**, 77–91.

Platt, D.C.M., 1973, 'Business Archives' in P. Walne (ed.), *A Guide to Manuscript Sources for the History of Latin America and the Caribbean in the British Isles*, London: OUP, pp. 442–513.

Platt, D.C.M., 1980, 'British Portfolio Investment before 1870: some doubts', *EcHR* **33**, 1–16.

Platt, D.C.M., 1980, 'Dependency in Nineteenth-Century Latin America: an historian objects', *LARR* **15**:1, 113–30.

Platt, D.C.M., 1983, 'Foreign Finance in Argentina for the First Half-Century of Independence', *JLAS* **15**, 23–47.

Platt, D.C.M., 1984, 'British Finance in Mexico, 1821–1867', *BLAR* **3**, 45–62.

Platt, D.C.M., 1985, 'Canada and Argentina: the first preference of the British investor, 1904–1914', *JICH* **13**, 77–92.

Platt, D.C.M., 1985, 'Dependency and the Historian: further objections' in Abel and Lewis (eds), *Latin America, Economic Imperialism, and the State*, pp. 29–39.

Platt, D.C.M., 1986, *Britain's Investment Overseas on the Eve of the First World War*, London: Macmillan.

Platt, D.C.M. (ed.), 1977, *Business Imperialism, 1840–1930: an inquiry based on British experience in Latin America*, Oxford: Clarendon Press.

Pollard, S., 1985, 'Capital Exports, 1870–1914: harmful or beneficial?', *EcHR* **38**, 489–514.

Pollard, S., 1989, *Britain's Prime and Britain's Decline: the British Economy, 1870–1914*, London: Arnold.

Prado Jr, C., 1949, *História econômica do Brasil*, São Paulo: Brasiliense.

Pratt, E.J., 1935, 'Anglo-American Commercial and Political Rivalry on the Plate, 1820–1830', *HAHR* **15**, 302–35.

Prebisch, R., 1986, 'Argentine Economic Policies since the 1930s: recollections' in Di Tella and Platt (eds), *The Political Economy of Argentina*, pp. 133–53.

Pregger-Román, C.G., 1978, 'The Role of the Banking and Insurance Sector in the Failure of the Industrial Revolution in Nineteenth-Century Chile', *Studies in Comparative International Devt* **13**, 76–95.

Pregger-Román, C.G., 1983, 'Dependence, Underdevelopment and Imperialism in Latin America: a reappraisal', *Science and Society* **47**, 406–26.

Pressnell, L. and Orbell, J., 1985, *A Guide to the Historical Records of British Banking*, Aldershot: Gower.

Pressnell, L.S., 1986, *External Economic Policy since the War. Vol. 1: the postwar financial settlement*, London: HMSO.

Ramírez Necochea, H., 1970, *Historia del imperialismo en Chile*, Santiago: Austral.

Randall, L., 1978, *An Economic History of Argentina in the Twentieth Century*, NY: Columbia UP.

Randall, R.W., 1972, *Real del Monte: a British mining venture in Mexico*, Austin: UTP.

Randall, R.W., 1985, 'British Company and Mexican Community: the English at Real del Monte, 1824–1849', *BHR* **59**, 622–44.

Rapoport, M., 1976, 'La política británica en la Argentina a comienzos de la década de 1940', *Desarrollo Económico* **16**, 203–28.

Rapoport, M., 1981, *Gran Bretaña, Estados Unidos y las clases dirigentes argentinas, 1940–1945*, Buenos Aires: Belgrano.

Reader, W.J., 1975, *Imperial Chemical Industries: a history. Vol. II: the first quarter-century, 1926–1952*, London: OUP.

Reber, V.B., 1979, *British Mercantile Houses in Buenos Aires, 1810–1880*, Cambridge, Mass.: Harvard UP.

Reckitt, B.N., 1951, *The History of Reckitt and Sons, Ltd*, London: A Brown & Sons.

Rector, J., 1975, 'Transformaciones comerciales producidas por la independencia de Chile', *RChHG* **143**, 106–26.

Redford, A., 1956, *Manchester Merchants and Foreign Trade. Vol. II: 1850–1939*, Manchester: Manchester UP.

Regalsky, A.M., 1989, 'Foreign Capital, Local Interests, and Railway Development in Argentina: French investments in railways, 1900–1914', *JLAS* **21**, 425–52.

Richmond, L. and Turton, A. (eds), 1987, *Directory of Corporate Archives*, London: Business Archives Council.

Richmond, L. and Stockford, B. (eds), 1986, *Company Archives: the survey of 1000 of the first registered companies in England and Wales*, London: Gower.

Ridings, E.W., 1982, 'Business, Nationality and Dependency in Late Nineteenth-Century Brazil', *JLAS* **14**, 55–96.

Ridings, E.W., 1985, 'Foreign Predominance among Overseas Traders in Nineteenth-Century Latin America', *LARR* **20**:2, 3–28.

Rippy, J.F., 1977 [1959], *British Investments in Latin America, 1822–1949: a case study in the operations of private enterprise in retarded regions*, NY: Arno Press.

Robinson, K., 1979, 'The Merchants of Post-Independence Buenos Aires' in W.S. Coker (ed.), *Hispanic-American Essays in Honor of Max Leon Moorhead*, Pensacola: Perdido Bay Press, pp. 111–32.

Robinson, R., 1972, 'Non-European Foundations of European Expansion: sketch for a theory of collaboration' in Owen and Sutcliffe (eds), *Studies in the Theory of Imperialism*, pp. 118–40.

Rock, D., 1975, *Politics in Argentina, 1890–1930: the rise and fall of Radicalism*, Cambridge: CUP.

Rock, D., 1986, 'The Argentine Economy, 1890–1914: some salient features' in Di Tella and Platt (eds), *The Political Economy of Argentina*, pp. 60–73.

Rock, D., 1987, *Argentina, 1516–1987: from Spanish colonisation to the Falklands War and Alfonsín*, London: Tauris.

Rock, D. (ed.), 1975, *Argentina in the Twentieth Century*, London: Duckworth.

Rodríguez, M., 1964, A *Palmerstonian Diplomat in Central America: Frederick Chatfield, Esq.*, Tucson: University of Arizona Press.

Rosenberg, E.S., 1975, 'Economic Pressures on Anglo-American Diplomacy in Mexico, 1917–1918', *JIASWA* **17**, 123–52.

Rosenberg, E.S., 1978, 'Anglo-American Economic Rivalry in Brazil during World War I', *Diplomatic Hist.* **2**, 131–52.

Roxborough, I., 1979, *Theories of Underdevelopment*, London: Macmillan.

Roxborough, I., 1984, 'Unity and Diversity in Latin American History', *JLAS* **16**, 1–26.

Royal Institute of International Affairs, 1937, *The Problem of International Investment*, London: OUP.

Sábato, H., 1983, 'Wool Trade and Commercial Networks in Buenos Aires, 1840s to 1880s', *JLAS* **15**, 49–81.

Sater, W.F., 1976, 'Economic Nationalism and Tax Reform in Late Nineteenth-Century Chile', *TAm* **33**, 311–35.

Sater, W.F., 1979, 'Chile and the World Depression of the 1870s', *JLAS* **11**, 67–99.

Saul, S.B., 1960, *Studies in British Overseas Trade, 1870–1914*, Liverpool: Liverpool UP.

Sayers, R.S., 1976, *The Bank of England, 1891–1944*, Cambridge: CUP.

Scalabrini Ortíz, R., 1958, *Historia de los ferrocarriles argentinos*, Buenos Aires: Devenir.

Scalabrini Ortíz, R., 1965, *Política británica en el Río de la Plata*, Buenos Aires: Plus Ultra.

Scobie, J.R., 1961, 'Los representantes británicos y norteamericanos en la Argentina, 1852–1862', *Historia* (Buenos Aires) **6**:23, 122–66; **6**:24, 85–128.

Scobie, J.R., 1964, *Argentina: a city and a nation*, NY: OUP.

Scobie, J.R., 1964, *Revolution on the Pampas: a social history of Argentine wheat*, Austin: ILAS.

Segreti, C.S.A., 1978, 'La política económica porteña en la primera década revolucionaria', *Investigaciones y Ensayos* **25**, 31–74.

Singh, K., 1989, 'Oil Politics in Venezuela during the López Contreras Administration, 1936–1941', *JLAS* **21**, 89–104.

Skidmore, T.E. and Smith, P.H., 1989, *Modern Latin America*, NY: OUP.

Skupch, P.R., 1971, 'Las consecuencias de la competencia de transportes sobre la hegemonía económica británica en la Argentina, 1919–1939', *Económica* **17**, 119–41.

Skupch, P.R., 1973, 'El deterioro y fin de la hegemonía británica sobre la economía argentina, 1914–1947' in M. Panaia, R. Lesser and P.R. Skupch (eds), *Estudios sobre los orígenes del peronismo*, Buenos Aires: Siglo XXI, II, 3–79.

Smith, J., 1978, 'New World Diplomacy: a reappraisal of British policy toward Latin America, 1823–1850', *IAEA* **32**:2, 3–24.

Smith, J., 1979, *Illusions of Conflict: Anglo-American diplomacy toward Latin America, 1865–1896*, Pittsburgh: Pittsburgh UP.

Smith, P.H., 1969, *Politics and Beef in Argentina: patterns of conflict and change*, NY: Columbia UP.

Smith, T., 1981, *The Pattern of Imperialism: the United States, Great Britain, and the late-industrializing world since 1815*, Cambridge: CUP.

Stang, G., 1982, 'Entrepreneurs and Managers: the establishment and organization of British firms in Latin America in the nineteenth and twentieth centuries', *Historisk Tidskrift* **1**, 40–61.

Stang, G., 1983, 'Aspectos de la política de personal de las empresas británicas en América Latina, 1880–1930' in AHILA, *Capitales, empresarios y obreros europeos en América Latina*, pp. 501–50.

Stein, S.J. and Stein, B.H., 1970, *The Colonial Heritage of Latin America: essays on economic dependence in historical perspective*, NY: OUP.

Stein, S.J. and Stein, B.H., 1980, 'D.C.M. Platt: the anatomy of "autonomy"', *LARR* **15**:1, 131–46.

Steiner, Z., 1970, 'Finance, Trade and Politics in British Foreign Policy, 1815–1914', *HJ* **13**, 545–52.

Stemplowski, R., 1976, 'Las potencias anglosajones y el neutralismo argentino, 1939–1945', *Estudios Latinoamericanos* **3**, 129–60.

Stemplowski, R., 1981, 'Castillo's Argentina and World War II: economic aspects of the Argentine-British-United States-German quadrangle', *Beiträge zur Wirtschaftgeschichte* **8**, 801–23.

Stone, I., 1968, 'British Long-Term Investment in Latin America, 1865–1913', *BHR* **42**, 311–39.

Stone, I., 1977, 'British Direct and Portfolio Investment in Latin America before 1914', *JEcH* **37**, 690–722.

Stopford, J.M., 1974, 'The Origins of British-Based Multinational Manufacturing Enterprises', *BHR* **48**, 303–35.

Street, J., 1953, 'Lord Strangford and the Río de la Plata, 1808–1815', *HAHR* **33**, 477–510.

Street, J.H., 1981, 'The Platt-Stein Controversy over Dependency: another view', *LARR* **16**:3, 173–80.

Sunkel, O., 1982, *Un siglo de historia económica de Chile, 1830–1930: dos ensayos y una bibliografía*, Madrid: Instituto de Cooperación Iberoamericana.

Svedberg, P., 1978, 'The Portfolio-Direct Composition of Private Foreign Investment in 1914 Revisited', *Economic Jnl* **88**, 763–77.

Tate, E.N., 1979, 'Britain and Latin America in the Nineteenth Century: the case of Paraguay, 1811–1870', *IAA* **5**, 39–70.

Teichova, A., Lévy-Leboyer, M. and Nussbaum, H. (eds), 1986, *Multinational Enterprise in Historical Perspective*, Cambridge: CUP.

Temperley, H., 1925, *The Foreign Policy of Canning, 1822–1827: England, the neo-Holy Alliance, and the New World*, London: G. Bell.

Tenenbaum, B.A., 1975, 'Straightening out some of the Lumpen in the Development: an examination of Andre Gunder Frank's explanation of Latin American history in terms of Mexico, 1821–1856', *LAP* **2**, 3–16.

Tenenbaum, B.A., 1986, *The Politics of Penury: debts and taxes in Mexico, 1821–1856*, Albuquerque: New Mexico UP.

Thomas, D., 1989, 'The United States Factor in British Relations with Latin America' in Bulmer-Thomas (ed.), *Britain and Latin America*, pp. 68–82.

Thompson, R., 1984, 'The Limitations of Ideology in the Early Argentine Labour Movement: anarchism in the trade unions, 1890–1920', *JLAS* **16**, 81–99.

Thomson, G.P.C., 1985, 'Protectionism and Industrialization in Mexico, 1821–1854: the case of Puebla' in Abel and Lewis (eds), *Latin America, Economic Imperialism, and the State*, pp. 125–46.

Thomson, G.P.C., 1991, 'Continuity and Change in Mexican Manufacturing, 1800–1870' in J. Batou (ed.), *Between Development and Underdevelopment: the precocious attempts at industrialization of the periphery, 1800–1870*, Geneva: Droz, pp. 255–302.

Thorp, R. and Bertram, G., 1978, *Peru, 1890–1977: growth and policy in an open economy*, NY: Columbia UP.

Thorp, R. (ed.), 1984, *Latin America in the 1930s: the role of the periphery in world crisis*, London: Macmillan.

Tischendorf, A., 1961, *Great Britain and Mexico in the Era of Porfirio Díaz*, Durham, NC: Duke UP.

Topik, S., 1979, 'The Evolution of the Economic Role of the Brazilian State, 1889–1930', *JLAS* **11**, 325–42.

Topik, S., 1980, 'State Interventionism in a Liberal Regime: Brazil, 1889–1930', *HAHR* **60**, 593–616.

Topik, S., 1985, 'The State's Contribution to the Development of Brazil's Internal Economy, 1850–1930', *HAHR* **65**, 203–28.

Topik, S., 1987, *The Political Economy of the Brazilian State, 1889–1930*, Austin: UTP.

Tulchin, J.S., 1971, *The Aftermath of War: World War I and US policy toward Latin America*, NYUP.

Tulchin, J.S., 1974, 'Decolonizing an Informal Empire: Argentina, Great Britain, and the United States, 1930–1943', *International Interactions* **1**: 3, 123–40.

Tulchin, J.S., 1975, 'Foreign Policy', in Falcoff and Dolkart, (eds) *Prologue to Perón*, pp. 83–109.

Tulchin, J.S., 1987, 'The Malvinas War of 1982: an inevitable conflict that never should have occurred', *LARR* **22**:3, 123–41.

Turner, L., 1978, *Oil Companies in the International System*, London: RIIA/George Allen & Unwin.

Van Aken, M.J., 1962, 'British Policy Considerations in Central America before 1850', *HAHR* **42**, 54–9.

Veliz, C., 1975, 'Egaña, Lambert and the Chilean Mining Associations of 1825', *HAHR* **55**, 637–63.

Veliz, C., 1977, 'The Irisarri Loan', *BELAC* **23**, 3–20.

Veliz, C., 1980, *The Centralist Tradition in Latin America*, Princeton: Princeton UP.

Venn, F., 1986, *Oil Diplomacy in the Twentieth Century*, Basingstoke: Macmillan.

Villalobos, S., 1965, *Comercio y contrabando en el Río de la Plata y Chile, 1700–1811*, Buenos Aires: Universidad de Buenos Aires.

Villalobos, S., 1968, *El comercio y la crisis colonial: un mito de la independencia*, Santiago: Universidad de Chile.

Villanueva, J., 1975, 'Economic Development' in Falcoff and Dolkart (eds), *Prologue to Perón*, pp. 57–82.

Waddell, D.A.G., 1959, 'Great Britain and the Bay Islands, 1821–1861', *HJ* **2**, 59–77.

Waddell, D.A.G., 1982, 'British Relations with Venezuela, New Granada and Gran Colombia, 1810–1829', in Lynch (ed.), *Andres Bello*, pp. 25–47.

Waddell, D.A.G., 1984, 'International Politics and Latin American Independence' in Bethell (ed.), *CHLA*, III, 197–228.

Waddell, D.A.G., 1987, 'British Neutrality and Spanish American Independence: the problem of foreign enlistment', *JLAS* **19**, 1–18.

Waddell, D.A.G., 1989, 'Anglo-Spanish Relations and the "Pacification of America" during the "Constitutional Triennium"' *Anuario de Estudios Americanos* **46**, 455–86.

Walker D.W., 1986, *Kinship, Business and Politics: the Martínez del Río family in Mexico, 1823–1867*, Austin: UTP.

Walker, G.J., 1979, *Spanish Politics and Imperial Trade, 1700–1789*, London: Macmillan.

Walter, R.J., 1982, 'The Socioeconomic Growth of Buenos Aires in the Twentieth Century' in S.R. Ross and T.F. McGann (eds), *Buenos Aires: 400 years*, Austin: UTP, pp. 67–126.

Warren, H.G., 1972, 'The Golden Fleecing: the Paraguayan loans of 1871–1872', *IAEA* **26**:1, 3–24.

Warren, H.G., 1978, *Paraguay and the Triple Alliance: the postwar decade*, Austin: UTP.

Warren, H.G. and Warren, K.F., 1985, *Rebirth of the Paraguayan Republic: the first Colorado era, 1878–1904*, Pittsburgh: Pittsburgh UP.

Weaver, F.S., 1976, 'American Underdevelopment: an interpretive essay on historical change', *LAP* **3**, 17–53.

Webster, C.K. (ed.), 1970 [1938], *Britain and the Independence of Latin America, 1812–1830: select documents from the Foreign Office archives*, 2 vols, NY: Octagon.

Weinstein, B., 1983, *The Amazon Rubber Boom, 1850–1920*, Stanford: Stanford UP.

White, R.A., 1978, *Paraguay's Autonomous Revolution, 1810–1840*, Albuquerque: University of New Mexico Press.

White, R.A., 1979, 'The Denied Revolution: Paraguay's economics of independence', *LAP* **6**, 4–24.

Wilkins, M., 1970, *The Emergence of Multinational Enterprise: American business abroad from the colonial era to 1914*, Cambridge, Mass.: Harvard UP.

Wilkins, M., 1974, *The Maturing of Multinational Enterprise: American business abroad from 1914 to 1970*, Cambridge, Mass.: Harvard UP.

Wilkins, M., 1986, 'The History of European Multinationals: a new look', *JEEH* **15**, 483–510.

Wilkins, M., 1988, 'The Free-Standing Company, 1870–1914: an important type of British foreign direct investment', *EcHR* **41**, 259–82.

Wilkins, M., 1988, 'European and North American Multinationals, 1870–1914: comparisons and contrasts', *BH* **30**, 8–45.

Will, R.M., 1960, 'La política económica de Chile, 1810–1864', *Trimestre Económico* **27**, 238–57.

Williams, John H., 1969 [1920], *Argentine International Trade under Inconvertible Paper Money, 1880–1900*, NY: Greenwood Press.

Williams, John Hoyt, 1972, 'Paraguayan Isolation under Dr Francia: a re-evaluation', *HAHR* **52**, 102–22.

Williams, John Hoyt, 1979, *The Rise and Fall of the Paraguayan Republic, 1800–1870*, Austin: ILAS.

Williams, J.B., 1935, 'The Establishment of British Commerce with Argentina', *HAHR* **15**, 43–64.

Williams, J.B., 1972, *British Commercial Policy and Trade Expansion, 1750–1850*, Oxford: Clarendon Press.

Wilson, C., 1954, *The History of Unilever: a study in economic growth and social change*, 2 vols, London: Cassell.

Wilson, C., 1968, *Unilever, 1945–1965: challenge and response in the post-war industrial revolution*, London: Cassell.

Winn, P., 1976, 'Britain's Informal Empire in Uruguay during the Nineteenth Century', *Past and Present* **73**, 100–26.

Wirth, J.D., 1977, *Minas Gerais in the Brazilian Federation, 1889–1937*, Stanford: Stanford UP.

Wright, W.R., 1967, 'Foreign-Owned Railways in Argentina: a case-study of economic nationalism', *BHR* **41**, 67–93.

Wright, W.R., 1974, *British-Owned Railways in Argentina: their effect on the growth of economic nationalism, 1854–1948*, Austin: UTP.

Wu, C., 1991, *Generals and Diplomats: Great Britain and Peru, 1820–1840*, Cambridge: CLAS.

Wynne, W.H., 1951, *State Insolvency and Foreign Bondholders: selected case histories of governmental foreign bond defaults and debt readjustments*, New Haven: Yale UP.

Yepes del Castillo, E., 1972, *Perú, 1820–1920: un siglo de desarrollo capitalista*, Lima: IEP.

Zahedieh, N., 1986, 'Trade, Plunder, and Economic Development in Early English Jamaica, 1655–1689', *EcHR* **39**, 205–22.

Zeitlin, M., 1984, *The Civil Wars in Chile (or the bourgeois revolutions that never were)*, Princeton: Princeton UP.

Ziegler, P., 1988, *The Sixth Great Power: Barings, 1767–1929*, London: Collins.

UNPUBLISHED THESES

Abreu, M. de P., 1977, 'Brazil and the World Economy, 1930–1945: aspects of foreign economic policies and international economic relations under Vargas', PhD thesis, Cambridge.

Bollinger, W.S., 1972, 'The Rise of United States Influence in the Peruvian Economy, 1869–1921', MA thesis, UCLA.

Henderson, S.P., 1984, 'Latin America and the Great War: a study of the effects of the First World War on economic and social conditions in Peru and Chile', PhD thesis, UEA.

Miller, R.M., 1978, 'British Business in Peru, 1883–1930', PhD thesis, Cambridge.

Oppenheimer, R.B., 1976, 'Chilean Transportation Development: the railroad and socio-economic change in the central valley, 1840–1885', PhD thesis, UCLA.

Maps

MEXICO

San Blas
Tampico
Mexico City • • Vera
Cruz
Havana
CUBA HAITI
BAY
IS. Santiago
JAMAICA
Mosquito
Coast
Cartagena
Panama
SANTO DOMINGO
(occupied by Haiti in 1822–44)

CURAÇAO
TRINIDAD (British)

UNITED PROVINCES
OF CENTRAL AMERICA

Caracas
Bogotá
R. Orinoco
GUIANAS

NEW
GRANADA
VENEZUELA
R. Amazon
Pará

ECUADOR
Quito

EMPIRE OF
BRAZIL
Recife
(Pernambuco)

PERU
Lima

La Paz
BOLIVIA
Sucre
PARAGUAY
R. São Francisco
Salvador
(Bahia)

Asunción
São Paulo
Rio de Janeiro

ARGENTINE
CONFEDERATION
R. Paraná

Valparaíso
Santiago
Córdoba
Buenos Aires
URUGUAY
Montevideo
Colônia do Sacramento

0   2000 km
0   1000 mls

FALKLAND ISLANDS
(British 1833→)

1   Latin America in 1830
After F. G. Dawson, *The First Latin American Debt Crisis*

MEXICO

2
1
3

4
CUBA

GUATEMALA
EL SALVADOR
NICARAGUA
COSTA RICA
PANAMA
COLOMBIA

HONDURAS
VENEZUELA
5

GUIANAS

ECUADOR
7
6
8
9
28
27
26

PERU
BOLIVIA
BRAZIL
PARAGUAY
10
11
12
25

Nitrate
zone
13
21
22
23
24

CHILE
14
15
17
18
19
20
URUGUAY

16
pampas

ARGENTINA

0   2000 km

0   1000 mls

Major Cities			
1 Mexico City	8 Guayaquil	15 Santiago	22 São Paulo
2 Tampico	9 Iquitos	16 Bahia Blanca	23 Santos
3 Vera Cruz	10 Lima	17 Córdoba	24 Rio de Janeiro
4 Havana	11 Arequipa	18 Rosario	25 Salvador
5 Caracas	12 La Paz	19 Buenos Aires	26 Recife
6 Bogotá	13 Antofagasta	20 Montevideo	27 Pará
7 Quito	14 Valparaiso	21 Asunción	28 Manáus

2   Latin America in 1913, showing principal railways
After C. M. Lewis, 'Latin America from Independence to Dependence' in R.
Morris (ed.), *Africa, America and Central Asia*

Index

Humphreys, R.A., 226
Hunt, Shane J., 94, 110
Huth Gruning, 100, 129
Huttenback, Robert A., 120
Hyslop, Maxwell and Wellwood, 39

ICI, 187, 211, 247
immigration, 11, 70
Imperial Preference, 5, 199, 205, 207, 209, 215, 218
imperialism, 15–19, 21, 22, 148, 238, 243
import substitution, 13, 19, 112–13, 207
independence, 6–7, 14, 27
    Brazil, 42–4
    Spanish America, 1–2, 33–42
indigo, 30
inflation, 164, 183, 198
Institute for the Permanent Defence of Coffee, 201
insurance, 3, 82, 100, 141, 180
investment, British, 5, 73, 116–17, 119–46, 184, 186–9, 211–14, 230, 235, 236–7, 246, 247
    in government loans, 2, 3, 38, 89–92, 124–8
    in mining, 2, 89, 92–3
    statistics, 120, 189
    (*see also* banks, manufacturing, railways, utilities)
Iquique, 174
Iquitos, 164
Irazusta, Rodolfo and Julio, 15
Irisarri, Antonio de, 91
Italy, 206, 209

Jamaica, 28, 29, 30–1
Japan, 140, 206, 209, 237
João, Dom (King João VI of Portugal), 42, 43
Johnston & Co, Edward, 101, 102, 160–1
Jones, Charles, 133
Joslin, David, 130

Juárez, Benito, 9
Juárez Celmán, Miguel, 154
Justo, Agustín P., 212, 220

Kay, Cristobal, 20
Kennedy, Paul, 60
Kiernan, V.G., 64–5
Kinder, Thomas, 91
Kindersley, Lord, 189
Kleinwort Sons & Co., 100
Knowles & Foster, 102

La Plata Cold Storage Co., 152
labour movements, 11, 12, 120, 143–6, 158, 173–4, 177, 195, 196, 213, 231, 245
Latham, Wilfrid, 83
lawyers, 10, 142, 143, 171, 173, 175, 198, 244
Lazard Brothers, 201, 222
League of Nations, 201
Leff, Nathaniel, 110
Leguía, Augusto B., 195
Lend-Lease, 225
Leopoldina Railway Co., 167
Lerdo de Tejada, Sebastián, 9
Lever Brothers (*see* Unilever)
Lewis, Colin, 158
liberalism, 7, 9, 14, 87, 88
Lima, 6, 84, 85
Liverpool Nitrate Co., 173
Lloyd Brasileiro, 165, 169
Lloyds Bank, 251
loans, forced, 50, 83, 85
Lobitos Oilfields Ltd., 143, 193
Lockett, Wm & Jno., 98, 169
Lomé Conventions, 246
London & Brazilian Bank, 130
London & River Plate Bank, 130
London Bank of Mexico and South America, 170–1
London Nitrate Co., 173
Lynch, John, 35, 52

machinery, 76, 100, 113, 115, 224, 228

Britain and Latin America in the Nineteenth and Twentieth Centuries

MacKintosh, Ewen, 58
MacLean Rowe (*see* Graham Rowe)
Maipo, Battle of, 34
maize, 149, 181, 197, 207, 217
Malvinas (*see* Falkland Islands)
Mamalakis, Markos, 173
Manáus, 163
Manchester, Alan K., 237
Mandeville, Henry, 52
manufacturing, 183, 190, 207, 219, 242, 246
   British investment in, 5, 104, 187–8, 189, 231, 236, 247
   in Brazil, 112–13, 160, 183
   in Mexico, 74, 82, 87–8, 112–13
Maranhão, 33
Marconi Co., 184, 192
Mariátegui, José Carlos, 15, 104
Marichal, Carlos, 158, 219
Martínez del Río family, 58
Mathew, W.M., 18, 47
Maximilian, 3
Mayo, John, 104
meat trade, 103, 106–7, 110, 149, 181, 197, 207, 215, 225, 228, 242
   Anglo-Argentine Commission, 218–19
merchant banks, 5, 62, 100, 125–6, 158, 201, 202–3, 221, 241–2, 244
merchants
   British, 2, 5, 38, 39–40, 41–3, 54, 58, 61, 64, 65, 78–85, 86–7, 88, 89, 94–5, 97–105, 114–15, 116–17, 191, 206, 235
   French, 42, 79
   German, 42, 79, 103, 114
   Latin American, 7, 14, 41, 42, 45, 79, 84–5, 163
   Portuguese, 98, 160, 163
   US, 42
Methuen Treaty, 32
Mexican Eagle Oil Co., 188, 193, 195, 196, 211, 213, 215, 230
Mexican Railway Co., 135
Mexico, 6, 8, 10, 12, 28, 49, 55, 59, 61, 98, 193

British investment, 5, 91–2, 96, 122, 125, 129, 133–4
British trade, 31, 73, 74
economic conditions, 84, 94
government finance, 82, 91–2
intervention in, 3, 7–8, 9, 16, 57, 60, 66, 67
manufacturing, 74, 82, 87–8, 112, 240
mining, 2, 76, 93
petroleum, 175, 183, 185, 188, 195–6, 206, 213–14, 237
Revolution, 11, 16, 189, 243
Midland Bank, 251
Miller, General William, 40
milling, flour, 100, 101–2, 104, 169
Milne Mission, 61
Minas Gerais, 161, 167, 168
mining, 2, 6, 7, 12, 76, 92–3, 119, 124, 187, 230
   (*see also* copper, gold, silver, tin)
Ministry of Agriculture, 214, 220
Miranda, Francisco de, 35
Mitre, Bartolome, 63–4
Mitre Law, 135, 156–7, 197, 229
monetary policies, 16, 160, 168, 174–5, 176, 180, 200, 240
Monroe Doctrine, 37–8
Montagu Mission, 201, 221
Montevideo, 39, 52, 72, 79, 136–7, 187
Morgan & Co., J.S., 125, 126, 127, 129
Morrow, Dwight, 213
Morton Rose & Co., 125
Mosconi, Enrique, 226–7
Mosquito Coast, 51, 55–6
motor vehicles, 114, 191
Mulhall, M.G., 149
Multi-Fibre Arrangement, 246
multinational firms, 102, 128, 130, 139–40, 187–8, 211, 236, 242
Murray, James, 51, 55, 56
Murrieta & Co., Cristóbal de, 125

322